cm

D0966392

THE GLOBALIZING LEARNING ECONOMY

The Globalizing Learning Economy

Edited by
DANIELE ARCHIBUGI
and
BENGT-ÅKE LUNDVALL

UNIVERSITY PRESS

3 38.064
G5622

OXFORD
UNIVERSITY PRESS

Great Clarendon Street, Oxford OX2 6DP

Oxford University Press is a department of the University of Oxford.
It furthers the University's objective of excellence in research, scholarship,
and education by publishing worldwide in

Oxford New York

Athens Auckland Bangkok Bogotá Buenos Aires Calcutta
Cape Town Chennai Dar es Salaam Delhi Florence Hong Kong Istanbul
Karachi Kuala Lumpur Madrid Melbourne Mexico City Mumbai
Nairobi Paris São Paulo Shanghai Singapore Taipei Tokyo Toronto Warsaw
with associated companies in Berlin Ibadan

Oxford is a registered trade mark of Oxford University Press
in the UK and in certain other countries

Published in the United States
by Oxford University Press Inc., New York

© The several contributors, 2001

The moral rights of the authors have been asserted
Database right Oxford University Press (maker)

First published 2001

All rights reserved. No part of this publication may be reproduced,
stored in a retrieval system, or transmitted, in any form or by any means,
without the prior permission in writing of Oxford University Press,
or as expressly permitted by law, or under terms agreed with the appropriate
reprographics rights organization. Enquiries concerning reproduction
outside the scope of the above should be sent to the Rights Department,
Oxford University Press, at the address above

You must not circulate this book in any other binding or cover
and you must impose the same condition on any acquirer

British Library Cataloguing in Publication Data
Data available

Library of Congress Cataloging-in-Publication Data
The globalizing learning economy/edited by Daniele Archibugi and Bengt-Åke Lundvall.
p. cm.
A collection of 15 revised papers first presented at the "European Socio-Economic Research
Conference," and held in Brussels on 28–30 April 1999 to present results of studies promoted
by the European Commission.
Includes bibliographical references and index.
1. Organizational learning—Europe—Congresses   2. Technnological innovations—Economic
aspects—Europe—Congresses.   3. Globalization—Congresses.
I. Archibugi, Daniele.   II. Lundvall, Bengt-Åke, 1941.   III. European Socio-Economic
Research Conference (1999: Brussels, Belgium)
HD58.82.G55   2001   338'.064—DC21   00–050499
ISBN 0-19-924109-0

1 3 5 7 9 10 8 6 4 2

Typeset by J&L Composition Ltd, Filey, North Yorkshire
Printed in Great Britain
on acid-free paper by
Biddles Ltd., Guildford & King's Lynn

NLA

BK Title: **PREFACE** *eds* .

This book reflects work pursued in the first generation of the European Commission's programme on socio-economic research TSER (Targeted Socio-Economic Research). It represents an attempt to contribute to one of the fundamental aims of TSER in the Fourth European Framework Programme, i.e. to let the results of socio-economic research feed into the knowledge base of public policy in Europe. TSER was the first major European effort to support and co-ordinate research in the field of social science and it supported research in three different areas: evaluation of science and technology policy options; social exclusion and inclusion; and, finally, education and training. This book is based primarily on research pursued under the first of these headings.

In selecting projects and contributors for this volume we had as a major criterion that they would contribute to the understanding of major new trends affecting the conditions for policy making in general and innovation policy in particular. This book is therefore addressed to students, scholars, policy makers, and others interested in understanding what are the major new challenges related to globalization and learning societies—and what can be done about them. We have preferred to use the title *The globalizing learning economy* rather than the more in vogue expression 'The global knowledge-based economy' because we want to emphasize that we are still a long way from a truly global economy and that there are still vast differences among countries, regions, and social classes in terms of the exploitation of the available knowledge. Moreover, what connotes the present era is not only the intense use of knowledge but also a learning process characterized by both knowledge creation and knowledge destruction—sometimes forgetting is a prerequisite for knowledge creation.

This book should give readers a feeling of optimism by pointing to the enormous potential in developing human resources in connection with new technologies and new forms of organization. It should, at the same time, raise big warning flags signalling that the globalizing learning economy may not be sustainable if left to itself. The challenge of growing social, regional, and global disparities, along with the environmental challenge, may undermine natural and social capital that are key inputs and prerequisites for the learning processes on which the whole system is founded. We also point out that in important respects Europe still seems to be unprepared to adapt successfully to the rapidly changing landscape. Several chapters highlight weaknesses of Europe in areas that are crucial for future well-being. A major policy effort at the European, national, and regional levels is required to allow the Old continent to run on a par in the new global economy.

University Libraries
Carnegie Mellon University
Pittsburgh PA 15213-3890

The analysis of most single chapters is based on large research projects involving interdisciplinary teams from many different European countries and taking place over a period of two to three years. In this book the reader gets the results from such large-scale research projects in a condensed form and with emphasis on the fact that it is *targeted* research. We have asked authors to emphasize the mapping of what they see as the most important new socio-economic trends in their field of research and to reflect upon policy implications at the European, national, and regional levels. Methodological problems and internal academic debates are important but they are discussed elsewhere.

The contributors broadly share an institutionalist perspective on the economy but they are not necessarily in agreement when it comes to interpreting what is happening and which policy measures should be preferred. The chapters are written by scholars with different disciplinary backgrounds, even if most of the authors are economists, sociologists, or organization theorists. We believe that the extreme specialization in academic work, as well as in policy making, needs to be compensated for by efforts to reintegrate different elements of knowledge. We are convinced that a lack of overview on how different pieces of knowledge are connected to each other and a lack of insight in how different policies interact in shaping reality are factors that undermine the sustainability of the globalizing learning economy. If anything, we should have liked to include expertise with an even broader set of perspectives and disciplinary backgrounds to capture the new social and economic trends.

The idea for this book came out of a major meeting held in Brussels on 28–30 April 1999, the 'European Socio-Economic Research Conference', which was devoted to the presentation of some of the most important results of the studies promoted by the European Commission. The majority of the papers were already available in advanced drafts then, but to generate a reasonably coherent book required additional efforts from the contributors. We are of course happy to be able to get so many interesting contributions from colleagues who, we know, are very busy and very much in demand as speakers and writers. The fact that they joined this effort and were willing to go through several rounds of revisions of their chapters may be taken as a tribute to the status of the TSER-programme. We wish, however, to thank them for their patience.

We want to address special thanks to Christopher Freeman, who was unable to join the conference but who let us have a presentation which is now a chapter of this book. Many of the authors in this volume owe him a lot in terms of intellectual and moral inspiration and he, together with Carlota Perez, was one of the first economists who told us that the IT revolution would fundamentally change our societies and the workings of the economy, long before 'the new economy' appeared as a standard concept in the columns of the business press.

We are very grateful for support from a number of EU officials connected to the TSER-programme and Directorate-General for Science, Research, and Development. First of all, we would like to thank Virginia Vitorino, who was active in preparing and organizing the meeting in Brussels, 28–30 April 1999, and who provided substantial help in the follow-up resulting in this book. We are also grateful to Director, Achilleas Mitsos, and Head of Unit, Andrew Sors, for their support for the initiative. Interesting debates with Ronan O'Brien and Peter Fisch have also been helpful in designing the project. We have also benefited from the insights and suggestions of our colleagues Cristiano Antonelli, Yannis Caloghirou, and François Chesnais.

All through this process we have depended very much on the assistance from Marcela Bulcu and Cinzia Spaziani in Rome and Dorte Køster in Aalborg. We owe them red roses for their kind support and many thanks for their professional work in preparing the typescript for the publisher. David Musson of Oxford University Press should be thanked for his early interest in this project, his positive and critical encouragement, but also for his tolerance in accepting our flexible deadlines. Sarah Dobson and Sally McCann should also be thanked for their patience in the preparation of the typescript. Our somewhat hectic working life would be terribly boring without the love and inspiration from Birte and Paola.

Daniele Archibugi and Bengt-Åke Lundvall

CONTENTS

Contents

LIST OF FIGURES

LIST OF TABLES

LIST OF ABBREVIATIONS

BETA	Bureau d'Economie Théorique et Appliquée, Université Louis Pasteur, Strasbourg, France
BRITE/EURAM	European Commission's Specific Research and Technological Development Programme in the Field of Industrial and Materials Technologies
CAP	European Common Agricultural Policy
CEC	Commission of the European Communities
CRAFT	European Commission's Specific Programme of Research and Technological Development in the Field of Industrial and Materials Technologies
CREI	Centre de Recherche en Economie Industrielle, Université Paris 13, Paris, France
CRIC	The ESRC Centre for Research on Innovation and Competition, UK
CSD	Commission for Sustainable Development
CSO	Central Statistical Office, UK
CTA	Constructive Technology Assessment
DBF	Dedicated Biotechnology Firms
DISKO	Danish Innovation System Research Project
DRUID	Danish Research Unit for Industrial Dynamics
DTO	Duurzame Technologische Ontwikkeling: Dutch Programme on Sustainable Technology Development
ECB	European Central Bank
EEC	European Economic Community
EFTA	European Free Trade Agreement
EIMS	European Commission's European Innovation Monitoring System
EMU	European Monetary Union
ESPRIT	European Strategic Programme for Research and Development on Information Technologies
ESRC	Economic and Social Research Council, UK
EU	European Union
EUREKA	European Research Coordination Agency
EUROSTAT	Statistical Office at the European Communities
FDI	Foreign Direct Investment
GATT	General Agreement on Trade and Tariffs
GDP	Gross Domestic Product

GNP	Gross National Product
HDTV	High Definition Television
ICT	Information and Communication Technology
IMF	International Monetary Fund
INRA/SERD	Institut National de la Recherche Agronomique / Sociologie et Economie de la R&D, Grenoble, France
IPTS	European Commission's Institute for Prospective Technological Studies, Seville, Spain
ISI	Fraunhofer Institute for Systems and Innovation Research, Karlsruhe, Germany
ITU	International Telecommunications Union
JIT	Just in Time Production
JRC	European Commission's Joint Research Centre
KBNO	Knowledge Based Networked Oligopolies
KIBS	Knowledge Intensive Business Services
LOK	Danish Project for Management, Organizations, and Competencies
M&A	Mergers and Acquisitions
MERIT	Maastricht Economic Research Institute on Innovation and Technology, The Netherlands
MNE	Multinational Enterprises
MTA	Material Transfer Agreements
NEPP	National Environmental Policy Plan, The Netherlands
NIC	Newly Industrializing Countries
NMT	Nordic Mobile Telephony Standard
OECD	Organization for Economic Cooperation and Development
RACE	European Commission's Specific Research and Technological Development programme in the Field of Communication Technologies
RMNO	Dutch Advisory Council for Research on Nature and Environment
R&D	Research and Development
RTD	Research and Technological Development
SME	Small and Medium Sized Enterprise
SPRU	Science and Technology Policy Research Unit, Sussex University, UK
TEP	The OECD Technology/Economy Programme
TMR	European Commission's Training and Mobility for Research Programme
TSER	Targeted Socio-Economic Research Programme of the European Commission
UMIST	University of Manchester Institute of Science and Technology, UK

UNCED	United Nations Conference on Environment and Development
UNCTAD	United Nations Conference on Trade and Development
UNESCO	United Nations Educational Scientific and Cultural Organization
UNWCED	United Nations World Commission on Environment and Development
VROM	Physical Planning and the Environment, Ministry of Housing, The Netherlands
WIFO	Osterreichisches Institut fur Wirtschaftsforschung: Austrian Institute of Economic Research
WTO	World Trade Organization

CONTRIBUTORS

DANIELE ARCHIBUGI	National Research Council, Rome, Italy
PATRICK COHENDENT	BETA, Université Louis Pasteur, Strasbourg, France
PEDRO CONCEIÇÃO	Center for Innovation, Technology and Policy Research, IN+, Instituto Superior Técnico, Lisboa, Portugal and The University of Texas at Austin, USA
BENJAMIN CORIAT	CREI, Université de Paris 13, Paris, France
CHARLES EDQUIST	Department of Technology and Social Change, Linköping University, Linköping, Sweden
JAN FAGERBERG	University of Oslo, Centre for Technology, Innovation, and Culture, Oslo, Norway
CHRIS FREEMAN	SPRU, University of Sussex, Falmer, Brighton, UK
CLAUS FRELLE-PETERSEN	Ministry of Trade and Industry, Copenhagen, Denmark
MANUEL V. HEITOR	Center for Innovation, Technology and Policy Reserach, IN+, Instituto Superior Técnico, Lisboa, Portugal
SIMONA IAMMARINO	National Statistical Institute, Rome, Italy
PIERRE-BENOÎT JOLY	INRA/SERD, Grenoble, France
BENGT-ÅKE LUNDWALL	Aalborg University, Aalborg, Denmark
FRIEDER MEYER-KRAHMER	Fraunhofer Institute for Systems and Innovation Research, Karlsruhe, Germany
LYNN K. MYTELA	Carleton University, Ottawa and Forum CEREM, Université Paris X (Nanterre), France
LARS NORMANN	Ministry of Trade and Industry, Copenhagen, Denmark
JENS NYHOLM	Ministry of Trade and Industry, Copenhagen, Denmark
MARK RIIS	Ministry of Trade and Industry, Copenhagen, Denmark
GERD SCHIENSTOCK	University of Tampere, Work Research Centre, Tampere, Finland
MARGARET SHARP	SPRU, University of Sussex, Falmer, Brighton, UK

LUC SOETE	MERIT, University of Limburg, Maastricht, The Netherlands
MARK TOMLINSON	ESRC Centre for Research on Innovation and Competition (CRIC), University of Manchester and UMIST, Manchester, UK
PETER TORSTENSEN	Ministry of Trade and Industry, Copenhagen, Denmark

530 f02

Introduction: Europe and the Learning Economy

BENGT-ÅKE LUNDVALL AND DANIELE ARCHIBUGI

Both the pace and the acceleration of innovation are startling; nay terri-
fying. . . . No-one can predict the . . . range of skills which will need to be
amassed to create and take advantage of the next revolution but one (and
thinking about the next but one is what everyone is doing. The game is
already over for the next).

(Bob Anderson, Director, Rank Xerox Research Centre, Cambridge
Laboratory, 'R&D Knowledge Creation as a Bazaar Economy', paper
presented at OECD–IEE Workshop on Competition and Innovation
in the Information Society, 19 March 1997)

The New Economic Context

The title of this book—*The Globalizing Learning Economy*—evokes probably
the two most significant aspects of contemporary economic and social life.
On the one hand, there is growing agreement that knowledge is now at the
very core of economic welfare and development. Nations, regions, industries,
and firms with a faster rate of growth are those which more successfully manage to generate and apply knowledge. The crucial role of knowledge is now
preached by a variety of academic, business, and policy sources. The OECD,
for example, has consistently stressed the move towards a *knowledge-based
economy* (OECD 1996; Foray and Lundvall 1996). However, we have preferred to refer to a slightly different concept, that of 'learning economy'
(Lundvall and Johnson 1994; Lundvall and Borrás 1998) because we believe
that this may capture even better the dynamics of our age. The concept is
based upon the hypothesis that over the last decades an acceleration of both
knowledge creation and knowledge destruction has taken place. Individuals
and institutions need to renew their competencies more often than before,
because the problems they face change more rapidly. And at the same time
the segments of society that are affected by accelerating change have grown
considerably. Therefore, in a wide set of economic activities what constitutes
success is not so much having access to a stock of specialized knowledge. The
key to success is, rather, rapid learning and forgetting (when old ways of
doing things get in the way of learning new ways). Narrowly defined skills
may actually even hamper rather than support economic success.

On the other hand, we also refer to the so-called globalization. In recent years the interconnections between geographically different parts of the world have considerably increased and this has also multiplied learning opportunities. But globalization is not a completed process. In some areas, such as markets for financial assets, it has developed very far, while in others more related to competence building and innovation national borders still remain crucial (Archibugi and Iammarino in this volume). Neither does the globalizing process provide advantages to all social groups and regions and it does not automatically reduce disparities. While some parts of the economy are at the core of the current trends, others have been marginalized. We have therefore preferred to refer to a 'globalizing' rather than to a 'global' economy to stress that the current state of the world remains far from one characterized by a trully global economy and society. Actually, the globalizing process contains dangers as well as opportunities and there are individuals, groups, regions, and nations which are not benefiting from the available potentialities and experience a worsening in their current well-being.

It is important to emphasize how the 'learning' economy and the 'globalizing' economy are strictly connected. It is obvious that knowledge and learning have always been a crucial component in human systems, but we should also ask why and how they have become more important in our age. One answer is connected to the opening of new scientific discoveries and technological innovations, but this alone would not be able to explain why knowledge and learning have become so crucial for economic success. A circular process has taken place. On the one hand, the development of an integrated world economy has allowed the acquisition of information, expertise, and technology at a faster pace and often at lower costs than in the past (see Archibugi and Iammarino in this volume). On the other hand, the current phase of globalization has been nurtured by a generation of new technologies. The major technological advances of the last quarter of a century have in fact occurred in fields which allow the production, communication, transmission, and storage of information. Information and Communication Technologies (ICTs) have in other words acted as the material devices to allow globalization to occur. Finance, production, media, and fashion would not be as global as they are today without the generation of new technologies. In this sense, the 'learning' and 'globalizing' dimensions of the world economy strongly reinforce each other (see Archibugi and Iammarino 1999).

An important element in this new context is that competition, as well as learning, has become more global and more intense in most parts of the economy. This is true especially in markets related to information technology: they are at the same time the carriers for the transmission of new knowledge, those where the rate of change is faster and those where competition has become extreme. But the production of traditional manufactured products such as textiles, toys, and ships has also experienced a more intense competition and substantial parts of these industries have moved out of Europe to other parts of the world. Service related activities such as shipping and software engineering are getting more and more exposed to global competition. Now also traditionally protected and regulated areas (telecommunications, collective transport, public utilities, health, and education), are becoming strongly exposed to competition.

There is little doubt that the breakthrough in information technology has had a major impact both on learning and globalization. Christopher Freeman (1984) and Carlota Perez (1983) signalled very early on that we were in the midst of a technological revolution that, after a period of institutional adaptation, might turn the world economy from a downturn to a long upswing. It is interesting to note that the scepticism they met a decade ago among standard economists now tends to be drowned by enthusiastic and somewhat uncritical references to 'the new economy' as based on information and communication technology by some of the same economists. The work done by Freeman and Perez on long waves and techno-economic paradigms is useful also in demonstrating that it is not the first time in history that the world has been through dramatic change that increases the need to learn and adapt. The industrial revolution and the different transformations connected to earlier technological revolutions were also dramatic in these respects. What might be different in this period is the extreme rate of change in certain areas related to the production and use of ICT and the breadth of the impact across regions as well as social groups (for an assessment of the 'new economy' on Europe, see Soete in this volume).

Other major driving forces have been political. The most critical political reform was the deregulation of currency policy and of international capital flows. After this first step had been taken it was almost unavoidable that the pressure for deregulating other activities would increase. For instance, the monetarist idea that macroeconomic policy should focus on monetary stability and leave the rest to the market found material support in the free movement of capital. The success of a specific policy package now had to be judged not so much by its impact upon a set of nationally prioritized economic political goals but rather by the more or less speculative reactions of international mobile capital.

Some of the deregulation initiatives have been intertwined with and motivated by radical changes in information technology. This is obviously true for mass media and telecommunications and it is also becoming the case for other areas such as education and health services, where the explosive expansion of the use of the Internet challenges the old ways of providing these services. Nevertheless, it is important to realize that the development has been quite strongly determined by policy choices. The perception that national and international policy making has been without influence on a predestined globalizing process is false and it might also be dangerous.

It is false because the design of national and international policies and institutions affects the rate, direction, and consequences of globalization. It is dangerous because abdicating from political responsibility and leaving the weakest segments of global and national society to carry the full burden of unhampered globalization leaves a lot of space for aggressive, populist, political movements, as European history has already taught once. In other words, the 'new economy' needs strong public policies in order to keep the polity working.

Learning as Social Process

In this volume we argue that the learning economy calls for new institutional set ups and new policy strategies at the level of the nation state and that of the European Community. One major conclusion is that not only is there a need to rethink specific policies related to, for instance, education, social issues, and industrial development, it is even more important to combine these specialized policies into holistic and coherent strategies. While knowledge production and policy making, through decades, have been characterized by growing specialization and by narrowing the fields of responsibilities for policy makers, the learning economy calls for lateral thinking and for a reintegration of separate perspectives and strategies. It is of special importance to take into account the importance of the social and ecological dimensions when considering innovation policy in the learning economy. This is because growth in the learning economy feeds upon social capital and that, if left to itself, it tends to undermine the very same social capital that it feeds upon.

Know-how is typically learnt in something similar to apprenticeship relationships where the apprentice follows his master and relies upon him as his trustworthy authority (Polanyi 1958/1978: 53 *et passim*). 'Know-who' is learnt in social practice and some of it is 'learnt' in specialized education environments. Communities of engineers and experts are kept together by a variety of linkages and networks such as reunions of alumni, professional societies, know-how trading among professional colleagues (Carter 1989). It also develops in day-to-day dealings with customers, sub-contractors, and independent institutes. Larger business communities exchange significant information which constitutes a vital input into their production process (on this, see Mytelka's chapter in this volume).

All this exchange of know-how will not be possible in a purely competitive economy. The learning economy thus needs a lot of trust in order to be successful. And, as Kenneth Arrow has pointed out, 'trust cannot be bought: and if it could be bought it would have no value whatsoever' (Arrow 1971). The fundamental role of trust raises strong doubts about how to interpret the standard assumption in economic theory that the most efficient economy is one where individuals act as 'economic animals' who *calculate* the outcomes of all alternatives in order to select the one which is best for themselves. *In the learning economy the importance of the ethical dimension and social capital increases enormously.* Little can be learnt and information cannot be used effectively in a society where there is little trust.

The most immediate benefits of intensified competition and accelerated change and learning are growing productivity, lower prices, and a higher level of consumption. Another more local benefit is that the employees of innovative and flexible organizations may earn a premium or at least avoid bankruptcy and unemployment. But there is also a clear and strong tendency towards polarization in the learning economy, as stressed in Schienstock's chapter in this volume. The distribution of the benefits and costs of economic development has become more uneven during the last decade, with the low-skilled of the labour force as the major losers (see OECD 1994: 22 *et passim*). Within Europe the catching up of the poorest regions has slowed down in this period (Fagerberg *et al.* 1997). At a global scale inequality between rich and poor countries has increased (see Freeman in this volume, World Bank 2000).

In the learning economy, there is a growing tension between the process that excludes a growing proportion of the labour force and the growing need for broad participation in the change process. It is not obvious that, in the long run, a learning economy can prosper in a climate of extreme social polarization. This is why there is a growing need at all levels of society to combine elements of the 'old new deal' with a 'new new deal' that puts the emphasis on a more even distribution of skills and competencies and especially on the capability to learn (Lundvall 1996).

Another, even broader, problem is that the speed-up of change puts a pressure on traditional communities. It contributes to the weakening of traditional family relationships, local communities and stable workplaces. This is important since the production of intellectual capital (learning) is strongly dependent on social capital. 'Social capital'—the social capability of citizens and workers to collaborate and share knowledge and information without too much friction—is not easily re-established if once devaluated. How new forms of social capital can be created and accumulated is a major issue in the learning economy. This is a major issue especially in the context of European integration since the formation of social capital has been so strongly connected to the national welfare states. To find ways of re-establishing the social capital destroyed by the globalization process is a major challenge for Europe.

The Impact of the Transformation

The focus of this book is on how 'innovation policy' needs to be designed in the new context. By 'innovation policy' we refer to a broader set of policies than are normally included in this concept and we will also try to take into account how other policy areas influence or are influenced by innovation (see

Edquist's and Lundvall's chapters in this volume). This approach reflects the fact that we see the present split of responsibilities among different institutions (such as ministries, directorates, commissioners, and other public agencies acting at the regional, national, or European levels) as one reason why it is so difficult to develop effective European strategies that counter the negative impact of globalization and exploit the positive opportunities it offers.

In Figure 1, some of the crucial aspects of the globalizing learning economy are illustrated with a simple model, where transformation pressure is linked to innovation and organizational change and to the costs and benefits of change. Through this model we can also see how different policy fields interrelate. In what follows we shall identify some of the strategic variables at each level and take into account how they have changed in the transformation to a globalizing learning economy.

Transformation Pressure

One of the most fundamental factors affecting the transformation pressure is *technical change*. New technological opportunities in the form of new products and new processes affect firms in different ways. They offer significant advantages but also new threats. A second major factor is the *competition regime*. New entrants into markets and extensions of markets bringing in new competitors located elsewhere are factors that increase the transformation pressure. The role of ownership and finance in managing the firms affects the intensity but also the direction of the transformation pressure. Finally the *macroeconomic stance* affects transformation pressure. For instance, a situation characterized by deflationary policies and an over-evaluated currency rate implies strong transformation pressure, as do aggressive trade union wage policies.

The Building up of Transformation Pressure

The development and widespread use of new technologies and especially of information and communication technologies have transformed such fundamental aspects of the economy as time and space. The wider set of

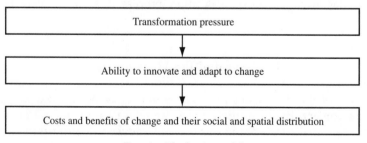

Fig. 1. *The basic model*

competitors in world trade also reflects deregulation of trade and international financial flows as well as transport technologies that make it less and less expensive to move commodities and people over long distances. Privatization and deregulation increase the transformation pressure on parts of the economy that have so far been sheltered. These are the main factors that have increased the transformation pressure. To this should be added mechanisms of cumulative circular causality. These reflect selection mechanisms in product and labour markets that favour change-oriented organizations and individuals and thus increase the transformation pressure further.

It is difficult to see what mechanisms within the economic sphere could halt this tendency. The full impact of information technology has yet to be felt: new entrants into world trade are on their way and further deregulation still lies ahead in most countries and are promoted by international organizations such as the OECD and IMF. The main limits to the process might be 'exogenous' and have to do with increasing costs in terms of potential social and environmental crises that might trigger popular resistance. The growing, if still modest, attention given to ethical, environmental, and social issues in big firms may reflect an insight that such developments, in the absence of both external regulation and self-restraint, might threaten the sustainability of the economic environment.

Ability to Innovate and Adapt to Change

A key to successful innovation is to have a strong knowledge base including an R&D capacity and a well-trained labour force (on the impact of new technologies on employment and skills, see Vivarelli and Pianta 2000). But as indicated by the concept 'innovation system' many different agents, organizations, institutions, and policies combine to determine the ability to innovate. Adaptation to change can take many forms and this is the subject of ongoing debates on economic policy. *Flexible labour markets* may be at the core of adaptation in some innovation systems while others adapt more through *functional flexibility* within organizations. *The creation of new firms* may be a key to adaptability and innovation in some systems while others rely more on *innovating and reorienting the activities of existing firms.* Increasingly important is the introduction of *learning organizations* and *network formation* as a response to a growing transformation pressure.

New Demands on the Ability to Innovate and Adapt to Change

The new demands on the ability to innovate reflect a new mode of knowledge production and give rise to a need to rethink most of the institutions and organizations that constitute the knowledge infrastructure. The new context puts a premium on interactivity within and between firms, and between firms and the knowledge infrastructure. These changes are reflected in new and more stringent demands regarding the qualifications of employees and management. The ability to combine abstract reasoning with social skills in communication and co-operation, including interdisciplinary co-operation, is now more important than before. The delegation of responsibility to employees is a response to the fact that rapid learning can take place only if the working environment is democratically organized. Services, and especially knowledge-intensive services, tend to become much more important, both in their own right and for overall industrial dynamics (see Tomlinson, in this volume. For an assessment of the innovative potential of the service industries see Evangelista 2000). These changes relate both to innovative and to adaptive capabilities. The characteristics of the innovative firm are not identical but they are overlapping with those of the functionally flexible firm (see Coriat, in this volume). The kind of external network relationships most conducive to innovation are also similar to those that favour flexible response.

Costs and Benefits of Change and Their Social and Spatial Distribution

The different forms of adaptability characterizing an innovation system will distribute the costs and benefits differently. Firms integrated in successful and dynamic networks may prosper when the transformation pressure increases while firms operating in formerly protected areas but now becoming exposed to new competitors will have to fight for their survival. The spatial distribution of costs and benefits will reflect regional and national abilities to innovate and to adapt to change. The nature of the transformation pressure may favour the particular institutional set ups prevalent in some innovation systems and inhibit others. What might be an ideal set up in one period may not be so in the next, and it usually takes decades rather than years fundamentally to reorient regional and national systems of innovation.

More Uneven Social and Spatial Distribution of the Costs and Benefits of Change

Data seem to indicate that, on balance, the distribution of benefits and costs has become more uneven during the last decade, at least within the OECD area (see respectively Schienstock and Freeman, in this volume). Profit shares have grown at the cost of wage shares in all parts of OECD since the middle of the 1970s (OECD 1994: 22). Earning differentials between skilled and unskilled workers have grown in the Anglo-Saxon countries and differences in employment opportunities between more and less skilled labour categories have increased in those, as well as in the other European countries (OECD 1994: 22–3). TSER research demonstrates that the differences in income between rich and poor regions in Europe remained substantial through the 1980s (Fagerberg *et al.* 1997).

It is important to note that the nature of the costs of change are quite different for those leading and pushing the process of change and those lagging behind. This is true for people as well as regions. People who are frontrunners may experience stress, a shortage of time, and work overload, while laggards may experience exclusion from the core of the economy and be relegated to passive consumption of mass-produced entertainment. In socio-economic terms there might be a trade off between extreme demands on the learning capability of the workforce promoting competitiveness and the costs represented by the fact that more people get excluded from active participation in the labour market. Another set of costs arising from rapid change and which now need to be tackled are those relating to global and local environmental problems: new industrialization and the intensification of transport increasingly threaten the basic conditions for human life (see Meyer-Krahmer, in this volume).

On the Importance of Feedback

The linear type of model presented above may be realistic for small regions and organizations since they have very limited impact on the transformation pressure to which they are exposed. But for units of a certain size it is important to understand the feedback between the three different levels. Starting from the bottom of Figure 1 there is a need to take into account how the distribution of costs and benefits affects the ability to innovate and adapt to change. An uneven distribution will typically create a strong negative attitude to change among those who register only the costs and negative aspects of change. If there are high degrees of insecurity among individuals they will tend to oppose change. This is one of the reasons why social cohesion is crucial for the learning economy.

The second feedback mechanism goes from the ability to innovate to the transformation pressure. Increasing the ability to innovate means building more flexible organizations and a selection of people and institutions that are change-oriented. This gives rise to a further increase in the transformation pressure. If there opens a wide cultural split between a change-oriented cosmopolitan élite and a defensive majority, social capital and learning will be undermined. Leaving social cohesion to be repaired by the nation states, *ex post*, and focusing the European integration exclusively on increasing the transformation pressure and on enhancing innovative capabilities may not be a sustainable strategy in the learning economy.

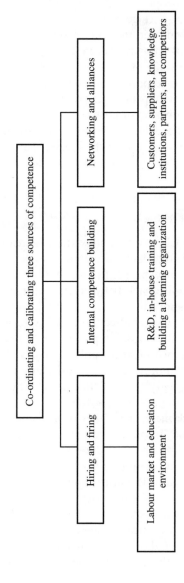

FIG. 2. *Knowledge management in the learning organization*

Innovation Policy in the New Context

Since innovation is strongly related to competence building at the firm level, we need to define the different roles of innovation policy by taking this as the starting-point. In Figure 2 we have sketched three major sources that firms may draw upon when building and renewing their competence.

The first source refers to hiring and firing in the labour market. The actual pattern of mobility of labour between regions, sectors, and firms, and the training efforts within and outside firms are crucial for how the hiring and firing mechanisms affect competence building at the firm level. The second source refers to internal competence building. Here the organizational set up of the firm is critical for its capability to learn. R&D investments and the investment in the training of employees are also important. Finally, firms will increasingly draw upon external sources of competence. These can originate from other firms operating as customers, suppliers, and competitors (Pavitt 1984; Von Hippel 1988; Archibugi *et al.* 1991). They may also be knowledge institutions such as laboratories, technical institutes, and training centres. Consultancy firms and other knowledge-intensive business service firms tend to become increasingly important as suppliers of competence. Science-based firms need to get into very close forms of interaction with universities (see Conçeicão and Heitor in this volume).

Traditionally, innovation policy has been thought of mainly as responsible for creating a public knowledge infrastructure and possibly creating links between this knowledge infrastructure and the firms. Another element of innovation policy has been firm incentives to invest in R&D through, for instance, tax subsidies. Finally, innovation policy may have focused on protecting the knowledge produced by private agents while in specific fields, such as agriculture, the main focus has been on diffusing knowledge. There has been agreement that there is a need for a public responsibility in relation to basic education and the functioning of labour markets but the criteria for designing these policies have only marginally referred to the impact on competence building and innovation in the private sector. There is still a long way to go before management and governments have fully responded to the need for strategies that take an integrated view of the three sources of competence building. There is a need to do so at the level of the firm, social partners, and governments.

Building Learning Organizations and Integrating Strategies of Competence Building at the Level of the Firm

If we ask ourselves how widespread is innovation among firms we will find that, contrary to what was predicted by Schumpeter, the number of innovating firms is substantial. Of course, not many of them are able to generate radical innovations but, from a public policy perspective, this seems to be less important than to create a vital fabric of innovating firms. The recent generation of surveys devoted to technological innovation, promoted by the OECD and the European Commission, have however shown that there is a substantial share of firms, both in the manufacturing and in the service industries, which do not innovate regularly (see Evangelista, Sandven, Sirilli, and Smith 1998). This has relevant implications for public policies since it calls for actions able to increase the number of firms active in technological innovation. Not only can firms innovate more, but more firms can innovate.

Equally important is to link product and process innovations to organizational change. Recent research linking organizational forms to innovation shows that there is a strong synergy between the introduction of new forms of organization and the performance and innovative capacity of the firm (Lundvall 1999; and Lundvall and Nielsen 1999. See also, in this volume, Coriat's chapter). Establishing the firm as a learning organization characterized by decentralized responsibility, team work, circulation of employees between departments, and investment in training has a positive impact on a series of performance variables. Flexible firms are characterized by higher productivity, by higher rates of growth and stability in terms of employment, and they are more innovative in terms of new products. The research cited above also shows that success in terms of innovation is even greater when such a strategy is combined with active networking in relation to customers, suppliers, and knowledge institutions.

But we also find that, so far, there is only a small minority of all firms (10–15%) that have introduced the major traits of the learning organization. There is an enormous unexploited reserve of economic competitiveness, especially in manufacturing and business service sectors in Europe. In some other sectors such as construction, agriculture, and transport, the efficacy of building learning organizations can be fully exploited only after a period of de- and re-regulation. Our conclusion is that a new kind of *integrated competence building strategy* is needed and that such a strategy should take into account how to combine the three different major sources of competence building: hiring and firing, internal competence building, and networking and alliances (see Figure 2).

Firms differ in how strongly they emphasize each of these elements both between and within national innovation systems. Japanese firms have emphasized internal competence building, while most high-tech firms in Silicon Valley depend on learning through high inter-firm mobility of employees within the industrial district. Hewlett Packard is one US firm that has given strong emphasis to internal competence building but it is now moving towards a compromise strategy with more openness to hiring experienced employees from other firms. In Denmark the institutional set up of the training system and labour market institutions promotes networking among firms and high mobility in the labour market, making it attractive for firms to locate in 'industrial districts'.

There is no single optimal strategy in this respect even if the relative success of IT-based firms in the US and the weakening of the Japanese firms might be interpreted as an indication that high inter-firm mobility of labour is an advantage in the learning economy context. Under all circumstances, management needs to be aware of its priorities in this respect and the different mechanisms need to be attuned to each other so that the firm can become an efficient competence creating system.

In this context, it is important to take into account that labour markets and education systems still have strong national characteristics. Strategies covering multinational operations need to take into account such differences—it is not possible to have one single global knowledge management strategy that neglects local and national specificity. This is true especially for Europe, where there is a multitude of quite distinct national labour market models.

Industrial Relations and the Role of Trade Unions in the Learning Economy

When Danish managers were asked about what factors stimulated or hampered the movement towards learning organizations, many of them referred to shop stewards (*tillidsmænd*) as a positive factor and only a small minority mentioned them as raising barriers to organizational change. This indicates that trade unions at the central and local level may be a positive factor when firms need to cope with the new challenges of the learning economy. The relative strength of organized labour in Europe may be regarded as a positive factor in global competition—at least potentially.

Giving workers and their representatives the right incentives to participate positively in building learning organizations may be a question of creating a minimum of security in processes of restructuring—in Denmark the unemployment support level, and its duration, has done so (in spite of high inter-firm mobility Danish workers express less worries of increased insecurity in their job situations than do workers in other European countries with much less labour mobility—see OECD 1997: 132).

The fact that access to learning capability is what constitutes success among the members of trade unions should affect the priorities of the trade union movement. When demanding shorter working hours they could combine such demands with requiring real access to skill upgrading for their members. Agreements between business and labour on the development of new forms of work organization and skill development become more and more important for both parties.

There is a risk that old priorities lead to short termism on both sides. Obtaining nominal wage increases for union members whose skill position is stagnating may be highly counterproductive to the long-term interests of those represented. On the business side, routine lamenting on tax levels and government regulation might get in the way of long-term considerations regarding the transformation of training systems and labour market institutions. Organizations on both sides may need to take on the task of convincing their members that the advent of the learning economy involves a new game to be played according to new rules.

A special new responsibility which affects both sides is that of coping with the growing tendency towards social exclusion and not least the exclusion of workers of foreign origin. There is a need at the central level for trade unions to focus on the upgrading of the learning capability of those segments of workers who have narrow skills and to find ways to shelter those segments of the workforce (older unskilled workers) that cannot take part in the learning race. In general, trade unions need to be prepared to develop new kinds of solidarity that focus on the redistribution of learning capabilities.

Management also has a responsibility for this problem. Our research shows a strong Mattheus syndrome in the human management strategy of most firms: it is primarily those with extensive training that are offered even more training within firms. It is tempting for firms to focus skill upgrading on those who are rapid learners and leave the rest to public training programmes. In the light of a growing scarcity of new entrants into the labour market and the need for broad participation of employees in learning organization, this might need to change in the future. Under all circumstances, co-ordinated efforts between business and labour to reduce social exclusion are necessary to make the remaining tasks of governments manageable. Also in the field of industrial relations there is a need for reintegrating functions and responsibilities. Traditional interests in terms of pay, working time, and job security must be linked to and assessed in relation to competence building and the distribution of learning capabilities. Again, European traditions of concertation between government, business, and labour may prove to be a comparative advantage if there is a willingness on all sides to take up these challenges.

The Need for a New Type of Policy Co-ordination at the European Level

As shown by Fagerberg (in this volume), the European economy is lagging behind in some of the most important aspects of the new learning economy. To bridge the gap is therefore a European imperative. There is a growing consensus on the need to focus on long-term competence building in firms and in society as a whole. At the same time, the prevailing institutional set up and global competition tend to give predominance to short-term financial objectives in policy making. At the institutional level this is reflected in the fact that ministries of finance have become the only agency taking on a responsibility for co-ordinating the many specialized area policies. Area-specific ministries tend to identify with their own 'customers' and take little interest in global objectives of society.

The concept of 'the learning economy' has its roots in an analysis of globalization, technical innovation, and industrial dynamics (Lundvall and Johnson 1994; Lundvall and Borrás 1998). But the concept also implies a new perspective on a broad set of policies including social policy, labour market policy, education policy, industrial policy, energy policy, environmental policy, and science and technology policy. Specifically, the concept calls for new European and national development strategies with co-ordination across these policy areas (for an assessment of the current European innovation policy, see Sharp in this volume). *Social and distributional policies* need to focus more strongly on the distribution and redistribution of learning capabilities. It becomes increasingly costly and difficult to redistribute welfare, *ex post*, in a society with an uneven distribution of competence. Therefore there is a need for stronger emphasis on a 'new new deal' where weak learners (regions as well as individuals) are given privileged access to competence upgrading.

The effectiveness of *labour market institutions and policy* has so far been judged mainly from a static allocation perspective. There is a need to shift the perspective and to focus on how far the labour market supports competence building at the individual level and at the level of firms. This implies, for instance, that some dimensions of flexibility and mobility are more productive than others and that there may be third roads aside from Anglo-Saxon maximum flexibility and Mediterranean contractual job security. One of the new roads can be represented by the Scandinavian model, characterized by a unique combination of relative income security, high participation, and mobility rates.

Education and training policy needs to build institutions that promote simultaneously general and specific competencies, learning capability and lifelong learning. This points towards a new pedagogy that combines individual learning plans with collective problem-oriented styles of learning. A real commitment among employers, employees, and policy makers to lifelong learning with a strong interaction between schools and practice-based learning is necessary. *Industrial policy* needs to align competition policy and policies aiming at developing learning organizations and competence-building networks. Intensified competition may stimulate superficial change rather than competence building if not combined with organizational change and new forms of inter-firm collaboration. *Energy and environment policies* need to take into account their impact on competence building in the economy. *Science and technology policy* needs to support incremental innovation and the upgrading of competence in traditional industries as well as the formation and growth of high technology industries. For instance, the reallocation of academically trained workers towards small- and medium-sized firms is a key also to the formation of networks with universities and other knowledge institutions.

These area-specific policies need to be brought together and attuned into a common strategy. In the learning economy it is highly problematic to leave policy co-ordination exclusively to ministries of finance and to central banks—their visions of the world are necessarily biased towards the monetary dimension of the economy and thereby towards the short term. Europe could decide to establish a *European high level council on innovation and competence building* with the president of the EU as its chairman and with at least as much political weight as the European Bank. Such a new institution could have as one of its strategic responsibilities to develop a common vision for how Europe should cope with the learning economy. The basis of such a vision must be a better understanding of the distinct European national systems of competence building and innovation. In the framework of such an understanding international bench-marking and policy learning at the European level becomes meaningful. Similar and corresponding new institutions need to be built at the national and regional levels within member states.

Even the most recent framework programme—the fifth—remains focused on the creation and use of *scientific* knowledge. Even if it is structured with reference to social and ecological needs it is still the scientific community and research ministries in member states that dominate when it comes to the detailed design and implementation. Europe could decide to develop a *Framework programme on innovation and competence building*, where science is treated as only one among several sources to competence building. The European High Level Council could be in charge of the design of the main lines of the programme. Again, similar efforts at the national and regional level within member states would make the initiative more forceful.

REFERENCES

ARCHIBUGI, D., CESARATTO, S., and SIRILLI, G. (1991). 'Sources of innovative activities and industrial organisation in Italy'. *Research Policy*, 20: 299–313.

——and IAMMARINO, S. (1999). 'The policy implications of the globalisation of innovation'. *Research Policy*, 28: 317–36.

ARROW, K. J. (1971). 'Political and economic evaluation of social effects of externalities', in M. Intrilligator (ed.), *Frontiers of Quantitative Economics.* Amsterdam: North Holland.

CARTER, A. P. (1989). 'Know-how trading as economic exchange'. *Research Policy*, 18: 155–63.

EVANGELISTA, R., (2000). 'Sectoral patterns of technological change in services'. *Economics of Innovation and New Technologies*, 9: 183–221.

——, SANDVEN, T., SIRILLI, G., and SMITH, K. (1998). 'Measuring innovation in European industry'. *International Journal of the Economics of Business*, 5/3: 311–33.

FAGERBERG, J., VERSPAGEN, B., and CANIËLS, M. (1997). 'Technology, growth and unemployment across European regions'. *Regional Studies*, 31/5: 457–66.

FORAY, D., and LUNDVALL, B.-Å. (1996). 'The knowledge-based economy: From the economics of knowledge to the learning economy', in D. Foray and B.-Å. Lundvall (eds.), *Employment and Growth in the Knowledge-based Economy*. Paris: OECD.

FREEMAN, C. (1984). 'Prometheus unbound'. *Futures*, 16/5: 494–507.

LUNDVALL, B.-Å. (1996). *The Social Dimension of the Learning Economy*, DRUID Working Paper, No. 1, April, Department of Business Studies, Aalborg University.

——(1999). *The Danish System of Innovation* (in Danish). Copenhagen: Erhvervs-fremmestyrelsen.

——and BORRÁS, S. (1998). *The Globalising Learning Economy: Implications for Innovation Policy*. Brussels: European Commission.

——and JOHNSON, B. (1994). 'The learning economy'. *Journal of Industry Studies*, 1/2: 23–42.

——and NIELSEN, P. (1999). 'Competition and transformation in the learning economy—illustrated by the Danish case'. *Revue d'Economie Industrielle*, 88: 67–90.

OECD (1994). *The OECD Jobs Study—Facts, Analysis, Strategies*. Paris: OECD.

——(1996). *Science, Technology and Industry Outlook 1996*. Paris: OECD.

——(1997). *Employment Outlook, July 1997*. Paris: OECD.

——(2000). *Knowledge Management in the Learning Society*. Paris: OECD.

PAVITT, K. (1984). 'Sectoral patterns of technical change. Towards a taxonomy and a theory'. *Research Policy*, 13: 343–73.

PEREZ, C. (1983). 'Structural change and the assimilation of new technologies in the economic and social system'. *Futures*, 15/5: 357–75.

POLANYI, M. (1958/1978). *Personal Knowledge*. London: Routledge & Kegan Paul.

——(1966). *The Tacit Dimension*. London: Routledge & Kegan Paul.

VON HIPPEL, E. (1988). *The Sources of Innovation*. Oxford: Oxford University Press.

VIVARELLI, M., and PIANTA, M. (2000). *The Employment Impact of Innovation*. London: Routledge.

World Bank (2000). *Entering the 21st Century; World Development Report 1999/2000*. New York: Oxford University Press.

PART I

Europe in Global Competition

1
The New Economy:
A European Perspective

LUC SOETE

1.1. Introduction

The last decade of this century and millennium—and if we are to believe historians reminiscent of earlier *fin de siècle* periods (Landes 1998)—has been a period of major structural transformations at the world level.[1] One witnessed the collapse of the former communist countries and the opening up to market-led economic incentives, with of course as the most extreme case of economic and political integration German unification; the rapid worldwide liberalization of financial capital markets; the further move to the European single market in other, non-manufacturing utilities and service sectors with deregulation of many, traditionally closed, domestic markets; the macroeconomic convergence to a monetary union with the formal introduction of the euro on 1 January 1999; and last but not least, the continuous dramatic reduction in the costs of information and communication processing, opening up an increasing number of sectors to international trade and restructuring. This has been a worldwide structural transformation process involving, however, some regions or areas much more than others. Europe has undoubtedly been at the centre of many of these structural transformations, yet in many ways, it seems to have benefited (as yet) least from the growth incentives behind these structural transformation processes.

While the impact of opening up to global international restructuring may still be in its infancy and take off only in the next century, it has rapidly brought to the forefront how degrees of freedom of national policy actions have shrunk dramatically in a wide variety of different fields. This holds not only for traditional macroeconomic policy but increasingly also for tax, social security, and other policies traditionally preserved at the national level. Among many policy makers and economic commentators these structural transformations and the widely different impact they seem to have on the economic performance of individual countries or regions in the world—an

[1] This chapter is based on research carried out within the framework of the TSER project 'Technology, economic integration and specialization' to be published in a forthcoming book *Europe and the New Economy* by Pascal Petit and Luc Soete. I am particularly grateful to Daniele Archibugi and Bengt-Åke Lundvall for critical comment on a previous draft and to Pascal Petit for the part of this chapter based an common work.

acceleration in growth in the US, a deceleration of growth in Asia—have become part of a wider debate whether one is not confronted with a *'new economy'*: an economy much more dominated by global influences and by the speed often in real time of information and communication across distance. Over the last decade the term 'new economy' became particularly popular in the US in a growing number of business and policy circles. In its (17) November 1997 issue, *Business Week* heralded the emergence in the US of such a new economy spurred by two new trends: globalization of business spurred by worldwide freer trade and deregulation, and widespread use of new information and communication technologies leading to a digitization as it was called of all information, leading to new companies and new industries. More recently, the same *Business Week* (24 August 1998) devoted in the midst of the August 1998 financial turmoil a special issue to this new, '21st century' economy with, as subtitle, 'Volatility is here to stay, but technology and globalisation will spur robust growth'. Most remarkably, it did so in the midst of what many predicted would become the rapid end of the longest US growth cycle of the post-war period. It did this also despite growing dismissing views of some of the most established economic policy writers in the field.[2]

In this chapter the account of the emergence of this 'new economy' is based on research carried out within the framework of the TSER project 'Technology and Employment'.[3] 'New' is of course a highly subjective concept. In a first section we review, albeit briefly, some aggregate economic evidence. The latter, because of its aggregate nature, remains of course obscured by many other trends and features. Nevertheless the divergence in growth pattern between the US and Europe and Japan over the last decade is remarkable. In a second section we then review some of the main new economy features as identified by *Business Week*: globalization and digitization. In a first sub-section some of the main features of globalization in terms of trade and foreign direct investment are discussed. Given the fact that these are the subject of some of the other chapters of this book, our analysis remains brief. Nevertheless, the new intangible features of international transactions appear to form the essence of what the 'new' economy is all about. Their expansion contributes to forge what can be qualified as a *new* dimension of globalization, spurred by the particular role of new information and communication technologies (ICTs). From this perspective, ICTs represent indeed the first 'global' technological transformation with

---

[2] In the meantime, the US economy has continued in 1997, 1998, and 1999, more or less unaffected, its remarkable 'new' long-term growth path. Its unemployment rate has further dropped to levels considered by most academic economists in 1997 to be unsustainable and inflation has reached a historic low; all this despite continuous warnings of a coming stock market and financial crash given the structural low US savings rate, rising medical costs, major consumer defaults following the stock market fall in the autumn of 1998, and increasing wage inflation.

[3] The interested reader is referred to a number of mimeo papers and articles published over the last two years (Petit and Soete, 1997, 1998, and 2000).

which our societies have been confronted. Their impact on the increased international tradeability of many service activities is an illustration of such global impact. In the third section, we briefly discuss the challenges such a more open, immaterial economy in which value generation is less related to material production than to information content, distribution, and consumer interaction poses for traditional economic concepts and in particular the functioning of markets. We conclude by drawing some policy conclusions. In emphasizing the US's growth performance we do not make any assessment of the various distributional problems with which the US economy has been confronted. Nor do we make any evaluation of the long-term sustainability of this growth path given the specific shortcomings of the US secondary education system.

1.2. A 'New Economy' Growth Divergence in the 1990s?

We start the analysis with a rough and brief statistical parenthesis based on Hollanders, Soete, and ter Weel, 1999. Post-war economic growth among the developed OECD countries has been characterized by growth convergence. Countries furthest removed from income levels of the US in the 1950s appear to have witnessed the most rapid subsequent growth performance.

Figure 1.1 shows the relative growth performance, i.e. growth of per capita GDP, of a sample of OECD countries relative to the US. On the horizontal axis one finds the relative distance of each country in terms of GDP per capita to the US level at the beginning of each period. On the vertical axis is the growth rate in GDP per capita compared to the US. Dots above the nil line imply catching up; below falling behind.

As shown by Figure 1.1, there has been a major shift from a general trend of catching-up to the US to a trend of the US increasing its lead in the most recent period 1991–8. The most recent period shows the EU as a group and Japan rapidly falling behind the US.

By contrast the period up to 1973 can be characterized as a period of rapid growth, particularly in the industrialized countries. From a more qualitative point of view this is indeed what appears to have occurred. It was a period dominated by catching-up phenomena: catching-up of European consumption patterns to US standards; significant growth in the centrally planned economies based on further exploitation of Tayloristic methods of labour organization in agriculture and the heavy industrial sectors,[4] and the end of the decolonization process in most Third World countries. It was in the logic itself of such a growth process that the gap between the US and these countries was to narrow down. By contrast, the US economy did, if

---

[4] The impulse to growth under communism would become based on the electricity revolution and the scientific Tayloristic division of labour organization.

Luc Soete

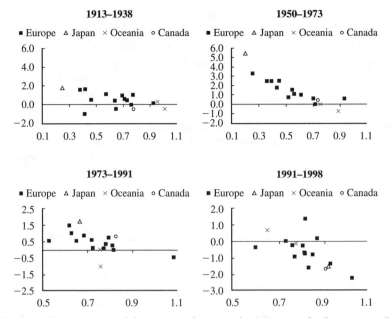

FIG 1.1. *Convergence and divergence relative to the US—growth of per capita GDP*
Source: Hollanders, Soete, and ter Weel 1999.

anything, show some major weaknesses, for example in relation to employment creation.[5]

By contrast, the period 1973–91 appears to be characterized by the disappearance of such strong catching-up features at least with respect to the European developed OECD world and Japan. This happened despite accelerated European economic integration with the subsequent enlargements of the European Community and the move from a customs union to an economic union. It also took place despite the gradual liberalization of financial markets. In fact the period was characterized first by a dramatic explosion of exchange rate volatility, inflation, unemployment, and public deficits. The failure of macroeconomic policies to contain inflation, reduce unemployment particularly in Europe, and control public spending are from this perspective both consequence and cause of the halt of growth convergence and what marked the end of what European economists referred to as *les trentes glorieuses*: the thirty wonder years of high growth, low inflation, and low unemployment.

The most recent period, from 1991 until 1998, appears to be characterized mainly by growth divergence between the US, Europe, and Japan; effectively a leap forward by the US. Once again, this US growth divergence took place

[5] See e.g. the various contributions to the so-called automation debate (US National Commission on Technology, Automation, and Economic Progress, 1966).

despite a major convergence in aggregate economic indicators such as inflation, long-term interest rates, and public spending. It is important to resitu-
ate in its recent historical context the continuing unexpected nature of this
emerging growth divergence. First and foremost, few authors predicted the
slowdown of Japanese growth. At the same time, many others predicted rapid
growth in Europe because of the internal economic integration deepening
process (the 1992 single market) and the expected rapid catching-up of
Eastern European countries to EU income and consumption levels. The ultimate paradox of macroeconomic convergence is probably best illustrated by
the arrival of the euro on 1 January 1999, accompanied by a significant slowdown of growth across EU member countries, again very much in contrast to
expectations and forecasts. However, the collapse of US growth predicted since
the mid-1990s as a result of its low savings rate, high trade deficit, and unsustainable growth in stock market prices failed to occur. Hence, growth divergence among the Triad countries has been a dominant feature of the 1990s.

Underlying the growth process over the last ten years, some other, new factors appear to have emerged, particularly in the US. More than any other
country in the world, the US economy appears to have benefited from faster
application and implementation of new technologies, more rapid uptake of
the new so-called information highways infrastructure, and more successful
worldwide commercial exploitation of these growth opportunities. In short,
the US seems to have been the most successful country in making its transition
to a 'new', more knowledge-, and more immaterial-based economy. This is not
the place to go into a discussion about the sustainability of such growth divergence process, particularly in view of the open, global financial and information networks. Nevertheless, the process as it appears to have evolved over the
last ten years is remarkable and is well worth some further investigation.

Before discussing some of the possible reasons explaining the US's success
in entering this 'new' economy, we turn to some of the characteristic features
of the new economy, starting with some of the dimensions of this new emerging open, global world economy.

1.3. Features of the New Economy

1.3.1. From Old to 'New' Globalization

As in many other areas of structural change, there is an ongoing debate about
the factual evidence surrounding globalization. We do not wish to discuss the
issue here in any detail given the fact that another part of this book is devoted
to the issue of globalization. Most of the traditional, readily available, evidence focuses on trade and foreign direct investment (FDI) flows. This evidence tends to suggest that there has been little increase in 'globalization'.
From a long-term perspective the ratio of exports or imports to GDP, or even

Luc Soete

the importance of FDI, is not unprecedented. The period 1870–1913 is often presented as a time of exceptionally rapid international integration (Bairoch and Kozul-Wright 1998), with trade flows that represented even a higher share of GDP in the UK, the Netherlands, or in Japan in 1913. Other critics underline that FDI flows are mainly intra-regional and globalization a process of regional integration (Hirst and Thompson 1996). Globalization is effectively a myth when it is viewed as a deterministic, entirely market-driven process.

However, from a more institutionalist perspective, one may say that globalization has reached an unprecedented phase, even if trade flows are not unprecedented and if FDI flows remain centred among developed economies. The fact that these trade and FDI flows now concern a much larger number of countries would be enough to characterize a new phase in the process of globalization. More important though is to consider the qualitative changes affecting international transactions. The very nature of these transactions and the institutional contexts in which they occur today are illustrative of the reality of a new phase in the globalization process.

Hence, what we would call the 'new' dimension of the process of globalization refers in the first instance to the intangible part in the fabric of international relations and transactions, based primarily on the internationalization of information and knowledge. Being intangible, these transactions no longer only reflect the financial counterpart of the real trade and investment flows but include now a wide variety of transactions some of which do not show up in the balance of payments, some only do so partially in some service transactions (beyond fees and royalties a lot of business and personal services imply some transfer of technology, information, and knowledge) and others are purely involved in financial arbitrage. These international intangible exchanges affect in very different ways the dynamics of trade and FDI flows. The common denominator is the widespread use of information and communication technologies.

Following Petit and Soete (1998), we track this dimension along five lines of development, from purely financial to scientific information flows:

(1) first and foremost, the particular case of finance, the ultimate (intangible) global tradeable good;
(2) second, the far-ranging deregulation move leading not only to the liberalization of trade and investment flows but also to the deregulation of many intermediate services which are central in the organization of markets and transactions;
(3) third, the practice of formalized (and publicly announced) international co-operation and agreements between firms;
(4) fourth, the free exchange of information and knowledge about new products and markets, that is conveyed by academic activities and media;
(5) fifth, the stock of expertise, experiences, and personal networks that have developed over years in the field of international relations and business,

mainly through the activities of internationalized business services but also through personal contact and cultural links.

The *area of finance* has of course always been highly volatile. However, the volume of transactions, fuelled by a large set of instruments and new means of transactions, has reached phenomenal levels. The growth in the 'globalization' of financial flows over the last two decades has been dramatic. Cross-border transactions in bonds and equities have increased in OECD countries over the last fifteen years from 10% of GDP in 1980 to between 150 and 250% of GDP in 1995. At the same time, the worldwide volume of foreign exchange trading has increased to a turnover of more than $1,200 billion a day (cf. Chesnais 1997). These financial flows are in no way compensatory of trade or FDI flows. They outline the development of new activities on money markets or in stock markets located in those financial centres that have been considerably deregulated. This realm of finance, where huge sums can be transferred instantaneously around the world, has of course become very risky. The speculative bubble that has outstretched the growth of some stock markets can blow up. The rush against some currencies, suddenly perceived as weak, can reach dramatic magnitude. Meanwhile after each 'local' alert the world of international finance tends to develop its own prudential rules to avoid a major systemic crisis. Whether the international financial regime, which is building up in this step-wise process, will prevent major chaos, remains a challenge. The question is too broad for existing international institutions like the IMF, while individual countries seem too divided on control issues (such as temporary exchange rate controls, forced deposit with domestic banks of a percentage of incoming funds, or a small flat rate tax on international capital flows to reduce their volatility as proposed by Tobin) to address such a global question.

Global finance also features an interesting, conservative trait: the importance retained by traditional financial areas such as London and New York. Despite the existence of new means of transacting, other financial areas have remained secondary, with the notable exception of Tokyo. Markets in Frankfurt or Paris find it difficult to remain competitive (even when new opportunities arise, such as EMU and more recently the euro). As for emerging markets that have developed in South East Asia in the trail of their economic upheaval, the financial crisis initiated in the summer of 1997 revealed their intrinsic weaknesses. Indeed the large development of the transactions led to the emergence of new locations and to the development of mid-ranking locations, but overall the hierarchy between financial areas has been more comforted than eroded in the last decade. This 'agglomeration' effect is also telling of the tacit knowledge, which, among other local conditions, is required to be durably successful at a worldwide level, a point that will be discussed below.

The *deregulation move* clearly gained some momentum in the late 1970s with the break up of the stringent regulatory frameworks that had been set up for most intermediary services (banking, transport, communication) in the late 1930s or in the post-war period. The trend to liberalize trade and investment started much earlier—it dates back to the post-war period, when some large international institutions like the GATT, the IMF, or the OECD were specially created to promote the idea of free trade and investment. This trend gained new momentum over the last two decades with, on the one side, the development of regional agreements and on the other side a more wide-spread and intensive adhesion of developing economies, whether forced by international money lenders to liberalize or induced by a new domestic balance of political power in favour of free markets.

While this trend accompanied the growth in trade and investment flows over the post-war period, the deregulation of intermediate services had its own impact on international restructuring. Deregulation is, in the first place, largely a consequence of the diffusion of new ICTs, which, in easing international access and provision, helped firms to bypass the limitations set by the old national regulatory frameworks. Deregulation forced at national levels has also been pushed forward and co-ordinated within regional agreements. Moreover, innovations in processes and products brought about in this new context stirred the interest for these services and increased the stakes of their restructuring. The privatization that often followed deregulation opened the doors to foreign multinational firms. But it also strongly induced the old monopolies to develop some global reach, in particular, by taking advantage of newly opened markets in developing countries. This all led, in some cases at least, to the creation of large international conglomerates or networks of allied multinational firms. A clear example is given in the telecommunications area, with British, French, and Deutsche Telecoms as major protagonists world wide, while deregulation of telecommunication industries was only just completed in January 1998. But large alliances of multinational firms have also recently developed in banking, insurance, and transport. This does not imply that the phase of liberalization is completed. In some developing countries the process is only starting; its pace, regarding external relations or domestic activities, depends on the outcomes of its policies, on the economic successes and financial difficulties of countries. Furthermore, invisible barriers to trade in advanced countries may be all the more lasting as product markets have become more complex, more differentiated. Some also argue that the liberalization of trade and investment around the world owes much of its dynamics in the past decades to regional agreements that will lock in the process of liberalization. This conflict between 'regionalization' and 'globalization' is either praised or blamed as promoting or hampering what the authors view as the final stage of the globalization process.

The third line of development to be considered is *the development of co-operation between firms* at an international level. We already alluded to this question when evoking the liberalization of intermediary service industries. Co-operation among firms at the international level (60% of inter-firm technical agreements are international) concerns all industries, even if they tend to concentrate in the high-tech sectors. This constitutes an important change, especially since these accords are public and publicized (the available databases have gathered information on the publicized accords only and they are likely to represent the tip of the iceberg—see Hagedoorn 1996) and because they structure the development of key innovative industries (ICTs and pharmaceuticals) at international levels (quite often beyond the regional level). These agreements have different objectives (production: 25%, R&D: 31%, marketing: 13%, mix of objectives: 30%. See OECD 1994, table 17). Their motivations are diverse. Sometimes firms are motivated to share high investment cost, or to avoid destructive competition; often they try to preserve some flexibility in the capacity of firms to adjust to external changes. Some alliances may appear contradictory, implying that they may be short in their duration. These agreements may last for different spans of time. They may also become obsolete before their term, they may fail or be successfully achieved and renewed. This whole fabric, with its history of past collaborations, sometimes more informal than others, can also take various legal and contractual forms (from joint venture and investment to loose agreements to share information), including arrangements between small firms and large firms as in franchising and the like. If one takes into account this diversity, then co-operation at the international level has been increasing over the past decades, even more intensively than it has domestically, precisely because it aimed to cope with the handicaps met by firms that want to produce abroad or access new markets (see Mytelka's chapter in this volume).

This process of co-operation is creating complex overlapping networks that continuously shape the fabric of global markets and internationalized production processes. Some of these networks may be regional (European, for instance). Most of such accords and alliances, however, are transcontinental and comprise, in various combinations, firms of the Triad (Europe, North America, and South East Asia) which directly transfer for a good deal of them into some FDI flows. Again it shows a meaningful level of global operations and strategies without implying that all international agreements between firms are global in their scope. Still it may be difficult to assess where we stand. Is there room for the development of such agreements? How do they impinge upon the dynamics of production processes and markets? How do they in particular relate to trade and FDI flows? Are they substitutes or preconditions (and therefore complementary)? So far this web of firms' arrangements is not integrated in a comprehensive way in our understanding of the working of our economies, although these arrangements are important, and being public, are also signals to the financial world, to competitors and to governments. They contribute to the process of globalization and are also linked to the treatment of information and knowledge that constitutes the third perspective we take on the intangible infrastructure backing the process of globalization.

The fourth line of the argument considers *the diffusion of information and knowledge by all the academic activities (scientific meetings and publications) and the media* (the press, general or specialized, as well as TV, radio, and the like). Universities and public research centres are considered as a pre-eminent vector in the globalization of innovation (cf. the taxonomy of Archibugi and Michie 1995, and Archibugi and Iammarino, in this volume). Even if indicators are still scarce, they do show a rise in international co-operation between academics and other public researchers. The ratio of internationally co-authored scientific papers (if compared with all co-authored scientific papers) has reached around 25% in the US and in Japan, and as much as 50% in Europe and the number of foreign students in postgraduate studies is approximately 24% in the US in 1994 (see Archibugi and Michie 1997).

The media are also an important international vector of information and knowledge, through not only the new global reach of TV, but also through the expansion of the technical press and professional international events (from traditional fairs to more professional seminars). The convergence between computing and telecommunication technologies broadens the scope for such international interactions among academics or professionals. In effect the potential of the new ICTs has become a key element in the diffusion of information and knowledge. The Internet in this respect is simply the latest stage of this process of free dissemination, with the worldwide web, which is telling on the globalization process as it develops itself in strong correlation with the levels of development of countries but also with a lot of countries lagging behind or forging ahead of this general trend.

The interesting thing is that information and knowledge are basically freely accessible (even if media are not free, they can provide specific information of high value for those who know how to exploit it, regardless of how information is priced, be it professional journals or more general press diffusing crucial information). Why is something that is costly to produce freely disseminated worldwide? We have a number of good reasons from which to choose. Traditions in academic spheres call for the publication and discussion of information within the scientific community. This is increasingly true as borders are disappearing through the use of English within the international community as a common language. Dissemination can also help to set standards, whether in science or in industry (one present reason is to set the norms of the new ICTs). Free dissemination also favours co-operation, not only around norms but also around projects, therefore avoiding duplications or incompatible varieties of new products. It may be intended for a small community of firms or professionals but at the cost of free riding by others, if they have the relevant knowledge that gives its price to the information under view. There is also the idea of reciprocity in a highly innovative world—where diffusing information may help the innovator to stay abreast of the next wave of innovations. Whatever the combination of reasons, a mass of information has been made available throughout the world: it can be both reached and used. The potential to access and use information depends on some knowledge which itself has to be built up. The development of higher education and of public research has helped strongly to reduce barriers. ICTs and regional arrangements have significantly contributed to the internal dissemination of information and knowledge. The codification of information that ICTs require has certainly facilitated this international dissemination. However, it is not a substitute for the tacit knowledge that is required in modern industries.

Again, one may question the extent to which the development of some internationalization of academic research and specialized media has contributed to the process of globalization. It is always difficult to appreciate the meaningfulness of some evolution when the laws of the underlying dynamics remain even sketchier. Somehow this discussion parallels the one on the effects that a globalization process could have on the systems of innovation that have been established as being strongly national specific in a recent past.

A strong argument stressing the limits of a globalization process has been to point out that R&D activities of multinational firms have been, until the late 1980s, for the most part realized in their home country (Patel and Pavitt 1991). First, R&D activities are at the core of the activities identifying a firm. Therefore any externalization of R&D activities, even partial, any 'delocalization' to affiliates, or any collaboration with competitors may be surprising. The level at which one should consider it as a critical change is difficult to assess.[6] Second, the economics of R&D is complex, and much of the international relations viewed above (the nexus of inter-firm agreements on technological issues or the transfers of information and knowledge through the networks of academics, researchers, and professionals) are major inputs in this process. Therefore one should be cautious in assessing the impact on national systems of innovations, and all the more so as the forms of competition have evolved on the highly differentiated markets that we featured in section 1.1. Such is the strain put on some systems of innovation that significant adjustments imply that some forms of internationalization are taking place which are becoming more obvious in the 1990s. Thus R&D expenditures by foreign affiliates in OECD countries in 1994 range from 2% (in Japan) to 68% (in Ireland) of total R&D, with significant figures in the UK (35%), in Germany (17%), and in France (15%) (Hatzichronoglou 1998). Although this is not even close to a complete globalization of R&D, it is already a distinct new system, with new external links, that are again very much country specific (see Patel and Pavitt 1999;

---

[6] Philips, the large Dutch multinational, realizes 40% of its R&D abroad, which may be considered as high or low accordingly. It should also be taken into account that R&D expenditures mix research and development activities which can be externalized and internationalized, both of them on very different grounds according to the sector, whether it is pharmaceutical, for instance, or automobile industry.

Cantwell and Janne 2000). The question therefore is: how will such a trend develop? Will there be hierarchies among clubs (or networks) of multinational firms of various countries within industries? Or will there be means for national systems to adjust to new norms of competition? Much depends on the abilities of countries to recreate the structural bases of idiosyncratic dynamics.

The fifth line of the argument focusing on the intangible logistics support-ing the globalization process underlines the role of *a comprehensive group of professionals* setting the norms of international transactions. The core of this group is composed of professionals working in business and financial serv-ices. They may not be directly involved in the international transactions that are part of the expanding trade in services. Still their work is directly con-cerned with the organization and supervision of international operations. Norms, rules, ethics are set by their own experiences.

One example is professionals managing pension funds. The criteria on which they manage their internationalized portfolios are crucial. They may use the information and knowledge that academics and the media diffuse, but mainly as inputs to help form their own opinions (which certainly have ir-rational and speculative aspects). Beyond this highly publicized example one finds a complex set of experts and special authorities, operating in insurance, law, finance, and accountancy. Just to illustrate their hold on businesses world wide one may recall (following Strange 1996) that the big six accountancy firms (Price Waterhouse, Peat Marwick, McClintock, Coopers & Lybrand, Ernst and Young, Deloitte Touche Tohmatsu, and Arthur Andersen) audit 494 of the Fortune 500 and that their worldwide fees total $30 billion (the GDP of Ireland). Their norms (rather inspired by US practices) tend to be imposed universally, especially through the symbiotic relationships that these accountancy firms have developed with banks and financial institutions. Such networking by international professionals or experts concerns a range of activities that goes beyond the ones we just mentioned, as it includes real estate (a high component of FDI), leisure (from international sport organ-izations to amusement parks), and cultural industries (with the technological convergence between computer and telecommunications technologies broad-ening the scope for worldwide markets of mass media products).

This last perspective shows how deeply rooted the changes in organizations and practices are that build up the kind of global reach suggesting the inter-national involvement of so many economic agents. On one side, it clearly shows that decisive moves within one country may follow from changes that occurred abroad, for example in norms, ethics, or knowledge, without the occurrence of any international transactions that could have been registered by the balance of payments. On the other side, it shows that this global inter-dependence does not display a clear ordering principle, neither a clear law of market competition nor a clear hegemonic power of one nation state.

Although we did not discuss this last issue, we return to it in assessing the room for manoeuvring left to the nation states. At this stage we have recalled the complexity of markets, with their high product differentiation and the segmented structure of countries' roles. We have then stressed above, with this third dimension of globalization, by which concrete means an accumulated base of information and knowledge has developed to support global strategies of economic agents, be they firms or individuals. Before we investigate the implications of this new context for nation states, it is worth calling specific attention to the one key factor contributing to this change of context, namely the diffusion of the new ICTs.

1.3.2. Digitization and the Expansion of Markets

In effect, if the world has entered into something of a new era in which global access has become a major characteristic of both production *and* consumption, then the cluster of new ICTs has been at the centre of this process. The ability they provide dramatically to reduce communication and information handling and processing costs has been the permissive condition for the expansion of the third dimension. This expansion has also forged the lines of development of these new technologies. The trend towards worldwide access is intrinsically linked with the ability of ICTs to codify information and knowledge over both distance and time and this global potential oriented the norms and the codes developed around the ICTs. It does not follow that ICTs have similar impacts on all sectors or on all countries. In some areas, such as finance, which is a major user of ICTs, and where this diffusion has been accompanied by an institutional liberalization and deregulation process, the globalization process has been most rapid: financial capital has in essence become fully internationally mobile.

In traditional manufacturing production, the decline in communication and information costs has further increased the international transparency of markets, reinforcing the scope to choose world wide where to produce and how to sell on different markets. It has also accelerated the rhythm of product innovation.

In areas such as services, new ICTs are often for the first time allowing cheap 'global' access to low-cost labour locations, thus facilitating the relocation of various 'routine' service functions and activities. Basically it also allowed for a much larger product differentiation and for the diffusion of finely discriminating tariffs (opening the way to yield managements). In the field of intermediary services, it enhanced a deregulation trend that deeply transformed these activities. Firms and organizations have come to discover both the benefits of international differences in labour costs in areas and conversely the advantage of the agglomeration of competencies (Freeman and Soete 1994).

It also follows that the benefit did not accrue evenly to all countries. ICTs contribute to global economic transparency in so far as they bring to the forefront the cost advantages as well as the specific competencies of alternative locations. But this is not a neutral clarification of pre-existing advantages. ICTs create their requirements in terms of individuals' and organizations' abilities or network facilities. Furthermore, if ICTs have positively affected international access to information and 'codified' knowledge (David and Foray 1995), which is useful to organize production processes and to access markets on a worldwide basis, its potential is limited by differences in local capacities to use or have the competency to transform such 'codified' knowledge. In effect the potential for catching up, in terms of competitiveness, based upon the economic transparency of advantages, strictly depends on some 'tacit' knowledge and other competency elements much more difficult to transfer by definition (Foray and Lundvall 1996; OECD 1996). The threat of rigid or widening segmentation it implies is one of the big challenges of this phase of *de facto* globalization, largely borne by the ability to master the ICTs.

There is little doubt that the US has been much more capable of benefiting from the emerging ICTs. There has been a dramatic revival of the US semiconductor industry following the US–Japanese semiconductor trade agreement effectively providing breathing space for such a revival. On the other hand, the alliance between the software and semiconductor industry has allowed for effective commercial exploitation of technological improvements in the computer industry. Authors such as John Zysman refer in this context to the notion of 'wintelism' (Borrus and Zysman 1998): the combination of continuous technological improvements (e.g. Pentium from Intel) in chip performance and operating systems such as windows (from Microsoft) requiring extensive performance capacity. Thanks to the combination of free local telecom access, expertise in hardware and software network technologies going back to DARPA and ATT (e.g. Sun and the software languages UNIX, Java, and now Jini), and the development of a universal Internet Protocol (Netscape), Internet use rose rapidly outside of the traditional scientific community and was quickly taken up by businesses and individuals. Finally, the availability of an extensive content (film, television, radio, press) sector provided a rapid take off in terms of new Internet content services.

The result has been that the US led the world with maybe one or two exceptions (Finland, Sweden), in Internet use and pricing, in number of websites, Information Service Providers, hits, sales on e-commerce, etc. (see also Fagerberg's chapter in this volume). The growth in employment in these ICT-related sectors has been significant and is expected to continue, as has been the volume of international trade generated. The international US competitiveness in these sectors has undoubtedly been greatly enhanced by the sometimes forceful imposition world wide (China) of strong intellectual property regimes (see, for instance, the systematic implementation methods of the Business Software Alliance in individual countries) in the area of copyrights, trademarks, and authorship rights (extended recently from fifty to seventy years).

But the final consumer end of these new ICT-based sectors is of course only one part of the 'new' growth story. Probably even more important has been the impact on firms' internal efficiency, the impact of so-called business-to-business e-commerce (OECD 1998). The increased potential for codification and transferability allowed for by ICT allows indeed also for significant reductions in transaction costs; for a process of 'de-intermediation' and decentralization of activities and more global direct distribution and access (Soete 1998).

The importance of access brings to the forefront the overriding importance of new communication infrastructures, as enabling factor for both cost reduction and the foundation of new markets.

1.4. New Economic Growth and New Market Rules

There is little doubt that one of the main achievements of economics has been the pervasive illustration that prices in well-functioning markets lead both in a static and in a dynamic sense to 'optimal' outcomes. In a static sense, 'free-market' prices solve in a better way than any other system the distribution of scarce commodities between consumers—anyone not willing to pay the market price will simply not be allowed to consume the commodity. In a dynamic sense, prices also signal profit opportunities to potential suppliers, their entry and competition with the incumbent, bringing prices in line with production costs. Under the well-known assumptions of free, well-functioning open markets, such market price systems will create the maximum amount of social surplus. It could be argued from this perspective that the failure of the planned-based, socialist system was in the first instance a failure to cope with the dynamic challenges. It failed to increase social surplus, precisely at a moment (the 1970s and 1980s) when changes in new production methods and new product opportunities were also challenging the capitalist market system.

However, for markets to function well three essential structural conditions need to exist: excludability, rivalry, and transparency. These conditions are to some extent intrinsic to the exchange of material goods.

Thus, the exchange between seller and buyer needs to involve the exclusive exchange of ownership over the particular product. Once traded the latter is no longer the property of the seller but the exclusive property of the buyer. It is this feature which is, of course, behind the notion of economic scarcity and provides the impulse for new output activities on the part of the seller. Another feature typical of material production and open markets is the notion of rivalry. While significant economies of scale are likely to exist in the production of most material goods, the selling of a single good will still imply that the same good cannot be sold to another buyer. At the same time, while there might be significant entry barriers, the threat of new entry will imply that suppliers will not be in a position to keep prices substantially above costs. Rivalry is in other words a major and essential condition for markets to generate optimal outcomes. Finally, the exchange of material goods involves a high degree of transparency: the buyer can see, feel, test, smell, in some cases even taste, the product on offer.

In the case of the exchange of a pure information 'electronic' good, it can be argued that none of these conditions holds. The owner of the digital commodity selling his product in the market-place will have difficulty in preventing buyers or anyone else for that matter from copying and reselling it. Excludability will typically be difficult if not impossible to achieve. Rather than a purchase and sale relationship, the nature of the exchange will look more like a gift. The creation and enforcement of excludability is hence an absolute and first condition for such markets to exist. Hence the focus on encryption, watermarks, and various other forms of tracing and monitoring property rights is central to most policy documents on e-commerce. Without these rules creating excludability, no optimal level of production can be achieved and little indication can be obtained of the sort of products that are wanted by potential buyers.

Yet the creation and strengthening of such property rules has, of course, immediate implications for the openness and the degree of competition in such markets. If property protection is absolute, whereas at the same time marginal production costs are minimal, possibly even nil as typical for many digital goods, many potential users will not consume, and compared to the social optimum, too little will be produced (as in the case of the virtual monopolist). At the same time, the individual producer is now being guaranteed a fixed property income and has little to fear both from competitors and consumers who can only choose to buy the particular product from him. This non-rivalry characteristic directly challenges the optimal market outcome. It raises a very large set of welfare questions characteristic of what has been called network economics and involving competition policy, regulation—for instance price control in the case of natural monopoly—standards, and inter-connectivity, etc.

Finally, despite the tremendous opening up of trading possibilities and the increase in market transparency, the actual exchange of a digital commodity will involve almost by definition a high degree of information asymmetry between seller and buyer. Many of the new forms of markets emerging on the Internet are typical illustrations of such problems of information asymmetry and well known in information economics. New intermediaries emerge assisting buyers in their search; alternatively, goods might be offered free, paid for by advertising or by subsequent upgrades; a limited preview of the good might be offered free; etc. Yet, what is clear is that the traditional physical market-place is being replaced by a far more complex and diversified set of exchange methods in which the value of what the content seller is offering is likely to differ strongly among individual consumers—hence the crucial importance of so-called versioning (Varian 1997)—and is becoming distributed among many intermediaries that have brought buyer in contact with supplier—with significant shifts in the value chain as highlighted in so-called attention or click economics.

On all three accounts it is difficult simply to subscribe to the notion that the newly created markets will, as in the exchange of physical goods, guarantee optimality. As Bradford de Long and Michael Froomkin (1998) put it forcefully: 'What used to be second-order "externality" corrections to the invisible hand have become first-order phenomena' in the cyberspace world. Nowhere else is this more clearly illustrated than in the artificial creation of excludability. In contrast to the old notion of the invisible hand of the market, excludability is human made. Its length, its height, its breadth as in the case of patent protection is likely to have major implications for market structure, competition, and more generally welfare. Furthermore, while national rules might be enforced and hence domestic excludability succeed in generating an optimal outcome, international differences in the protection of property rights might undermine such domestic attempts at strengthening intellectual property. In other words, the human-made rules of excludability involve practically by definition particular sectoral and/or national lobbies. Excludability is also questioning the traditional arguments about the welfare gains from trade: for example, strengthening the imposition of the international property regime world wide might well shift the terms of trade in favour of countries specialized in digital goods and content at the disadvantage of countries more specialized in manufactured commodities.[7] This may well be one of the underlying 'real' factors behind the Asian crisis.

1.5. New Policy Challenges to the Nation State

In most debates, the globalization process tends to be associated with the end of nation states. One has to take a much more balanced view. Entering a new phase of globalization certainly transforms and alters the power of the old nation states. But an assessment of the new room for policies that nation states have kept or can develop is crucial to reconstruct any active structural policy (see Lundvall and Archibugi and Iammarino, in this volume). The limits set to the power of the old nation states are obvious.

During the past 'fordist' period of rapid growth of the now-developed economies, states and governments have been involved at an unprecedented level in economic activities. Besides the enlargement of public sectors and the enrichment of regulatory frameworks, standard macroeconomic Keynesian

[7] Once again, there is no superior invisible hand in arguing about such a shift. For many centuries, the now-developed countries have freely taken from now less-developed countries their ideas, technologies, and knowledge.

policies, with their monetary and fiscal instruments, played a central role in this monitoring of economies. The new context, providing economic agents more or less directly with some global reach, limits the power and scope of these policies, while favouring a trend of deregulation and of privatization of the public sectors. Even if this statement requires many specifications,[8] it remains that the old tools that allowed individual nation states more or less to successfully monitor their economies have been drastically constrained. While this does not imply that new room for manoeuvre does not exist, it highlights the need for a new policy framework. The new challenge to nation states may be precisely to articulate policy actions at each level which allow them to take mutual and significant advantage of a tamed process of globalization. We briefly present these reasons, starting from a more local level and moving towards a more universal one, concluding with some future perspectives on the EU.

1.5.1. **Around Industrial and Structural Policies**

The first level refers to the change of context for industrial and structural policies induced by the present phase of the globalization process. The structural changes on which we focused, with the development of new forms of competition on products markets and of new relations with multinational firms at local levels, enhanced by the diffusion of new technologies, somehow enlarged the scope for policies taking care of the general environment of economic activities. Industrial and structural policies seemed in that respect to be given a new opportunity, all the more welcome since standard macroeconomic policies had been further constrained in the process. Still at the same time the balance of power between the local, national, and international levels of government has changed. The question is then to reassess, in a schematic way, the perspective left to nation states to develop comprehensive structural policies, e.g. policies that transform the context in which an economy operates. In effect, the economic efficiency and competitiveness of a territory depends greatly on the quality and range of its infrastructure. A good match of a territory's infrastructure with the geographic, historical, and cultural background increases positive external effects, helping to create competitive advantages. The infrastructures under view are mainly of two kinds: those in charge of education and training of the labour force; and those organizing by means of large network services (transport, communications, distribution, finance) all the 'intermediations' implied by the functioning of markets and the running of production processes. A whole economic literature on endogenous growth theory has been pointing at the potential importance of such infrastructure

---

[8] Thus one should speak of a radical change in the orientations of the regulation frameworks more than of a deregulation trend. It is clear in the case of finance where a deregulation of a regulatory framework which segmented activities tends to favour a more prudential-oriented reconstruction of regulations.

effects. Much emphasis has been put on national levels. Still little is known on the idiosyncratic dimension of this supportive action: how can specific combinations of these factors increase the positive externalities and at which level, local, national, or regional, should they be organized? We stressed above that structural change developed a new relationship between the local and the global level. We also underlined the importance of the regional organization of nation states. Both evolutions affect the primacy that nation states had in the building up of infrastructures. Local authorities will be tempted to favour symbiotic moves adjusting closely infrastructures to local characteristics (searching for new industrial districts or science parks). Regional authorities will, on their side, favour a greater regional harmonization of the infrastructures. Much depends on the type of infrastructure under view. In some cases, as in telecommunications, the deregulation and the regional if not global harmonization of service provisions is well advanced. In the case of education and training the monitoring is still national, with more or less autonomy left to local levels.

Nation states have thus a complex role to play. Regarding logistics, which are basically organized under international regulations, they may help to develop schemes 'downstream', facilitating specific uses of the logistics (aiming at special groups of people or special local regions). As for infrastructures that would be strongly influenced by local needs, nation states may avoid a too stringent specialization and provide schemes allowing some adjustment, as in the case of education, possibilities of mobility, and retraining.

To conclude, the structural changes over the last decades seem to have brought new opportunities for comprehensive industrial policies but nation states cannot straightforwardly make use of these possibilities. They have to take into account the new balance of government between local, national, regional, and global levels. Nation states are thus led to articulate their actions accordingly. This shift still leaves them with a potential of intervention, if they make an adjustment which basically attempts to monitor comprehensive learning processes on how to use the new 'market' logistics, instead of monitoring directly the provision of these services (as was done previously with the 'public' services). They remain key actors, with a unique legitimacy and historically rooted know-how, to launch such schemes at a meaningful scale, even if the complexity of this set of policies strongly limits their political appeal.

1.5.2. **At the Heart of the Working of International Regimes**

Globalization also proceeds through the organization of some sectoral issues at a world level. The notion of international regime precisely considers *per se* the relative autonomy of such international organization with its own rules, historical experiences, and balance of power. The most common example of such international regime has been given by the oil industry.

The political power of nation states is an important factor in establishing the rights and the prices of the exploitation and the distribution of oil. The hierarchy between nation states and the more or less hegemonic power detained by the US, at various periods, contributed to the high specificity of this global market. Financial markets are another example of such international regime, with the role of the nation state being completely different. Localizing market activities around the world, even in fiscal heaven, strongly give the impression of a footloose 'industry'. We have stressed that such was not fully the case, as the core of this activity remained in historically financial places. But even more important is the fact that nation states one way or the other are the only actors likely to prevent the system from running unacceptably high risks and collapsing. It is not at all certain at this stage that states will be able to co-ordinate their actions and avoid such chaos. Still the lessons from the financial crises of the last decades is that beyond the limits of specialized international financial institutions, states' interventions have been rapid and forceful, even if they did not put an end to the financial turmoil. One of the big paradoxes of this financial regime is precisely that without this credo—that states will end up bailing out the bankruptcies—a deep lack of confidence would rapidly bring to an end the expansion of the financial sphere. This importance of nation states, that shows up in the governance structure of such rather accomplished international regimes as the ones we just mentioned is also pointing at the area of intellectual property rights which plays a crucial role in the present forms of competition. In effect these rights condition the existence and duration of nearly all the rents of innovation and therefore of the whole dynamics of non-price competitiveness, which has gained in importance in the last decades. The fact that the most successful firms in the past decades have been selling intangibles (such as Microsoft) strongly illustrates this strategic importance.

The widespread and 'hierarchized' international organization of production processes in key high-tech industries (such as electronics or pharmaceuticals) is based largely on the nexus of national and international laws, private inter-firm agreements, and public co-operation which constitutes the regime of intellectual property rights.[9]

In all the above examples the importance of nation states shows up clearly, but this power is here severely limited by the place of the country for this special activity in the concert of nations. Such a context is often governed by a hegemony, basically the US or a club of countries. It is in such fields that regionalism may lead to construct a more or less asymmetric triadic pattern. Still the disconnected nature of these international regimes, concerned with

---

[9] The new competition era, qualified of wintelism by Borrus and Zysman (1998), to echo the success of the strategies of Intel and Microsoft to set norms, standards, and pace of technical change in the electronics industry, is obviously strongly conditioned by this regime of intellectual property rights.

different activities, limits the collusion between issues. Thus Europe, where the regional integration process is most advanced, has in effect no common energy policy (but instead a common agriculture policy) and is more a follower than a leader regarding property rights or global financial issues. More generally nation states do not seem to take large initiatives in the ruling of these regimes, being more inclined to follow in each field the hierarchy of power inherited from the post-war period.

1.5.3. On the Forefront of Really Global Policy Issues

There are large numbers of issues which are in essence global and require some explicit international co-ordination that no other agents can initiate but nation states or at a broader level regional entities such as the EU. We have already stressed that globalization, as a process induced by market forces, was by no means heading towards some well-ordered world with a desirable or acceptable ranking of priorities. Differences in national trajectories tend to make adjustments more costly and erratic than desired (Boyer and Drache 1996) and the whole market process seems awkwardly short sighted. On two grounds these drawbacks are unbearable and should force countries to co-operate. Nation states or within the boundaries of the EU treaties, the European Commission are the only legitimate actors that can launch the process of co-operation and forge its institutions, taking into account that non-governmental organizations (NGOs) have a limited autonomy and capacity, and act mainly as instigators for the actions of countries. One of these crucial fields is science and technology; the other is the field of environmental threats.

One can easily see their complementarity. Once the complexity of science and technology is taken into account in all its dimensions, the advantages of international interaction, networking, and co-ordination (as is *de facto* taking place in the private sector with respect to privately funded research) of government-sponsored basic and long-term research is an obvious opportunity. When the challenge of environmental threats is at stake, this scientific co-operation on basic science becomes imperative.

These 'global' advantages have been most evident in the case of the so-called 'mega science' research efforts, where a single country or even Triad block such as the EU can no longer cover the full variety and diversity spectrum of scientific disciplines, approaches, and methodologies, let alone the rapidly increasing equipment and material costs of such very costly research. It first raises the question of the responsibility of the richest, most-developed countries for sharing the international burden of such 'big science' research efforts. There are in effect major differences between the OECD countries in the share of GDP devoted to basic research. This global responsibility is even more striking once the 'global' demand side and the truly global environmental problems the world is confronted with are introduced in the analysis (but also famine, diseases, desertification, energy, etc.). Environmentally sustainable development requires a wide range of complementary policies, if only to support the investment in the new environmental technologies that is needed. International agreements on environmental regulations, probably the most explicit expression of positive integration, do raise formidable policy challenges. No existing international institution can face such challenges of environmental problems of the magnitude we are alluding to. Most of them have been created with a precise mandate and, strangely enough, their room for manoeuvre and their autonomy seem to have reduced while the globalization process was deepening. Only nation states can, up to now, try to co-ordinate their actions and set up the relevant institutional bodies. However, such co-operation is not an easy task.

Given the international character of environmental problems, the goal of environmentally sustainable development is important to all of the different regions and nations of the world. In practice it requires a widespread diffusion of relevant technologies and supporting institutions. The multinational character of both the problems and the solutions suggests a strong role for new supra-national organizations. At the same time the localized nature of many of the sources of pollution and differences in the institutions and solutions that have developed to solve environmental problems require an extensive involvement at the regional, national, and local levels. All of which calls for the creation, through the co-operation of nation states, of a whole new set of institutions, meeting the criteria of transparency and non-bureaucracy, common in most countries nowadays. Defining and developing a consensus around specific environmental goals is, however, a thorny problem, particularly when environmental goals require substantial changes to systemic and interlocked technologies. Examples of such chains of implications could be drawn from agriculture, with the reduction in the use of some intensive methods or transport; with a reduction in the use of private cars. These types of major changes to the techno-economic system cannot be achieved without political debate. How to achieve such political debate at the global level with the many different interests and trade offs remains largely an open question.

REFERENCES

ARCHIBUGI, D., and MICHIE, J. (1995). 'The globalisation of technology: A new taxonomy'. *Cambridge Journal of Economics*, 19: 121–40.
——(1997). 'Technological globalisation or national systems of innovation', in D. Archibugi and J. Michie (eds.), *Technology, Globalisation and Economic Performance*. Cambridge: Cambridge University Press.
BAIROCH, P., and KOZUL-WRIGHT, R. (1998). 'Globalisation myths: Some historical reflections on integration, industrialisation and growth in the world economy', in

R. Kozul-Wright and R. Rowthorn (eds.), *Transnational Corporations and the Global Economy*. Houndmills: Macmillan.

BORRUS, M., and ZYSMAN, J. (1998). 'The rise of wintelism as the future of industrial competition'. *Industry and Innovation*, 4/2: 141–67.

BOYER, R., and DRACHE, D. (1996). *States Against Markets. The Limits of Globalisation*. London: Routledge.

CANTWELL, J., and JANNE, O. (2000). 'Globalisation of innovatory capacity', in F. Chesnais, G. Ietto-Gillies, and R. Simonetti (eds.), *European Integration and Global Corporate Strategies*. London: Routledge.

CHESNAIS, F. (1997). *La Mondialisation du Capital*. Paris: Syros.

DAVID, P., and FORAY, D. (1995). 'Accessing and expanding the science and technology knowledge base'. *Science Technology Industry Review*, 16: 14–68.

DE LONG, J., and FROOMKIN, A. (1998). 'The next economy ?', in D. Hurley, B. Kahin, and H. Varian (eds.), *Internet Publishing and Beyond: The Economics of Digital and Intellectual Property*. Cambridge, Mass.: MIT Press.

FREEMAN, C., and SOETE, L. (1994). *Work for All or Mass Unemployment? Computerised Technical Change into the 21st Century*. London: Pinter Publishers.

FORAY, D., and LUNDVALL B.-Å. (1996) (eds.). *Employment and Growth in the Knowledge-based Economy*. Paris: OECD.

HAGEDOORN, J. (1996). 'Trends and patterns in strategic technology partnering since the early seventies'. *Review of Industrial Organisation*, 11: 601–16.

HATZICHRONOGLOU, T. (1998). 'L'Internationalisation de la R-D industrielle: structure et tendances'. Paris: DSTI/OCDE, 15–16 juin.

HIRST, P., and THOMPSON, G. (1996). *Globalisation in Question*. Cambridge: Polity Press.

HOLLANDERS, H., SOETE, L., and TER WEEL, B. (1999). 'Trends in growth convergence and divergence and changes in technological access and capabilities'. Paper presented at the Lisbon Workshop on Cliometrics, Econometrics and Appreciative History in the Study of Long Waves in Economic Development. 11–13 March, Lisbon.

KOZUL WRIGHT, R., and ROWTHORN, R. (1998) (eds.). *Transnational Corporations and the Global Economy*. Houndmills: Macmillan Press.

LANDES, R. (1998). *The Apocalyptic Year 1000: Then and Now*. http: //www.mille.org/ 1000thennow.html.

OECD (1994). 'Globalisation of industrial activities'. Background report. Paris: DSTI/OECD.

——(1996). 'Technology, productivity and job creation'. 2, analytical report. Paris: OECD.

——(1998). 'The competitive dynamics of internet-based electronic commerce'. Paris: OECD.

PATEL, P., and PAVITT, K. (1991). 'Large firms in the production of the world's technology: An important case of non-globalisation'. *Journal of International Business Studies*, 22: 1–21.

——(1999). 'Global corporations and national systems of innovation: who dominates whom?', in D. Archibugi, J. Howells, and J. Michie (eds.), *Innovation Policy in a Global Economy*. Cambridge: Cambridge University Press.

PETIT, P. (1998). 'Transnational service corporations in the process of globalisation', in R. Kozul-Wright and R. Rowthorn (eds.), *Transnational Corporations and the Global Economy*. Houndmills: Macmillan.

PETIT, P., and SOETE, L. (1997). 'Technical change and employment growth in services: Analytical and policy challenges'. November, mimeo.

—— ——(1998). 'Service sector productivity and the productivity paradox'. May, mimeo.

—— ——(2000). *Europe and the New Economy*. (forthcoming).

SOETE, L. (1998) 'Electronic commerce and the information highway'. September, mimeo.

STRANGE, S. (1996). *The Retreat of the State.* Cambridge: Cambridge University Press.

US National Commission on Technology, Automation, and Economic Progress (1966). 'Technology and the American economy'. Report to the US Congress, 6 vols., Washington.

VARIAN, H. (1997). 'Versioning information goods'. Paper prepared for Digital Information and Intellectual Property. Harvard University, 23–5 Jan.

2

Europe at the Crossroads: The Challenge from Innovation-based Growth

JAN FAGERBERG

2.1. Introduction

Europe's performance relative to the US and countries in Asia is a topic that greatly preoccupies policy makers who are concerned that the EU is losing ground compared to other, more dynamic, parts of the world.[1] Although the recent crises in Asia gave a timely reminder that the grass often looks greener on the other side of the fence, this chapter points to trends in EU performance that European policy makers will find disconcerting. Productivity growth has slowed down relative to competitors. Export competitiveness has deteriorated in all areas except agriculture and raw materials. The losses have been manifest in the technologically most sophisticated industries, particularly ICT. Europe has also failed to create employment on a scale at all comparable with the US or Japan, with obvious repercussions for unemployment. While until recently there was a tendency towards convergence in productivity and income between European regions, there are now signs of a reversal of this trend. Redressing this relatively disappointing performance will be neither easy nor quick, but if enduring answers to Europe's problems are to be found, it is essential that the scale and nature of these problems are carefully diagnosed and solutions found.

2.2. A Long View

In terms of productivity (as measured by GDP per capita), Europe seems to be surpassed not only by the United States, but also by Japan and—if the trends from the past decades prevail in the next century—by a number of other Asian economies as well. How did this happen? One or two centuries

[1] This chapter summarizes some of the findings from the TSER project 'Technology, Economic Integration and Social Cohesion' co-ordinated by Bart Verspagen, MERIT, University of Maastricht. It has benefited from comments and suggestions from the editors of this volume, for which I am grateful. An earlier and shorter overview of results from the project has been published as Fagerberg (1999). For a more detailed account the reader is referred to Fagerberg, Guerrieri, and Verspagen (1999a). I wish to thank my co-authors, particularly Iain Begg, Paolo Guerrieri, and Bart Verspagen, for their permission to use our joint work for this purpose.

ago, the situation was entirely different. During most of the nineteenth century the UK was the leading capitalist country in the world, with a GDP per capita about 50 per cent above the average of other leading capitalist countries (Table 2.1). However, during the second half of the century, the United States started to catch up with the UK and eventually—around 1910—surpassed it. In retrospect it becomes clear that US growth was based on a new technological system, based on large-scale production and distribution systems well suited for the large, fast-growing, and relatively homogenous US market (Chandler 1990; Nelson and Wright 1992).

That Europe initially failed to take advantage of these innovations is perhaps not so difficult to explain. The European markets were smaller and less homogenous. Hence, it is not obvious that US methods, if applied to European conditions in this period, would have yielded superior results. This is what Abramovitz (1994) has dubbed a lack of 'technological congruence'. Two world wars and an intermediate period of protectionism and slow growth added to these problems (Abramovitz 1994). Hence, the US lead increased even further and peaked around 1950, when GDP per capita in the United States was about twice the European level.

While the period between 1820 and 1950 was one of divergence in economic performance between leading capitalist countries, the following period has generally been one of convergence. The productivity gap between the United States and Europe has been significantly reduced. This reduction, most of which occurred during the 1950s and 1960s, was related to the potential for rapid productivity advance in Europe through imitation (of superior US technology). European production and exports in industries such as cars, domestic electrical equipment, electronics, and others grew rapidly from the 1950s onwards. The gradual reduction of barriers to trade within Europe from the 1950s onwards has generally been regarded as an important contributing factor to this process, as has the general rise in living standards (Abramovitz 1994; Maddison 1991).

European countries were not alone, however, in exploiting the window of opportunity given by superior US technology. From the 1950s onwards Japan, later joined by other Asian economies, aggressively targeted the very same industries as those that had grown rapidly in Europe (Johnson 1982; Wade 1990). Initially this did not give much reason for concern among European policy makers or industrialists. But during the 1970s and 1980s it became evident that Japanese suppliers outperformed their European and US competitors in many cases, and that this could not be explained solely by low wages. It became clear that the Japanese, as the Americans before them, had made important innovations in the organization of production, innovations that have led to both increased quality and higher productivity (Von Tunzelmann 1995), and which US and European competitors—despite serious efforts—have not yet managed to imitate to the extent that they would have wished.

TABLE 2.1. *GDP per capita in the industrialized world, 1820–1994 (thousand 1990 US$ per head)*

	1820	1870	1910	1950	1970	1980	1990	1994	Growth 1820–1950	Growth 1950–94(90)
USA	1.3	2.5	5.0	9.6	14.9	18.3	21.9	22.6	1.5	2.0
Japan	0.7	0.7	1.3	1.9	9.4	13.1	18.5	19.5	0.8	5.3
Germany	1.1	1.9	3.5	4.3	11.9	15.4	18.7	19.1	1.0	3.4
France	1.2	1.9	2.9	5.2	11.6	15.0	17.8	18.0	1.1	2.8
Italy	1.1	1.5	2.3	3.4	9.5	13.1	16.0	16.4	0.9	3.6
United Kingdom	1.8	3.3	4.7	6.8	10.7	12.8	16.3	16.4	1.0	2.0
Canada	0.9	1.6	3.9	7.0	11.8	16.3	19.6	18.4	1.6	2.2
Belgium	1.3	2.6	4.0	5.3	10.4	14.0	16.8	17.2	1.1	2.7
Netherlands	1.6	2.6	3.7	5.9	11.7	14.3	16.6	17.2	1.0	2.5
Korea[a]				0.9	2.2	4.1	9.0			5.8
Taiwan[a]			1.0	0.9	2.7	5.6	10.3			6.0
Hong Kong[a]				2.0	5.3	10.0	17.1			5.4
Europe(6)[b]										
Mean	1.3	2.3	3.5	5.2	11.0	14.1	17.0	17.4	1.0	2.8
Coeff. of Var.	0.18	0.26	0.22	0.21	0.08	0.07	0.05	0.05		
All countries except Asia NICs										
Mean	1.2	2.1	3.5	5.5	11.3	14.7	18.0	18.3	1.2	2.7
Coeff. of Var.	0.25	0.35	0.32	0.38	0.14	0.11	0.10	0.10		
All countries										
Mean				4.4	9.3	12.7	16.5			3.3
Coeff. of Var.				0.59	0.4	0.32	0.21			

Notes: [a] For Korea, Taiwan, and Hong Kong, the final period is 1950–90, not 1950–94.
[b] Europe (6) is the six European countries in the table.

Sources: Fagerberg, Guerrieri, and Verspagen 1999b based on data from Maddison 1995 and unpublished data kindly supplied by Angus Maddison.

While Europe, Japan, and other countries started to catch up in many typical 'American way of life' products, US industry leaped forward in another area: science-based industry, in part due to massive public investments in R&D during the Second World War and the 'cold war' that followed. Gradually, however, European countries and Japan started to devote more resources to science and R&D (Table 2.2). By the mid-1970s many of these countries used a larger share of their available resources on civil R&D than did the United States. Hence, the US lead started to be challenged in this area as well. Following the Japanese example, some of the Asian NICs started to invest massively in R&D from the 1970s onwards.

TABLE 2.2. *Estimates of non-defence R&D as a percentage of GDP* (selected years)

	1963	1973	1981	1993
USA	1.5	1.7	1.9	2.1
Japan	1.4	1.9	2.4	2.8
Germany	1.3	2.0	2.4	2.3
France	1.2	1.5	1.7	2.1
Italy	0.7	0.9	1.0	1.3
United Kingdom	1.5	1.6	1.9	1.8
Canada	1.0	1.1	1.2	1.6
Belgium	1.0	1.4	1.4	1.6
Netherlands	2.0	2.0	1.9	2.0
Sweden	0.9	1.4	2.0	3.0
Switzerland	2.5	2.3	2.3	2.6
Korea	0.3	0.3	0.8	2.3
Taiwan	0.4	n.a.	0.7	1.8
Europe (6)				
Mean	1.3	1.6	1.7	1.9
Coeff. of var.	0.3	0.2	0.2	0.2
All countries except Asian NICs				
Mean	1.4	1.6	1.8	2.1
Coeff. of var.	0.4	0.2	0.2	0.2
All countries				
Mean	1.2	1.4	1.7	2.1
Coeff. of var.	0.5	0.4	0.3	0.2

Note: Estimates of civil R&D are available for most OECD countries for selected years. These estimates show that for all but a few countries (notably the USA, the UK, France, and Sweden) differences between civil and total R&D are small. Hence, for some countries and years, total R&D is used instead. Since data are not always available annually, the data reported here will in some cases be based on information from a preceding and/or following year. For definition of Europe (6), see Table 2.1.

Sources: Fagerberg, Guerrieri, and Verspagen 1999*b*, based on data from OECD Science and Technology Indicators Database and UNESCO/national sources (Korea, Taiwan).

During the 1980s European catch-up *vis-à-vis* the United States came to a halt, while Japan continued to increase productivity (GDP per capita) at a faster rate than both the United States and Europe. As a consequence Japan now enjoys a higher level of GDP per capita than Europe. The Asian NICs (Hong Kong, Korea, and Taiwan) have—at least until recently—continued to experience very rapid productivity growth, i.e. to catch-up relative to the United States and other countries.

2.3. Europe in the Global Market

Technological catch-up (or lack of such) and structural changes are intimately related with trade performance. In fact, one of the striking findings from studies of successful catch-up is that it is associated with both a general improvement in trade performance and a radical change in the composition of trade. For instance, the catch-up of Europe and Japan in scale- and capital-intensive technologies from the 1950s onwards was associated with rapidly increasing export market shares for products embodying these technologies. However, since then the locus of growth within manufacturing has changed to science-based industries.

How has Europe adapted to these changes in the global market? To map these developments this chapter makes use of a taxonomy in which industries are allocated to sectors depending on the nature and sources of technological knowledge. In principle this taxonomy, based on earlier work by Pavitt (1984, 1988) and Guerrieri (1992), could have been applied to both goods and services, but because of data limitations the analysis was confined to the former. The taxonomy identifies five type of industries: *agricultural products and raw materials, traditional manufactures, scale-intensive, specialized suppliers* (of various types of machinery, instruments, etc.) and, finally, *science-based* industries (such as professional electronics, pharmaceuticals, and aerospace). The two former depend largely on technology developed in other sectors, while the two latter are typical 'technology producing' sectors serving the entire economy. Scale intensive industry is in an intermediate position in this regard, it receives a lot of its technology from others, but it also has significant in-house technological accumulation (learning). Among these industries, the science-based sector has displayed the highest growth recently. Between 1970 and 1995 the share of science-based products in total world trade more than doubled, largely at the expense of agricultures and raw materials (Fagerberg, Guerrieri, and Verspagen 1999a).

Table 2.3 reports market shares (ratio of national exports to world exports) for four major players in the global economy, Europe (15), the United States, Japan, and the Asian NICs between 1970 and 1995. The market shares for Europe reported in the table include intra-European trade, and this explains why Europe's market shares are so high compared to the United States and

TABLE 2.3. *Market shares, 1970–1995* (ratio of national exports to world exports[a], per cent)

		Agricultural and raw material Products	Traditional industries	Scale-intensive	Specialized Suppliers	Science-Based	Total
Europe (15)	1970	24.1	57.0	55.7	61.2	48.6	44.6
	1988	30.3	47.6	51.2	56.0	41.3	44.0
	1995	31.6	40.1	47.3	47.6	33.8	39.6
	Change 1970–95	7.5	−16.9	−8.4	−13.6	−14.8	−5.0
USA	1970	13.1	7.4	14.5	22.3	29.5	14.8
	1988	13.4	5.2	9.4	12.2	19.8	11.6
	1995	11.0	6.7	10.3	13.7	17.9	11.8
	Change 1970–95	−2.1	−0.7	−4.2	−8.6	−11.6	−3.0
Japan	1970	1.2	9.3	13.8	6.4	7.7	6.7
	1988	1.1	4.1	17.1	15.6	16.7	10.1
	1995	1.4	3.2	12.8	15.7	14.3	9.0
	Change 1970–95	0.2	−6.1	−1.0	9.3	6.6	2.3
Asian NICs	1970	2.0	6.1	1.0	0.8	1.0	2.1
	1988	2.6	14.5	5.6	4.0	9.1	6.7
	1995	3.4	16.2	8.7	8.8	17.8	10.8
	Change 1970–95	1.4	10.1	7.7	8.0	16.8	8.7

Notes: Europe (15): Austria, Belgium, Denmark, Finland, France, Germany, Greece, Ireland, Italy, Luxembourg, Netherlands, Portugal, Spain, Sweden, United Kingdom.
Asian NICs: Hong Kong, Korea, Singapore, Taiwan.
[a] Goods exports (trade in services not included). For the definition of sectors see Fagerberg, Guerrieri, and Verspagen 1999b.

Source: Fagerberg, Guerrieri, and Verspagen 1999b, based on UN and OECD data from the SIE World Trade data base.

Japan. However, similar calculations were made excluding intra-European trade, and the trends (changes through time)—which is what commands interest here—were basically the same. Between 1970 and 1995 Japan and the Asian NICs gained market shares at the expense of the United States and Europe. In particular, the Asian NICs showed a spectacular performance; between 1970 and 1995 its overall market share increased more than five times, from 2.1 to 10.8 per cent of the global market. It is also noteworthy that the rapid growth of Japan and the Asian NICs was accompanied by very rapid structural changes that totally changed the specialization pattern of these countries. In the case of Japan, in spite of overall market share growth, the market shares for traditional and scale-intensive industries actually contracted, while those of specialized suppliers and science-based industry increased rapidly, so that by the end of the period Japan had its major strength in the latter (followed by scale-intensive industry). For the Asian NICs a similar development took place, with a much stronger growth in science-based industry and specialized suppliers than in the traditional area of strength (traditional industries).

In contrast to the Asian experience, both Europe and the United States lost overall market shares. Moreover, these losses were generally more manifest in high-technology sectors, particularly science-based industries, than elsewhere. As a consequence, in the 1990s Europe was no longer specialized (i.e. having an above-average market share) in science-based industry. The only area in which Europe gained market shares was agricultural products and raw materials. Hence, European competitiveness, whether measured through its growth or trade performance, is deteriorating. Moreover, slow growth and declining market shares, particularly in the most advanced and fast-growing industries, go hand in hand with increasing unemployment problems (Table 2.4).

2.4. **European Economic Integration**

It is pertinent to ask what European integration has to do with all this. Forty to fifty years ago, when the first steps towards the present-day European Union

TABLE 2.4. *Unemployment as a percentage of the total labour force*

	1960–73	1974–9	1980–9	1990–5
Europe (15)	2.3	4.6	9.2	9.8
USA	4.8	6.7	7.2	6.4
Japan	1.3	1.9	2.5	2.5
Korea	n.a.	3.8	3.8	2.4

Source and definitions: Fagerberg, Guerrieri, and Verspagen 1999*b*, based on data from OECD Historical Statistics 1960–95.

were taken, priority was given to the creation of a common market for natural resource-based industries such as the coal and steel industries and agriculture. Because of the political sensitivity of these industries, the steps towards a common market were often combined with subsidies for high-cost, uncompetitive producers, and in many cases these subsidies became of a permanent (or semi-permanent) nature. In agriculture, a strong and costly incentive scheme was created, the Common Agricultural Policy (CAP), that encouraged agricultural production. As a result, Europe has become self-sufficient for most agricultural products and a problem of surpluses has occurred that is being resolved through, among other things, subsidized exports. Hence, it comes as no surprise that Europe has increased its market shares internationally for agriculture and raw materials.

The other main element in the European economic integration process has been a continuous drive towards economies of scale through enlargement and homogenization of markets. After the Second World War various schemes were developed in order to facilitate trade across national borders in Europe. From the late 1950s onwards a process of trade liberalization took place within two European trading blocks, EEC and EFTA. By the early 1970s internal trade in manufactures was virtually free of tariffs and other restrictions within these two blocks. These developments clearly strengthened the catch-up of Europe in many scale-intensive industries previously dominated by US industry, such as cars, domestic electrical equipment, and consumer electronics.

The drive towards economies of scale through enlargement of markets continued in the 1970s with the integration of the member countries of the two former trading blocks, EEC and EFTA. By the mid-1980s Western Europe had become a free-trading area for manufactures. However, this failed to produce positive growth effects of the type that had been associated with previous integration efforts. Partly as a result of this the EU launched its plan for a revitalization of the internal European market ('Europe 1992'). This plan was based on the idea that there were large unexploited economies of scale in European industry, the exploitation of which had been prevented by the existence of so-called 'non-tariff barriers' to trade, commonly assumed to be related to discriminatory actions by governments in one way or another. Hence, the heart of the plan has been to abolish these barriers. The fact that Europe's trade performance has been slightly better in scale-intensive industry than in manufacturing as a whole indicates that although it is difficult to detect an effect on overall growth, the strong emphasis on scale in European integration efforts may have had an impact on its pattern of specialization.

To sum up, European integration has favoured natural resource-based and scale-intensive industries, and this is consistent with the observed change in its pattern of specialization. However, given that modern growth is increasingly knowledge-based (Fagerberg 1994), it seems relevant to ask to what extent this move away from the technologically most advanced and fast-growing parts of manufacturing poses a problem for Europe's future growth and welfare.

2.5. Challenges from Innovation-based Growth

Traditional economic theory tells us that specialization is beneficial in itself because it leads to more efficient use of available resources. However, unless this has a positive effect on technological progress (so-called 'dynamic economies of scale'), it will not lead to higher growth in the long run. The evidence (Begg *et al.* 1999) shows that what matters for growth and competitiveness is not so much increasing the degree of specialization in general, as the ability to exploit areas of high technological opportunity, which in recent years have been dominated by information and communication technologies (ICTs).

However, as pointed out above, during the last decades Europe has lost ground in the technologically most progressive industries, and ICT is no exception to this trend. In fact, the research shows that, with the exception of telecommunication equipment, Europe has fallen behind the United States and Japan as suppliers to non-EU markets, and is increasingly vulnerable in software and services as well (Dalum, Freeman, *et al.* 1999). The diffusion of ICT products and services in Europe is also slow (Table 2.5), particularly when compared to the United States, and very uneven across Europe. While some smaller countries, especially the Nordic ones, have diffusion rates similar (or superior) to the US level, most countries in Europe (particularly in the south) are laggards when it comes to use of ICTs.

This raises the issue of what policy makers can and should do to reverse this uncomfortable trend. Arguably, transforming the education and training systems in order to equip individuals with the skills needed for an environment in which the major new technology is pervasive should be high on the policy agenda. The continuing skill shortages in software testify to the failure of Europe to meet this challenge, and it is evident that this deficiency has slowed the diffusion of ICTs beyond the immediate sectors that developed and applied them. However, acquiring skills is only a necessary first step. Skills also have to be put to uses that improve diffusion and learning. Therefore a combination of enhancement of skills and diffusion-oriented policies centred on social needs is required. Mobile communications in the Nordic area is a good example of how public regulation and support managed to bring together new technology, skills, and existing social needs in a way that both led to rapid diffusion of the new technology and—through learning—the development of globally competitive firms and industries (Dalum, Fagerberg, and Jørgensen 1988). The possibility that similar policies also may work for other types of ICT applications should encourage

TABLE 2.5. *Some indicators on the use of ICT, 1996*

	Cellular phone[a]	Internet hosts[b]	Internet users[b]	Personal computers[a]	ISDN subscribers[b]	Overall rank[c]
Norway	28.7	34.2	113.8	28.5	10.0	1
Finland	29.2	61.3	167.8	19.5	7.0	2
Denmark	25.0	20.3	57.0	30.4	5.7	3
US	16.5	37.9	78.8	36.2	3.3	4
Switzerland	9.3	18.7	52.1	40.9	17.7	5
Sweden	28.2	26.9	90.5	21.5	2.2	6
UK	12.2	12.4	43.0	19.3	4.5	7
Canada	11.4	20.1	66.7	24.4	0.1	7
Germany	7.1	8.4	30.5	23.3	23.7	9
Netherlands	5.2	17.4	58.0	23.2	6.4	10
Japan	21.4	5.8	55.7	12.8	4.2	11
Austria	7.4	11.0	37.2	14.9	5.2	12
Belgium	4.7	6.4	29.5	16.7	5.4	13
Ireland	8.2	7.6	22.7	17.0	0.0	14
France	4.2	4.1	8.6	15.1	7.3	15
Italy	11.2	2.6	10.2	9.2	1.8	16
Portugal	6.7	2.4	23.2	6.7	2.0	17
Spain	3.3	2.9	13.4	9.4	0.9	18
Greece	5.3	1.6	14.3	3.5	0.0	19
Europe[d]	8.8	8.7	29.7	16.9	8.4	—

Notes: [a] subscribers per 100 inhabitants, [b] per 1000 inhabitants, [c] mean rank of previous 5 columns, [d] weighted mean of countries above.

Source: Dalum *et al.* 1999, based on data from ITU World Telecommunications Development Report, 1998.

policy makers to experiment further with diffusion-oriented policies centred on users and social needs.

In a way the challenge for policy makers is no less than devising solutions which restore the dynamism and creativity that characterized the European economy in earlier periods. Part of the answer has to do with getting a proper understanding of the 'system of innovation', the mix of characteristics, infra-structure, and policies that determines how well an economy is able to exploit opportunities afforded by new technologies. In fact, differences in invention and innovation would not matter much if knowledge spread readily from region to region. However, the research reveals that the greater the geographical distance between regions, the lower the degree of knowledge flows between them (Maurseth and Verspagen 1999). Moreover, knowledge flows are greater within countries than between them, suggesting that the national element in innovation systems remains strong. The research also shows that knowledge flows are most intense between regions with similar or complementary specialization patterns, as well as between technologically linked sectors. These results suggest powerful influences leading to the formation of geographically concentrated clusters of technologically related activities at work in Europe's economy.

Economic and social cohesion—usually defined in terms of equity considerations such as regional disparities or social inclusion—is a fundamental aim of the EU articulated in Article 2 of the Treaty. However, research shows that regional disparities in economic performance remain substantial, and have increased in many member countries in the last decade (Fagerberg and Verspagen 1996; Cappelen, Fagerberg, and Verspagen 1999), see Table 2.6. This gap is especially marked as regards innovative activity. Hence, what seems to be a fairly robust finding is that there exists a subgroup of high

TABLE 2.6. *Dispersion of GDP per capita in EU regions and countries, 1960–1995*

	1960	1970	1980	1995
Regional standard deviation EU9	0.34	0.27	0.20	0.21
National standard deviation EU9	0.26	0.23	0.18	0.17
Share of total regional dispersion in EU9 due to:				
Between country dispersion in per cent	64	79	52	41
Within country dispersion in per cent	36	21	48	59

Note: Regional standard deviation measures the dispersion across European regions independent of which country the regions belong to. National standard deviation measures the dispersion across European countries (disregarding the dispersion between regions within countries). EU 9 includes Denmark, Be-Ne-Lux, France, Germany, Ireland, Italy, and UK. All figures based on PPS (purchasing power standard). The regional disaggregation is more detailed from 1980 onwards, and this biases the figures before 1980 for EU9 downwards.

Source: Cappelen, Fagerberg, and Verspagen 1999, based on data from EUROSTAT (REGIO Data Base).

R&D, high-income regions in Europe with its own internal dynamics. What distinguishes these high R&D regions from the rest is mainly that R&D matters a lot in the former, while it is of little importance (or contributes negatively) in the latter. Thus, there is a risk that a faster rate of innovation, which is vital for European growth and competitiveness in general, might further aggravate regional disparities.

Although data are scarce on many factors of potential relevance for regional growth, the evidence clearly indicates that most low-income regions have failed to exploit the potential for technology diffusion. This points to a need for policies aimed at enhancing the capacity of such regions to absorb new technologies, especially ICTs. Similar issues arise in relation to the eastern enlargement anticipated in the next few years (Grabbe, Hughes, and Landesmann 1999). The research also drew attention to the potential for the local science base, in the form of university research, to contribute to local learning processes and, hence, regional development (Dalum, Holmen, *et al.* 1999). Furthermore, the low rate of diffusion is often associated with a structure of activity dominated by agriculture or 'older' industries, and a corresponding lack of high-tech activities, often combined with relatively high unemployment. One strategy for change would be to reorient policies in this area towards accelerating structural change. But it is important to design policies in a way that does not lead to a further increase in long-term unemployment, as this is itself a factor hampering diffusion and growth (Fagerberg, Verspagen, and Caniëls 1997).

Perhaps the most important problem facing EU policy makers is how to combat the persistent high rate of unemployment in Europe (Table 2.4), which threatens social cohesion. It is important to stress that innovation is, in itself, no 'quick fix' for unemployment. Product innovation may increase employment through increased demand for products embodying the new technologies. But process innovation aimed primarily at rationalization of existing production processes may also reduce employment in a specific industry and/or location, if not compensated by indirect income and demand effects. In contrast to the situation in the other parts of the 'triad', the latter (employment-reducing) type of outcome is in fact the most common in Europe (Pianta and Vivarelli 1999). This is especially evident in industry (Table 2.7). What this implies is that Europe's industrial structure is orientated towards sectors most open to labour saving, mostly mature industries characterized by a high degree of process innovations.

Thus the challenge for policy makers is not only to increase innovation diffusion but also to do so in a way that is more 'employment friendly'. This requires a shift from the traditional emphasis on process innovations and reduction of labour costs to a stronger focus on product innovations and increases in quality. It should be evident that Europe can never hope to compete with newly industrialized countries in Asia and elsewhere on the basis of labour costs alone, and that the long-run outlook for Europe is also influenced by

TABLE 2.7. *The relationship between growth of employment and growth of GDP/value added (elasticity), 1975–1996*

Country	Whole economy	Industry	Services
United States	0.6	0.4	0.6
Japan	0.3	0.2	0.4
Europe (15)	0.1	−1.2	0.4

Source: Pianta and Vivarelli 1999, based on data from the OECD, UN, and Datastream.

the quality of what it produces. The research shows that there is great scope for raising quality as the core competitive advantage of the EU through a strategy based on product innovation, upgrading of skills, and increased R&D efforts (Jansen and Landesmann 1999).

2.6. Conclusions

To some extent Europe's current problems are the price to be paid for past successes. European integration, most recently through the single market programme, has made product and factor markets more open and paved the way for the realization of economies of scale and a more efficient allocation of resources. From a long-run perspective, these policies have been extremely successful. Without them, it is doubtful whether Europe would have managed to catch up with the United States to the extent that it did. However, the rewards to catch-up in capital- and scale-intensive sectors producing for the mass markets have been cashed in long ago, and now the rules of the game have changed. In the last decades, science-based industries, especially those drawing heavily on ICTs, have become the main driver of technological change and economic growth. Although the ICT revolution has been under way for a long time, its major effects are just beginning to be felt and it is clear that Europe's performance in ICT, however measured, is far from satisfactory. Arguably, if appropriate steps are not taken now, the current trends towards slow growth, increasing inequality and unemployment are likely to persist, threatening social cohesion, the social model, and the democratic values that Europeans hold dear.

The story is easily told. Slow growth is mainly the result of failure to exploit the technological opportunities inherent in new and fast-growing technologies. This is not mainly a question of failing to be competitive in, say, the production of computers or other products embodying ICT, but embedding the new technology in society at large. Regional disparities have been exacerbated by the very uneven diffusion of new technology, which has, hitherto, disproportionately favoured high-income, high-R&D regions specialized in high-tech manufacturing and—above all—services. By contrast, traditional agricultural regions or regions in the rustbelt have benefited very little if at all. Rather, what has happened is that the relative prices of their products and factor services have declined. High unemployment is the flip side of this coin. Europe's continuing specialization in increasingly mature industries characterized by labour-saving innovation has meant that relatively few new jobs have been created. Low labour mobility has made matters worse by inhibiting effective redeployment of resources and has, arguably, been an impediment to technological advance (Fagerberg, Verspagen, and Caniëls 1997).

Although the diagnosis is clear, agreeing on remedies is much less easy. What makes the problem so challenging is the need for actors and trends at very different levels to pull together. On the one hand, as the research shows, the creation of technological advantage is in most cases a very local affair. At the other extreme, radical technological changes, particularly the ICT revolution, affect nearly all aspects of life, so that a holistic approach to change aimed at exploiting the opportunities afforded by these new technologies is needed. Because of path dependency in local technological, institutional, and economic systems, and the complex conditions for getting the most out of ICT, this is very difficult to realize in practice. Thus, there is a large co-ordination problem here, and this emphasizes the need for a strategic view on European growth. Arguably, what is needed is a much more prominent role for the EU, not only in policy co-ordination, but in discussing policy change, experimenting with policy alternatives, evaluating the results, and providing benchmarking for government at various levels. Moreover, a much greater emphasis needs to be placed on stimulating more rapid, pervasive, and effective innovation in technologies, organizations, and institutions.

The core message from the research presented in this chapter is that the problems that Europe faces in key areas such as growth, equality, and employment are all related to its failure to take sufficient advantage of technological advances, particularly the ICT revolution. Consequently, a coherent European strategy for upgrading technological capability and quality competitiveness is long overdue. This cannot be limited to providing support to selected industries (or companies) in order to make them more competitive in global markets. Rather, what Europe has to do is to take steps to embed new technologies in society. This should bring together macroeconomic policy, regulation, science and technology policy, and employment initiatives. The complementarities between policy areas, in particular, should be stressed. Equally, it is vital at the outset to recognize that change will not happen overnight and that boosting the long-run ability of the economy to create and use new technologies will require concerted action.

REFERENCES

ABRAMOVITZ, M. (1994). 'The origins of the postwar catch-up and convergence boom', in J. Fagerberg, B. Verspagen, and N. von Tunzelman (eds.), *The Dynamics of Technology, Trade and Growth*. Aldershot: Edward Elgar.

BEGG, I., DALUM, B., GUERRIERI, P., and PIANTA, M. (1999). 'The Impact of specialization in Europe', in J. Fagerberg, P. Guerrieri, and B. Verspagen (eds.), *The Economic Challenge for Europe: Adapting to Innovations-based Growth*. Aldershot: Edward Elgar.

CAPPELEN, A., FAGERBERG, J., and VERSPAGEN, B. (1999). 'Lack of regional convergence', in J. Fagerberg, P. Guerrieri, and B. Verspagen (eds.), *The Economic Challenge for Europe: Adapting to Innovations-based Growth*. Aldershot: Edward Elgar.

CHANDLER, A. D., Jr (1990). *Scale and Scope. The Dynamics of Industrial Capitalism*. Cambridge, Mass.: The Belknap Press.

DALUM, B., FAGERBERG, J., and JØRGENSEN, U. (1988). 'Small countries in the world market for electronics: The case of the Nordic countries', in B.-Å. Lundvall and C. Freeman (eds.), *Small Countries Facing the Technological Revolution*. London: Pinter Publishers.

DALUM, B., FREEMAN, C., SIMONETTI, R., VON TUNZELMANN, N., and VERSPAGEN, B. (1999). 'Europe and the information and communication technologies revolution', in J. Fagerberg, P. Guerrieri, and B. Verspagen (eds.), *The Economic Challenge for Europe: Adapting to Innovation-based Growth*. Aldershot: Edward Elgar.

DALUM, B., HOLMEN, M., JACOBSSON, S., PRÆST, M., RICKNE, A., and VILLUMSEN, G. (1999). 'Changing the regional system of innovation', in J. Fagerberg, P. Guerrieri, and B. Verspagen (eds.), *The Economic Challenge for Europe: Adapting to Innovation-based Growth*. Aldershot: Edward Elgar.

FAGERBERG, J. (1994). 'Technology and international differences in growth rates'. *Journal of Economic Literature*, 32: 147–75.

——(1999). 'The need for innovation-based growth in Europe'. *Challenge,* 42: 63–79.

——VERSPAGEN, B., and VON TUNZELMAN, N. (1994) (eds.). *The Dynamics of Technology, Trade and Growth*. Aldershot: Edward Elgar.

—— ——(1996). 'Heading for divergence? Regional growth in Europe reconsidered'. *Journal of Common Market Studies*, 34: 431–48.

—— ——and CANIËLS, M. (1997). 'Technology, growth and unemployment across European regions'. *Regional Studies*, 31: 457–66.

——GUERRIERI, P., and VERSPAGEN, B. (1999*a*) (eds.). *The Economic Challenge for Europe: Adapting to Innovation-based Growth*. Aldershot: Edward Elgar.

—— ——and——(1999*b*). 'Europe-a long view', in J. Fagerberg, P. Guerrieri, and B. Verspagen (eds.), *The Economic Challenge for Europe: Adapting to Innovation-based Growth*. Aldershot: Edward Elgar.

GRABBE, H., HUGHES, K., and LANDESMANN, M. (1999). 'The implications of EU enlargement for EU integration, convergence and competitiveness', in J. Fagerberg, P. Guerrieri, and B. Verspagen (eds.), *The Economic Challenge for Europe: Adapting to Innovation-based Growth*. Aldershot: Edward Elgar.

GUERRIERI, P. (1992). 'Technological and trade competition: The changing position of US, Japan and Germany', in M. C. Harris and G. E. Moore (eds.), *Linking Trade and Technology Policies*. Washington, DC: National Academy Press.

JANSEN, M., and LANDESMANN, M. (1999). 'European competitiveness: Quality rather than price', in J. Fagerberg, P. Guerrieri, and B. Verspagen (eds.), *The Economic Challenge for Europe: Adapting to Innovation-based Growth*. Aldershot: Edward Elgar.

JOHNSON, C. (1982). *MITI and the Japanese Miracle: The Growth of Industrial Policy, 1925–1975*. Stanford: Stanford University Press.

MADDISON, A. (1991). *Dynamic Forces in Capitalist Development*. New York: Oxford University Press.

——(1995). *Monitoring the World Economy, 1820–1992*. Washington, DC: OECD.

MAURSETH, P., and VERSPAGEN, B. (1999). 'Europe: one or several systems of innovation?', in J. Fagerberg, P. Guerrieri, and B. Verspagen (eds.), *The Economic Challenge for Europe: Adapting to Innovations—based Growth*. Aldershot: Edward Elgar.

NELSON, R. R., and WRIGHT, G. (1992). 'The rise and fall of American technological leadership: The postwar era in historical perspective'. *Journal of Economic Literature*, 30: 1931–64.

PAVITT, K. (1984). 'Sectoral patterns of technical change: Towards a taxonomy and a theory'. *Research Policy*, 13: 343–74.

——(1988). 'International patterns of technological accumulation', in N. Hood and J. E. Vahlne (eds.), *Strategies in Global Competition*. London: Croom Helm.

PIANTA, M., and VIVARELLI, M. (1999). 'Employment dynamics and structural change in Europe', in J. Fagerberg, P. Guerrieri, and B. Verspagen (eds.), *The Economic Challenge for Europe: Adapting to Innovations-based Growth*. Aldershot: Edward Elgar.

VON TUNZELMANN, G. N. (1995). *Technology and Industrial Progress. The Foundations of Economic Growth*. Aldershot: Edward Elgar.

WADE, R. (1990). *Governing the Market. Economic Theory and the Role of Government in East Asian Industrialization*. Princeton: Princeton University Press.

PART II

New Trends in Firm Organization, Competition, and Co-operation

3

The Production of Technological Knowledge: New Issues in a Learning Economy

PATRICK COHENDET AND PIERRE-BENOÎT JOLY

3.1. Introduction

The mode of knowledge production in society is changing fundamentally. Recently, a growing field in the theoretical literature and evidence from empirical facts have strongly emphasized the emergence of new features of production of technological knowledge. For example:

1. The drastically increasing costs of innovation, the growing need of inter-disciplinarity in scientific and technological areas, and the tighter meshing of research and demand have induced some major changes in the relationships between research and industry. The line between research laboratories and firms is becoming fuzzy: in some fields such as biotechnologies firms invest massively in fundamental research; in some academic disciplines, growing numbers of industrialists are publishing research papers or present academic lectures in colloquia; more and more researchers are running their own enterprises; new ways of designing contracts or co-operative agreements are constantly being implemented between firms and laboratories, etc.

2. The 'geography' of knowledge production is changing dramatically. There is an increasing internationalization of basic research. The development of new information technologies and cheaper transport and communication costs have increased the flow of knowledge across national borders; basic research is one area where internationalization has gone very far. The links between domestic investments in basic research and national performance are becoming even more complex through this process. 'A new paradigm of transnational research and technology emerges, characterised by intense market and technology interaction, with few centres of competence at different geographical locations and interactive technology transfer' (Meyer-Krahmer 1998).

3. The increasing technical possibilities to codify knowledge that are offered by the development of ICT (simulation techniques, symbolic communication, aided-memory devices, etc.) have significant impacts on the efficiency of research activities. As pinpointed by Foray and Lundvall (1997), codification is in general an important process for economic activity and

development for four main reasons: first, codification reduces some of the costs in the process of knowledge acquisition and technology diffusion. Secondly, through codification, knowledge picks up more and more properties of a commodity. This implies that market transactions are facilitated by codification, reducing uncertainties and information asymmetries in transactions involving knowledge. Thirdly, codification facilitates knowledge externalization and allows a firm to acquire more knowledge than previously for a given (but not necessarily lower) cost. And, finally, codification directly affects the speeding-up of knowledge creation, innovation, and economic change.

The change is such that the transformation could be considered as marking a distinct shift towards a new mode of knowledge production ('Mode 2') which is replacing and reforming established institutions, disciplines, practices, and policies ('Mode 1'). According to Gibbons *et al.* (1994: page vi, preface), who promoted this idea,

The new mode operates within a context of application in that problems are not set within a disciplinary framework. It is transdisciplinary rather than mono- or multi-disciplinary. It is carried out in non-hierarchical, heterogeneously organised forms which are essentially transient. It is not being institutionalised primarily within university structures. It involves the close interaction of many actors throughout the process of knowledge production and this means that the process of knowledge production is becoming more socially accountable. One consequence of these changes is that the new mode makes use of a wider range of criteria in judging quality control. Overall, the process of knowledge production is becoming more reflexive and affects at the deepest levels what shall count as good science.

This radical approach has been questioned by some authors (Pestre 1997), who advocate that the two modes always had coexisted in society (as, for instance, in agro-food research). However, all the authors agree at least on the fact that Mode 1 was until recently by far the dominant mode, and that there is growing evidence that it is increasingly challenged by Mode 2 in many loci of production of knowledge.

This contribution will investigate the new ways of producing technological knowledge in society. Beyond understanding the mechanisms at stake in this transformation, one can draw major conclusions for science and technology policy, in particular for the organization and incentives within the public research domain. From this perspective, in the first part of the contribution, the main features of the traditional vision of knowledge production will be briefly recalled. A second part will be devoted to an analysis of the new mode of production of knowledge. The last part will deduce the consequences of the change of paradigm on public policy.

It must be emphasized that this contribution is focused mainly on the new mode of production of knowledge related to research and used in industry, and does not address the issue of learning processes and skill formation as outcomes of the process of knowledge production (on this broader issue, see OECD 1999). Also, on many aspects this contribution takes a complementary view to the Conceição and Heitor chapter on the role of European universities in the new mode of knowledge production in this volume, by focusing more systematically on the general theoretical profiles of the process of knowledge production.

3.2. The Traditional Vision of Knowledge Production and its Questioning

3.2.1. The Main Features of the Traditional Vision

The traditional vision of knowledge production was characterized by a simple dichotomy: on the one hand, the distinction between science and technology which is logically deduced from the vision of a linear model of innovation; and, on the other hand, the distinction between private and public research which is related to the fact that science was considered as a public good.

1. The separation between fundamental research and applied research is a consequence of the linear model of the process of innovation that supposes a kind of division of labour between the two types of research: first, the role of fundamental research is to increase (through publications of scientific articles, conferences, seminars) the stock of knowledge of society. Secondly, the role of applied research is to transform the stock of knowledge of society and shape the technological results obtained (through patents, licences, copyrights, etc.) into useful applications.

2. The separation between public and private research is related to the fact that science was considered as a pure public good. More precisely, the production of fundamental research, assimilated to the production of some new piece of (codified) information, has limited appropriability that discourages private investments (Arrow 1962). Because of this nature of codified information that characterizes the results of fundamental research, the part the private investor obtains is generally too small compared with the benefits reflected in knowledge spillovers appropriated by competitors, users, and consumers. From this Arrow deduced that basic research should be 'open', accessible, and public, while applied research should be protected by strong property rights devised to discourage any 'free riding' of competing imitators.

Thus, the distribution of roles that results from the traditional dichotomy is the following: on the one hand, public research ('open science') was supposed to produce scientific results independently from applications, contributing to the growing (and free access) stock of knowledge of society. On the other hand, industry was supposed to be in charge of applied research, that is to try to appropriate and transform the scientific results into technological solutions, with the prospect to reach useful and profitable applications.

This traditional vision supposes that the production of knowledge is equivalent to the production of a flux of information that will be cumulated in a knowledge stock. More precisely, one can distinguish three different stocks of knowledge. There is first scientific knowledge. This knowledge is cumulated through the process of production of information by academics who follow some commonly shared modes of learning. In the traditional vision, academic problems are supposed to be set and solved within a disciplinary context which is governed by the interests of a specific academic community. Each discipline (mathematics, physics, chemistry, etc.) presents different patterns of learning, languages, rules, norms, attitudes, expressed in specific search 'practices'. For instance, the ways in which academics articulate different processes of learning (producing different categories of scientific knowledge from the more generic forms to the more specific) over time, or are organized to publish, validate, duplicate, or test new forms of knowledge, exhibit some commonalities through all the scientific communities.

Second is the knowledge produced by applied research. If applied research 'digs' into scientific knowledge to find new useful applications, it also contributes to the cumulation of two types of knowledge: technological knowledge at the level of industry; and engineering knowledge at the level of firm.

Technological knowledge refers to the fact that industries often share particular and technological parameters, and understandings concerning technical functions, performances, characteristics, and use of materials. This is the 'generic' level of industry: 'On the one hand, a technology consists of a body of knowledge, which I shall call generic, in the form of a number of generalisations about how things work, key variables influencing performance, the nature of the currently binding constraints, and approaches to pushing these back, widely applicable problem-solving heuristics. I have called this the "logy" of technology. . . . Generic-(technological) knowledge tends to be codified in applied scientific fields like electrical engineering, or material science, or pharmacology, which are 'about' technology' (Nelson 1987).

Engineering knowledge is used for industrial practices oriented by problem-solving activities and focused on learning constantly to improve individual and collective know-how. Here each organization exhibits specific ways of arranging learning processes to reach such goals. For instance, as mentioned by Hatchuel and Weil (1995) there are many ways to orient learning processes towards increasing know-how: one can distinguish between 'doing know-how' (referring to the generation of consistent pre-established prescriptions for actions in specific contexts); 'understanding know-how'(referring to the generation of plausible interpretations for some questions); and 'combining-know-how' (referring to the generation of a sequence of prescriptions which allow certain desired outcomes to be achieved).

According to the traditional approach, the production of knowledge in society requires a division of labour and a high degree of specialization of each of these three stocks of knowledge. These blocks are supposed to be governed by different norms and practices. They are managed independently from one to another, and each one contributes in the linear sequence to the process of innovation.

The consequences of this broad traditional vision, that assimilates knowledge to mere information, were considerable. Since the knowledge generated by the different research activities possesses the generic properties of public goods, it cannot be optimally produced or distributed through the workings of competitive markets. Here is the justification for government subsidization of science, technological, and engineering research, and for innovative activity more generally. This vision shaped the conception of public intervention in R&D during decades. It justified the role and creation of public laboratories, of centres of research, of public programmes of R&D, of public institutions (patent offices, for instance), of public infrastructure for transfer of technology, etc.. It explained why public efforts in R&D were generally disconnected from applications and why arguments about the existence of spillovers from public research programmes were so important to justify public money spent on R&D. It suggested that scientific production was in fact considered as exogenous to the economic sphere, and governed by rules and behavioural norms (reputation effects, peer reviews, etc.) that were drastically different from the norms and behaviour of industry (seeking profit and technical efficiency). In particular in this perspective, the choices of research themes by academics should remain independent of the objectives of industry.

3.2.2. The Questioning of the Traditional Vision

As it was mentioned in the introduction, this traditional vision is nowadays strongly questioned in the literature, by a growing number of scholars who reject, on theoretical grounds, this simple dichotomy.

Firstly, the linearity of the model of innovation has been severely questioned. These changes are partly related to the evolution of production processes. With the growing importance of flexible automation and dedicated products, firms ought to integrate the users' needs as inputs in the innovation processes. The activities of *design* become topical and do not accommodate any more with the linear model of innovation which is based on clear-cut distinctions between basic research, applied research, and product development. 'Technology creation' involves recurrent interactions between basic and applied research as keys of efficiency in a process of innovation. This means that the choices of research themes by academics are not necessarily independent of the preferences of industry. An interactive model of innovation conveys the idea that the quality and frequency of interactions between academic laboratories and private firms is a key element in the success of the innovative process. The focus is thus more on the interfaces between basic, applied, and industrial R&D, than on the amount of resources allocated to each of these activities. The interactive processes of innovation are associated here with an increasing codification of knowledge used in productive activities.

But a second important point is that the idea that research produces only codified information is also strongly questioned. Dosi (1988) and Pavitt (1984), among others, stated that research does not produce information, but knowledge of which some is coded and the rest tacit. Tacit knowledge is extremely localized and circulates with high costs and difficulties. Because they focus on the analysis of the two faces of R&D (innovation and learning), Cohen and Levinthal (1989) argued that the degree of spillovers and imitation depends on both the nature of knowledge and the absorptive capacity of firms. All things being equal, the more knowledge is codified, the easier its absorption will be. But even in the case of codified knowledge, the user or imitator needs certain know-how and technical ability to benefit from the knowledge. To appropriate the results of academic research, even if it is codified, one has 'to know the code'.[1] From this point of view, to quote Joly and Mangematin (1996: 905) research activity has two complementary facets: 'It naturally contributes to the creation of information and knowledge, but it is also a learning process which helps to increase absorptive capacity. Not only are externalities not evenly distributed but they increase when the knowledge bases of firms are similar. In such contexts, external research cannot be substituted for internal research: the two are complementary.'

Also, such considerations allow us to understand better that the circulation of knowledge is not only related to its degree of codification. It is also a function of the state of the networks within which it circulates. Such a statement is corroborated by the studies in sociology and anthropology of science, as shown by Callon (1999). Callon shows that a fluid circulation of knowledge and information appears in 'stabilised networks' which emerge as a result of

---

[1] On this critical issue, Saviotti (1998: 848) proposed a relevant synthesis: 'We can argue that a piece of knowledge is never completely appropriable, but that there is a range of situations varying from the completely appropriable to the completely public. Even if it were the case that knowledge is completely codified, it would still not be true that a completely codified piece of knowledge does not confer upon its discoverer any competitive advantage. Traditionally, knowledge was considered a public good because it is impossible for its creator to prevent it being used by economic agents who do not pay anything in exchange of it. However, even a completely codified piece of knowledge could not be used at a zero cost by anyone. Only agents who know the "code" can use the piece of knowledge at zero (imitation) cost. Agents who do not know the "code", if they realise the economic value of a given piece of knowledge, have to know the code before being able to retrieve and to imitate. The cost of learning has to be included among the costs of imitation. Such conclusions may be rationalised in two different ways. First as pointed out before, knowledge has a retrieval structure: the agents possessing a certain type of knowledge can retrieve both information based on this knowledge and other similar pieces of knowledge. Second, the concept of absorption capacity tells us that in order to be able to access a piece of knowledge, we must have done R&D on something similar. As a consequence, we have included among the variables determining the degree of appropriability, not only the degree of codification, but also the fraction of agents knowing the code and the distribution of agents with respect to the frontier.'

a collective learning process which involves many 'translations' in order to allow various actors to speak the same language.

These considerations warrant further theoretical investigations of the foundations of the production of knowledge to clarify the actual characteristics of what can be called a new mode of production of knowledge. However, we believe that at this stage, we can already describe some of the main tendencies that emerge from the observation of research activities and suggest a significant deviation from 'Mode 1'.

3.3. Three Main 'Stylized Facts' Concerning the New Mode of Knowledge Production

During the last two decades significant numbers of qualitative changes in the production of knowledge have been observed. They suggest an in-depth re-examination of the theoretical approach of knowledge production. We propose to review these changes in a somewhat stylized manner.

We first focus on three 'stylized facts' (which are converging and to some extent overlapping). The first stylized fact is that codification of knowledge increases the level of externalities, which may be very frequently positive, as noted by many observers. The second stylized fact is related to the drastic changes in the role and behaviour of private and public research. The third stylized fact partly results from the previous two and may be phrased in a more analytical way. Many signals call for a reconsideration of the issue of incentive mechanisms and draw the attention to the issue of co-ordination.

We then formulate an analytical proposition which, to some extent, sums up the various properties highlighted through the analysis of the stylized facts.

3.3.1. Stylized Fact 1: 'The Increasing Ways of Codifying Knowledge Contribute to Enhancing the Generation of Knowledge Externalities'

The growing possibility to use codification in the production of knowledge has a dramatic impact. These impacts can be analysed into many different dimensions: new technologies of information and communication contribute to change the ways researchers are accessing, storing, retrieving, exchanging, and transferring knowledge. Reducing redundancies, reducing delays and costs, and increasing quality are among the main attributes that are related to the introduction of new technologies in research. Of specific importance is the possibility offered to reduce delays and redundancy from the 'prototype' at the level of the laboratory, to the achievement of the actual production of a given product at the level of the plant. Automobile manufacturers have notably benefited from simulation techniques and computer-aided graphics methods that have in fact contributed to 'reduce the distance' between research and applications. The extensive use of codification techniques in research leads to a major impact at the society level: the possibility to 'reduce the distance between research and applications'. An example (Cohendet *et al.* 1989) has shown that, in the domain of new materials, the change of paradigm results from the general advance in the microscopic mastery of matter that relies on dramatic increases in the codification of knowledge by research. In the transition from an old style production system based on standardiz-ation and efficiency of scale to a new system founded on the diversity of products and variety-based economics, the codification of knowledge plays a key role in many perspectives in a shift from former 'screening' practices in research to tailor-made approaches involving a broad range of competencies, in the extensive use of material data bases, in the redesign of the materials for packaging, with an ever growing support for codification and information on the quality of products and the physical models underlying the design of production process, in the very significance of this new paradigm which implies that from now demand may drive the direction of research efforts. There are strong possibilities that the new paradigm due to new codifi-cation techniques in research that has been observed in the domain of new materials could also be analysed in domains such as biotechnologies or electronics.

Such phenomena that contribute to increase the efficiency of the global system of research have been well investigated by numerous studies, and we shall not insist on them here. However, one specific aspect should be empha-sized: the increasing ways of codifying knowledge contribute to enhance the generation of 'knowledge externalities'.

The process of knowledge generation is cumulative and integrative. Cumu-lative forms of knowledge are those in which today's advances lay the foun-dation for succeeding rounds of progress. Scotchmer (1991), when emphasizing the cumulative nature of inventive activity, compared it to the effect of 'raising the height of the shoulders of giants' from which one can see further, rather than obscuring the view. Thus, the process of knowledge gen-eration produces positive learning externalities. The generation of a new piece of knowledge increases the probability of creating useful new products, processes, and ideas arising from novel and unanticipated combinations. The more is invented, the easier it becomes to invent still more.

These positive learning externalities are based on various knowledge interactions, such as in the 'mining analogy' proposed by David and Foray (1996): 'First knowledge is like surveying: it generates maps that raise the return to further investment in exploration and exploitation' (David, Mowery, and Steinmueller 1994). Second, it has been observed that mineral produc-tion in an area leads to localization of exploration, so that at least for some time, mineral reserves become larger in the territories where exploita-tion is underway. When discovery increases the probability that others will undertake exploration in the neighbourhood, producing knowledge is likely to generate positive externalities for the explorers and each agent has an interest in diffusing the product of his discovery so as to profit from the results of others.

At the very least, information about where others have failed to make a discovery will be valuable in guiding one's own search. This third aspect of positive externalities deals with the migration of young investigators into new fields—colonizing new areas with tools and concepts developed elsewhere. As in the case of exploitation of minerals, this 'frontier expansion' requires falling yields in colonized areas to generate breakthroughs into new territory.

Many studies have shown that the introduction of new techniques of codification of knowledge has positive impact on each of the steps of the mining analogy (increasing the ability to design better maps at a lower cost, increasing the diffusion of the 'results of the mining', improving the possibility to reproduce elsewhere efficient schemes of discovery), which implies significant possibilities for an increase in general positive externalities. Thus, as emphasized by Mowery (1994), basic research generates 'orientation knowledge', that can make some key contributions to technological innovation: first, by enhancing the economic returns from applied research with a subsequent impact on growth; second, through the training of scientists and engineers; and third, through the development of new instruments and techniques for use in basic research programmes and laboratories.

3.3.2. Stylized Fact 2: Changes in the Role and Behaviour of Private and Public Research

An increasing complementarity between public labs and private firms. The traditional hypothesis of the independence of science and industry is seriously questioned by many changes of behaviour that are observed in the ways firms as well as laboratories are conducting their research activities.

On the one hand, Cohen and Levinthal (1989) clearly show that firms, whatever their size, must invest in basic research to create the capability to recognize, exploit, and assimilate knowledge produced elsewhere. Investing in basic research allows firms to gather knowledge from academic contacts. The motivation and aims of firms to improve their links to basic research have been discussed in a recent paper by Hicks (1995). She suggested that originally, the purpose of corporate research laboratories was to develop internal technological resources in order to identify and evaluate external technology. Nowadays, they have a strong tendency to emphasize interactions with external sources of knowledge. Hicks shows that firms in science-based industry (chemistry, for instance) do publish an increasing number of scientific papers in academic journals. As Meyer-Krahmer (1996) pointed out, firms release information in publications for a variety of reasons. Important among these are their need to participate in the barter-governed exchange of scientific and technical knowledge and to send market signals beyond those reflected in prices. Publications signal the existence of tacit knowledge and other unpublishable resources, thus building credibility needed to find partners in knowledge exchange. By signalling the existence of unpublishable resources, papers also allow researchers to search, select, and evaluate their tacit knowledge. Thus, papers are integral to the moving knowledge: not only do they convey formalized information, they point to the unpublishable. Thus, the growing tendency of firms to publish can be interpreted as an attempt to find new access to external knowledge by entering the club of academic researchers in a given field, one of their objectives being to detect the most promising researchers. By becoming 'members of the club' of academic activities, by paying an implicit fee to access the 'epistemic communities of researchers', the firm clearly expects a right of access to the academic tacit knowledge in a given field.

On the other hand, for basic research laboratories, the increasing share of their private financing becomes a key issue. This implies that research themes will be more and more influenced by applications. Knowledge and scientific theories are supposed to be partly dependent on the context in which they are produced. The scientific themes are not only constructed from the accumulated expertise of researchers, but also from strategies adopted by the laboratories for securing access to resources. Researchers have incentives to exploit more and more the opportunities offered by industry to complement their private funding: by doing so, they participate in the economic competitiveness of firms, and contribute to reinforcing the co-evolution of research and industry. This tendency varies from one discipline to another, but it can be shown that in certain areas, such as biotechnologies, the development of 'strategic' basic research strongly supported by private funds is an ever-growing phenomenon. This tendency will modify the nature of scientific knowledge. Research themes will be more and more dependent on the strategies of firms, in particular in the perspectives of the strategic reorganization of firms along their 'core-competencies', which can be interpreted as specific bodies of competitive knowledge accumulated, controlled, and managed by firms. The risk is to render this knowledge base more fragile, because mainly irrigated by veins of short-term considerations. Also, it has to be emphasized that the knowledge bases of particular firms are highly localized: firms tend to have one or a few technologies which they understand well and which form the basis of their competitive position. The highly specific character of this knowledge is not simply technical: it is also social, concerning the way in which technical processes can be integrated with skills, production routines, use of equipment, explicit or tacit training, and management systems. These potential biases in the accumulation of knowledge lead to a possible fragmentation of the scientific knowledge.

Geuna (1997) has studied the respective financing of British universities by government and firms in the period 1989–93. The analysis developed offers some evidence to support the hypothesis that policies oriented towards decreasing state financing of university research may be disappointing in two senses: firstly, industrial funding is not likely to be large enough to replace major cuts in public support for R&D, so that the net effect is a contraction of R&D. Second, universities hit hardest by budget cuts are pushed to do routine contract research for industry, which neither leads to high publications (and spillovers) nor does it lay a basis for long-term fundamental innovations.

The nature of the contractual relationships between laboratories and industry is changing. Certain exchanges amount to a subsidy from the firm to the laboratory, with the firm expecting a right of access to the laboratory network, rather than a specific service. Similarly, firms and public laboratories maintain numerous relations which are not based on commercial exchange but on the rules and norms of reciprocity (Cassier 1995).

Cassier used a case study of contracts between the Technical University of Compiègne and various industrial partners to explain the new forms of co-ordination modes between universities and industry. He noted the coexistence of two broad forms of contractual research: one is based on a logic of diffusing the results accumulated by the laboratory; while the other consists in a dynamic process of joint creation on more fundamental themes which are less directly applicable by the firm. As Joly and Mangematin (1996) noted, only a part of industry/university research contracts correspond to a R&D purchase on the market. Certain exchanges amount to a subsidy from the firm to the laboratory, with the firm expecting the right of access to the laboratory's network, rather than a specific service. Similarly, firms and public laboratories maintain numerous relations which are not based on commercial exchanges but on the rules of norms and reciprocity. The research agreements as studied by Cassier correspond to a model of *'unified technology research'*, that allows for two types of outputs: one towards the academic world (articles, theses, etc.); and the other towards the industrial world (methods, patents, etc.). He clearly shows that the only division is expressed in terms of results from unified technological research. Thus, what is behind a research contract is a project of joint production and mutual dependence between research laboratories and industry. If the production and circulation of some codified pieces of knowledge are anticipated as one of the results of the collaboration, it clearly appears that this is not by far the main expected output. Tacit forms of exchange are also expected. To give an example of these new forms of contractual relationships between laboratories and firms, one can quote cases where laboratories were given private financial funds by firms to do their own research (on themes that are selected by the sole laboratory). The counterpart for the company, being the right of priority access (not 'to possess') to academic papers to be submitted for publications in academic journals by the members of the laboratory.

3.3.3. Stylized Fact 3: The Reconsideration of the Incentive Mechanisms in the Production of Knowledge: From Incentives to Co-ordination

In the traditional vision, the main economic variable considered is the ownership status of knowledge. We were observing the incentives of agents to produce knowledge, with regards to the issue of appropriability. Another characteristic of the behaviour of agents that can be considered is the disclosure/secrecy dimension. This issue has been brought forwards in particular by David and Foray (1996):

> The extent of disclosure is a continuous variable bounded by full disclosure at one limit and total secrecy at the other. The degree of disclosure required is not uniform across intellectually property rights regimes, and even with a given regime, different kinds of text may be protected by varying completeness of disclosure. Computer software, for example, may be copyrighted without revealing the source code, and in some instance even the full body of object code does not have to be disclosed. Standards of disclosure may be defined not only by the statute laws and intellectual-property agencies such as patent offices, but also by the policies of the journals in which scientific papers are published. For example, professional journals may or may not insist upon the exact co-ordinates of complex proteins whose molecular structure is being reported, or required disclosure of the computational algorithm used in analyzing experimental observations.

The introduction of both the appropriability dimension and the disclosure dimension of economic agents *vis-à-vis* knowledge has an important consequence: the institutional settings, as expressed by norms, rules, and standards to be followed, govern to some extent disclosure among members of different social organizations. In particular, the modes of organizing research activities strongly influence the costs of transferring the knowledge that has been produced. This debate is a key one in the economics of knowledge and it is presently a very active one among the community of researchers in the domain. The point of focus is again the production of new knowledge, with regard to the differences between fundamental and applied research. Callon (1999) recently emphasized what he considers to be two extreme visions among economists of the main ways to produce knowledge.

1. On the one hand, there is the vision proposed by Romer (1993), for whom the main difference between basic research and applied research resides in the difference in the contents of knowledge which are manipulated (basic science consisting essentially in codified statements having a large degree of generality, and applied research consisting essentially in manipulating private tacit knowledge in forms of know-how incorporated in workers or equipment).

2. On the other hand, the vision proposed by Dasgupta and David (1994) is that the difference would not be found in the contents of knowledge (which, a priori, would exhibit a 'cognitive equivalence' that leads to a strong substitutability between the two forms), but rather in the institutional settings. The incentive schemes and norms edicted by the institutional settings

are the main explanation for why codified forms are preferred by some agents (researchers who have incentives to publish articles, theorems, and treaties), while tacit forms are preferred by others (engineers working in private firms). As expressed by David and Foray (1996):

The true nature of new knowledge does not stem from any intrinsic differences between knowledge that is scientific rather than technological, nor between basic and applied scientific knowledge. The critical factor governing the distribution and the utilization of new findings are those regarding the rules structures and behavioral norms about information disclosure that dominate in the particular social organizations within which the new knowledge is found or improved.

The above considerations emphasize the role of incentives as shaping the nature of the production of knowledge. This issue is still a quite controversial one. For example, when considering the status of incentives for research in the US, Stephan and Levin (1997: 45) mentioned:

Why have researchers in the US focused so extensively on individuals as opposed to groups and why has this focus persisted despite widespread evidence that science is becoming increasingly a collaborative effort? It is virtually impossible for a scientist to survive and have a career at a university without becoming a 'principle investigator' (PI) and directing a lab. The research the PI directs is collaborative, but the majority of the collaborators are graduate students *and* postdocs—statuses which by their very definition are temporary.

This individualistic vision of incentives is in accordance with the mertonian model of scientific activity, where the individual trajectory of the researcher and his/her capacity to accumulate a stock of credibility is the main driver of the academic domain. This leads for instance to the well-known 'Matthews effect': as public fundings of scientific research is related to previous accomplishments, the system may give disproportionate recognition to scientists who attained early discoveries (Diamond 1996). A very different point of view on incentives has been recently taken by other countries, for example the UK, where the 'lab' is the unit of reference for reputation and other mechanisms of incentives. In some cases, one can see a tendency to reward beyond the frontier of the lab, the network of research centres and laboratories that have produced the new knowledge. A recent example, quoted by Joly (1997), is the publication in *Nature* of an article on the sequence of chromosome III in yeast. The article was signed by 147 researchers from forty different institutions of research. It is one among many signs of the tendency to consider research as a real collective enterprise. Depending on the types of incentives mechanisms that will be promoted in the future by public authorities that support research, this tendency has some chances to become a dominant mode of production of research.

The increasing importance of collective research is attested by scientometric analysis (see Stephan 1996). It is explained by the conjunction of: (i) increasing costs of innovation; (ii) increasing level of externalities; and

(iii) increasing level of knowledge codification. Let us come back to genomic research in order to focus on current organizational changes associated with these trends.[2] In the proliferation of material transfer agreements (MTA) which become the general norm under which exchanges of data are performed, MTAs will protect the laboratory, which produced the results. At this stage MTAs are private contracts signed between two researchers. The researcher who receives the research material undertakes in the MTA not to use the genetic material for purposes other than those for which she or he requested it, and not to use it for any commercial applications. Some MTAs stipulate the modalities for citing the team that provided the genetic material (citation, acknowledgement, co-authors). MTAs have a relatively standardized form and are available on the Web or in certain publications by research teams (rice genome letter, for example).

MTAs cover all genetic material or, more generally, experimental material. Software may also be included. They may also accompany the dissemination of certain documents with a limited circulation. They are a flexible form of bilateral or multilateral agreements. Therefore, the classical distinction between public and private data is blurred. The yeast programme shows the functional importance of the 'grey area', which is based on 'pooled data'. This does not mean that private data replace public ones but that, at least for a given period, the data will not be accessible. This does not mean, as Dasgupta and David (1994) claim, that it will lead to an increasing amount of tacit instead of codified data. It is the contrary since, by definition, genomics is all about codification. Therefore, the main issue here is not codification but *standardization*, since the agreement on common standards is the necessary condition for data to circulate freely. Standardization may not be expected as the result of competition. It has to be constructed through *ex-ante* co-ordination. This is precisely why national and international consortia are so important in this area.

Theoretically, consortia could be just about producing public standards and public data. However, this is not the case. One of the reasons that explain the shortcomings of such a solution is the high level of private investment. In such a configuration, creating an island of standard public data in an ocean of private actors risks resuming to wishful thinking. If the level of incentives for private actors to co-operate is not enough, the risk is to get a kind of jeopardized standard or, finally, to see a private standard becoming the *de facto* standard.

3.3.4. Proposition

A rich and intensive knowledge-based environment will certainly favour an intense use of rights of access with a rather weak system of property rights to ensure the dynamic efficiency of the innovative network and the development

---

[2] These lines are extracted from Joly and Mangematin (2000).

of a dynamics of creation and circulation of knowledge. Networking between academic institutions and private enterprises is a growing phenomenon. This growing phenomenon could be explained by numerous reasons. The first is related to the fact that the knowledge exchanged between agents is never a pure form of codified knowledge, even if the amount of codified knowledge is always increasing. In such a perspective, one should not worry too much about excessive uncontrolled spillovers and risks of excessive imitation, precisely because of significant transaction costs. Imitating is very costly, and loose co-operation in informal networks that allows a certain control of the diffusion of spillovers between agents can be an efficient form of collaboration that ensures incentive compatibility between them.

Second, networks offer a way to share and exchange knowledge complementarities. What differentiates an agent from another is its specific body of tacit knowledge. Through networks, agents can organize an efficient circulation of codified knowledge through a structure that renders compatible different segments of specific tacit forms of knowledge. Agents accept increasing specialization in a given tacit form of knowledge because they are confident that the other agents will increase their specialization in complementary forms. This reduces the risks of overspecialization, but relies intensively on the building of mutual trust in the production of knowledge. Taking into account the degree of trust raises an important issue which has to do with the choice between specialization and co-operation in the production of knowledge. As mentioned by Zuscovitch (1998),

Trust is a tacit agreement in which rather than systematically seeking out the best opportunity at every instant, each agent takes a longer perspective to the transactions, as long as his traditional partner does not go beyond some mutually accepted norm. Sharing the risks of specialization is an aspect of cooperation that manifests an important trust mechanism in network functioning. Specialization is a risky business. One may sacrifice the 'horizontal' ability to satisfy various demands in order to gain 'vertical' efficiency in an effort to increase profitability. Any specializing firm accepts this risk, network or not. A risk-sharing mechanism is essential because, while aggregate profits for participating firms may indeed be superior to the situation where firms are less specialized, the distribution of profits may be very hazardous. To make specialization worthwhile, the dichotomous (win–lose) individual outcome must be smoothed somehow by a cooperative principle of risk sharing.

'Trust' is relevant in regard to reliability of other specialized producers of complementary knowledge. The institutionalization of incentives as validation processes (peer referring processes, for instance) in epistemic communities may vary widely. The choice for an agent A to specialize in one domain of knowledge (and to accept to bear the sunk costs for that) in co-operation with other agents that would accept to specialize in turn in the complementary types of knowledge that are necessary for A (while A's knowledge would be considered as complementary viewed by the other agents) seems to be one of the main lines of research to understand the management of knowledge by organizations.

In the above perspectives, one of the key issues that determine the functioning of innovative networks is the constant trade off by agents involved in these networks between the delimitation of property rights, on the one hand, and the determination of rights of access to complementary forms of knowledge, on the other.

3.4. Conclusions: Consequences of the New Tendencies of the Production of Knowledge for the Policy of Research and Technology

The tendency towards a new mode of knowledge production raises several issues when considering the policy maker's point of view.

1. The new mode seems to undermine the concept of science as a public good (Dasgupta and David 1994) . As has been seen, the problem of innovators in a context of knowledge production is not so much a problem of being protected by strong property rights but rather of having the internal capabilities to access and absorb knowledge produced externally, and to negotiate with selected partners the rights of access to their knowledge. As a result, the increasing production of knowledge by private entities raises the problem of the role of public institutions of knowledge production (public laboratories, public centres of research, etc.). Market forces are penetrating the 'republic of science' to such an extent that many voices call for the need to protect the specific traits of the research system. One of the major supports for the strengthening of the system of science came from Dasgupta and David (1994). The main characteristics of their message is that the specific features of the scientific domain must be preserved for reasons of economic efficiency. One of the associated risks is that in a period of budgetary cross-cutting, governments will focus their attention on the larger and politically more visible items of the basic science budget, namely the large-scale research facilities. David (1993) explained why such a decision will be damaging for the whole system of research, and the competitiveness of industry.

2. In the perspective of a new mode of knowledge production, new arguments should be developed to justify the involvement of public entities in the production of knowledge. Among these arguments, three of them appear as essential.

First is the need for public authorities to ensure an efficient system of distribution and access to knowledge for increasing the amount of innovative opportunities. As David and Foray (1996) pointed out, the activity of diffusing economically relevant knowledge is not a natural one. Rather, it is socially constructed through the creation of appropriate institutions and conventions, such as open science and intellectual property rights. Improving what they termed 'the distribution power' of the system of innovation has often been portrayed as a desirable objective that has to be sacrificed in order to provide stronger market incentives for private investments in organized R&D, since copyright, patent, and trade secrecy laws create obstacles to access and restrict the commercial utilization of knowledge.

Second is the need for public authorities to promote 'positive knowledge externalities' (Cohendet, Foray, Guellec, and Mairesse 1999). Classical ways of stimulating knowledge externalities, such as the definition of patents, could be reviewed in the light of the new economics of knowledge. In some cases, other than the definition of too strong property rights that would hamper the diffusion of innovation, governments should favour direct discussions and agreement between the entities that are concerned. In many cases, the real problem is not to hold property rights, it is to avoid free-rider attitudes. In other contexts, mainly when radical innovations are at stake, governments should envisage buying directly the property rights better to diffuse it, as was the case for the 'Daguerrotype' (in 1839 the French government bought the property right of the photographic process from Daguerre). Besides these two main directions, other arguments for justifying public involvement in the research system could be mentioned, such as the preservation of diversity, the possibility to invest in long-term options, the capability to certify, verify, or memorize the advances in the production of knowledge.

Third, as stated by Callon (1994), one of the aims of public research is to counterbalance the tendency towards the reduction of technological variety. This tendency is linked to the intensity of economic increasing returns which are all the more important when externalities are high. Thus, if what has been stated previously is right, public research institutions face a major trade off. Because of the efficiency of innovation 'Mode 2' and because of the level of positive externalities, they are highly integrated into technological networks. If they want to widen the level of technological variety, they have to be able to build new networks, and indeed, to be independent of the stabilized networks.

3. The new vision inspired by the interactive model of innovation plays an important role in the perspective of the development towards a learning economy. As Meyer-Krahmer (1996) mentioned, 'the growing degree of internalisation and the acceleration in the rate of diffusion of codified knowledge imply that the capability to absorb the results from basic research pursued abroad is becoming increasingly important. A strong position in basic science is important in this context, but a stronger emphasis on international competitive advantage may be called for.' This argument for government to invest in basic research is relevant at a moment where some argued that the scope for free riding has increased, weakening the interest of governments to invest in science (this risk is also weakened by the consideration of tacit knowledge as a key strategic asset).

4. As we have mentioned, the 'geography' of the production of knowledge is going to be drastically modified. Multinationals are establishing and expanding R&D abroad, benefiting from the possibilities offered by ICT to internationalize the learning processes along the whole of the value chain. In this movement, 'multinational companies set priorities for some leading edge locations where the best conditions for excellent research on the one hand and lead marketing on the other hand are located' (Meyer-Krahmer 1998). The paradox is that simultaneously in the middle of the 1990s some of them have apparently reduced their innovative efforts (AT&T, IBM, General Electric, Xerox, Kodak), in particular in the domain of fundamental research. But this movement should be carefully interpreted. In many cases it corresponds to an outsourcing of some research activities to external centres as university laboratories. In such cases, an efficient innovative network is substituting a centralized activity of R&D. To be able to do so, these companies relied on internal absorptive capabilities that have been strongly reinforced.

Small and medium enterprises will benefit from new opportunities in terms of innovative potential, provided that a number of conditions are satisfied: the progressive building within these companies of internal absorptive capabilities, the existence of a strong 'power of distribution of knowledge', the existence of services (KIBS, knowledge-intensive business services) and institutions supporting the development and circulation of knowledge. In the development of this infrastructure of support, public authorities should be extremely careful not to develop the risk of a 'crowding-effect', that is to develop within the centres that help SMEs exclusive absorbing capabilities instead of developing them within SMEs. The effect in the long run would then be totally the opposite to the one expected.

REFERENCES

ARCHIBUGI, D., and IAMMARINO, S. (1999). 'The policy implications of the globalisation of innovation'. *Research Policy*, 28: 317–36.

AGHION, P., and HOWITT, P. (1992). 'Un modèle de croissance par destruction créatrice', in D. Foray and C. Freeman (eds.), *Technologie et Richesse des Nations*. Paris: Economica.

ARROW, K. (1962). 'Economic welfare and the allocation of resources for invention', in R. R. Nelson (ed.), *The Rate and Direction of Inventive Activity*. Princeton, NJ: Princeton University Press.

BACH, L., and LHUILLERY, S. (1998). 'Recherche et externalités: tradition économique et renouveau', in D. Foray and J. Mairesse (eds.), *Innovations et performances: Approches interdisciplinaires*. Paris: Editions de l'EHESS.

BETA (1993). 'Les effets économiques des programmes Brite-Euram'. Rapport à la Commission Economique Européenne. Strasbourg: BETA, Université Louis Pasteur.

CALLON, M. (1994). 'Is science (still) a public good?'. *Science, Technology and Human Values*, 19/4: 395–425.

——(1999). 'Le réseau comme forme émergente et comme modalité de coordination', in M. Callon, P. Cohendet, and N. Curlien (eds.), *Réseau et coordination*. Paris: Economica.

CASSIER, M. (1995). 'Les contrats de recherche entre l'université et l' industrie'. Thèse de doctorat, Ecole des Mines, Paris.

COHEN, W. H., and LEVINTHAL, D. (1989). 'Innovation and learning: The two faces of R&D'. *The Economic Journal*, 99: 569–96.

COHENDET, P., LEDOUX, M. J., and ZUSCOVITCH, E. (1989). *New Materials: Economic Dynamics and European Strategy*. Berlin: Springer Verlag.

COHENDET, P., FORAY, D., GUELLEC, D., and MAIRESSE, J. (1999). 'La gestion des externalités positives de la recherche', in D. Foray and J. Mairesse (eds.), '*Innovations et performances: Approches interdisciplinaires*'. Paris: Editions de l'EHESS, Springer Verlag.

COHENDET, P., LLERENA, P., STAHN, H., and UMBHAUER, G. (1998) (eds.). *The Economics of Networks: Interaction and Behaviours*. Berlin: Springer Verlag.

DASGUPTA, P., and DAVID, P. (1994). 'Towards a new economics of science'. *Research Policy*, 23/5: 487–522.

DAVID, P. A. (1993). 'Knowledge, property and the system dynamics of technological change', in L. Summers and S. Shah (eds.), *Annual Bank Conference on Development Economics*. Washington, DC: World Bank.

——and FORAY, D. (1996). 'Accessing and expanding the science and technology knowledge-base'. *STI Review*, 16: 13–68.

——MOWERY, D., and STEINMUELLER, W. E. (1994). 'Analysing the economic payoffs from basic research'. *Economics of Innovation and New Technology*, 2/4: 73–90.

DIAMOND, A. (1996). 'The economics of science'. *Knowledge and Policy*, 9/2–3: 6–49.

DOSI, G. (1988). 'Sources, procedures and microeconomic effects of innovation'. *Journal of Economic Literature*, 26: 1120–71.

FORAY, D., and LUNDVALL, B.-Å. (1997). 'Une introduction à l'économie fondée sur la connaissance', in B. Guilhon, P. Huard, M. Orillard, and J. B. Zimmermann (eds.), *Économie de la Connaissance et Organisations*. Paris: L'Harmattan.

GIBBONS, M., LIMOGES, C., NOWOTNY, H., SCHWARTZMAN, S., SCOTT, P., and TROIW, M. (1994). *The New Production of Knowledge*. London: Sage.

GUELLEC, D. (1995). 'Externalités et asymétries d'information dans un modèle de croissance. *Revue Economique*, 4/3: 837–47.

GEUNA, A. (1997). 'Allocation of funds and research output: the case of UK universities'. *Revue d'Economie Industrielle*, 79: 143–63.

HATCHUEL, A., and WEIL, B. (1995). *Experts in Organizations*. Berlin: Walter de Gruyter.

HICKS, D. (1995). 'Published papers, tacit competencies, and corporate management of the public/private character of knowledge'. *Industrial and Corporate Change*, 4: 401–24.

HIRSCHLEIFER, J. (1971). 'The private and social value of information and the reward to inventive activity'. *American Economic Review*, 61: 561–74.

JOLY, P. B. (1992). 'Le rôle des externalités dans les systèmes d'innovation'. *Revue Économique*, 43/4: 785–96.

——(1995). 'A quoi servent les brevets en biotechnologie', in M. Basl (ed.), *Changement institutionnel et changement technologique*. Paris: CNRS Éditions.

JOLY, P. B. (1997). 'Chercheurs et laboratoires dans la nouvelle économie de la science'. *Revue d' economie industrielle*, 79: 77–94.

——and MANGEMATIN, V. (1996). 'Profiles of public laboratories, industrial partners and the organization of R&D'. *Research Policy*, 25: 901–22.

——(2000). 'Data circulation and public management of techno-scientific production: The example of genomics', *Research Policy* (forthcoming).

KREMER, M. (1997). 'Patent buy-outs: A mechanism for encouraging innovation'. National Bureau of Economic Research Working Paper no. 6304.

MEYER-KRAHMER, F. (1996). *Strategies of Applied Research.* London: Cartermill.

——(1998) (ed.). 'Internationalisation of Research and Technology'. EUR 18762. Brussels: European Commision.

MOWERY, D. (1994). *Science and Technology Policy in Interdependent Economies.* Boston: Kluwer Academic Press.

NELSON, R. R. (1987). *Technical Change as an Evolutionary Process.* Amsterdam: North Holland.

OECD (1999). *Unlocking Knowledge in the Learning Economy.* Paris: OECD.

PAVITT, K. (1984). 'Sectoral patterns of technical change: Towards a taxonomy and a theory'. *Research Policy*, 13: 343–73.

PESTRE, D. (1997). 'La production des savoirs entre académie et marché: Une relecture historique du livre *The new production of knowledge*'. *Revue d'Economie Industrielle*, 79: 163–75.

ROMER, P. (1986). 'Increasing returns and long run growth'. *Journal of Political Economy*, 94/5: 1002–37.

——(1990). 'Endogenous technical change'. *Journal of Political Economy*, 98/5: 97–102.

——(1993). 'Implementing a national technology strategy with self-organizing industry boards'. *Brooking Papers on Economic Activity. Microeconomics* 2: 345–99.

SAVIOTTI, P. P. (1998). 'On the dynamic of appropriability, of tacit and of codified knowledge'. *Research Policy*, 26/7–8: 843–57.

SCOTCHMER, S. (1991). 'Standing on the shoulders of giants: Cumulative research and the patent laws'. *Journal of Economic Perspectives*, 5/1: 29–41.

STEPHAN, P. E. (1996). 'The economics of science'. *Journal of Economic Literature*, 34: 1199–235.

——and LEVIN, S. G. (1997). 'The critical importance of careers in collaborative scientific research'. *Revue d'economie industrielle*, 79: 45–61.

YOUNG, A. (1995). 'Growth without scale effects'. NBER Working paper no. 5211.

ZUSCOVITCH, E., (1998). 'Networks and trust', in P. Cohendet, P. Llenna, H. Stahn, and G. Umbhauer, *The Economics of Networks: Interactions and Behaviours.* Berlin: Springer Verlag.

4

Universities in the Learning Economy: Balancing Institutional Integrity with Organizational Diversity

PEDRO CONCEIÇÃO AND MANUEL HEITOR

4.1. Introduction

The important strategic role that universities can play in helping nations to meet public goals has been extensively recognized. These roles have a multi-faceted nature, including such diverse aspects as public safety, quality of life, health care, environmental protection, and economic development and growth (e.g. Clark 1995; Lucas 1996; Noll 1998). The specific ways in which universities have played these roles are dominated by activities associated with the creation and distribution of knowledge (Rosenberg 1998). The generation and diffusion of knowledge is translated, for example, in improved competencies and skills in the labour force, and in the development and commercialization of new technologies. However, in face of continuous and ever-more demanding public scrutiny, traditional suppliers of knowledge—such as schools, universities, and training organizations—as well as businesses and knowledge based organizations in the public sector (growing users of knowledge) are urgently seeking fundamental insights to help them nurture, harvest, and manage the immense potential for their knowledge assets to excel at the leading edge of innovation.

To a certain extent, it can be argued that a trend is emerging which is leading to a breakdown of the institutional boundaries that separated companies and universities. This process of 'institutional convergence' can be understood as a result of two forces that come together to impose an ever-closer identification of firms and academic institutions, and vice versa. The first force results from the fact that the creation of added value and wealth is increasingly associated with the production of knowledge, so it is natural that companies look to the way universities function for inspiration on how to perform creative tasks. Secondly, the universities find themselves facing difficulties in obtaining sufficient funds for their basic tasks of teaching and research (see Caraça, Conceição, and Heitor 2000), so it is also natural that they look to companies to learn how to derive commercial benefits from their intellectual assets and endeavours.

As various studies have shown, while this convergence is, to a certain extent, to be welcomed, it can also be dangerous. Rosenberg and Nelson (1996), Dasgupta and David (1994), David (1993), and Pavitt (1987) argue that this convergence is 'acceptable' as long as it does not harm the institutional integrity of the university. Companies and universities have evolved in a social context to the point of attaining what these authors call 'institutional specialization'. Thus, whereas companies are concerned with obtaining private returns for the knowledge that they generate, universities have traditionally made it public. By means of this specialization, or 'division of labour', the accumulation of knowledge has taken place at a rapid pace, as is shown by the unprecedented levels of economic growth since the end of the Second World War (Rosenberg and Nelson 1996). These authors show that the universities we know today, despite their long historical inheritance, are relatively new institutions, namely in the way they relate to their surrounding social and economic context. And universities have defined themselves almost as *non-firms*, in the sense that they produce knowledge that is publicly available. To do this effectively, a complex set of incentive structures and organizational features has emerged, which are relatively easy to destroy, despite the long time it took for them to evolve.

The argument on the dangers of harming the institutional integrity of the university is analysed in detail in the context of the knowledge-based economies in Conceição, Heitor, and Oliveira (1998). The threats to a university's institutional integrity in fact go beyond the extension of its activities to links with society, which, if excessive, could lead to resources being spread too thinly. The analysis is based on the more serious problems that may arise if universities take the path of privatizing the ideas that they produce and the skills that they develop.

In other words, an evolutionary metaphor could, with some liberties, be used here. Both firms and universities have evolved over time as institutions adapted to an environment where different types of knowledge were generated by each institution for mutual benefit. Thus, in a simplified way, while firms were able to commercialize and diffuse technologies, universities specialized in advancing the knowledge frontier at the forefront of the unknown. No insurance mechanism or system of private rewards could possibly lure investors into this most risky of ventures. Universities assumed this role, with a structure of incentives which never penalizes too much for failure but that also does not reward exceedingly for successes. This is particularly true in Europe, where university professors are, to a large extent, civil servants, and their salaries are rigidly structured by the civil servant system in which seniority carries a very heavy weight, and there is not much possibility for competition along the salary dimension (Rosenberg 1998). The danger addressed in this chapter is in the 'extinction' of one of the knowledge-creating 'institutional species' identified above. If universities become, at least in the way they deal with knowledge, very much like firms, we shall be in fact witnessing the death of an institution!

Therefore, our chapter suggests two important ideas. First, we propose that the *institutional integrity of the university needs to be preserved.* Universities are a special type of learning organization specialized in producing and diffusing knowledge in unique ways. Second, we argue that, important as universities are, they are not enough to guarantee prosperity, and there *is a need to promote a diversity of organizational arrangements,* even at the higher education level. Indeed, this organizational diversity could be a major contributor to ensure the institutional integrity of the university.

Our analysis is based on the way organizations deal with knowledge, that is, the way organizations promote 'learning', where learning is understood as the mechanisms through which knowledge is produced and diffused. Therefore, we start, in section 4.2, by describing a conceptual framework where we make explicit our understanding of *learning* as a process of knowledge accumulation. In section 4.3 we discuss the application of the model to the context of the university. Finally, in the concluding section 4.4 we summarize the main arguments of the chapter.

4.2. Learning as Knowledge Accumulation: A Conceptual Framework

From our perspective, learning is understood, broadly, as *knowledge accumulation.* There are different levels of 'learning entities', from individuals, to organizations, to whole economies. Our discussion of universities is based, as we indicated above, on the exploration of the ways in which universities promote learning and, thus, contribute to knowledge accumulation. A first important step in our discussion is the clarification of our conceptual understanding of terms such as 'knowledge' and 'learning', often loosely used with dramatically different meanings. This conceptual clarification of our understanding of learning as knowledge accumulation is the objective of this section.

We find it useful, as developed in more detail in a previous paper (Conceição and Heitor 1999), to follow Nelson and Romer's (1996) differentiation between ideas and skills, or *software* and *wetware,* to use these authors' nomenclature. These two kinds of knowledge differ in the way they are used, diffused, and produced. However, they are strongly interdependent in the learning processes that lead to the accumulation of knowledge.

The conceptual difference between software and wetware lies in the level of codification. While ideas correspond to knowledge that can be articulated in words, symbols, or other means of expression, skills cannot be formalized but always remain in tacit form. Under this taxonomy, knowledge is divided into two worlds: the world of codified ideas (*software*) and the world of non-codified skills (*wetware*).

The difference in the level of codification has implications in terms of the 'economic properties' of the two types of knowledge that we consider. The most important implication is associated with the differences in the rivalry associated with the consumption of each type of knowledge. Since the knowledge underlying software is codified, it is easily articulated and reproduced by simple, inexpensive means. In general, the costs of disseminating ideas are extremely low, especially in comparison with the costs of producing them. Indeed, the ease, speed, and low cost of distribution are characteristic of virtually all codified knowledge. Consequently, rivalry in the consumption of software is low, in the sense that many people can share exactly the same ideas (software) without precluding each other from joint consumption. By contrast, the transmission of skills (wetware) is complex, expensive, and slow. Skills result from a combination of factors, ranging from their largely innate quality, through individual experience, to formal training. Thus, rivalry is comparatively higher in the consumption of wetware.

The differences in rivalry between software and wetware have important implications for knowledge production. The non-rivalry of ideas, and their low distribution costs, mean that it is very hard to assign property rights to them and to protect those rights, on the one hand, and on the other that ideas tend to be abundant, especially given advances in information technology and telecommunications which enable codified knowledge to be easily and inexpensively used and transmitted. In contrast, the rival character of wetware means that, in principle, the market provides incentives to produce this type of knowledge, at least when it is analysed in isolation.

From this perspective, what type of incentives exist for the production of ideas? Dasgupta and David (1994) suggest that there are basically two choices. The first consists of *intervention by the state* in the production of ideas, by means of direct production (such as occurs, for instance, in state-controlled research laboratories), or by subsidizing production, such as funding of university R&D. The alternative consists of granting property rights for the creation of ideas, that is by defining regulations for *intellectual property*, specific instruments that include patents, registered trade marks, and copyright (see Conceição, Heitor, and Oliveira 1999, for a more comprehensive analysis). Therefore, the conclusion from this analysis is that the production of ideas requires more complex institutional mechanisms than those provided by the market. As for skills, the market provides a large proportion of the incentives needed for their production, at least when these are analysed in isolation. We shall see below that we challenge this interpretation, and, in fact, suggest that the role of institutions and of public support probably needs to be much stronger than is normally acknowledged, even when the production of skills is at stake.

We bring our own understanding to the process of knowledge accumulation when each of the categories of knowledge ceases to be seen in isolation and the interaction between them is explored. Considering the two types of knowledge together is a requirement, since it is the accumulation of knowledge as a whole that we are interested in, which means that the way ideas and skills are related to each other needs to be taken into account.

The idea of interaction between ideas (software) and skills (wetware) is crucial to our model of learning. In fact, each fuels the other. Without skills, ideas may be irrelevant. What good is a car if we lack the skills to drive it? And without ideas, there is no need for new and better skills. Why should we need to further our knowledge of computers if new applications were not continuously forthcoming? Analysis of the interaction between ideas and skills leads us to explore the learning processes associated with the generation of each type of knowledge in a more integrated and dynamic way, beyond the mere accumulation of ideas and skills, each in isolation.

Indeed, according to Soete (1996), ideas and skills are no more than two sides of the same coin, two essential aspects of the accumulation of knowledge. Herbert Simon, quoted by Varian (1995), puts the argument as follows:

What information [in the sense of ideas, according to our terminology] consumes is rather obvious: it consumes the attention of its recipients. Hence, a wealth of information [that is, of ideas] creates a poverty of attention, and a need to allocate that attention efficiently among the overabundance of information sources that might consume it.

It is worth while to restate our argument, which is that without skills, ideas may be irrelevant, and without ideas, there may be no need for new and better skills. The invention of writing (one important idea) required the development of writing skills. Similarly, the widespread diffusion of another important idea, the computer, requires increasing computer skills. New ideas spur the development of the skills required to use those new ideas. The bridge from the production of ideas to the usage of ideas is established by producing new skills. Increased use of an idea, which requires its diffusion, will lead to a constellation of other ideas, aimed at improving and extending the initial idea, which will lead to the need for further skills and so on, in a self-reinforcing cycle that leads to the accumulation of knowledge. The accumulation of knowledge results from the production, usage, and diffusion of both software and wetware. Figure 4.1 summarizes this understanding of the learning processes that leads to knowledge accumulation.

To systematize the close and complex interdependence between ideas and skills that leads to overall knowledge accumulation, we suggest two major categories of learning processes. *Learning by codifying* (Foray and Lundvall 1996)—the production of ideas, through the codification of knowledge: this includes new scientific and technological results but also major ideas of relevance to the progress of humankind, such as democracy, the equality across race and gender, but also ideas of relevance to a single person or a firm. *Learning by interpreting* (OECD 1997)—the production of skills, through the usage, or more broadly, the interpretation of ideas, of codified knowledge,

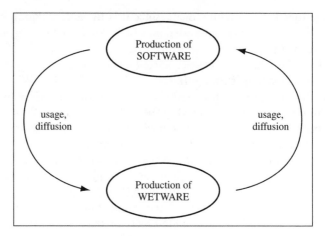

FIG. 4.1. *The self-reinforcing learning cycle leading to knowledge accumulation*

including machines, which can be regarded as embodied ideas: this includes skill development as a result of training or of experience.

The mere *production* of skills and ideas is, nowadays, well rewarded economically, namely through the public and private mechanisms which include those associated with the institutional arrangements in universities. Learning processes that result in the codification of knowledge (generation of new ideas) include R&D and artistic creation. In both cases, the creators of the ideas (scientists and artists) are rewarded economically as a result of their efforts.

However, the substantial gains in wealth and knowledge generation are to be found in the usage and *diffusion* of knowledge. In fact, history is full of examples in which producers of ideas and skills, by not using and diffusing them, were surpassed by others that did use the new ideas, even though they were not the initial innovators. Two examples, one at the grand scale of the history of civilization, the other at the much smaller scale of contemporary corporate warfare, serve as illustrations.

China developed what was, after the invention of writing, one of the most important ideas for the progress of humankind: the movable type printing press. This idea produced an unprecedented increase in the possibilities of codifying knowledge. However, Imperial China restricted its usage to the affairs of the emperor and its court. It was Europe that was able to capitalize on this invention, by promoting its widespread usage and diffusing it vastly and quickly (the historical account is taken from Elvin 1973; Landes 1998). At a more prosaic level, the history of the invention at Xerox PARC of what would become the basis of today's Windows operating system is well known. Not even Apple, initially more successful than Xerox, was able to capitalize fully on the potential of wealth in these new ideas, by underestimating the returns that could accrue from a widespread diffusion and promotion of usage. In the end it was Microsoft that reaped most of the potential benefits.

Thus, with Figure 4.1 we achieve our main objective for this section, making explicit the way in which we understand learning as knowledge accumulation, which is a result of a complex set of learning processes where there is considerable interdependence between the accumulation of ideas and of skills. Our next challenge is to examine how universities, and other institutions, fit into these processes.

4.3. Universities in the Learning Economy

Our conceptualization of the mechanisms through which learning occurs emphasizes the importance of the learning processes. This section discusses how these concepts can be used to analyse the challenges facing universities in the emerging learning economy. The university as an institution is recognized primarily through two important functions: teaching and research. However, universities have recently also committed themselves to a range of additional activities, normally grouped together under the heading of 'links with society' (for detailed discussions on the context of the university's mission in Europe, see Caraça, Conceição, and Heitor 1998, and in the United States, Lucas 1996).

At the same time, there is a growing tendency to classify companies as 'learning organizations'. Nonaka and Takeuchi (1995) are perhaps the classic example of this trend, with the publication of their book *The Knowledge-creating Company*. Against this background, is the university still the 'knowledge factory', as described by the *Economist* (1997)? Or, given the profusion of activities associated with university extension, should it structure itself along business lines? At the same time, companies themselves are becoming involved in the production of knowledge, when they are not set up and run from the beginning along similar lines to a university, as is the case with Microsoft (*Economist* 1997). In short, will the trend towards a breakdown of the institutional boundaries between companies and universities become a fact of life in knowledge-based economies?

To a certain extent, the description already given of recent developments in companies and universities indicates that there will be a convergence. This convergence is the result of two forces that come together to drive an 'identification' of companies as universities, and vice versa. Firstly, the creation of value added and wealth is increasingly associated with the production of knowledge (OECD 1996), so it is natural that companies look to the way universities function for inspiration on how to become more creative. Second, the universities find themselves facing difficulties in obtaining sufficient funds for their basic tasks of teaching and research (see Caraça, Conceição, and

Heitor 1998), so it is also natural that they should look to companies to learn how to derive commercial benefit from their intellectual assets.

The issue we want to address is the extent to which this convergence is to be welcomed. As we suggested, companies and universities have evolved in a social context to the point of attaining an 'institutional specialization'. Whereas companies are concerned about attaining private returns for the knowledge that they generate, universities have traditionally made it public. This argument is analysed in detail, in the context of the knowledge-based economies, in one of our previous papers (see Conceição, Heitor, and Oliveira 1998). In the scope of that article, we started by analysing the university function of *teaching*, which was understood as contributing to the accumulation of knowledge, specifically of skills, through the formal process of learning through education. The development of the paper continued with an analysis of *research*; it noted that the great majority of the ideas that are generated in universities are of a public nature, this being the essence of the specific contribution that the university makes to the accumulation of ideas. Incentives for the production of these public ideas come from a complex system of reward and prestige within the academic community.

Our conclusion in that paper was that the institutional integrity of the university should be preserved, and one important point in terms of public policy was that state funding of universities should not be reduced. In terms of teaching, and besides the well-known externalities associated with university education which justify state support for education in virtually every country in the world with the possible exception of Japan (Eicher and Chevalier 1993), we discussed the need to provide skills that accompany the growth in codified knowledge. The threat of increased privatization of teaching could thus cause serious problems, in that it would lead to a reduction in the resource that really could be in short supply: the skills to use and interpret ideas. This conclusion does not cast doubt on the contributions currently made by students, but rather questions a possible trend that could jeopardize the institutional integrity of the university itself. Similarly, in terms of research we described the risks of following the temptation of privatizing university research results, which could threaten fundamental aspects of the way universities work and could harm their essential contribution to the accumulation of ideas.

The current chapter extends the arguments outlined in the paragraph above by addressing issues that were not dealt with in the original paper. Firstly, in Conceição, Heitor, and Oliveira (1998) we focused on the contribution of universities to augment the *levels* of science and human capital, and said very little about the *processes* of learning. Second, from a more pragmatic viewpoint, society's demands from the universities are more complex than we allowed for in the 1998 paper. These demands include rapid and unforeseeable changes in the structure of the employment market, and the need to furnish its graduates with new skills beyond purely technical ones, particularly learning skills.

Here we suggest that the response to the complex and mutating demands of society involves the design of arrangements that combine the strengthening and preservation of the institutional integrity of the university with a second ingredient. The universities cannot actually be expected to foresee and respond to all the demands. If they were to try to do so, this would certainly entail jeopardizing the university's institutional integrity. A solution to this problem is to develop that second ingredient: *a diversified higher education system*, which would include various institutions with different vocations, in a way that promotes a functional stratification of the system. This could be the way to ensure *sustained flexibility* capable of providing society with the instruments it needs to deal with instability in employment and, more generally, the inevitable changes in technology, tastes, markets, and needs. This seems moreover to be the way to meet the challenge of maintaining excellence. The expansion of university education is obviously irreversible in the emerging society, but this fact cannot be allowed to stand in the way of creating centres of excellence. On the contrary, it should encourage their development, notably by means of the stratified system suggested above.

The US education system can give some pointers towards a possible path to follow. According to the Carnegie Foundation for the Advancement of Teaching, which produces a semi-official classification of US higher education institutions, there are around ninety 'research universities', being those that have generally been called simply 'universities'. These ninety institutions operate within a system of 3,706 institutions (not counting the 6,256 others that provide only vocational training), with a total of over 14 million students enrolled. In this way, the diversity and functional stratification of the system as a whole helps it to respond to rapid changes in society's demands, particularly through those institutions oriented more towards teaching and with shorter graduation times, without putting undue pressure on the universities.

But beyond suggesting a diversified and stratified higher education system, there is also a need to analyse further the way in which the university can contribute to creating a truly enhanced culture of learning where its unique contributions to knowledge generation are enhanced and nurtured.

To explore the role of the university further, we begin by constructing a model that, building on the general learning model presented in Figure 4.1, intends to codify the learning processes that are promoted in universities. Figure 4.2 is an expansion of our simplified learning model. To begin with, skills appear as a cluster of small ovals, reflecting the individual nature of the skills of people, ideas appear as a single oval. This represents the indivisibility of ideas (David 1993), meaning that, once created, an idea remains at least potentially accessible everywhere, and there is no need to rediscover it. Figure 4.2 also shows more detail in terms of the several learning processes that have been analysed in various places in the literature. Our two main categories of learning processes are now presented more thoroughly:

- *cycle 1*—codification of knowledge: the great number of existing ideas that are the starting point or 'feedstock' for new ideas to be constructed using existing skills
- *cycle 2*—interpretation of codified knowledge: using existing skills as a starting-point or instrument to decode the ideas which are being studied or used, leading to improved skills.

Cycle 1 covers learning processes that result in the *codification of knowledge*, that is the generation of new ideas. Specific examples within universities include R&D and artistic creation. In both cases, ideas are generated as a result of a process of exploration, searches in science, or in artistic forms of expression. This type of learning is convergent, meaning that on the basis of different and unique skills, ideas are generated that have the potential for common use.

Cycle 2, on the other hand, relates to learning by *assimilation of knowledge*, which results from activities such as education, experience, and social interaction. Through the *interpretation* of existing ideas, different skills emerge. Imagine a mathematics class: all the students are using the same book, they attend the same classes, they do the same exercises. However, the ways in which they assimilate and interpret these are different, meaning that the learning process is *divergent*.

In terms of the university functions, we think that expanding the way research is performed at universities is the way to intensify the learning skills that people are required to have in order to sustain a society wide learning culture. Research can be viewed as various sub-functions, not always clearly defined, but which should be the subject of separate public policies and forms of management, as follows:

1. R&D, Research and Development, which aims at the accumulation of ideas through convergent learning processes, which are associated with the processes of codification represented in Figure 4.2. This is the commonest form of research, particularly in the context of economic development and from the standpoint of the relationship between universities and companies.
2. R&T, Research and Teaching, in which research functions as a way of developing teaching materials, as well as of improving the teaching skills of the teaching staff, and which is also associated with the convergent processes of knowledge codification represented in Figure 4.2.
3. R&L, Research and Learning, in which the value of the research is not necessarily in the creation of ideas, but in the development of skills that enhance opportunities for learning. Research appears as a divergent function, associated with the process of interpretation represented in Figure 4.2.

According to the definitions of the learning processes, R&D and R&T are convergent learning processes, the purpose of which is the creation of ideas.

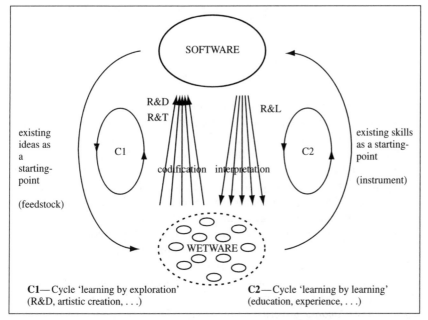

FIG. 4.2. *Learning processes and different aspects of university research*
(R&D: Research and development; R&T: Research and Training; R&L: Research and Learning)

In this context, *selectivity* is required in the choice of individuals with suitable skills for these types of activity. In turn R&L is associated with a divergent learning process, which seeks to develop learning skills through the experience of doing research. It is important to *disseminate* these opportunities, presenting research as a cultural factor.

In these circumstances, a diversified system could respond effectively to the different demands made of it in the emerging economy, by being selective in R&D and R&T, and comprehensive in R&L. Indeed, the comprehensive nature of R&T should be extended beyond the university to cover the whole education system, as a way of promoting learning skills. In this situation, it seems essential to place renewed emphasis on education and, to a certain extent, to reinvent its social and economic role. Educational institutions must rethink their relationships with the individuals, families, and communities among which they find themselves, presenting themselves as vital providers of opportunities to develop formal learning processes, while at the same time encouraging a way of life that promotes learning through social interaction.

We regard these types of initiatives as a way to deal with one of the main challenges facing the university and the education system in general: the need for lifelong learning, going beyond formal teaching to participatory learning, which is directly associated with continuous (lifelong) training. Furthermore, the fact that informal learning processes are shared between a varied range of institutions opens up new possibilities for the universities' ability to create and disseminate knowledge.

4.4. Conclusions

Over the past decade there has been an increased discussion on how universities can play a more effective role in contributing to promote wealth creation. A significant stream of that discussion has regarded US universities as a reference and has resulted, within the diverse range of institutions in the European higher education system, in various organizational and strategic arrangements that go far beyond the traditional roles ascribed to education and research. The unifying characteristic of these different arrangements is provided by the unique characteristics of 'the university' as a societal environment for *exploration and interpretation of knowledge*. Exploring and interpreting knowledge are two sides of the learning process. Therefore, in this chapter we attempted to look at the university as a *learning organization*, exploring its role in the broader context of the learning economy. In this context, we described a conceptual understanding of the relationship between *learning and economic prosperity*. Our analysis led us to suggest that while the role of the university needs to be re-examined, the *institutional integrity of universities must be preserved*. The analysis also shows that the variety of demands and the continuously changing social and economic environment surrounding higher education organizations is calling for *diversified systems* able to cope with the need to produce policies that nurture and enhance the learning economy.

To sum up, rather than presenting a detailed plan of public policy options and forms of management for the universities, this chapter sets out to show how our conceptualization of *learning as knowledge accumulation* can be used to analyse the challenges facing the university. Among our substantive conclusions are the importance of preserving the institutional integrity of the university by maintaining the academic character of its basic functions of *teaching and research*. In a situation in which education should promote learning skills, we put forward the need to identify and understand the different components of university research, so as to enhance the *selectivity of the Research & Development* and *Research & Training* sub-functions, while ensuring the *widespread availability of Research & Learning*. It is argued that a diversified higher education system can free the universities of many of the pressures that they are experiencing today by helping to ensure the preservation of their institutional integrity.

The ideas put forward in this chapter are largely exploratory, and we hope they will trigger the development of lines of research. In terms of future research, we advocate an approximation between the more formal work on *economics* with more appreciative (or institutional) perspectives on *learning and knowledge.* This task, though difficult, for at the root of the differences are often epistemological considerations, may be key to illuminating the process by which the role of existing institutions can be enhanced in the emerging knowledge based economies.

One final point has to do with the role that university leaders can, and should, play in the process of rethinking the role of the university, in the larger context of the higher education system, as a 'learning engine' that contributes in unique ways for knowledge accumulation. We did not touch this issue in this chapter, but it is up to university management to give visibility to a research agenda for the role of the university.

REFERENCES

CARAÇA, J., CONCEIÇÃO, P., and HEITOR, M. V. (1998). 'A contribution towards a methodology for university public funding'. *Higher Education Policy*, 11/1: 37–58.
——(2000). 'On the definition of a public policy towards a research university'. *Higher Education Policy* (forthcoming).
CLARK, B. (1995). *Places of Inquiry—Research and Advanced Education in Modern Universities.* Berkeley: University of California Press.
CONCEIÇÃO, P., and HEITOR, M. V. (1999). 'On the role of the University in the knowledge Economy'. *Science and Public Policy*, 26/1: 37–51.
—— ——and OLIVEIRA, P. M. (1998). 'Expectations for the university in the knowledge based economy'. *Technological Forecasting and Social Change*, 58/3: 203–14.
—— —— ——(1999). 'On the need of new mechanisms for the protection of intellectual property of research universities', in A. Inzelt (ed.), *Technology Transfer: From Invention to Innovation.* Dordrecht: Kluwer.
DASGUPTA, P., and DAVID, P. (1994). 'Toward a new economics of science'. *Research Policy*, 23: 487–521.
DAVID, P. (1993). 'Knowledge, property, and the system dynamics of technological change', in L. H. Summers and S. Shah (eds.), *Proceedings of the World Bank Annual Conference on Development Economics 1992.* Washington, DC: The World Bank.
Economist (1997). 'A survey of universities—the knowledge factory', 4 October.
EICHER, J.-C., and CHEVALIER, T. (1993). 'Rethinking the finance of post-compulsory education'. *International Journal of Educational Research*, 19: 445–519.
ELVIN, M. (1973). *The Pattern of the Chinese Past.* Stanford, Calif.: Stanford University Press.
FORAY, D., and LUNDVALL, B.-Å. (1996). 'The knowledge-based economy: From the economics of knowledge to the learning economy', in OECD, *Employment and Growth in the Knowledge-based Economy.* Paris: OECD.
LANDES, D. S. (1998). *The Wealth and Poverty of Nations: Why Some are so Rich and Some so Poor.* New York: W. W. Norton & Company.
LUCAS, C. (1996). *Crisis in the Academy—Rethinking Higher Education in America.* New York: St. Martin's Press,.

LUNDVALL, B.-Å. (1992) (ed.). *National System of Innovation—Towards a Theory of Innovation and Interactive Learning.* London: Pinter Publishers.

NELSON, R. R., and ROMER, P. (1996). 'Science, economic growth, and public policy', in B. L. R. Smith and C. E. Barfield (eds.), *Technology, R&D, and the Economy.* Washington, DC: Brookings.

NOLL, R. G. (1998). *Challenges to Research Universities.* Stanford, Calif.: Brookings Institute Press.

NONAKA, I., and TAKEUCHI, H. (1995). *The Knowledge-creating Company.* Oxford: Oxford University Press.

OECD (1996). *Employment and Growth in the Knowledge-based Economy.* Paris: OECD.

——(1997). *Technology and Industrial Performance.* Paris: OECD.

PAVITT, K. (1987). 'The objectives of technology policy'. *Science and Public Policy*, 14: 182–8.

ROSENBERG, N. (1998). 'Knowledge and innovation for economic development: should universities be economic institutions?', in P. Conceição, D. Gibson, and M. Heitor (eds.), *Knowledge for Inclusive Development.* Austin, Tex.: Quorum Books.

——and NELSON, R. R. (1996). 'The roles of universities in the advance of industrial technology', in R. S. Rosenbloom and W. J. Spencer (eds.), *Engines of Innovation.* Cambridge, Mass.: Harvard Business School Press.

SOETE, L. (1996). 'The challenges of innovation'. *IPTS Report*, 7: 7–13.

VARIAN, HAL R. (1995). 'The information economy'. *Scientific American*, 273/3: 200–2.

5

A New Role for Business Services in Economic Growth

MARK TOMLINSON

5.1. Introduction

This chapter[1] attempts to synthesize and summarize the main results of some recent quantitative macroeconomic analyses of the impact of services on economic performance. We provide some background explanations of the phenomena considered and adumbrate some policy issues that arise from this new research. It has been shown that, although there are differing levels of knowledge-intensive service activity in different countries, the impact that these services have on economic performance is highly significant in all the countries studied so far. This has several implications regarding the way in which services are viewed *vis-à-vis* manufacturing and it also has important consequences for industrial policy.

We begin the chapter with a brief discussion of the role of services in economic development and how the theoretical underpinnings of older debates are now being challenged. We then discuss a selection of the results of analysing knowledge-intensive services from more recent literature at the macroeconomic level. Discussion and conclusions following from this are then presented.

5.2. The Traditional Role of Services in Economic Development

In the past business services, and indeed services in general, have been seen as a peripheral sector relative to manufacturing industry and of relatively minor importance in understanding the nature of production in capitalist societies. This is partly as a result of theories of economic development that placed services as a tertiary category after everything else had been accounted for (for example, the Fisher–Clark model, Fisher 1935; Clark 1940). This is also one of the reasons why the service sector is such a heterogeneous category.

---

[1] Several pieces of work have been carried out for the TSER project 'Services in Innovation, Innovation in Services' (SI4S) which attempt to measure the changes in intensity and the impact of knowledge-intensive business services on the economic performance of several 'post-industrial' economies. A detailed report of the project can be found in Hauknes (1998). This chapter summarizes many of these results.

Now that services dominate modern economies, their role is seen as an increasingly important component of overall economic activity (Miles 1993). This has had positive as well as negative interpretations in the literature.

Advocates of 'post-industrial society' (for example, Bell 1973) suggest that as society develops its needs fundamentally change and demand for non-material goods takes on an enhanced importance. On the other hand, scholars such as Cohen and Zysman (1987) insist on the remaining importance of manufacturing. The reality is more likely to lie somewhere between these two extremes. Manufacturing still matters, but the role that services play in economic development is taking on an increased significance. This is especially the case with respect to the 'knowledge economy' and hence knowledge-based services in particular. Policy makers are increasingly concerned with institutions being able to adapt to the rapidly changing nature of production as well as the nature of non-material production. For instance, 'the role of technology needs to be seen in the context of an ongoing transformation of OECD economies from industrial to knowledge-based economies where the creation and distribution of knowledge underpins the process of growth' (OECD 1998: 55).

Knowledge-intensive business services in particular are now seen by some to play a pivotal role in several respects: such as contributing to innovation and knowledge in a wider economic sense; helping to transform firms into learning organizations; or facilitating flows of knowledge and information from one sector to another (including manufacturing). The interaction of these types of services with other firms is now seen as potentially profitable for all parties concerned (see, for instance, Hauknes 1998: 50–1).

Moreover, many services are more knowledge intensive than other sectors in the economy in terms of the number of highly skilled workers they have or innovation expenditure, etc. Recent research on intangibles in the service industries has begun to reveal the extent to which certain services outstrip many manufacturing sectors in some important respects (Peneder *et al.* 1999). Although manufacturing sectors spend more on R&D, for example, many services do in fact conduct a substantial amount of R&D themselves and when the definition of technological innovation spending is widened to include things such as marketing, training, and acquisition of new technologies, many services have much higher spending than average. For instance, the business sector in the UK spends over 12% of turnover on innovation (broadly defined) compared with a mean of 6.75% for the entire population. The R&D service sector spends 47%, the computer service industry 12%, etc. (see Peneder *et al.* 1999: 68)[2]. Unfortunately the information available is rather scattered and unsystematic as there is substantial bias in reporting and data collection towards manufacturing in most national statistical organizations.

---

[2] These figures were derived from the second UK Community Innovation Survey of 1997.

If one views the economy from a network-oriented perspective, it becomes clear that certain services have a crucial role to play in mediating between and contributing to production in other sectors. The development and flow of knowledge and information within an economic system is to a large extent facilitated by knowledge-intensive services. Enhanced communication and crossover between knowledge-based and non-knowledge-based entities can then become a vital adjunct to improved performance (Nelson 1982; Antonelli 1995; Howells 1996).

Several scholars emphasize that learning and knowledge are essential to the efficient operation of the economy as a whole (Lundvall 1992, 1998; Lundvall and Borrás 1998; Lundvall and Johnson 1994). A recent paper has also shown that learning at the employee level is taking place to a significantly greater extent in knowledge intensive service sectors than in other sectors of the British economy (Tomlinson 1999*a*). This implies that from a learning economy perspective the 'human capital' of service workers is outstripping other employees, which raises important issues for employment policy. What should be done about workers who are falling behind in this regard? There are thus positive and negative aspects of the growth of knowledge-intensive business services that must be addressed. This is returned to below.

There are at least two other major reasons why services' interactions (and knowledge-intensive business services' interactions in particular) are important to study. Firstly there is the concept of 're-penetration' and second the idea of 'co-production'. The use of these concepts allows us to understand aspects of the economic models described below. By re-penetration we mean the idea that a service firm can adopt new ideas or utilize new technology and then re-penetrate older structures and transform their capabilities:

the traditional professional services are often intensive and advanced users of new IT, and there is some cross-over from traditional professional services to KIBS [knowledge intensive business services], reflecting the general process of knowledge-intensification. 'Spin-offs' and new firm formation occur where KIBS emerge from traditional professional services. For example, professionals with experience of new technology—in particular IT—establish vertical niche markets promoting the application of technology into their old specialisms (or sometimes to their old clients). (Tomlinson and Miles 1999)

In the 1980s many service firms were created as a result of increased outsourcing by manufacturing enterprises. This has in part led to the phenomenon of re-penetration. It must also be borne in mind that this re-penetration by services is not new. It has happened at several junctures in history where economic and social change has rendered old structures redundant (see Berg 1994; Tomlinson 1999*b*). What is different now is the proliferation of new technologies (such as ICTs, the Internet, etc.) along with socio-economic changes (such as globalization) that are enabling new forms of services to thrive.

The second important phenomenon to consider is co-production. Several innovations in services and manufacturing take place as a result of the interaction of different firms. According to Miles (1996: 29), knowledge-intensive business service transactions involve two types of learning: the service firms themselves learn about their clients' operations and requirements; while the client learns about the service firm and the services on offer. Both sides emerge with a better understanding of their problems as a result of the knowledge generated by the interaction. In other words innovation is often a co-production of interaction between more than one enterprise—very often including a service enterprise.

How do these two phenomena manifest themselves in national accounts? One of the ways in which the analysis of knowledge, as transmitted or facilitated by knowledge-intensive business services, has been carried out is through the use of input–output tables from various countries. Input–output tables show the flows of goods and services from each sector to every other sector in the economy at a specific point in time. Thus flows of goods and services can be traced between sectors and their relative contributions to economic output, value-added or productivity can be estimated. So if the phenomena of re-penetration and co-production lead to any real gains in efficiency with respect to knowledge-intensive business services, the volume of transactions between knowledge-based service sectors should be correlated with higher performance (in terms of productivity, say) in the consuming sectors.

Figure 5.1 shows the increasing trend of knowledge-based service inputs to several economies in terms of intermediate inputs. That is the percentage of these services as a proportion of the total sectoral inputs to all sectors. The data in this case were derived from OECD input–output tables. At the present time, detailed statistical analyses of this type of data have been carried out on the following countries: Greece (Katsoulacos and Tsounis 2000), the UK and Japan (Tomlinson 2000), the UK, Japan, Netherlands, and Germany (Windrum and Tomlinson 1999) and Italy, the UK, Germany, and France (Antonelli 1998).

5.3. A Summary of the Analysis of the Input–Output Tables

The contributions are all slightly different in their formulations of the problem, but they generally draw similar conclusions regarding the relative importance of knowledge-intensive business services for economic efficiency. The results of some of these analyses are summarized below. This is not a complete description of the work. The reader is referred to the actual papers for a more detailed account.

Firstly, both Katsoulacos and Tsounis (2000) and Antonelli (1998) show that there is a high correlation between the consumption of communication

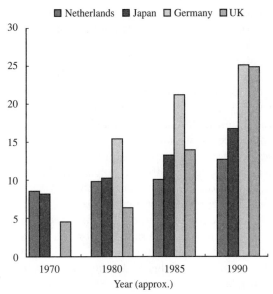

Fɪɢ. 5.1. *Knowledge-intensive service sector inputs as a percentage of total intermediate inputs to all sectors*

Note: (No data are available for Germany 1970)

Source: Derived from OECD data used in Windrum and Tomlinson 1999.

services and of business services towards the end of the 1980s by all sectors. Furthermore they also show that the growth in consumption of these two inputs is highly related. This implies that there is a strong co-evolution of business and communication services consistent with the idea that both business and communication services play increasingly important roles in facilitating knowledge and information flows throughout the economy. According to Antonelli (1998), it is by means of new ICTs that knowledge-intensive services would increase their grip on the knowledge economy.

Katsoulacos and Tsounis (2000) and Antonelli (1998) also outline and test a 'production function' approach to assess communication and business service inputs into the economy. The general idea is to estimate an equation such as equation 1 below and some variations of it:

$$Q = AK^bL^cCBS^d \qquad (1)$$

Which leads to:

$$\log Q = a + b \log K + c \log L + d \log CBS \qquad (2)$$

Where Q = value added, K = capital stock, L = labour costs, CBS = inputs of communications and/or business services to each sector and a, b, c, d are coefficients to be estimated.

This treats various knowledge-intensive and communication service inputs as a separate factor of production along with fixed capital and labour in an equation of similar form to the well-known Cobb–Douglas production function. This is an attempt to show that these 'knowledge' inputs to other sectors are significantly related to value added. If there are significant coefficients on the services variable then we have evidence that re-penetration and co-production via business and communication services enhance productivity. Antonelli estimates separate models using business services and communication services. Katsoulacos and Tsounis estimate the model using just business services for Greek input–output data.[3]

Some studies use a slightly different approach. Tomlinson (2000) and Windrum and Tomlinson (1999) present a modified version of the above approach. Rather than applying a production function in the traditional way, they consider the interaction of labour with two types of intermediate goods ('material' and 'non-material'). The rationale for this is that the only way to produce output is by labour interacting with material goods (i.e. from manufacturing) and/or using knowledge and information (reflected in the purchases from knowledge-intensive services). So the assumption is that labour within each sector interacts with intermediate material goods consumed in the production process as well as knowledge-intensive business services.

Q (which is gross output in these models rather than value added as above) is therefore thought of as a function of the quantity of intermediate material goods purchased, the quantity of communication and business services purchased by each sector and labour. Labour is still reflected by the wage bill of the sector, which represents a composite indicator of the quantity and quality of labour available.

This approach leads to two basic functions to be estimated. The first function to be estimated is of the form:

$$\log Q = a + b \log M + c \log B + d \log L \qquad (3)$$

Where Q = gross output, M = material inputs, B = communication and business services, and L = the sectoral wage bill. Again a, b, c, and d are to be estimated.

With a similar logic, equations for productivity are derived and an equation of the following form is estimated:

$$\log Q/L = a + b \log(M/L) + c \log(B/L). \qquad (4)$$

The results of the analyses based on these equations show, almost without exception, that there appears to be a highly significant relationship between value added, gross output, and productivity and the value of knowledge-

---

[3] All the studies referred to in this chapter use slightly different definitions of knowledge-intensive services and communication services. The data used are from a variety of different sources and the reader is referred to the original articles for more detail.

intensive business services purchased by each sector after taking into account labour and capital. The only exception is with communication services and value-added in the German case (Antonelli 1998). However, the modified model (Windrum and Tomlinson 2000) does show the significance of knowledge-intensive business services in Germany with respect to gross output rather than value added. This gives us significant evidence that re-penetration and co-production via knowledge-intensive business services has significant benefits in terms of economic performance.

So the analysis indicates that there are underlying economic gains relating to the intensity of communication and business services consumed. However, some caution must also be exercised with respect to the rapid growth of knowledge-intensive services. The promotion of the unfettered expansion of these types of services without any consideration for the economic network of which they form a part would not necessarily be beneficial. One study (Tomlinson 2000) compared the growth and development of services in Japan and the UK. Although there has been steady growth in the knowledge-intensive business service sector in Japan it is smaller and it has been expanding at a slower rate than in the UK. However, the analysis of input–output tables for several years revealed that the impact that these services had on the Japanese economy was far more effective even as far back as 1970 than it was in the UK. In the UK case the impact was negligible using 1979 data and only became significant using 1990 data. So the impact of knowledge-intensive business services appears to be weaker in the UK even though they appear much more developed than in Japan, as Figure 5.2 shows.

These results suggest that the impact of knowledge-intensive services in Japan on output and productivity has been much more effective even though

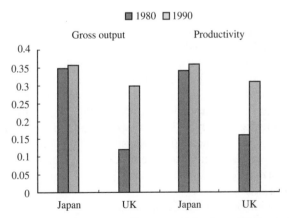

Fig. 5.2. *Levels of the impact of KIBS measured by the coefficients derived from models of gross output and productivity in the UK and Japan*
Source: Derived from Tomlinson 2000.

they appear to form a smaller proportion of the economy and have a relatively slow growth rate. In both 1980 and 1990 Japan had a higher coefficient
on both models. The impact of knowledge-intensive business services in the
UK appears to be approaching, but has still not reached, Japanese levels. The
implications of this analysis are that the growth of these services in itself will
not necessarily lead to major improvements in productivity. The nature of the
economic system of which the services are a part is of vital importance.

The Japanese have a long history of maintaining strong production networks as long ago as the pre-Meiji period (see, for instance, Scott 1986). For
example the *keiretsu* (and its predecessor, the *zaibatsu*) form of organization,
where groups of companies are 'tied together through reciprocal share-
holdings, credit relations, trade relations, and interlocking directorships'
(OECD 1992: 100), is considered to be a significant source of Japanese competitive advantage. The advantages that the Japanese appear to have in the
previous analysis probably stem from their long-standing skills in maintaining these networks.

One of the further consequences of this analysis then is that the precise
nature of the linkages between business services, communication services,
and other entities in economic knowledge-based systems must be explored.
There may be substantial differences in the efficiency of services in the knowledge economy that may depend on more qualitative aspects of networks such
as corporate cultures, organizational forms, and national systems of production and innovation. These things are hard to quantify at a national level, but
may help to explain the differences between countries revealed by the macroeconomic analysis.

5.4. Conclusions

The analyses of knowledge-intensive business services undertaken so far
imply a broadening of the study of economic performance to include the role
of services as components of economic networks, learning economies, and
systems of innovation. Rather than maintaining artificial divisions between
manufacturing and non-manufacturing sectors, certain services appear to
have an essential role in improving economic efficiency. It has been demon-
strated that there are underlying links between productivity, value added, and
output and the input of knowledge-intensive business services, but there are
important national differences to be considered. A narrow focus on manufacturing performance without considering producer services would be somewhat inappropriate.

Policy must confront these issues as soon as possible, for it is far from clear
what the effects of the growth of knowledge-based services or an increasing
reliance on non-material production will be in the long term. The UK–
Japanese analysis revealed that there are substantial differences between

countries with respect to knowledge-intensive business services. This implies that the nature and embeddedness of these services within national or regional systems of innovation will be a key factor for long-term national economic performance.

We know that in many European countries there is rapid change taking place and the expansion of knowledge-based services is proceeding apace. In order to create efficient innovation networks it would be foolhardy to neglect the role of services in economic development. It is crucial for governments to tap into this expansion effectively by providing a useful and flexible framework within which services can operate and interact with the economy as a whole. Services as drivers of innovation are becoming essential for maintaining growth and competitiveness. In terms of regional policy, for example, the promotion of knowledge-intensive business services in less-developed areas should be a priority. More recent work has in fact suggested that even less-developed countries, such as those in Asia and Latin America, are benefiting from the service sector even though it is relatively underdeveloped (Tomlinson 1999*b*). One way of stimulating the economic development of backward regions might be to foster consortia of firms interacting strongly with knowledge-intensive business enterprises as a central hub.

This brings us to the global question. Not only are knowledge-intensive business services and other services crucial at national level but also they are increasingly becoming part of globalized structures of innovation and knowledge transmission. Barriers to participation by services in global networks as well as national ones should be weakened (for instance, see the collection in Archibugi *et al.* 1999). The usefulness of knowledge-intensive services in transmitting knowledge and information across space should certainly not be underestimated. It is therefore important that these services should be encouraged to interface with global knowledge and learning structures so that knowledge and expertise can be transmitted from global to national and regional sub-systems. The globalization of economic activity does not negate the importance of national and regional systems of innovation (see, for instance, Howells 1999: 85–6).

Finally we consider the labour market aspects of services. It has already been alluded to above that there is a growing polarization of skills between those employees who work in knowledge-intensive services and other workers. There also appear to be significant barriers preventing workers from moving between certain sectors or occupations (Tomlinson 1999*a*). This was particularly marked with respect to manufacturing workers. The OECD jobs strategy has also highlighted the problems of those workers who are falling behind in terms of training and skills and who find it extremely difficult to bridge the skills gap (see OECD 1994, 1999). Clearly, if workers are to maintain an ethic of lifelong learning and improve their abilities there will have to be significant policies directed at removing these barriers to entry into certain professions and sectors. This may involve substantial programmes that will have to take account of the growth of services. Assistance may be needed for those employees who find themselves in redundant industries and find it difficult to move into new, mainly service or knowledge-oriented, ones.

New institutional arrangements and regulatory frameworks will prove increasingly necessary to support the efficiency of the linkages between knowledge-intensive services and other economic and non-economic entities. These services clearly have a new role to play in economic growth that must now be addressed. The main traditional focus of economic policy on manufacturing is becoming of less relevance.

REFERENCES

ANTONELLI, C. (1995). *The Economics of Localized Technological Change and Industrial Dynamics*. Norwell, Mass.: Kluwer Academic Publishers.

——(1998). 'Localized technological change, new information technology and the knowledge-based economy: The European evidence'. *Journal of Evolutionary Economics*, 8: 177–98.

ARCHIBUGI, D., HOWELLS, J., and MICHIE, J. (1999) (eds.). *Innovation Policy in a Global Economy*. Cambridge: Cambridge University Press.

BELL, D. (1973). *The Coming of Post-industrial Society*. London: Heinemann.

BERG, M. (1994). *The Age of Manufactures, 1700–1820: Industry, Innovation and Work in Britain*. London: Routledge.

CLARK, C. A. (1940). *The Conditions of Economic Progress*. London: Macmillan.

COHEN, S. S., and ZYSMAN, J. (1987). *Manufacturing Matters: The Myth of the Post-industrial Economy*. New York: Basic Books.

FISHER, A. G. (1935). *The Clash of Progress and Security*. London: Macmillan.

GUINET, J. (1997). 'Knowledge flows in national innovation systems', in OECD, *Industrial Competitiveness in the Knowledge-Based Economy: The New Role of Governments*. Paris: OECD.

HAUKNES, J. (1998). 'Services in innovation—Innovation in services'. STEP Group, SI4S final report, Oslo.

HOWELLS, J. (1996). 'Tacit knowledge, innovation and technology transfer'. *Technology Analysis and Strategic Management*, 8/2: 91–106.

——(1999). 'Regional systems of innovation?', in D. Archibugi, J. Howells, and J. Michie (eds.), *Innovation Policy in a Global Economy*. Cambridge: Cambridge University Press.

KATSOULACOS, Y., and TSOUNIS, N. (2000). 'Knowledge intensive business services and productivity growth: The Greek evidence', in I. Miles and M. Boden (eds.), *Services in the Knowledge-Based Economy*. London: Cassell.

LUNDVALL, B.-Å. (1992) (ed.). *National Systems of Innovation: Towards a Theory of Innovation and Interactive Learning*. London: Pinter.

——(1998). 'The learning economy: Challenges to economic theory and policy', in K. Nielsen and B. Johnson (eds.), *Institutions and Economic Change: New Perspectives on Markets, Firms and Technology*. Cheltenham: Edward Elgar.

——and Borrás, S. (1998). *The Globalising Learning Economy: Implications for Innovation Policy*. Brussels: European Commission.

——and Johnson, B. (1994). 'The learning economy'. *Journal of Industry Studies*, 2/1: 23–42.

Miles, I. (1993). 'Services in the new industrial economy'. *Futures*, 25/6: 653–72.

——(1996). *Innovation in Services: Services in Innovation*. Manchester: Manchester Statistical Society.

Nelson, R. R. (1982). 'The role of knowledge in R&D efficiency'. *Quarterly Journal of Economics*, 97: 453–70.

——(1993) (ed.). *National Systems of Innovation*. Oxford: Oxford University Press.

OECD (1992). *Technology and the Economy: The Key Relationships*. Paris: OECD.

——(1994). *The OECD Jobs Study: Facts, Analysis, Strategies*. Paris: OECD.

——(1995). *The OECD Input–Output Database*. Paris: OECD.

——(1997). *Industrial Competitiveness in the Knowledge-based Economy: The New Role of Governments*. Paris: OECD.

——(1998). *Technology, Productivity and Job Creation: Best Policy Practices*. Paris: OECD.

——(1999). *OECD Employment Outlook*. Paris: OECD.

Peneder, M., Miles, I., and Tomlinson, M. (1999). 'Intangible investments, industrial sectors and competitiveness: International comparison'. Report prepared for the European Commission, DG III/A5. Vienna/Manchester: WIFO/CRIC, University of Manchester.

Scott, J. (1986). *Capitalist Property and Financial Power*. Brighton: Wheatsheaf Books.

Tomlinson, M. (1999a). 'Learning economies and embodied knowledge flows'. CRIC Discussion Paper no. 26. University of Manchester and UMIST.

——(1999b), 'Services and economic development: A network approach'. Paper presented at the MIT workshop on 'Innovation in Services', Massachusetts Institute of Technology, 28–29 October.

——(2000) 'Information and technology flows from the service sector: A UK–Japan comparison', in I. Miles and M. Boden (eds.), *Services in the Knowledge-based Economy*. London: Cassell.

——and Miles, I. (1999). 'The career trajectories of knowledge workers'. Paper for the OECD workshop on S&T labour markets, Paris, 17 May.

Windrum, P., and Tomlinson, M. (1999). 'The impact of knowledge-intensive services on international competitiveness: A UK, Netherlands, German and Japanese comparison'. MERIT research memorandum 99–025, University of Maastricht.

PART III

The Globalizing Innovation Process

F02
632
638
L52
F23

6

The Globalization of Technology and National Policies

DANIELE ARCHIBUGI AND SIMONA IAMMARINO

6.1. Introduction

New technologies are a fundamental ingredient of the current economic globalization. Without aeroplanes, telecommunications, satellites, and the Internet it would not be possible to transfer the amount of information across the world which allows so-called globalization in areas as different as finance, production, media, fashion, and culture. In the last few years, however, too many heterogeneous phenomena have been lumped together under the label 'technological globalization' and the concept has thus lost much of its original clarity. This chapter proposes to identify three different categories which compose the globalization of technology with a view to understanding what is the impact of each of them on the national economies and, above all, what public policies can do to exploit the available technological knowledge for welfare and growth.

The next section analyses the effects of the globalization of innovation for single nations according to a taxonomy which breaks down into three categories: the international exploitation of technology; the global generation of innovations; and global technical collaborations. The third section of the chapter explores the implications of each of these three typologies of the globalization of technology for public policies. It suggests that no single strategy can be used to address all three globalization processes. But contrary to what is held to be the dominant *laissez-faire* view, we argue that the dynamics of globalization need a more active role of governments to allow national economies to exploit the available opportunities. A much broader battery of public policy instruments than those currently being used in the majority of countries are needed today.

6.2. The Impact of the Globalization of Innovation on National Economies

In the last few years, too many heterogeneous phenomena have been lumped together under the label 'the globalization of innovation', and the concept has thus lost much of its original clarity. We thus attempted (Archibugi and

Michie 1995, 1997) to find our way in the labyrinth of the globalization of innovation by identifying three main categories. The aim of this taxonomy is to classify individual innovations and areas of technological competence according to their main forms of generation, transmission, and exploitation. Both at single enterprise and national levels, the categories are complementary, not alternative. Enterprises, especially large enterprises, generate innovation following all three procedures described. The categories of this taxonomy and the main forms through which the three processes manifest themselves (for their empirical importance, see Archibugi and Iammarino 2000) are shown in Table 6.1.

The first category includes the attempts of innovators to obtain economic advantages by exploiting their technological competencies on markets other than the domestic. We have preferred to label this category 'international' as opposed to 'global', since the players that introduce innovations preserve their own national identity, even when such innovations are diffused and marketed in more than one country. This first category may also comprise production activity in the host foreign countries (through direct investment abroad), but not when it also envisages the creation of additional technological capacity *in loco*. If this kind of capability were generated, then we would move from the first category to the second.

The second category is represented by the global generation of innovations. It includes innovations generated on a global scale: only innovations produced by multinational enterprises fit into this category. Save for a few exceptions (such as Shell and Unilever), it is so easy to identify the country of origin of these enterprises that some observers speak in terms of national enterprises with multinational operations (Hu 1992).

Recently, another form of globalization of innovative activities has asserted itself, midway between the two categories described above. We have in fact witnessed a growing number of agreements between enterprises, often situated in two or more countries, to develop given technological innovations together. The need to cut the costs of innovation has created new forms of industrial organization and new proprietary arrangements, which are now expanding beyond the technological sphere (cf. Mytelka 1991 and her chapter in this volume; Dodgson 1993). In a sense, enterprises have imitated a method of generating and transmitting knowledge typical of the academic community. Indeed, the academic world has always had a transnational range of action, with knowledge being transmitted from one scholar to another without any economic compensation to the supplying party.

How far processes of globalization of innovation affect national economies or not depends on a multiplicity of factors. The benefits and costs may be substantial and are closely influenced by the characteristics of the players who take part and by their interactions. Growing globalization implies, first and foremost, more intense, fiercer competition between enterprises, between national and local systems, and between governments. Simultaneously,

TABLE 6.1. *A taxonomy of the globalization of technology*

Categories	Actors	Forms
International exploitation of nationally produced innovations	Profit-seeking firms and individuals	Exports of innovative goods Transfer of licenses and patents Foreign production of internally generated innovative goods
Global generation of innovations	Multinational firms	R&D and innovative activities in both the home and the host countries Acquisitions of existing R&D laboratories or greenfield R&D investment in host countries
Global techno-scientific collaborations	Universities and public research centres National and multinational firms	Joint scientific projects Scientific exchanges, sabbatical years International flows of students Joint ventures for scientific innovative projects Production agreements with exchange of technical information and/or equipment

Source: adapted from Archibugi and Michie 1995.

however, the increased interdependence of the different players provides greater opportunities for collaboration both inside and outside national boundaries. These changes, which are largely occurring in the most developed areas of the world, may have beneficial or adverse consequences on economic performance and on the innovative capacity of national and local systems. Differences between strong and weak regions are thus also prone to become more marked.

In fact, the trends currently in progress do not reveal an unequivocal convergence towards higher levels of economic and technological activity, neither within the group of the most advanced countries nor among their regions. Considering each of the three aspects of globalization separately, it is possible to distinguish the impact which they have on national economies and enterprises. Table 6.2 sums up these differences.

6.2.1. The International Exploitation of Technology

One of the oldest methods used by firms to exploit their innovating products in foreign markets is to trade them. As a growing literature has shown, technological advantage is more and more a key determinant of international trade. As already anticipated by Thirlwall (1979) and Kaldor (1981), non-price factors have become more important in determining competitiveness in the last decade (Fagerberg 1996; Amendola, Guerrieri, and Padoan 1998).

The increase in the volume of international trade, also connected to new international agreements to reduce trade barriers, has made it more important for each country to select its own sectoral strengths and weaknesses. The tendency for international specialization to increase plays a fundamental role in growth dynamics, since technological innovation does not affect all sectors of economic activity uniformly. In other words, a given model of specialization can in no way be seen as being on a par with others; countries specialized in sectors which register a relatively faster growth in exports—usually the most technology-intensive—not only register higher growth rates but also see their position in the international division of labour strengthened thanks to the cumulative character of technical progress (Lucas 1988).

Many studies have addressed the problem of convergence from the point of view of dedicated efforts of industrialized economies to improve their innovative capacity (Archibugi and Pianta 1992, 1994; Patel and Pavitt 1998). Looking at industrialized countries, what emerges is a limited tendency towards convergence in both per capita product levels and innovation potentials. However, instead of univocally reducing international differences through the faster diffusion of technology, the opening up of exchanges and internationalization processes would appear to trigger economic convergence among countries whose technological profiles are becoming increasingly dissimilar due to sharp sectoral specialization (Cantwell 1995; Vertova 2000).

TABLE 6.2. *The globalization of technology: Implications for the national economies*

Categories	Inward flows	Outward flows	Tendency towards convergence/divergence
International exploitation of nationally produced innovations	Low learning in consumption goods, medium learning in capital goods and equipment	Expansion of the market and of the areas of influence Maintenance of national technological advantages	Limited but significant economic convergence (GDP per capita) Divergence of technological profiles across countries
Global generation of innovations by MNE	Acquisition of technological and managerial capabilities Increased dependence on the strategic choices of foreign firms	Missing technological opportunities for the internal market. Strengthening of the competitive position of national firms. Tapping into the expertise of host locations.	Increasing regional/local divergence both in economic and innovation variables
Global techno-scientific collaborations	Increased techno-scientific flows For developed countries, diffusion of their knowledge For developing countries, acquisition of knowledge and learning opportunities		Convergence of technological profiles across countries

The complementary relationship which exists between international trade and foreign direct investment also tends to amplify their impact, creating virtuous and vicious circles both in the investor's country of origin and in the recipient country (Cantwell 1987). To exploit their competitive advantage, enterprises that relocate their production activities abroad may (though not necessarily) improve local productive capacity by increasing the competitiveness of the recipient market and investment-associated technology transfers. The impact may either consolidate or weaken the national production and technological base depending upon the respective patterns of sectoral specialization and the strengths of both the country of origin and the host economy.

6.2.2. The Global Generation of Innovation

The second category in the taxonomy concerns the global generation of innovation by multinational enterprises. This implies not only the transfer of innovative activities outside the borders of the country of origin, but also, and above all, a higher degree of interdependence between the various units which go together to form the multinational enterprise, through the setting up of 'networks' inside and outside the enterprise itself.

The location of the innovative activities of multinational enterprises in host countries often goes hand in hand with the location of their production activity. However, though the correspondence can be very strong, it is never complete. The centralization and decentralization of technological activities by MNEs, in fact, entails advantages and disadvantages. The primary advantages of centralization, which derive mainly from economies of scale and scope in R&D, from the control which may be exercised on innovation and from linkages with the national entrepreneurial and institutional environments, are, however, increasingly counterbalanced by those associated with decentralization. From the investor's point of view, these latter advantages may be summed up in direct ties between innovative activities and production, markets, suppliers, and local customers and in the possibility of exploiting the fields of technological excellence in the host countries (Pearce and Singh 1992; Howells and Wood 1993; Miller 1994).

The possible effects on national economies are both direct and indirect (Dunning 1993). The branches of multinational enterprises may generate innovations in the host countries. But in doing so they may give rise to a displacement effect on innovations produced by local enterprises. The global generation of innovation by multinational enterprises may thus facilitate the advancement of the innovative capabilities of the host location just as, in unfavourable circumstances, it may weaken them.

The appearance of cumulative causation mechanisms triggers either virtuous or vicious circles depending essentially on the sectoral and technological profile of the economies involved. The growing tendency of multinational enterprises to establish networks for innovation, on the one hand, accelerates the decentralization of innovative activities through internal integration (within the enterprise) which crosses national boundaries. On the other hand, networks increase the advantages of geographical agglomeration within national boundaries through sectoral integration between foreign affiliates and local enterprises in the host country. In other words, multinationals take decisions to locate innovative activities on the basis of a 'hierarchy' of regional centres, strengthening geographical agglomeration according to the position occupied by the region in the scale of their innovation strategies (Cantwell 1994; Cantwell and Iammarino 1998, 2000). The 'competitive bidding' to attract direct investment in innovative activities is thus likely to become fiercer, both among the centres of technological excellence of the advanced economies and among less technology-intensive locations, increasingly threatened by emerging competition from the less-developed countries. A sharpening of regional disparities may thus also increase inside national boundaries, since the strategies of multinationals foster the strengthening of centres of excellence and penalize technologically backward regions.

6.2.3. Global Technological Collaborations

As we have seen, the business world is increasingly affected by strategic global technological alliances. The most frequently cited motivations for this are the so-called 'propulsive' factors (Howells 1997), identifiable as alliances forged to address the complexity of new, increasingly knowledge-intensive technologies and to share the costs and risks of innovative activity (Katz and Ordover 1990; Baumol 1992). What makes these collaborations stand out is the fact that the enterprises involved maintain distinct proprietary arrangements, albeit agreeing explicitly to exchange and/or generate, bilaterally or multilaterally, technical and scientific information and knowledge (Mowery 1992). 'Recall' factors are the degree of attraction exercised over external sources of technological competence with respect to the enterprise's internal assets and the desire to extend the range of scientific and technical capabilities.

It is possible to argue that the concept of collaboration reveals a tie with that of competition. Strategic co-operation agreements are, in the final analysis, a source of comparative advantage. They encompass mainly sectors in which competition is most intense, largely characterized by oligopolistic market structures, and based on a sharp differentiation of products and/or markets (for example, emerging technological sectors, such as biotechnology, information and communication, and new material technologies). Collaborations are increasingly configured as determinants of competitiveness which, after all, increasingly depends upon joint efforts for innovation.

As we have already pointed out, the phenomenon of global collaboration does not boil down only to strategic inter-firm agreements, since the academic world has always established global co-operation relations. In so far as the scientific world influences industrial activity, its globalization acts as a vehicle of transmission of knowledge and competencies. This is one reason why technological alliances and scientific agreements may contribute significantly to the strengthening of the innovative base of national economies and to processes of technological convergence between regions and countries.

6.3. Implications for Public Policies

In technology, as in other spheres of economic and social life, globalization processes are also a challenge for public policies. More specifically, governments that exert a definite power over a given territory find themselves in a situation in which their choices are strongly influenced by processes not entirely under their control (Holland 1987; Held *et al.* 1999). In the present debate on innovation policies, two different tendencies have emerged. One school of thought regards government policies to strengthen the technological competencies of the country as irrelevant, since the resources invested would not necessarily generate a national advantage (Ohmae 1990). This 'techno-laissez-faire' vision is implicitly founded on the idea that knowledge and technology may be transferred geographically without any great difficulty, and that the innovative activity of enterprises has no need for the externalities produced by the public system. A second view believes that it will take a broader spectrum of public policies than the present one to equip every nation for the technological change in progress and for the increase in globalization. This is the thesis argued by the approach founded on national innovation systems (Lundvall 1992; Nelson 1993; Freeman 1995; Archibugi and Michie 1997).

The premiss is that it is an advantage for any nation to boost its technology-intensive activity. It is thus possible to pay higher wages to create a demand for a better skilled workforce and, in the long term, to sustain higher growth rates for added value and employment. Technological activities generate a set of externalities from which the entire production system benefits. Table 6.3 sums up the principal objectives of the public policies and tools available for each of the three categories of globalization.

6.3.1. The International Exploitation of Technology

As we have seen, this form of globalization is the oldest of the three considered here. It would appear to entail no radical rethinking neither of theories nor of the policies to be implemented. This, moreover, is the form with the greatest quantitative relevance and the highest speed (Archibugi and Iammarino 2000); which is why it is logical for governments to focus attention on it. It is also the one that evokes international competition directly,

TABLE 6.3. *Public policies: Targets and instruments for the globalization of technology*

Categories		Targets	Instruments
International exploitation of national innovations	Inflows	Achieving lower foreign dependency and filling technology gaps. Increasing learning	Incentives to national infant industries. Promoting collaborations between national firms and leading firms. Incentives to selected FDI in the country
		Obtaining competitive supply prices	Negotiations on imports with the firms of other countries
	Outflows	Supporting national firms to appropriate their innovations	Export incentives for high-tech industries. Property rights negotiations
Global generation of innovations by MNEs	Inflows	Preserving and developing competitive advantages in high-tech industries	Public support to basic research and technology dissemination. Ensuring fair competition. Reinvesting profits in new innovative projects of international scope
		Enhancing national technological capabilities	Providing real incentives to the location of new innovative activities with foreign capital. Upgrading S&T infrastructures and institutions
		Keeping control on foreign capital	Monitoring the technology strategies and location choices of MNEs
	Outflows	Strengthening the competitive position of national firms	Assessing the need of home-based MNEs to invest abroad in R&D and innovative activities

TABLE 6.3. *Continued*

Categories		Targets	Instruments
	Scientific	Upgrading the scientific competence of the nation	Scientific exchange programmes Incentives to international scientific projects Participation to international S&T organizations
Global techno-scientific collaborations	Techno-industrial	Allowing the country to become a junction of technical and industrial information Applying knowledge to production	Developing infrastructures for techno-collaborations (science parks, consortia, etc.) Promoting university/industry linkages Participation to international organizations for technical and industrial collaborations

since each country has an interest in developing its competencies on foreign markets to the full and, symmetrically, to minimize the costs associated with the acquisition of the competencies of others.

Certain generic policies have to be implemented to allow national enterprises to exploit their technological competencies on the world market as well. Incentives to export, real business services, and efficient diplomatic services foster the access of a country's firms to foreign markets no less than the availability of world information networks. These policies are not sectorally selective and may be applied generally to shoes as well as to semiconductors. They stress the central role innovation plays in all industries, not only in those commonly defined as high tech. Moreover, the success of national enterprises on the global market will increasingly depend on the capacity to monitor and regulate flows of technology (whether incorporated in tangible goods or otherwise). For example, the need for governments to control the quality of inward and outward foreign direct investment becomes increasingly pressing in a context of growing globalization.

In the contemporary world, no single country has a clear advantage in all industries characterized by high technological opportunities (Pianta 1988; Nelson and Wright 1992). This forces all industrial countries, the largest included, to choose the fields of technology in which they intend to assert themselves on global markets and those in which they intend to rely on imports. Hence, one of the factors which allows a country successfully to exploit its own technological competencies on foreign markets is a careful selection of the sectors it intends to target, bearing in mind the competencies it already possesses, which *per se* reduces its leeway to search for new opportunities. In a world in which the international exploitation of technology is increasing, it is not a problem for a country to have glaring weaknesses in certain technological sectors, provided they are compensated for by as many outstanding strengths.

Although it is by no means easy—and not often possible—to 'shift' a country's specialization towards different sectors, a number of actions can be taken to reinforce the competitiveness of national enterprises in sectors with sophisticated technological competencies. They include: public aid to basic research and the connected infrastructure, which effectively facilitates all sectors of economic activity; competition policies, which may stimulate innovation by increasing domestic competition, especially in the most sensitive sectors (i.e. strategic or technologically emerging); increased dissemination of technology and participation mechanisms to facilitate in particular small and medium enterprises; incentives both to pre-competitive R&D in new strategic sectors and to market-oriented R&D in fields in which technological advantages already exist. In a world characterized by increasingly intense exchanges and mounting competition for the exploitation of innovation, the problem is not to be able to do everything, but to be able to negotiate on equal terms.

6.3.2. The Global Generation of Innovation

Vis-à-vis this form of globalization, governments have, in the words of the title of an influential essay (Hu 1992), to deal with 'national enterprises with international operations'. So which interests does a government have to pursue in this case? On the one hand, it finds itself with national enterprises that have been formed, grown up, and become competitive thanks to the resources of the national economy. In order to broaden their range of business and maintain their competitiveness, such enterprises might have to decentralize some of their technological activities to third countries. But from the country's point of view this de-location may prove negative, since the domestic market may miss out on technological opportunities as a result. On the other hand, the national government finds itself dealing with foreign enterprises (and, as such, with preferential ties with the governments of other counties) which intend to strengthen their own position by investing in the country. This means an inflow of new capital for the host country and the frequent creation of skilled jobs, but also risks of weakening national enterprises. As the competencies and capabilities connected with foreign investments in R&D are becoming increasingly important, proprietary arrangements become less significant. Most of the advantages of learning are incorporated in individuals and institutions, and domestic enterprises may draw substantial benefits from the investment in innovation and in local human capital of major multinational groups (Sharp and Pavitt 1993). Public policies ought to try to distinguish between the investment earmarked to create new technological capabilities in a country from that allocated solely for acquisitions. Governments thus have to observe both aggregate and incoming/outgoing investment in high technology to understand the extent to which their country provides an environment conducive to the development of innovative projects. If inflows prove structurally scarce, it is necessary to pinpoint the reasons why. The problem may be due to insufficient levels of infrastructure, obsessive institutional rigidities, or a lack of suitable partners in universities and public research centres. Each of these factors may be addressed with appropriate policies, the aim of which should be not so much to maximize the value of national ownership as to stimulate high added value activities in local contexts and communities. Furthermore, it is increasingly important to study the distribution of the costs and benefits of globalization inside national boundaries. As has been suggested, the global generation of innovation by multinational enterprises may aggravate regional imbalances: the link between 'global' and 'local' has thus to be supported by public intervention.

6.3.3. **Global Technological Collaborations**

Unlike the two previous forms of globalization, the third and last does not necessarily trigger international competition. On the contrary, it would appear to be characterized by a positive-sum game in which all the economic players that take part may gain an advantage. The prime concern of public authorities ought to be to assure a sufficiently high level of competition on the domestic market. It is important to focus greater attention on technological collaboration agreements to establish to what degree they boil down to collusion detrimental to consumer interests, or whether instead they lead to general advantages by acting as vehicles for the dissemination of knowledge which would otherwise remain localized. To protect the national interest, a government is bound to help its own enterprises—especially small and medium enterprises—to take part in this form of international integration and put them in a position to establish a virtuous circle leading from collaboration to learning and from learning to innovation. This can be done either through intergovernmental agreements or through the setting up of international organizations (for example, the Eureka project and the various framework programmes of scientific and technological research promoted by the European Commission). Institutional—bilateral or multilateral—agreements apart, it is the job of public authorities to create infrastructure on their own territories to make their country an attractive partner for collaboration. However, although a country will obviously be more attractive as a partner the greater its technical and scientific potential, this cannot suffice in itself, since technological capabilities may be compromised by 'institutional failures' (Abramovitz 1986). The modernization of institutions for the diffusion of science and technology is a crucial factor and the lack of appropriate linkages between the education system and industry, or between the worlds of finance and business, may seriously hamper the development of technical and scientific collaborations.

In the long term, it would appear that this type of globalization is the one which most often will strengthen a country's scientific and technological potential. It allows the country to become a crossroad of information, and hence to acquire knowledge in a broad range of technologies, especially when collaborations involve different actors—enterprises, governments, and institutions—and indirectly but substantially influence its competitive position.

6.4. **Conclusion**

In this chapter, we have discussed the role of public policies in processes of globalization of innovation in terms of their possible impact on national economies. Our main conclusion is that no single strategy exists—neither for enterprises nor for governments—to address all three types of globalization identified. Although they overlap in part, the three categories constitute three separate challenges for policy makers and it is necessary to deal with them separately. It is, however, important to stress that none of the three processes makes public policies obsolete. On the contrary, as long as nations are able to capitalize on the opportunities offered by the globalization of innovation, it will be necessary to widen the range of public policies from that implemented to date in the majority of countries.

REFERENCES

ABRAMOVITZ, M. (1986). 'Catching up, forging ahead and falling behind'. *Journal of Economic History*, 46/4: 299–313.

AMENDOLA, G., GUERRIERI, P., and PADOAN, P. C. (1998). 'International patterns of technological accumulation and trade', in D. Archibugi and J. Michie (eds.), *Trade, Growth and Technical Change*. Cambridge: Cambridge University Press.

ARCHIBUGI, D., and IAMMARINO, S. (2000). 'Innovation and globalisation: Evidence and implications', in F. Chesnais, G. Ietto-Gillies, and R. Simonetti (eds.), *European Integration and Global Corporate Strategies*. London: Routledge.

——and MICHIE, J. (1995). 'The globalisation of technology: A new taxonomy'. *Cambridge Journal of Economics*, 19: 121–40.

—— ——(1997) (eds.). *Technology, Globalisation, and Economic Performance*. Cambridge: Cambridge University Press.

——and PIANTA, M. (1992). *The Technological Specialization of Advanced Countries. A Report to the EEC on International Science and Technology Activities*. Boston: Kluwer.

—— ——(1994). 'Aggregate convergence and sectoral specialization in innovation'. *Journal of Evolutionary Economics*, 4: 17–33.

BAUMOL, W. J. (1992). 'Horizontal collusion and innovation'. *Economic Journal*, 102: 129–37.

CANTWELL, J. A. (1987). 'The reorganization of European industries after integration: Selected evidence on the role of multinational enterprise activities'. *Journal of Common Market Studies*, 26/2: 127–51.

——(1994) (ed.). *Transnational Corporations and Innovatory Activities*. United Nations Library on Transnational Corporations, 17. London: Routledge.

——(1995). 'The globalisation of technology: What remains of the product cycle model?'. *Cambridge Journal of Economics*, 19: 155–74.

——and IAMMARINO, S. (1998). 'MNCs, technological innovation and regional systems in the EU: Some evidence in the Italian case'. *International Journal of the Economics of Business*, 5/3: 383–408.

—— ——(2000). 'Multinational corporations and the location of technological innovation in the UK Regions'. *Regional Studies*, 34/4: 317–32.

DODGSON, M. (1993). *Technological Collaboration in Industry*. London: Routledge.

DUNNING, J. H. (1993). *Multinational Enterprises and the Global Economy*. Wokingham: Addison-Wesley.

FAGERBERG, J. (1996). 'Technology and competitiveness'. *Oxford Review of Economic Policy*, 12: 39–51.

——and VERSPAGEN, B. (1996). 'Heading for divergence? Regional growth in Europe reconsidered'. *Journal of Common Market Studies*, 34: 431–48.

FREEMAN, C. (1995). 'The national system of innovation in historical perspective'. *Cambridge Journal of Economics*, 19: 5–24.

GRANSTRAND, O., HÅKANSON, L., and SJÖLANDER, S. (1992) (eds.). *Technology Management and International Business. Internationalization of R&D and Technology*. Chichester: Wiley.

GUERRIERI, P., and MILANA, C. (1995). 'Changes and trends in the world trade in high-technology products'. *Cambridge Journal of Economics*, 19: 225–42.

HELD, D., MCGREW, A., GOLDBLATT, D., and PERRATON, J. (1999). *Global Transformations. Politics, Economics and Culture*. Cambridge: Polity Press.

HOLLAND, S. (1987). *The Global Economy*. London: Weidenfeld & Nicolson.

HOWELLS, J. (1997). 'Research and development externalisation, outsourcing and contract research'. Paper presented at the Conference on 'Collaboration & Competition in R&D and Innovation Programmes: Lessons for the Public and Business Sectors', Cambridge, 9–11 June.

——and WOOD, M. (1993). *The Globalisation of Production and Technology*. London: Belhaven Press.

HU, Y. S. (1992). 'Global or stateless corporations are national firms with international operations'. *California Management Review*, 34: 107–26.

KALDOR, N. (1981). 'The role of increasing returns, technical progress and cumulative causation in the theory of international trade and economic growth'. *Economie appliquée*, 34: 593–617.

KATZ, M. L., and ORDOVER, J. A. (1990). 'R&D co-operation and competition'. *Brookings Papers on Economic Activity. Microeconomics*, 20: 137–203.

LUCAS, R. E. (1988). 'On the mechanisms of economic development'. *Journal of Monetary Economics*, 22: 3–42.

LUNDVALL, B.-Å. (1992) (ed.). *National Systems of Innovation*. London: Pinter Publishers.

MILLER, R. (1994). 'Global R&D networks and large-scale innovations: The case of the automobile industry'. *Research Policy*, 23: 27–46.

MOWERY, D. (1992). 'International collaborative ventures and US firms' technology strategy', in O. Granstrand, L. Håkanson, and S. Sjölander (eds.), *Technology Management and International Business. Internationalization of R&D and Technology*. Chichester: Wiley.

MYTELKA, L. K. (1991) (ed.). *Strategic Partnership. States, Firms and International Competition*. London: Pinter Publishers.

NELSON, R. (1993) (ed.). *National Systems of Innovation*. New York: Oxford University Press.

——and WRIGHT, G. (1992). 'The rise and fall of American technological leadership: The postwar era in historical perspective'. *Journal of Economic Literature*, 30: 1931–64.

OHMAE, K. (1990). *The Borderless World: Management Lessons in the New Logic of the Global Market Place*. London: Collins.

PATEL, P., and PAVITT, K. (1998). 'Uneven (and divergent) technological accumulation among advanced countries: Evidence and a framework of explanation', in D. Archibugi and J. Michie (eds.), *Trade, Growth and Technical Change*. Cambridge: Cambridge University Press.

PEARCE, R. D., and SINGH, S. (1992). *Globalizing Research and Development*. London: Macmillan.

PIANTA, M. (1988). *New Technologies Across the Atlantic*. Hemel Hempsted: Harvester & Wheatsheaf.

SHARP, M., and PAVITT, K. (1993). 'Technology policy in the 1990s: Old trends and new realities'. *Journal of Common Market Studies*, 31/2: 129–51.

THIRLWALL, A. P. (1979). 'The balance of payments constraint as an explanation of international growth rate differences'. *Banca Nazionale del Lavoro Quarterly Review*, 32: 45–53.

VERTOVA, G. (2000). 'Stability in national patterns of technological specialisation: Some historical evidence from patent data'. *Economics of Innovation and New Technologies*, 8: 331–54.

7

Mergers, Acquisitions, and Inter-firm Technology Agreements in the Global Learning Economy

LYNN K. MYTELKA

During the 1980s inter-firm technology co-operation agreements emerged as an important phenomenon in the advanced industrial countries. One indicator of this is the steep rise in the number of such agreements over the period 1975–96. From an annual average of only 63 per year in the period 1975–9 (Hagedoorn and Schakenraad: 1990, Tables 1, 2, and 3), the number of agreements rose steadily over the 1980s, reaching 502 per year in 1988–91 and 626 in 1992–5. In 1996 some 650 such agreements were signed (UNCTAD 1998: 23).[1] In contrast to the five-year period 1975–9, during which a total of 317 inter-firm technology agreements had been concluded, by the mid-1990s, nearly twice that number of agreements were being signed *each* year. Information technology and the life sciences industry[2] account for 55%, of these agreements (Figure 7.1).

Not only were firms spontaneously engaging in inter-firm R&D collaboration but the growing importance of partnering activity for international competitiveness led governments in Japan (Fransman 1990; Levy and Samuels 1991), and later in Europe (Aaltonen *et al.* 1991; Mytelka 1991, 1995) and the United States (Alic 1991; Vonortas 1997) to initiate and/or finance a wide variety of different programmes designed to promote strategic partnerships. Among the most well-known R&D-consortia are the Japanese Very Large Scale Integration (VLSI) and Fifth Generation Computer projects, the Semiconductor Research Corporation, SEMATECH, in the United States, and the European ESPRIT (Strategtic Programme for Research and Development in Information Technology) and EUREKA programmes.

---

[1] The MERIT/UNCTAD database includes only strategic inter-firm technology agreements, that is those involving the long-term position of firms or products. It originated at CATI in the Netherlands, was developed by MERIT, University of Maastricht under the direction of John Hagedoorn and subsequently modified by UNCTAD. The MERIT/UNCTAD version contains a total of 8,254 agreements. All entries are drawn from published sources. The database is thus biased towards formal agreements that have been publicly announced in newspapers and professional publications, most of which report agreements involving US, European, and to a lesser extent, Japanese firms. Its coverage of agreements involving firms from the developing world is exceedingly limited.

[2] Life sciences is the term by which the new biotechnology giants in pharmaceuticals and agrobusiness now designate themselves.

FIG. 7.1. *Number of inter-firm technology agreements in information technology and life sciences, 1980–1996*

Source: MERIT/UNCTAD database.

Accompanying the sharp rise in strategic partnering activity was a dramatic increase in cross-border mergers and acquisitions (M&As) since the 1980s. This contrasts with the 1950s and 1960s when greenfield investment was the predominant form of foreign direct investment (FDI). By 1986 the value of such deals had reached nearly 100 billion US dollars. In 1997 cross-border M&As had risen to $342 billion and accounted for approximately 58% of total foreign direct investment inflows in that year (UNCTAD 1998: 18–19). M&As are also taking place within national borders, furthering a process of concentration at both national and global levels.

The purpose of this chapter is to assess the contribution of international inter-firm technology agreements to enterprise learning and innovation. To do so it situates these agreements in the broader context of changes in the structure of industry on a global scale and of competition within it. Section 1 presents a taxonomy that distinguishes traditional forms of one-way inter-firm agreements from two-way collaborative partnerships in research and development (R&D), production, and distribution and illustrates the way in which the latter have contributed to joint knowledge production and sharing in industries as diverse as information technology, biopharmaceuticals, and automobiles. Section 7.2 explores in greater depth the role that R&D-consortia play in strengthening the potential for innovation, particularly in small and medium-sized enterprises and in industries undergoing a process of catch-up. As firms encounter each other across multiple technology partnerships, opportunities for learning each other's strategies also increase and so, too, do the incentives for collusion. Section 7.3 draws a distinction between the static barriers to entry that result from mergers and acqusitions and traditional forms of oligopoly, and the dynamic entry barriers that are made possible through the emergence of knowledge-based networked oligopolies on a global scale. These, the chapter argues in conclusion, have the potential to become powerful selection mechanisms that create differential access to learning across firms and geographical space.

7.1. **Strategic Partnerships and M&As: A Learning-Based Taxonomy**

Strategic technology partnerships can be distinguished both from conventional forms of investment, such as mergers and acquisitions, and from more traditional inter-firm agreements in production or technology, such as joint ventures, licensing, or sub-contracting arrangements, by three main characteristics. Firstly, they are two-way relationships focused on joint knowledge production and sharing as opposed to a one-way transfer of technology. The knowledge component in strategic technology partnerships may involve the development of new products, new production processes, or new routines within the firm or in its ability to manage inter-firm contractual relationships. Whereas more traditional one-way agreements have been particularly important to the firm in catching up with the industry's frontrunners, managing a portfolio of collaborative or two-way partnerships has become central for firms at the technological frontier.

Second, unlike traditional joint ventures, strategic partnerships tend to be contractual in nature with little or no equity involvement by the participants. Even when strategic partnerships take the form of a joint venture their aim is less one of control than, as in biopharmaceuticals, providing the partners with key complementary assets to ensure the further development, production, and marketing of new products.

Third, such partnerships are strategic in the sense that they are part of the longer term planning activity of the firm rather than simply an opportunistic response to short-term financial gains. As with tacit knowledge learning to manage two-way partnerships takes time and involves the building up and the sustaining of relationships of trust.

Although the focus in this chapter is mainly upon strategic partnerships in R&D, these are not the only form of collaborative activity in which firms have engaged. Figure 7.2 provides a taxonomy that includes older, unidirectional forms of linkages as well as some examples of the newer forms of partnering activity in R&D, production, and marketing that became more prominent over the 1970s and 1980s.

In Figure 7.2 some linkages are classified as both two-way and more traditional one-way relationships. This is done to underscore the mutability of traditional relationships. Consider the joint venture. Some, but not all, strategic partnerships are joint ventures but when they do involve an equity arrangement, as, for example, in biotechnology industry, the intention is less to exercise control than it is for the larger firm, usually a major pharmaceutical or chemical company, to provide the financial and marketing

	R&D	PRODUCTION	DISTRIBUTION
ONE-WAY agreements	licensing cross-licensing early efforts to commercialize public sector R&D joint ventures	sub-contracting OEM (TV sets, PCs) acquisitions	franchizing (Mcdonald's) (Benetton)
TWO-WAY partnerships	R&D-Consortia (ESPRIT) (EUREKA) (SEMATECH) (VLSI project)	co-production use of common components (across automobile models) modularization (auto dashboards) (aircraft)	joint marketing system-products (the wired house) standardization of interfaces
	customer–supplier networks (textiles, electronics, autos)		
	inter-firm tech. collaboration agreements	joint ventures (biotechnology)	
	university/industry partnerships (Carnegie Mellon's Robotics Institute) (Stanford's Ctr for integrated systems)	new forms of sub-contracting	

FIG. 7.2. *Inter-firm technology agreements: A matrix of linkages*
Source: adapted from Mytelka 1993: 109.

resources that the smaller dedicated biotechnology firm lacks. Similarly the emergence of some sub-contractors as partners engaged in a dialogue with their 'principals' has been documented in both the textiles and clothing and the electronics industries.[3]

Customer–supplier relationships have also changed considerably as suppliers are drawn into joint research and collaboration in the design of new products for their clients and take on additional responsibility for the manufacture of whole modules subsequently assembled into complete products by their customers, notably in the automobile (Humphrey 1998) and the aircraft (Mowery 1991) industries. Data from the MERIT/UNCTAD database for the years 1980 to 1996 show a marked shift away from the quasi-exclusive reliance on one-way linkages to the development of two-way collaborative relationships in the 1990s (Figure 7.3).

Underlying the upsurge in inter-firm technology agreements and the shift to two-way technology partnerships are three factors related to changes in the

---

[3] For a discussion of these newer relationships in textiles and clothing see Mytelka (1991), and in electronics Ernst and O'Connor (1992).

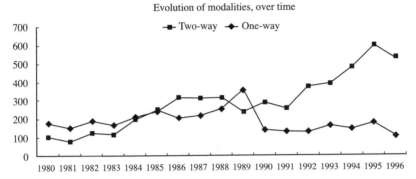

FIG. 7.3. *Evolution in the type of inter-firm technology agreement, 1980–1996*
Source: MERIT/UNCTAD database; WIR 1998: 25.

pattern of production and in the nature of competition that have been underway since the 1970s.[4]

(1) the growing knowledge-intensity of production across a wide range of
industries, where knowledge is understood to include R&D as well as
other intangibles such as design, engineering, training, marketing, and
management.
(2) the emergence of an innovation-based mode of competition leading to
an increase in the speed with which new products are developed and
moved to market. This shortened product life cycles and raised the costs,
risks, and uncertainties of R&D. To amortize the higher costs of R&D
under these conditions, companies sought access to wider markets;
(3) the rapid diffusion of an innovation-based mode of competition as pressures mounted for the deregulation of domestic markets around the
globe and for the liberalization of trade and investment guaranteed by
international agreements.

As competition globalized, it gave impetus to a wave of mergers and
acquisitions aimed at strengthening traditional size barriers to entry in
R&D, consolidating positions at home and accessing markets abroad. But
mergers and acquisitions, while they create critical mass, also add to the
inertia of the firm precisely at a time when flexibility is needed to respond
to the uncertainties generated by the rapid pace of innovation, the erosion
of frontiers between industries, and discontinuities in what were previously
incremental technological trajectories. Strategic alliances in R&D, production, and marketing emerged as one means to resolve these contradictory
pressures. Indeed, participation in such networks and the skill with which a
portfolio of partnerships is managed have since become critical elements in

---

[4] Elsewhere I have discussed these factors in detail. See Mytelka (1991, 1995).

the firm's ability to access new knowledge and markets. This is particularly true in science-based and/or R&D intensive industries, information technology (IT), and the life sciences, for example. But strategic partnering activity also has become a competitive asset in industries, such as automobiles, that are currently undergoing major organizational changes in which tacit knowledge plays a key role along with inter-industry linkages that are R&D intensive.[5]

7.2. Learning Through Partnership

During the 1980s state support for research consortia in the US and Europe stimulated considerable growth in R&D partnering. Over the period 1983–96, the European Strategic Programme for Research and Development in Information Technology (ESPRIT), for example, sponsored more than 1,500 R&D-consortia (see Sharp's chapter in this volume). EUREKA, which got underway somewhat later than the EU programmes, led to the creation of 1,031 R&D-consortia from 1985 to 1996.[6] In both cases partnerships were formed overwhelmingly with other European firms and research institutions.

Since the passage of the National Cooperative Research Act in 1984 the number of R&D consortia among US firms has grown as well, though at a much slower rate. Data collected by the US Justice Department show that over the period 1985–95 a total of 575 R&D-consortia were registered (Vonortas 1997: 581). Data from the MERIT/UNCTAD database also show that over the 1980s and 1990s US firms significantly increased the level of their technology partnering activities and the share of these agreements involving a US partner rose from 47.4% in 1983–9 to 58.8% in the period 1990–6. In contrast, the number of technology agreements involving a European firm declined by 8% between 1983–9 and 1990–6 and was accompanied by a sharp fall in the share of intra-EU partnerships from 47.6% to 29.3 % (data are drawn from the MERIT/UNCTAD database).[7] To some extent, this reflects a rough division of labour in which intra-European partnerships, notably through programmes such as ESPRIT, tended to support a catch-up strategy on the part of participating firms, while market-based EU–US partnerships are frontier-oriented.

State sponsored R&D partnering activity has been particularly important for small and medium-sized enterprises who are faced with much larger rivals and in sectors where catching-up is needed. The IT industry in Europe fell

---

[5] Alliances involving automobile assemblers, fuel cell manufacturers, component suppliers, and oil companies are one such example.

[6] Data on ESPRIT are derived from the CEREM database (Nanterre) for the period 1983–91. ESPRIT data for the period 1992–6 and EUREKA data for 1985–96 come from the database developed under TSER project CT-97-1075 (co-ordinator: Yannis Caloghirou).

[7] Data are drawn from the MERIT/UNCTAD database.

into both categories in the early 1980s. Prior to the launching of the ESPRIT programme in 1983 firms in Europe, when they engaged in partnerships with other firms, universities, and research institutes at all, did so primarily with firms and research institutions in their own country, occasionally with those from the United States but very rarely with firms or research institutions in other European countries. ESPRIT, the first of the major European R&D programmes, would radically alter these habits and practices.[8]

In 1980, aware of the difficulties facing European information technology firms, far smaller and less involved in R&D than their US rivals, inspired by the rapid movement of Japanese firms towards the technological frontier made possible by state-promoted inter-firm R&D-consortia and empowered by Article 235 of the Rome Treaty to promote the competitiveness of European industry, Etienne Davignon, then Commissioner of Industry in the European Community, invited Europe's twelve largest information technology firms to draw up a work programme for their industry. The ESPRIT programme which resulted had three objectives:

(1) to promote intra-European industrial co-operation in R&D in five main information technology areas;
(2) to furnish European industry with the basic technologies that it would need to bolster its competitiveness through the 1990s; and
(3) to develop European standards.

ESPRIT I began with a pilot year in 1983 and ran until 1987. It was renewed as ESPRIT II, for an additional four-year period in 1988. By 1992 a total of 561 projects was underway or had been completed. ESPRIT was renewed under the Third (1991–4) and Fourth (1994–8) framework programmes. ESPRIT contributed to learning and innovation in two ways. The first was to induce changes in the traditional habits and practices of European firms with regard to partnering and to partnering across Europe. The second was to increase the participation of SMEs in such partnerships.

In large part ESPRIT's rules of operation provided considerable inducement for firms to join R&D-consortia. To qualify for funding a project must include a minimum of two firms located in at least two different EC countries. This ensures that projects tend to be user oriented rather than technology driven by universities or research institutes. That 50% of project costs are funded by the EU provides a considerable incentive to small and medium-sized enterprises. The user orientation is also reflected in the continuous consultation with industry in the elaboration of both the overall objectives and the yearly work programmes for the ESPRIT programme. Initially this involved only the big-12 companies, but increasingly small and medium-sized companies (SMEs) have been active in the various consultative groups that

[8] This case study draws upon Mytelka: 1990, 1991, 1995; and Delapierre, Lemettre, Mytelka, Zimmermann and Vavakova 1988.

structure the work programme and participate in the project selection process each year. Special actions to encourage SME participation were also gradually introduced in the Second and Third Framework programmes. By the end of 1989, of the 678 participating firms in the ESPRIT programme, 386 were small and medium-sized enterprises (CEC 1990: 4). During the Third Framework programme (1991–4), however, a total of 1,130 SMEs participated in ESPRIT and in the first two years of the Fourth Framework programme (1994–6) alone, some 979 SMEs had already become participants (CEC 1997: 6).

Catching-up through ESPRIT was not as rapid as the Japanese experience in the VLSI project had shown it could be. Nearly 65% of the projects accepted under ESPRIT I were pre-competitive and many of these had four- to five-year terms. As a result, four years after start-up only 37 projects had been completed. Despite their long terms, moreover, much of the R&D undertaken during the first phase of ESPRIT consisted in efforts to catch up in older technologies (Mytelka 1991). Although Europe's IT firms were particularly weak precisely because they specialized in older, less dynamic, technologies, such as bipolar integrated circuits and silicon substrates (Hobday 1993), ESPRIT projects were not initially used to move more quickly to the existing frontier. Not until ESPRIT II, for example, did a concerted drive to develop design and production technologies for Application Specific Integrated Circuits (ASICs) begin. Thus catching up did not enable Europe's information technology firms to keep up with a moving technological frontier and their market share continued to erode throughout the 1980s.[9]

Towards the end of that decade, however, ESPRIT began to move closer to the market by consciously selecting projects for their commercial potential. In consequence the number of pre-competitive R&D projects in ESPRIT II fell from nearly two-thirds to 37% (Mytelka 1991, 1995). To further increase the commercial impact of the ESPRIT programme, integrated project clusters were also formed under ESPRIT II. These consisted of sets of projects that had a number of partners in common and undertook different aspects of a related technological problem. Perhaps the best-known integrated project cluster within ESPRIT is the PCTE—Portable Common Tool Environment—which spawned over fifteen applications and extension projects. Follow-up projects and under the Third framework programme, larger scale targeted projects were still other means to ensure that work done in ESPRIT found its way to the market. By 1989 data furnished by the ESPRIT secretariat showed that ESPRIT had produced 313 major results, of which 152 contributed directly to products or services (CEC 1990: 2). Three years later, with 800 projects completed or underway, the total number of results had risen to 721, of which 417 contributed directly to marketable products or

---

[9] The chapters by Archibugi and Iammarino and by Fagerberg in this volume address the problem of catch-up in the broader context of convergence among European countries and regions.

services, 72 were contributions to international standards, and 232 consisted of tools and methods used outside ESPRIT (CEC 1992: 8).

For French SMEs, in particular, ESPRIT opened hitherto unavailable market opportunities. The software industry, for example, had been heavily engaged in work for captive markets, frequently involving military applications and was described by one respondent from the industry as singularly 'non-innovative'. This significantly changed as these firms, through their ESPRIT projects, begin to compete in the wider European market. Today the French software industry is among Europe's most dynamic IT sectors. For small, relatively new firms, the opportunities that this openness offered were particularly important since a close relationship between the state and large firms in France had earlier constituted a serious barrier to entry in the domestic market for these firms.

Participation levels, outputs, and ESPRIT's contribution to enterprise growth are among the classic indicators of success or failure in strategic partnering. Less frequently assessed, however, are the intangibles and particularly those accruing to the SME sector. Two surveys of firms that had participated in at least one ESPRIT project provide data on the impact of the ESPRIT programme during the 1980s and early 1990s on small and medium-sized enterprises from France, Italy, Germany, the UK, and the Netherlands.

In terms of knowledge acquisition ESPRIT was of critical importance for SMEs since it assured partners of access to all research results emanating from within their own projects and it provided for the dissemination of information across projects on a privileged basis for ESPRIT partner firms and research organizations. For many small and medium-sized firms this access to research results has created a multiplier effect that considerably enlarged the impact of their own R&D effort and expenditure.

In addition, these interviews revealed that ESPRIT has

• enabled Europe's SMEs to increase or maintain R&D levels
• stimulated firms to incorporate R&D within longer term strategic planning;
• enhanced knowledge accumulation by SMEs, thereby increasing their resistance to takeovers
• enabled subsidiaries to remain active in R&D by complementing the R&D decentralization strategies of parent firms
• speeded-up the process of innovation by creating critical mass in R&D, and
• encouraged networking through which new forms of supplier–client partnerships were established.

7.3. Shaping the Global Learning Economy

The formation of traditional oligopolies is based on three relatively static pillars: the ability to identify a small number of competitors, mainly other domestic firms, among whom mutual interdependence and forbearance are practised; the set of products or the industry within which oligopolistic competition takes place; and the technological trajectory which these products will follow.[10] Catch-up consortia which followed an incremental technological trajectory were ideal environments within which defensive oligopolistic market structures could be formed.

As Japanese firms in the IT and automobile industries cut dramatically into the market share of their competitors, rival consortia in these industries emerged in Europe and the United States. During the first two phases of ESPRIT, Europe's big-12 IT firms, for example, were able to build the bases for a 'defensive oligopoly' through high rates of participation in the ESPRIT programme and their multiple linkages across the 561 R&D projects that were created in this period (Mytelka 1995). Firms like Thomson, Siemens, Bull, and Philips were each involved in over seventy of these R&D-consortia and encountered each other in many of the core technology projects of the period. Prometheus, an eight-year EUREKA programme, was designed to strengthen Europe's role in the growing automotive electronics market. It included all leading European-owned car companies and over one hundred of their suppliers (Graves 1989). Nearly absent from all these consortia were rival US and Japanese firms. R&D-consortia in the United States exhibited similar characteristics (Vonortas 2000). Sematech, for example, was launched in 1987 primarily as a means to help stem the loss of market share by US semiconductor firms to their Japanese rivals. The US government supported this exclusive club of semiconductor firms and their suppliers with an annual grant of $100 million dollars over eight years (Alic 1991). In the automobile industry, the 'Initiative for a New Generation of Vehicles' launched by the Clinton administration in 1993 involved only the big-3 US automobile manufacturers and their suppliers.

The globalization of knowledge-based competition, however, has made it increasingly more difficult to identify potential rivals. Even more difficult to predict in this period of technological discontinuity are one's competitors when these may emerge from other 'industries' through a combination of hitherto unrelated generic technologies as has taken place in what is currently known as the life sciences and the information and communications industries. Indeed, what constitutes an industry is itself uncertain since *horizontal segments*, as opposed to vertical divides such as the therapeutic categories which characterize the traditional pharmaceutical industry,[11] can emerge within any existing industry and become a potential platform for the configuration of new industrial sectors. The reconfiguration of the data processing industry away from the wholly integrated manufacturer towards three distinct

---

[10] This discussion of traditional oligopolies was originally developed in Delapierre and Mytelka (1988), Mytelka and Delapierre (1997 and 1999).

[11] Market niches such as designer clothes or Application Specific Integrated Circuits (ASICs) are similar to vertical divides in this respect.

industries—the semiconductors, software, and computers—loosely linked into an IT industry is a case in point.

Horizontal segments with some degree of exclusivity can emerge within any industry and just as they emerge, they can also disappear. Which segments are critical for one's own industry, moreover, is not generally clear at the outset. Yet all firms require some degree of predictability in planning investments and in developing new products. There is thus a need for some measure of agreement on what constitutes an industry and what the rules of competition are within it. It is in this context that knowledge-based networked oligopolies have a strategic role to play.

The new oligopolies share three principal characteristics:

(1) They are knowledge based i.e. involve collaboration in the generation of, use of, or control over the evolution of new knowledge. As a result, the new knowledge-based oligopolies are dynamic, seeking to organize, manage, and monitor change as opposed to rigidifying the status quo.

(2) They are composed of networks of firms rather than of individual companies. Alliances thus form the basic structure and building-blocks of the global oligopoly.

(3) In terms of their organization, the new oligopolies can form within or across industry segments and sometimes do both at the same time. They are moving and reshaping themselves to include new actors when the assets they bring to the network are complementary and eliminating others whose resources are no longer critical. The IT industry over the 1980s and 1990s reflects the continually changing opportunities for reconfiguration as the focus of potentially rival firms has shifted from the interactive TV to the Internet.

Knowledge-based networked oligopolies emerge within industries in which the three pillars upon which traditional oligopolies can be constituted—rivals, industries, technologies—are themselves undergoing radical change. The erosion of these bases for the construction of traditional oligopolies tends to occur when one or more 'ruptures'—a technological discontinuity, a radical policy change, the emergence of a new category of consumers or a significant change in competitive strategy—open opportunities for the creation of new horizontal segments within an existing industry precisely because these ruptures are systemic in nature. They thus allow the bypassing or the destruction of an existing barrier to entry (Mytelka and Delapierre 1997, 1999).

New horizontal segments, however, are only potential platforms for the development of new industries. Which factors transform the potentiality inherent in a new segment into the actuality of a new industry? Two stand out in particular. Firstly, a segment is more likely to become a platform for reshaping an industry if its products are generic in nature. Firms in this segment are thus able to reduce their vulnerability by widening the range of potential users. Cost, quality, and availability of the new products will undoubtedly affect the speed with which the population of users increases. But to the extent that the market grows rapidly, firms on this segment will be well positioned to generate the revenues and acquire the size and/or other skills needed to change the mode of competition by establishing new rules of the game and creating new barriers to entry.

Both software and semiconductors cut across all products in the old computer industry and, in time, spread well beyond it. Through the strategic alternation of standardization which widened the range of potential users and customization which locked them in, and through the development of strategic partnering activities which spread the risks, costs, and uncertainties of rising R&D expenditures and shortening product life cycles, software and semiconductor firms were able to institute an innovation-based mode of competition in their emerging industries. The new mode of competition in the semiconductor industry, for example, was based on a set of dynamic entry barriers that included:

(1) innovation-based competition with rapid movement down the performance/cost curve;
(2) equally rapid movement down the manufacturing learning curve in order to ensure higher yields, rapid ramp up in volume to reduce costs; but
(3) speed and flexibility in changing over to new product generations as the product life cycle shortened; and,
(4) increased use of strategic partnering to reduce the high costs and risks of R&D needed to maintain the pace of innovation; and
(5) maintain positions within the core group of firms in a knowledge-based networked oligopoly through which the industry's future was increasingly shaped.

Second is the extent to which firms that composed the traditional oligopoly were able to absorb the new segment by transforming themselves into a knowledge-based networked oligopoly and establishing a new mode of competition in the 'old' industry (Delapierre and Mytelka 1988; Mytelka 1995). To maintain their position within these shifting hierarchies, however, traditional firms must be able to create new entry barriers that set industry standards, rules, and competitive practices, control the evolution of technology, and reduce the shocks of radical change. Knowledge-based networked oligopolies (KBNOs) have been one vehicle for doing so. In the IT industries these have emerged in, among others, the markets for Drams and Risc technologies (Delapierre and Mytelka 1998) and for HDTV (Mytelka and Delapierre 1999). In the automobile industry they are currently forming around the new fuel cell technology and may also emerge through the increasingly closer links that are being formed between sets of first-tier suppliers and their auto assembler partners. In the life sciences they are evident in the fusion of agro-business and pharmaceuticals around core genetic engineering techniques and the rival alliances of Monsanto, Novartis, Dupont, and Rhone Poulenc Rorer/Hoechst that are beginning to emerge.

7.4. Technology Agreements and Global Oligopolies

In a recent study Archibugi and Michie analysed the process of globalization along three dimensions: the international exploitation of technology as measured by exports, licensing, and Foreign Direct Investment (FDI); the global generation of innovation, as reflected in R&D investments at home and abroad; and global techno-scientific collaboration involving universities, research institutions, and firms (see also Archibugi and Iammarino, in this volume). From this analysis they concluded that 'the globalization of technological activities has not led to a convergence either in the methods adopted by countries to innovate or in their profiles of sectoral specialisation' (Archibugi and Michie 1997: 173). This is particularly paradoxical, if, as they argue with respect to techno-scientific collaboration, the transfer of knowledge is enhanced by seeking to partner with firms based in countries which have endowments lacking in the home country (Archibugi and Michie 1997: 181).

Strategic technology partnerships enable firms to window on a wide variety of ancillary technologies thus widening access to new knowledge. They reduce the risks and uncertainties associated with knowledge production at the frontier by involving potential users at the research phase and they reduce the cost of continuous innovation by leveraging in-house R&D and strengthening supplier–client relations (Mytelka 1991, 1993). These gains from partnering would also suggest that inter-firm collaboration would contribute to convergence across industrialized countries. The analysis presented in this chapter provides a number of arguments for why this is not occurring.

Inter-firm agreements must be understood in their context. The contribution of inter-firm collaboration to knowledge production, sharing, and diffusion can thus be expected to differ across industries and in function of the dynamics of change in the structure and mode of competition within that industry. As these change overtime, there is a dynamic element to the process which makes the projection of trends in an industry problematic. Technology partnerships in the semiconductor segment of the information technology industry, for example, are set within a context marked by dynamic entry barriers based on knowledge generation and chip-production capacity that enable the firm to capture the rents from R&D rapidly. Both of these have a size dimension that recalls more traditional oligopolistic market structures. KBNOs form and reform among semiconductor manufacturers and between those in the semiconductor sector and clients from a wide range of user industries. These create still other barriers to entry for smaller firms, but opportunities for learning and innovation, particularly in niche markets, are still present.

In automobiles, alliances complement three significant changes: new forms of supplier–client relationship; cross-industry linkages; and an intensification of mergers and acquisitions among firms in the auto parts segment of the industry as well as among automobile assemblers. This is leading to rapid increases in concentration within the industry and to radical changes in the locus of knowledge generation and the appropriation of knowledge rents. Inter-firm technology partnerships are at the cutting edge of the division between insiders and outsiders in this process.

In pharmaceuticals a rash of M&As brought about the disappearance of an independent 'biotechnology' segment and is now transforming the core of the pharmaceutical industry into a part of the new life sciences industry. In both bio-agriculture and bio-pharmaceuticals dedicated biotechnology firms (DBFs) were too small and specialized to emerge as dominant players on a new horizontal market segment. A long period of research and testing was required to turn the new genetic engineering techniques into approved prod-ucts. This further weakened the DBF's ability to generate revenues and sus-tain the R&D process on its own. Complementarities between DBFs have not been significant enough to compensate for these size factors. Traditional financial and size barriers in R&D, clinical or field testing, and marketing remained important and sustained the larger pharmaceutical and chemical firms in their position of dominance within the vertical markets in which they were established—especially the very large markets for cancer and cardiovas-cular drugs, antidepressants, antibiotics, seeds, pesticides, and herbicides—in all of which biotechnology plays an increasingly important role.

Generalizing across time and industries conceals these dynamics and their impact on enterprise learning. Monitoring industry dynamics is thus critical for effective policy making.[12] Equally important, in this context, is the need to analyse the way in which M&As and alliances are working in tandem to shape opportunities for learning and for change in specialization. Figure 7.4 shows the close parallels in the trend between M&As and technology part-nering activity.

Large firms use M&As to build further upon the advantages derived from size and scope. These static advantages may include the management of 'stocks' of competencies as embodied in patents and trademarks. Patenting creates a number of cost-barriers to entry for latecomer firms. It enables patent holders to oblige licensers, for example, to acquire whole packages of patents and to accept restrictions on the use of such licences. By selecting which firms can become licensees and under increasingly broader definitions of patent applicability and more stringent conditions applying to the processes for obtaining compulsory licences, the patent holder can signifi-cantly slow down the catch-up process and the emergence of rivals. Size advantages also inhere in the use of trademarks and advertising as well as in

---

[12] This applies as much to innovation as to competition. See Lundvall and Borrás (1998).

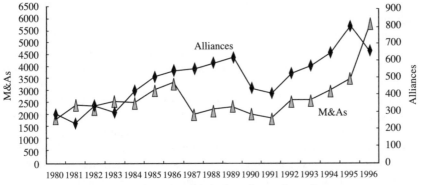

FIG. 7.4. *Number of M&A deals and inter-firm alliances*
Source: MERIT/UNCTAD database.

after sales service, all of which are reinforced through the waves of M&As that are raising levels of concentration on a global scale. Local markets as the basis for start-ups and for catching up are increasingly vulnerable to pressures for liberalization, while M&As bring the competition home even when traditional trade barriers are still in place. The restructuring of the automobile and telecommunications industries worldwide and the tendency towards the stripping of knowledge assets that has resulted need to be better monitored and their impact on the ability of national and local innovation systems to emerge and become dynamic will need to be more thoroughly analysed.

As a complement to M&As and to traditional oligopolistic market behaviour, large firms have also been able to use strategic partnerships to build dynamic advantages based on knowledge. KBNOs, for example, enable these firms to manage the 'flow' of knowledge and shape technological trajectories, remain flexible, and widen the knowledge base. Partnerships serve to create research barriers to entry, help to orchestrate the pattern of diversification in the industry and shape the direction of R&D which, in turn, influences the standards for new products, the timing of their commercialization and the price at which they will be offered on the market. They have become a selection mechanism that locks out rivals and locks in potentially large clients, monopolizing downstream or upstream markets as effectively as vertical integration did in the past, yet they also bring about a measure of flexibility that is critical in industries undergoing rapid technological change. Through technological lock-in, the welfare consequences in terms of future opportunities and constraints on technological change, however, are potentially enormous. It is within this new and rapidly changing context that the future of convergence within Europe must be posed and the broader issue of globalization and its consequences addressed.

In sum, if strategic partnering activity has opened new opportunities for enhanced learning in the short term, paradoxically, it has also provided the means whereby technological change can be channelled and shaped over the longer term through knowledge-based networked oligopolies at the global level. These new oligopolistic market structures create dynamic barriers to entry for newcomers and affect the ability of competitors to keep up with a rapidly moving frontier. In combination with traditional strategies of merger and acquisition, which raise size barriers to entry and affect the distribution of gains from knowledge, a powerful selection mechanism is created that results in differential access to learning across firms and geographical space. This potentially has a bearing on patterns of national specialization and opportunity in the future. Three sets of policies might mitigate the effects of the increasingly dominant role that large firms in knowledge-based networks are playing in the global learning economy. These are the maintenance of publicly funded R&D; the promotion of co-operative linkages among SMEs and between SMEs and public research and technology development institutions; and the closer monitoring of the combinatory effects of M&As and strategic alliances. The latter will require the development of new tools of analysis, as this chapter has shown.

REFERENCES

ALIC, J. (1991). 'From weakness or strength: American firms and policies in a global economy', in L. K. Mytelka (ed.), *Strategic Partnerships and the World Economy.* London: Pinter Publishers.

AALTONEN, M., LINDGREN, U., PENNANEN, I., KAURANEN, I., and VALTONEN, P. (1991). *Promoting the Start-up of International Strategic Alliances of Technology-intensive Companies.* Helsinki: Helsinki University of Techonology.

ARCHIBUGI, D., and MICHIE, J. (1997). 'The globalisation of technology: a new taxonomy', in D. Archibugi and J. Michie (eds.), *Technology, Globalisation and Economic Performance.* Cambridge: Cambridge University Press.

AUDRETSCH, D., and STEPHAN, P. (1991). 'How and why does knowledge spill over? The case of biotechnology'. Centre for Economic Policy Research, Discussion Paper Series no. 9.

CEC (1990). *ESPRIT 1989 Annual Report.* Brussels, DGXIII.

——(1991). *ESPRIT 1990/91 Annual Report.* Brussels, DGXIII.

——(1992). *ESPRIT 1991/1992 Annual Report.* Brussels, DGXIII.

——(1997). *Framework Programme IV, SME Participation 1994–1996.* Brussels, DGXII, 18 February. Mimeo.

DELAPIERRE, M., and MYTELKA, L. K. (1988). 'Decomposition, recomposition des oligopoles'. *Economie et sociétés,* 12/11, 55–81.

—— —— (1998). 'Blurring boundaries: New inter-firm relationships and the emergence of networked, knowledge-based oligopolies', in M. Colombo (ed.), *The Changing Boundaries of the Firm Explaining Evolving Inter-firm Relations.* London: Routledge.

DELAPIERRE, M., LEMETTRE, J.-F., MYTELKA, L. K., ZIMMERMANN, J.-B., and VAVAKOVA, B. (1988). *Cooperation Between Firms and Research Institutes: The French Case*, prepared for the EUREKA workshop on Collaboration between Enterprises and Research Institutes. Milan: Bocconi University.

ERNST, D., and O'CONNOR, D. (1992). *Competing in the Electronics Industry. The Experience of Newly Industrializing Economies*. Paris: OECD Development Centre.

FRANSMAN, M. (1990). *The Market and Beyond: Cooperation and Competition in Information Technology in the Japanese System*. Cambridge: Cambridge University Press.

GRAVES, A. (1989). 'Prometheus: A new departure in automobile R&D?' Cambridge, Mass.: MIT, IMVP Automobile Policy Programme, May.

HAGEDOORN, J., and SCHAKENRAAD, J. (1990). 'Inter-firm partnerships and cooperative strategies in core technologies', in C. Freeman and L. Soete (eds.), *New Explorations in the Economics of Technical Change*. London: Pinter Publishers.

HOBDAY, M. (1993). 'Les opérations de croissance externe dans l'industrie européenne des semi-conducteurs', in F. Sachwald (ed.), *L'Europe et la globalisation Acquisitions et accords dans l'industrie*. Paris: Masson.

HUMPHREY, J. (1998). 'Globalisation and supply chain networks in the auto industry: Brazil and India'. Paper presented to the International Workshop on Global Production and Local Jobs: New Perspectives on Enterprises, Networks, Employment, and Local Development Policy. Geneva: ILY, 9–10 March.

LEVY, J., and SAMUELS, R. (1991). 'Institutions and innovation: research collaboration as technology strategy in Japan', in L. K. Mytelka (ed.), *Strategic Partnerships and the World Economy*. London: Pinter Publishers.

LUNDVALL, B.-Å., and BORRÁS, S. (1998). *The Globalising Learning Economy: Implications for Innovation Policy*. Brussels: European Commission.

MOWERY, D. (1991). 'International collaboration in the commercial aircraft industry', in L. K. Mytelka (ed.), *Strategic Partnerships and the World Economy*. London: Pinter Publishers.

MYTELKA, L. K. (1990). 'Technological and economic benefits of the European Strategic Programme for Research and Development on Information Technologies (ESPRIT)', A Report to the Department of Communications, Government of Canada. Ottawa.

——(1991). 'States, strategic alliances and international oligopolies: The European ESPRIT programme', in L. K. Mytelka (ed.), *Strategic Partnerships and the World Economy*. London: Pinter Publishers.

——(1993). 'Strategic alliances', in F. O. Hampson and C. Maule (eds.), *Global Jeopardy*. Ottawa: Carleton University Press.

——(1995). 'Dancing with wolves: Global oligopolies and strategic partnerships', in J. Hagedoorn (ed.), *Technical Change and the World Economy*. Cheltenham: Edward Elgar.

—— and DELAPIERRE, M. (1997). 'Industrial dynamics, knowledge-based networked oligopolies and the emergence of new modes of competition'. Paper presented at the DRUID Summer Seminar on Competition and Industrial Dynamics, 1–3 June, Skagen.

————(1999). 'Strategic partnerships, knowledge-based networked oligopolies and the state', in C. Cutler, V. Haufler, and T. Porter (eds.), *Private Authority and International Affairs*. Binghamton: Suny University Press.

UNCTAD (1998). *World Investment Report: Transnational Corporations, Market Structure and Competition Policy.* New York and Geneva: United Nations.

VONORTAS, N. S. (1997). 'Research joint ventures in the US'. *Research Policy,* 26: 577–95.

——(2000). 'Multimarket contact and inter-firm cooperation in R&D'. *Journal of Evolutionary Economics,* 10: 243–71.

PART IV

New Challenges in Europe: Inequality, Sustainability, and Organizational Innovation

8

The Learning Economy and International Inequality

CHRIS FREEMAN

This chapter is in five parts. Section 8.1 introduces briefly the theme of widening gaps between rich and poor countries. Section 8.2 discusses the analogous
problem of widening gaps in the distribution of income within countries. Section 8.3 links these problems of inequality to long-term changes in technology
and to the problems of 'catch-up' by countries that have fallen behind. Section 8.4 relates this discussion to contemporary problems of catch-up in information and communication technology (ICT). The final section presents
conclusions and points to some important differences between the international and national dimensions of inequality.

8.1. Introduction

According to economic historians (e.g. Bairoch 1981) the very large gaps
which now exist between rich and poor countries opened up only in the eight-
eenth century. Before that, there were certainly enclaves of wealth for small
numbers of people, as for example, in the city states of medieval Italy, but the
huge systematic differences between large populations characteristic of the
contemporary world economy did not yet exist (Table 8.1).

It is relatively non-controversial that the emergence and widening of these
huge international disparities in the nineteenth and twentieth centuries is
attributable to changes in technology during and since the industrial revolution and, more controversially, to variations in the 'social capability' for
catching up in technology and management of the economy.

This chapter argues that the phenomenon of international inequality and
the related problem of inequality within countries may best be understood in
the light of a systematic theory of technical change and of long cycles in economic growth. Schumpeter did not himself much study either the problems
of international inequality or the problems of inequalities within nations, but
his theory of successive industrial revolutions nevertheless offers a basis for
the interpretation of both phenomena. We take first the question of inequality within countries.

TABLE 8.1. *Estimates of pre-industrial per capita GNP*
(at 1960 US dollars and prices)

Countries now developed	Period	GNP per capita
United Kingdom	1700	160–200
United States	1710	200–260
France	1781–90	170–200
Russia	1860	160–200
Sweden	1860	190–230
Japan	1885	160–200
Countries now less developed		
Egypt	1887	170–210
Ghana	1891	90–150
India	1900	130–160
Iran	1900	140–220
Jamaica	1832	240–280
Mexico	1900	150–190
Philippines	1902	170–210

Source: Bairoch 1981.

8.2. **Long Swings in Social Policy and Inequality**

Concern with social inequality is a recurrent theme of political life. Ever since the Old Testament prophets, if not earlier, many people have found something morally repulsive about the coexistence of extremes of wealth and poverty, especially when the highest incomes and the largest fortunes were not earned by hard work or by exceptional creativity. This ethical concern has been periodically reinforced by fear and by prudence—the fear of rebellions and social unrest and prudence in attempting to avert rebellion by timely reforms. Although seldom, if ever, approaching a truly egalitarian distribution of income and wealth (which was in fact rarely advocated), these pressures did lead periodically to a wave of social reforms which mitigated the worst hardships in the lives of the poor and the socially excluded (to use today's fashionable terminology).

In the 1980s and 1990s it has sometimes seemed that both the ethical concern and even the prudence had disappeared. In the United Kingdom and the United States especially, but also in many other European countries, the trend of fiscal policy which had been flowing strongly in favour of progressive taxation ever since the Second World War, was reversed. After the war, high levels of taxation on high incomes had been widely advocated and accepted as the norm. So general was this trend that Williamson and Lindert (1980: 33), historians of wealth and poverty in the United States, committed themselves in 1980 to this generalization: 'In contrast with the previous periods of wealth levelling, the twentieth century levelling has not been reversed.'

Unfortunately for their generalization very soon afterwards, of course, it was reversed, not only in the United States but worldwide. Even in countries like Sweden, fiscal regimes were modified in a regressive direction and the biggest changes of all came in the former communist countries, from a rather egalitarian distribution of income to an extremely unequal distribution (and often no income at all for the poorest). This trend has also been strong in countries like China, which have remained nominally communist, whilst moving towards free-market economies. In the UK, the share of the lowest 20% of household disposable incomes fell from 10% in 1979 to 6% in 1992, while the share of the top 20% rose from 35 to 43% (Table 5.19 of *Social Trends*, CSO 1995).

That was a pretty drastic and rapid change in the space of little more than a decade in the 1980s, brought about mainly by a combination of mass unemployment on the one hand and big tax reductions for the rich on the other. It was a major reversal of the social policies pursued by all the major political parties in the UK from the 1940s to the 1970s. These policies, advocated by economists such as Keynes, and social reformers such as Eleanor Rathbone and William Beveridge, found their embodiment in the 'welfare state', a typical creation of this period in many other European countries as well as in the UK.

From the example of the twentieth century in Europe, it seems that there have been long swings in attitudes towards inequality and social policy. Brian Berry and his colleagues in the University of Texas found evidence of similar long swings over two centuries in the United States:

In the two-hundred year history of American macro-economic development there have been four great surges in inequality. Each followed a stagflation crisis and was accompanied by a turn of the electorate to more conservative commercially-oriented candidates for the Presidency and Congress. Each surge was followed in turn by an egalitarian backlash in which a political agenda dominated by technological innovation, efficiency and growth was replaced by one concerned with social innovation, equality and redistribution   (Berry *et al.*, 1995, abstract).

Should these long swings be attributed simply to electoral pendulum-type changes in political mood over successive generations or are they related in some way to changes in the economy and in technology?

Eleanor Rathbone, like her two great fellow reformers, Beveridge and Keynes, had little or nothing to say about technology or technical change, and it may therefore seem odd to link their great reforming achievements to this topic. Not only did they and many other economists ignore technical change but most engineers and scientists also would not see any connection between technology, inequality, and social justice. However, this chapter will attempt to show that there is indeed a connection.

8.3. Long Waves and Technology

At the simplest level, it is of course obvious that the standard of living for all of us depends on the achievements of science and technology. Since Adam Smith's *Wealth of Nations* and Marshall's comments on *Knowledge as the Chief Engine of Production* the role of technical change in economic growth has been universally accepted by all schools of economists. The so-called new growth theory gives to research, development, and education a more central role than earlier growth models, but no economist of repute had ever denied their importance.

Schumpeter suggested in his magnum opus, *Business Cycles* (1939), that waves of new investment were generated by the diffusion of new technologies. In his theory, the ability and initiative of entrepreneurs, drawing upon the discoveries and ideas of scientists and inventors, create entirely new opportunities for investment, growth, and employment. The exceptional profits made from these innovations are then the decisive signal to swarms of imitators generating bandwagon and multiplier effects throughout the system. Following the Russian economist Nikolai Kondratieff, he argued that successive industrial revolutions led to long cycles of about fifty years' duration (Table 8.2 and Figure 8.1). Schumpeter studied the extraordinarily rapid growth of the cotton and iron industries in the first industrial revolution, of steam power and railways in the second, and of electrification in the third. He observed that innovations tend to cluster together in relation to new infrastructures, so that the growth of the economy depends on a succession of industrial revolutions.

In a passage which is seldom referred to Keynes (1930) fully acknowledged the significance of these influences on investment behaviour:

> In the case of fixed capital it is easy to understand why fluctuations should occur in the rate of investment. Entrepreneurs are induced to embark on the production of fixed capital or deterred from doing so by their expectations of the profits to be made. Apart from the many minor reasons why these should fluctuate in a changing world, Professor Schumpeter's explanation of the major movements may be unreservedly accepted.

The big investment booms and full employment, whether in the 1850s and 1860s, or the 'belle epoque' before the First World War, or the 'golden age' of the 1950s and 1960s, were followed by fairly prolonged periods of recession, depression, and high unemployment. In Schumpeter's scheme, these recessions were the result of the erosion of profits from the previous wave of technology and the necessity for a new infrastructure and new industries to unleash the next wave.

Unemployment in periods of deep structural change is itself one of the main sources of inequality. These periods have been well described as 'crises of structural adjustment' because there is a mismatch between the skills and

TABLE 8.2. *Long waves in the world economy*

Kondratieff Wave	Dominant technological regime	Emergence and formation of the constellation	Core inputs	Carrier branches	Other leading sectors	Infrastructures
1st Age of cotton, iron and water power	1790s–1840s	1750s–1790s	Iron	Cotton	Potteries Water wheels Iron products	Canals Water power
2nd Age of railways, steam power, and mechanization	1840s–1890s	1790s–1840s	Coal Iron	Railways Steam engines	Machine tools Coal gas Iron steam ships	Iron rail networks Telegraph Shipping lines
3rd Age of steel, electricity, and imperialism	1890s–1940s	1850s–1890s	Steel	Electrical products Heavy engineering	Steel ships Steel products Copper Heavy chemicals	Electric power generation and distribution Steel rail networks Global shipping
4th Age of oil, automobiles, mass production, and total war	1940s–1990s	1900s–1940s	Oil Gas	Automobiles Aircraft	Refineries and refinery products Synthetic materials Consumer durables Tankers	Motor highways Airlines Service stations Airports
5th Age of computers, semiconductors, and Internet	2000–?	1950s–1990s	Micro-electronics (chips)	Computers Software	Video Information Services	Telecommun-ications Internet Air freight

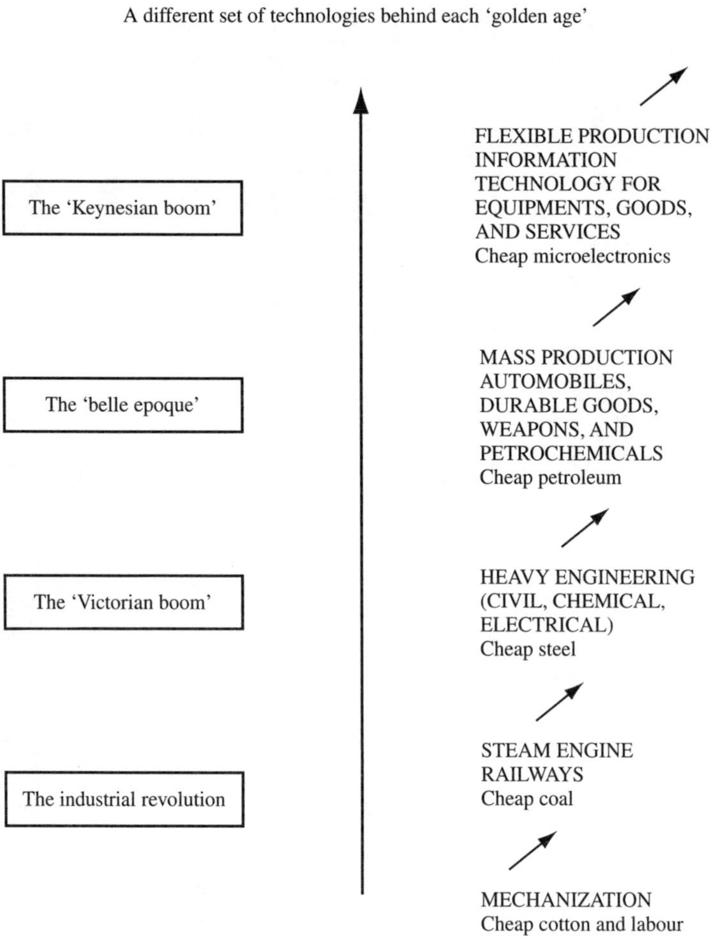

A different set of technologies behind each 'golden age'

The 'Keynesian boom'	FLEXIBLE PRODUCTION INFORMATION TECHNOLOGY FOR EQUIPMENTS, GOODS, AND SERVICES Cheap microelectronics
The 'belle epoque'	MASS PRODUCTION AUTOMOBILES, DURABLE GOODS, WEAPONS, AND PETROCHEMICALS Cheap petroleum
The 'Victorian boom'	HEAVY ENGINEERING (CIVIL, CHEMICAL, ELECTRICAL) Cheap steel
The industrial revolution	STEAM ENGINE RAILWAYS Cheap coal

MECHANIZATION
Cheap cotton and labour

FIG. 8.1. *Historical experience*

institutions of the older technologies and those that are needed for the new wave of technologies. Shortages and surpluses exist side by side, as in the case of the shortage of software designers and engineers which has persisted ever since the 1970s right through a period of massive unemployment. It was for this reason that Schumpeter maintained that aggregate statistics of GNP or of industrial production can conceal as much as they reveal, since they are the outcome of diverse trends in the economy. There is general agreement that structural unemployment has been the main problem from the 1970s onwards, especially in Europe. However, although it has often been severe and threatens now to become more severe worldwide, unemployment has not been the only source of growing inequality over the last twenty years. Changes in earnings have also been a major source of inequality.

The effects of the uneven distribution of social costs and benefits are clearly visible in the statistics of earnings for the 1980s and 1990s (Table 8.3). Twelve out of seventeen OECD countries showed an increased dispersion of earnings in the 1980s, four showed no change and only one (Germany) showed a decrease. In the 1970s the reverse was true. In that decade only one country showed an increase in inequality—the United States—while most others showed a decrease in dispersion. These statistics are for income before tax. Taking into account that, as we have seen, fiscal changes in the UK and many other countries have been regressive in this period, the increase of inequality in incomes has been substantial for those in employment.

Similar changes took place in previous waves of technical change: the earnings of engine drivers and fitters in the nineteenth century, of electricians in the 1890s, of assembly line workers in the 1940s and 1950s, and of software

TABLE 8.3. *General pattern of changes in the dispersion of earnings in the 1970s and 1980s hourly earnings or earnings of fulltime workers*

	1970s	1980s	Comments on extent and type of changes in dispersion
Australia	−	+	Increase in the dispersion from 1979 onwards
Austria	−	+	Increase from 1980 to 1989
Belgium		+	Slight increase due to gains at top over 1983–8
Canada	0	+	Increase mainly due to gains at top
Denmark		0	Slight gains at top and bottom
Finland	−	0	Slight gains at top and bottom
France	−	−/+	Decrease in dispersion ended in 1983
Germany	0	−	Decrease mainly due to gains at bottom
Italy	−	0	Gains at top and bottom
Japan		+	Increase due to gains at top
Netherlands	0	−/+	Slight decrease to 1984, then slight increase
Norway		0	Gains at top and bottom
Portugal		+	Increase between 1985 and 1990
Spain	− −/0	+	Sharp decrease in mid-1970s; rise in 1980s
Sweden	0	0/+	Increase after 1986, except for low-paid women
United Kingdom	−	++	Increase from 1979 onwards
United States	+	++	Increase for men only in 1970s; strong gains at top in 1980s

Key:
+   Increase in dispersion
++   Strong increase
−   Decrease
− −   Strong decrease
0   No clear change (perhaps changes at top and bottom working in opposite directions)
+/−   Increase followed by decrease (etc.)
Blank No information available

Source: OECD 1993.

engineers and programmers in the 1980s were all above the average earnings of the time. It is obvious that in any market system the shortage of workers in rapidly expanding occupations will have these effects because of lags in supply.

As the notion of 'information rich' and 'information poor' households suggests, social inequality is not only a question of employment and unemployment. Each new wave of technical change brings with it many social benefits in the form of new more skilled occupations and professions, and higher standards of living for many people based on the growth of new industries and services. But each wave also brings high social costs in the form of erosion of old skills and occupations, the decline of some older industries, services, and industrial areas. This uneven distribution of social costs and benefits occurs also on an international scale, with some nations taking full advantage of the new technologies and others unable to do so.

The combined effect of prolonged periods of high unemployment together with increased dispersion of earnings and increasingly regressive taxation has been to create or to enlarge an 'underclass' in the UK, Russia, France, Spain, and many other countries. A huge underclass already existed in Mexico, Brazil, and most other countries of Latin America and Africa, and this is growing even faster now in Asia also. A rise in social tensions, crime, and ethnic hostility was observable almost everywhere in the 1980s and was clearly associated with the loss of social cohesion and increasing insecurity of employment. The reduction in crime in the United States in the 1990s was not simply due to new methods of policing but also to the temporarily lower levels of unemployment.

The international dimension of the growth of inequality is even more serious than the domestic problems in the richer countries since the poverty in the Third World is far more extreme (Table 8.4).[1] Abramovitz (1986) coined the expression 'social capability' to describe that capacity to make institutional changes which led to this divergence in growth rates. He was himself one of the pioneers of 'growth accounting' but, as he cogently pointed out, the accumulation of capital and increase in the labour force are not in themselves sufficient to explain these varying rates of economic growth. The huge divergence in growth rates which is so obvious a feature of long-term economic growth over the past two centuries must be attributed in large measure to the presence or absence of social capability for institutional change, and especially for those types of institutional change that facilitate and stimulate a high rate of technical change, i.e. innovation systems. Institutional changes were, of course, essential for the accumulation of capital itself.

---

[1] According to the *World Development Report 1999/2000*, the gap in terms of income per capita between rich and poor countries kept growing all through the period 1970–95 (World Bank 1999: 14).

TABLE 8.4. *Estimates of trends in per capita GNP* (1960 US$ and Prices, 1750–1977)

Year	(1) Developed countries Per capita 1960 US$ and prices	(2) Third World Per capita 1960 US$ and prices	(3) Gaps Ratio of the most developed to the least developed
1750	182	188	1.8
1800	198	188	1.8
1860	324	174	4.5
1913	662	192	10.4
1950	1054	203	17.9
1970	2229	380	25.7

Source: Bairoch 1981: 7–8.

The rise of pervasive new technologies involves the emergence of some qualitatively new features in the social and economic system. Partly as a result of historical accidents and partly as a result of deliberate policies and their domination of international institutions, some countries have proved more adept in exploiting the potential of these new technologies both in world trade and in domestic growth. Until the 1990s some of the East Asian countries were good examples of accelerated catch-up. Both their rapid catch-up in the 1970s and 1980s and the crisis that they experienced in the mid-1990s demand some explanation in terms of technical and institutional change.

8.4. Catch-up in ICT and International Inequality

Whereas real per capita incomes were actually falling over the 1980s in Africa and Latin America, they were rising quite fast in South Asia and very rapidly in East Asia (Table 8.5). The East Asian countries were especially successful in expanding their production and exports of electronics and telecommunication equipment, which were by far the fastest growing sectors in world trade. Although they are all relatively new, the electronic industries vary in their skill intensity and technology intensity. The general pattern is clearly for the most skill- and technology-intensive activities to remain in Japan, with the least skill-intensive increasingly based in the second tier of South East Asian countries or in South Asia. The 'four tigers' and China occupy an intermediate position, but analysis of the trends in their exports shows a steadily rising ratio of skill-intensive and technology-intensive products. This shift was made possible by active education, industrial, and technology policies within these countries (Amsden 1991, 1992; Amsden and Hikino 1991; Wade 1990).

TABLE 8.5. *Comparative growth rates sub-continental regions, 1965–1999*

GDP, % p.a.	1965–80	1980–9	1990–9 (est.)
East Asia	7.5	7.9	7.2
South Asia	3.9	5.1	5.5
Africa (Sub-Sahara)	4.0	2.1	2.7
Latin America	5.8	1.6	3.1
GDP per capita, % p.a.	1965–80	1980–9	1990–9 (est.)
East Asia	5.0	6.3	5.7
South Asia	1.5	2.9	3.4
Africa (Sub-Sahara)	1.1	−1.2	0.2
Latin America	3.5	−0.5	1.2

Source: World Bank 1991. Own estimates 1990s.

What the post-war experience demonstrates therefore is an extremely uneven process of catch-up by developing countries, depending upon their technical capability and on imports of technologies. But the import of the technologies is very far from the costless diffusion of perfect information assumed in pure versions of neo-classical economic theory. Technologies cannot be taken 'off the shelf' and simply put into use anywhere. Without infrastructural investment in education, training, R&D, and other scientific and technical activities, very little can be accomplished by way of assimilation of imported technologies. The Asian countries were by far the most active in promoting these policies. Hobday (1995) has pointed to the variety of strategies in the East Asian countries, all designed in different ways steadily to upgrade local technological capability. The contrast between the rapid rise in the performance of in-house R&D in firms in both South Korea and Taiwan, and its low level, stagnation, or non-existence in firms in most developing countries, is especially notable.

The rise of in-house R&D in the 1970s led to an extraordinary increase in numbers of patents (Table 8.6) and this is perhaps the most striking confirmation of the active learning system in South Korea and Taiwan. Between 1977–82 and 1990–6, the number of patents taken out in the USA by Brazil, Argentina, Mexico, and Venezuela nearly doubled from 570 to 1,106, but in the same period the numbers taken out by the 'four tigers' increased nearly 30 times over, from 671 to 18,763. This contrast has been well described by Viotti (1997) as a contrast between active and passive learning systems.

In the case of Korea nearly half of the patents taken out between 1969 and 1992 were in six technical fields in the electronics area (semiconductors, computers, imaging and sound, instruments, electrical devices, and photocopying). In the case of Taiwan the increase in total numbers of patents was even more remarkable and they were spread over a wider technical area, including especially metal products and machinery as well as electrical and electronic

TABLE 8.6. *Emerging sources of technology in terms of ownership of US patents*

Year	1983–9	Share	1990–6	Share
Taiwan	2,292	0.41	11,040	1.43
S. Korea	580	0.10	5,970	0.77
Israel	1,507	0.27	2,685	0.35
Hong Kong	633	0.11	1,416	0.18
S. Africa	699	0.12	787	0.10
Mexico	289	0.05	314	0.04
Brazil	212	0.04	413	0.05
China P. Rep.	142	0.03	353	0.05
Argentina	135	0.02	187	0.02
Singapore	65	0.01	337	0.04
Venezuela	122	0.02	192	0.02
India	96	0.02	204	0.03
East and Central Europe	2,417	0.43	1317	0.17
Sub-total	9,189	1.62	25,215	3.26
Other developing countries	902	0.16	1,494	0.19
Total US Patents	565,739	100.00	772,927	100.00

Source: US Patents and Trademarks Office (1997).

devices (Choung 1995). Firms in both Korea and Taiwan were so successful in their catch-up that they began to export technology themselves and to invest overseas in older industrial countries like the UK as well as in the less-developed countries of South-East Asia. However, despite their great success in the 1970s and 1980s and indeed, partly because of it, the global economy in the 1990s presented new and acute problems for those catch-up countries that made good progress in closing the gap in manufacturing. The liberalization of capital movements which has taken place exposes all countries to the instability and shocks that occur in any part of the system. Events during 1997 and 1998 showed that these shocks can be propagated throughout the system and that however good the national innovation system it is always still part of a broader global economic and political system.

Many of the comments on the East Asian crisis of 1997–8 are characterized by emphasis on the supposed sins of the Asian governments. In particular, they have blamed corruption of governments for some of the unwise and inept investment decisions of the 1990s. Of course, there has been corruption in many Asian countries and in some, especially Indonesia, it has been on a very large scale. There has also been corruption in European countries and in the United States. But it is fanciful to put the whole blame for the collapse on corruption and to ignore the misallocation of private investment. As Jeffrey Sachs (1997) has put it: 'It is somehow comforting, as in a good morality tale, to blame corruption and mismanagement in Asia for the crisis. Yes, these exist, and they weaken economic life. But the crisis itself is more pedestrian.

No economy can easily weather a panicked withdrawal of confidence, especially if the money was flooding in just months before'.

He continues:

The problems emerged in the private sector. In all of the countries, international money-market managers and investment banks went on a lending binge from 1993 to 1996. To a varying extent in all of the countries, the short-term borrowing from abroad was used, unwisely, to support longterm investments in real estate and other non-exporting sectors.

The problems of catch-up in technology will now be aggravated by acute social tensions engendered by the investment crisis and the IMF medicine. In a region previously characterized by rather high levels of employment and a strong demand for labour, unemployment is becoming a major social problem. The president of the World Bank, James Wolfensohn, was one of the first to recognize that the social problems associated with high unemployment would now require major policy attention, including World Bank programmes:

The region must tackle social issues if it is to foster sustainable economic recovery and East Asia's financial crisis risks undermining one of the most remarkable economic and social achievements of modern history. What began as a financial crisis has spilled over into the real economy, severely hitting both production and employment.

In that case, was the miracle a mirage? Emphatically not. No other group of countries in the world has produced more rapid economic growth and dramatic reductions in poverty.

They did it by getting the fundamentals right—with high savings, a commitment to education, sound fiscal policies and an outward orientation. But as the crisis has revealed, political, financial and corporate structures were not well suited to cope with the demands of an increasingly globalised economy' (*Financial Times*, 29 January 1998).

As recent events have shown, dependence on the global economy, and on the IMF and World Bank, can be a mixed blessing. If these institutions were operating as Keynes had originally envisioned, there would be much greater reason for optimism. In the present state of globalization, the instability of the system and the repercussions of the Asian crisis in Eastern Europe, Latin America, and, ultimately, in Western Europe and the United States itself seem more likely to aggravate the turbulence.

This means that the reform of the IMF is now becoming an urgent question for the management of the global economy. Again, as Jeffrey Sachs (1998) has pointed out, the lack of accountability and transparency in the operations of the IMF means that disagreement with its advice is now often regarded as synonymous with a sinful rejection of financial rectitude punishable by the markets. Yet its advice has often been mistaken and not only in East Asia. It forecast growth of 1.5% in Mexico in 1995 after the Mexican financial crisis, but actual growth was minus 6.1%, and again in Argentina forecast growth was 2% and actual growth minus 4.6%. Its handling of successive crises in Latin America in 1995, in Bulgaria in 1996, and East Asia in 1997 and 1998 calls into question its ability to handle the volatility of the private capital market in a way which does not damage future growth in countries in which the 'fundamentals' for sustained growth are relatively favourable.

8.5. Conclusions

Those economists and technologists who see in computer technology, information technology, and the Internet an enormous potential for new employment and a new wave of high investment and high growth are not mistaken. There is indeed such a potential but all previous experience shows that when a new pervasive technology enters the economic system, it can do so only after a prolonged social process of learning, reform, and adaptation of old institutions. It was Carlota Perez (1983) who pointed out that there would be a mismatch between the institutions created to regulate the previously dominant technology and those needed to regulate a new one. The technical, political, and economic uncertainties are so great that an uneven and conflict-ridden process is the rule rather than the exception. Temporary over-capacity in the fastest growing new industries was characteristic of all the big technologies in the past, as in semiconductors and computers today. There was huge over-capacity in the Detroit automobile industry in the 1930s, and in the British cotton industry in the 1830s. No-one can predict accurately at the time what will be the future size and characteristics of such new markets; still less the share of the individual firms or countries. These uncertainties are compounded by waves of euphoria and panic in the financial markets and by the general instability of investment in a capitalist market economy.

In the 1920s some US economists and businessmen had assumed that Henry Ford had superseded Karl Marx and that a bull market on the stock exchange could continue long into the future. This neglect of both long and short business cycles was repeated in the 1990s when references were frequently made to the supposed 'end of history' and 'a new paradigm' of low inflation, full employment, and high growth was supposed to have eliminated the business cycle. Alan Greenspan showed some doubts about this.

Cycles of over-capacity and of shortages are a familiar accompaniment of waves of technical change. The huge over-capacity in Asia in the production of electronic consumer goods was one such episode and the over-capacity in memory chips and semiconductors is another episode in a story which has long been familiar to economic (Kaplinsky 1998: 35).

These phenomena in the 'real' economy interact with political events and with financial markets to generate the instability characteristic of the periods of structural 'crises of adjustment'. In the 1890s as in the 1990s outward flows of speculative investment to 'emerging economies' aggravated this instability. The headlong deregulation and liberalization of capital movements in the 1970s and 1980s have created a particularly unstable situation in the world economy at the turn of the millennium, as both the speed and scale of capital movements are greatly increased by the use of information technology and of ingenious financial innovations such as derivatives. The mathematical pretensions of the derivatives models which underlie the speculative investments of the 'hedging funds', even if they are developed by Nobel prize-winners, would be laughable if they were not tragic in their consequences.

The present phase of the 'information revolution' therefore calls out more than ever, as Carlota Perez insisted in her original work, for institutional and social innovations that could create a stable regulatory framework for the constructive application of this extraordinary powerful technology in world-wide economic growth. Another *belle époque*, in which the potential productivity gains of information technology are more fully realized is by no means inevitable. It depends on the policies which are now adopted.

This chapter has argued that both the increases and reductions in inequality within nations and the disparities between nations are related to the long waves of technical change. However, there is an important difference between the two phenomena with respect to timing. The widening gap within countries develops mainly during the crises of structural adjustment in those countries which are leading in technical innovation, and is associated with the unemployment, skill changes, and organizational changes in the production system. The reduction of inequality occurs mainly once a major new technology has become the dominant regime, the economy recovers to a state of full or near-full employment, new skills are widely diffused and socialized, and new movements for social reform have addressed some of the main sources of social conflict.

The timing of catch-up by countries which have fallen behind the world technological frontier is a rather different matter. There is inevitably a time lag before even those countries with strong social capability are able to assimilate complex new technological systems. There may be major barriers in the form of intellectual property rights as well as barriers in the availability of finance, skills, and market access. Nevertheless, latecomer countries may enjoy some advantages of the kind identified by Gerschenkron, provided they adopt the type of policies for science and technology which Perez and Soete (1988) have indicated, and which have been briefly discussed in section 8.4. As they have shown, costs of diffusion and imitation, as well as of original innovation, can be reduced once an autonomous capability has been established. For all these reasons, the most favourable period for closing international gaps and inequalities is likely to be during the years of a dominant technological regime and perhaps even more when profitability of that regime is becoming eroded in the leading countries. At this stage, finance capital is likely to be searching for new areas of profit; investment in catch-up countries can provide one such opportunity. The flows of foreign investment to Third World countries before and after the First World War and again in the 1970s and 1980s provide illustrations of this phenomenon.

REFERENCES

ABRAMOVITZ, M. (1986). 'Catching up, forging ahead and falling behind'. *Journal of Economic History*, 46: 385–406.

AMSDEN, A. H. (1991). 'Diffusion of development. The late industrialising model and Greater East Asia'. *American Economic Review*, 81/2: 282–6.

——(1992). 'A theory of government interaction in late industrialisation', in L. Putterman and D. Rueschmeyer (eds.), *The State and Market in Development*. New York: Lynn Riener.

——and HIKINO, T. (1991). 'Borrowing technology or innovating: An exploration of two paths to industrial development'. Working Paper 31, New School for Social Research. New York.

BAIROCH, P. (1981) 'The main trends in national economic disparities since the industrial revolution', in P. Bairoch and M. Levy-Loboyen, *Disparities in Economic Development Since the Industrial Revolution*. London: Macmillan.

BERRY, B. J. L., HARPHAM, E. J., and ELLIOTT, E. (1995). 'Long Swings in American Inequality, the Kuznets conjecture revisited'. *Papers in Regional Science*, 74/2: 153–74.

CHOUNG, J.-Y. (1995). 'Technological capabilities of Korea and Taiwan: An analysis using US patenting statistics', Steep Discussion Paper, 26, SPRU, University of Sussex.

CSO (1995). *Social Trends*. London: HMPO.

HOBDAY, M. (1995). *Innovation in East Asia: The Challenge to Japan*. Aldershot: Edward Elgar.

KEYNES, J. M. (1930). *A Treatise on Money*. London: Macmillan.

OECD (1993). *Employment Outlook*. Paris: OECD.

PEREZ, C. (1983). 'Structural change and the assimilation of new technologies in the economic and social system'. *Futures*, 15/5: 357–75.

——and SOETE, L. (1988). 'Catching up in technology: Entry barriers and windows of opportunity', in G. Dosi, C. Freeman, R. Nelson, G. Silverberg, and L. Soete (eds.), *Technical Change and Economic Theory*. London: Pinter.

SACHS, J. D. (1997). 'IMF orthodoxy isn't what Southeast Asia needs'. *International Herald Tribune,* 4 November.

——(1998). 'Out of the frying pan into the IMF Fire'. *Observer*, 8 February.

SCHUMPETER, J. A. (1939). *Business Cycles*, 2 vols. New York: McGraw Hill.

US Patents and Trademarks Office (1997). TAF Special Report: AU Patents, Washington, DC.

VIOTTI, E. B. (1997). 'Passive and active national learning systems'. Ph.D. dissertation, New School for Social Research.

WADE, R. (1990). *Governing the Market: Economic Theory and the Role of Government in East Asian Industrialisation*. Princeton, NJ: Princeton University Press.

WILLIAMSON, J., and LINDERT, P. H. (1980). *American Inequality: A Micro-economic History.* New York: Academic Press.

WOLFENSOHN, J. (1998). 'Asia, the long view'. *Financial Times*, 29 January.

World Bank (1991). *World Development Report*, 1991. New York: Oxford University Press.

——(1999) *World Development Report, 1999/2000.* New York: Oxford University Press.

9
Social Exclusion in the Learning Economy

GERD SCHIENSTOCK

fo2
H55
I38
630

9.1. Introduction

Social exclusion has become the key concept in the international social policy debate. At the end of this century, as Touraine (1991) argues, the point is no longer a matter of being 'up or down', but of being 'in or out'. The notion of social exclusion implies a relative and process-linked vision of degradation and deterioration with respect to a certain status and situation experienced previously. At the end of this process, people find themselves cut off from all circles of social exchange. Integrated subjects can become vulnerable because of organizational transformation in the working environment and these vulnerable people can fall into the precipice of social exclusion.

Although recognizing the complexity of the phenomenon of exclusion, we will here focus on the sphere of work (see also Nasse 1992). Employment is seen as the core of the social tie that links individuals with society, as our modern societies have privileged economic exchange and thus remunerated work (de Foucauld 1992). In the following, we shall analyse the impact the emerging learning economy may have on processes of social exclusion.[1]

9.2. Globalization and the Learning Economy

There is widespread agreement that we are living through a period of time characterized by rapid and fundamental economic changes. Some authors refer to the present stage of development as a learning economy (Lundvall and Johnson 1994; Lundvall 1996). The growing importance of learning in economic life can be attributed to the process of globalization of markets. Globalization not only leads to an intensification of competition but also to the establishment of new rules of the 'competition game'.

There is no doubt that the ability to produce the required number of quality products just in time and within a reasonable cost framework is a prerequisite

[1] Surprisingly, the system approach in innovation theory has not so far taken up the problem of social exclusion, although conceptual tools are available, such as the 'unintended consequences of purposeful action' or 'feedback loop'.

for modern enterprises to hold their own in worldwide competition. But these criteria develop more and more into entrance barriers to the global market, while economic success nowadays depends upon companies' capability to innovate rapidly and continuously to develop new products that meet market demands.

The capacity of companies to produce incremental innovations continuously depends on their learning capabilities a great deal. Global innovation competition can be seen as the key driving force behind the new developments that are likely to enlarge the learning capability of companies and thus increase and accelerate companies' innovation activities. These new developments include a change in the nature of work, the introduction of new organization forms, the increasing application of modern information technology and its intelligent use, and a growing investment in human resources.

In a learning or reflexive economy, as Lash (1994) calls it, a greater proportion of the production process than heretofore must be accounted for by a knowledge-intensive design process and a smaller proportion by the material production process. Furthermore, companies' innovativeness depends upon their competence to interpret and translate new scientific knowledge; otherwise they can hardly make use of this 'public good'. There is also increasing demand for other knowledge-intensive business services: marketing, management, organization, training, or documentation, not to mention new ICT-related services (see, for example, Miles 1995).

In a situation of global innovation competition, companies must be able to cope with great uncertainty, a situation for which the traditional Fordist production model is not designed. Therefore, new organization forms allowing for more flexibility, adaptability, and learning have to be applied. Companies move to leaner and flatter corporate structures by introducing group work and cross-functional design teams (Kanter 1991). This strategy of vertical de-integration is accompanied by an organization strategy of functional or horizontal integration, aiming at intensifying internal information and knowledge exchange. We can conclude that the learning economy is based on the network as a central governance mechanism. Intra-organizational network structures develop among sub-units, replacing the bureaucratic governance regime; these increasingly include global production networks. At the same time, an inter-organizational network structure develops among companies, replacing the market as the traditional mode of co-ordinating exchange.

So far, modern ICTs have been used mainly to control or automate the work process. However, it may be more efficient to use ICTs for supporting the introduction of new organization forms that foster innovation and learning, as these technologies do not determine organization structures but provide options for designing work and business processes according to other drivers of change. Furthermore, modern ICTs can be used as media to exchange huge amounts of information and knowledge rapidly within and between companies. As they bridge both time and space, they will likely improve and speed up the innovation process.

It is generally accepted that, in the current stage of global innovation competition, the development of human resources is inextricably linked with the economic success of companies. Too little investment in human resources often becomes a limiting factor in relation to innovation and economic success (OECD 1998). However, when we talk about the need to invest in human capital, we have to go beyond the argument of a general trend towards higher qualification or re-skilling. Instead, we have to point to particular forms of knowledge, skills, competencies, work orientations, and work virtues. Digital knowledge, multi-skilling, social competencies, management competencies, quality consciousness, creativity, and entrepreneurship are some of the new qualifications needed to draw the maximum gain from the new organization forms and continual innovations.

9.3. **Learning Organizations and Social Exclusion**

The move into a learning economy will have major consequences for working people. Due to the growing transformation pressure, they face an increasingly unstable environment. The average worker is confronted with new tasks and problems and has to develop new skills and competencies more frequently than before. To be able to cope with unclear and unknown situations, workers have to learn how to learn. Slow learners, among them the unskilled, handicapped and elderly, will have difficulties in preparing themselves all the time for new tasks and problems; continuous learning may be beyond their capacity. Being under pressure to innovate continuously, companies may select only rapid learners, while they may dismiss slow learners (Lundvall and Nielsen 1999). This means that particularly unskilled or less-skilled workers are at risk of becoming unemployed.

The restructuring of firms stimulated by global competition and supported by information technology leads to a fundamental transformation of work regulation: the individualization of work in the labour process. The traditional form of work, based on fulltime employment, a career pattern over the life cycle, clear-cut occupational assignments, standardized working hours, and a collectively agreed wage, is shrinking continuously. The fastest-growing categories of work are temporary labour and part-time work. School leavers starting their working life rarely get a fulltime job. Also, self-employment is becoming a substantial component of the labour force. Although the broader category of 'flexible work' in various industrialized countries takes different forms (part-time, temporary work, and self-employment), we can clearly identify a general trend: in all countries traditional fulltime employment is increasingly replaced by 'flexible work'. In these countries, flexible work nowadays accounts for about 30–40% of the workforce (Castells 1996). As these 'flexible' workers are not covered by collective agreements, they may experience serious social disadvantages.

The introduction of the new organization form also leads to the desta- bilization of bureaucratic career structures enjoyed by a large proportion of managerial and professional staff. Fewer of those in such occupations can now be guaranteed lifelong employment and continuous career advancement. With the demise of the bureaucratic business structure, these groups of work- ers have to accept flexible careers; an inevitable feature of 'flexible work' and 'flexible career' patterns is that they are inherently insecure (Brown 1995).

A consequence of this development is that unemployment constantly affects new categories of people. The workers who have been employed for a long time in 'normal', that is to say non-precarious, conditions are now made redundant (Yépez del Castillo 1994). Of course, low-skilled workers are more threatened with becoming unemployed than qualified workers, but the lay- offs caused by outsourcing, streamlining, and restructuring often affect the middle management and narrowly trained experts in particular. In these cases, not only individual, less-qualified people are selected to become redun- dant; sometimes whole work groups and departments are closed down.

Restructuring strategies, caused by global competition, have contributed significantly to the massive increase in unemployment that has taken place in many industrial countries during recent years. What is striking, however, is not only the scale of unemployment but also its structuration. It is the increasing and long-lasting nature of the phenomenon that causes severe problems, since the share of the long-term unemployed among people with- out a job has been growing continuously in recent years. The proliferation of unstable forms of employment is an important factor that causes long-term unemployment. In a situation of decreasing labour demand, it becomes more and more difficult for the unemployed to find normal, non-precarious employment. Instead, the newly unemployed are constantly moving from one insecure and unskilled job to another, while young and highly qualified people are often the beneficiaries of newly created, more demanding jobs. A great number of the newly created jobs offer only atypical work contracts.

For those who are unemployed, the risk of becoming long-term unem- ployed and finally totally excluded from the labour market increases expo- nentially with the length of unemployment. 'This dual trend—precarious employment and recruitment of over-qualified workers—continuously pushes to the back of the queue those among the unemployed who are con- sidered to be the least productive' (Yépez del Castillo 1994). Women, unskilled workers and people over the age of 50 are the groups that are most at risk of becoming long-term unemployed.

Our future society is often described as being highly segmented. We can expect, it is argued, that only a small group of core workers will have a secure work status and contracts of indefinite duration. Core workers are the ones whose skills are most essential to the main activities of the firm. They are required to accept 'functional flexibility', which concerns the employer's ability to vary the allocation of work within the organization so that changes in their jobs can easily be made when required.

There is, however, another form of flexibility, often known as 'numerical flexibility'. This takes the form of varying the size of the workforce in response to changing requirements, whether these involve seasonal fluctuations, responses to changes in customer demand, or market changes. These forms of flexibility may involve the introduction of temporary working, part-time working, home-working, on-call working, or casual labour (Atkinson 1995). Workers in this segment can be called peripheral workers; they conduct the activities that are less critical to the firm's core activities. Many of these forms of flexible working involve the employment of women. These flexible workers may well find themselves outside the remit of social protection regulations, precarious, poorly paid, and socially marginalized (Huws 1998).

The third group comprises external workers distanced from the enterprise; generally they are service suppliers, sub-contractors, or self-employed workers. They do not have conventional career perspectives or employment security. It is likely that their employment status will change very often. People may be employed on the basis of a short-term conventional labour contract; they may work as independent consultants; or they may become unemployed for some time. They often work in temporary groups on a project basis; as soon as a project has been completed, the group dissolves and its members start to work in another group, often with different partners.

Our traditional understanding of core and peripheral workers does not seem to hold true any longer. Obviously, the new vulnerability of labour under the conditions of unrestrained flexibility does not concern only less-skilled or unskilled workers. We can see new risk groups developing, such as middle management, foremen, or some specialist groups, which were for a long time seen as core workers, sheltered by 'internal labour markets'. Evidently, for some groups of employees, formerly conceived of as core workers, these internal labour markets are about to disappear. Castells (1996) mentions that the jobs of the employees over 50 years of age are the first in line for any potential downsizing.

We can, on the other hand, no longer equate peripheral or external workers with those who have a weak labour market position. Among them we can identify at least two groups: low-skilled workers performing routine jobs (data processing), on the one hand; but also highly qualified self-employed specialists, on the other. The second group of workers actually has a very strong labour market position, drawing on their extensive networks and renewed knowledge to ensure effectiveness (Robins and Webster 1997). These 'networked people' can easily mobilize all the knowledge needed to solve complex problems. While a core labour force is still the norm in most firms, sub-contracting and consulting are fast-growing forms of obtaining professional work (Castells 1996).

No doubt self-employment has some advantages, such as independence and taking more responsibility. But not all people concerned have chosen 'self-employment' voluntarily; they are often forced to accept this new employment form as the result of the outsourcing strategies of companies. We can speak of the 'fictitious self-employed' as *de facto* they work as employees dependent on decisions taken by the management of the core company. The fact that the normally employed workers are replaced by the 'fictitious self-employed' may become a major problem as the latter are not covered by the protection mechanisms of labour and social laws (Enquete Kommission 1998). Labour is losing institutional protection and becomes increasingly dependent on individual bargaining conditions in a constantly changing labour market.

9.4. Regional Exclusion

Due to global competition, companies are forced to look for the most supportive environment for specific functions or products. The cost of leadership has to be combined with high quality, quick delivery, and product differentiation, companies break down their value chain into discrete functions and locate them where they can be performed most effectively (Ernst and Lundvall 1997). Cost-sensitive production is transferred to the regions[2] with cheap labour, whereas knowledge-intensive production and services will be located in regions with highly qualified labour and a developed information infrastructure.

New information technologies facilitate the global organization of companies' production and innovation processes. Moreover, as production becomes more science based, advantages such as a developed research infrastructure, a highly qualified workforce, or an innovative milieu are becoming more important environmental factors than natural resources, which means that a supportive environment for companies can deliberately be created. To become attractive for companies, nations or regions can set up specific organizations and institutions to support companies' innovation and production strategies. Scott (1996) stresses the importance of spatial proximity to co-ordinate economic activities, as the possibility to interact continuously facilitates collective learning processes. Obviously, this means that 'region-states' are now more appropriate for designing supportive environments than nation states.

It is argued that the globalization of markets will lead to economic convergence, as it allows each region to specialize and develop specific advantages that will attract large transnational companies to invest and set up a business. This argument neglects the fact that regional specialization is always tied up with the aims of companies. Companies' strategies, in order to organ-

---

[2] Here the term 'region' is understood as a sub-national territory.

ize their production processes on a global scale, do not only create opportunities for a 'high road development'. They also produce 'low road development' perspectives (Sengenberger and Pyke 1992), since for some of the products or parts, cheap labour and less-restrictive environmental regulations are seen as advantages which particular regions can offer. Due to the fact that companies, when organizing their production processes globally, are looking for both a 'high road' and a 'low road' environment, only a limited number of regions can acquire the position of a knowledge and decision centre in global business networks (Amin 1993). Many regions, although they are integrated in global production networks, are caught in the trap of a 'low road development'; less value creation per capita seems to be their fate. A less qualified workforce, traditional value patterns, ineffective institutions, and traditional regulation practices often reinforce this development, which makes the changeover from a low road to a high road development strategy very unlikely. Instead, the less-developed regions compete against each other; in this context, economic development becomes a 'zero sum game'; one region loses what the other gains. In their attempt to catch up with the high road regions, less developed regions start to overshadow each other through low wages, permissive environmental regulations, and open-handed subsidies (Schienstock 1997). Social exclusion, we can conclude, is no longer a phenomenon associated with individual courses of life only, but it is a collective fate of people living in 'low road' regions.

9.5. Information Economy and Social Exclusion

It is often argued that the transformation of the traditional industrial economy into what is called the 'information economy' or 'knowledge economy' will lead to new forms of social exclusion. Two trends are mentioned to underline this argument. One aspect is that the emerging organization forms of business processes and the developing network economy will result in the prioritization of certain types of occupations and workers. Robins and Webster mention the following groups: 'Those which manage and operate across global networks, those which are capable of offering design intensity, those which can provide high added value to products and services through scientific excellence, imaginative skill, financial acumen, or even effective advertising' (Robins and Webster 1997). It is assumed that in the future these symbolic analysts will make up about 30% of the whole workforce.

At the same time, modern ICTs have increased and will further increase the possibilities to codify large parts of human skills. The more knowledge becomes codifiable, the more the remaining non-codifiable part is likely to become even more crucial. People become de-skilled, as their knowledge is no longer an asset needed in the production process. Together with the widespread use of modern ICTs, 'skills mismatches' are more likely to be of a more pervasive and general nature (Soete 1996). This does not mean, of course, that tacit knowledge becomes less important in the information economy. Often, the codification of knowledge creates the need for new tacit knowledge, for example, for a worker to be able to sort out relevant information and to use it effectively.

The growth of a group of highly skilled and very flexible knowledge workers, on the one hand, and the increasing codification of knowledge, on the other, may lead to a process of segmentation in society. Authors like Reich (1991) and Castells (1996) assume that while the 'symbolic analysts' will rise in the upper ranks of companies, the great majority of workers, whose knowledge can be codified and whose work can be automated, will form a new underclass which will be more or less irrelevant for the information economy. The information age, according to the authors, will be one which excludes a great majority of people, not only in less developed parts of the world but also in the metropolitan societies.

Freeman and Soete reject the notion of skills-biased technical change as being too simple. Modern ICTs, they argue, have much more contradictory consequences. According to them, the substantial growth and employment potential of networking is typical of the most recent set of ICTs. 'At the same time, however, not being linked up to information networks necessarily implies being locked out of the efficiency gains associated with the use of ITs. Moreover, it implies being prevented from participating in the learning activities associated with new and more efficient uses of IT' (Freeman and Soete 1994). Lash argues in a similar way, speaking of 'reflexivity winners' and 'reflexivity losers'. 'Life chances in reflexive modernity are a question of access not to productive capital or production structures but instead of access to and place in the new information and communication structures' (Lash 1994).

9.6. Social Security and Policy Implications

There is a danger that, due to the individualization of work in the labour process, our work system will evolve into multifaceted, generalized flexibility for workers and working conditions (Castells 1996). Of course, the new work arrangements can have some transformation value for social life. As Hewitt (1993) argues, they may improve family relationships and may contribute to more egalitarian patterns between genders. At the same time, however, increasing job insecurity, growing unemployment or underemployment, and increasing inequality will lead to a widespread deterioration of living and working conditions. The transformation of the working system, according to Castells (1996), has already shaken our institutions, inducing a crisis between work and society. Of course, all these trends do not stem from the structural logic of the learning society but are helped by the powerful tools provided by modern ICTs and facilitated by the new organization forms. There is a need for stabilizing work and improving social security together with the transformation into a learning society.

9.7. Individual-targeted Strategies

Various approaches have been developed to prevent or combat social exclusion. They are based, as de Foucauld (1992) argues, on a concept of social justice different from the one underlying the post-war social consensus, which simply insured the population against predictable risks. We can distinguish between individual-targeted and general approaches. The individualistic approaches often define social exclusion in connection with citizenship and social rights. The Observatory on National Policies to Combat Social Exclusion, for example, states that social exclusion 'can be analysed in terms of the denial—or non-realization—of social rights' (Room 1995).

The right to work can be seen as a key social right. The emphasis here is on employment, not on income compensation through social welfare; integration into the work process is the aim of strategies to combat social exclusion. Therefore, the unemployed and school leavers having difficulties in finding a job are the main target groups. Three measures of an active labour market policy can be seen as key strategy elements:

(1) the readjustment of the unemployed to new labour market demands;
(2) the appropriation of wage subsidies for the creation of new jobs in firms; and
(3) the promotion of employment outside the labour market.

Training to readjust the unemployed to new labour market demands cannot be reduced to training workers in specialized knowledge only. Instead, it becomes more important to strengthen their labour market positions, as an increasing number of workers have to cope with the prospect of flexible careers in the future. Therefore, a variety of different skills and competencies, such as social skills, learning how to learn, digital skills, and management competencies, are becoming increasingly important.

Embracing intensive training programmes for long-term solutions is not sufficient. Job creation programmes for unskilled workers also have to be financed. There is, however, always the risk that wage subsidies for firms will not create new jobs or at least any stable employment. On the one hand, it is argued that companies will employ only those workers they need anyway; on the other hand, it is very likely that companies will hire only temporary workers. In the private sector, it is therefore important to combine employment based on wage subsidies with a qualification element.

In addition, including programmes that have a high growth potential to create jobs for the unskilled in community and personal services is needed.

Although ICTs will be used in this sector of the economy, the criteria and imperatives of international competition will not exert the same pressure to conform to the needs of the international markets (Freeman and Soete 1994). The promotion of employment in sheltered areas outside the labour market dissociates work from employment; this means that people become socially integrated, although they are not occupationally integrated. Furthermore, such a strategy helps people to manage 'non-employment' (Yépes del Castillo 1994). The promotion of employment outside the labour market is often combined with a policy of guaranteeing employment for those people who have been unemployed for a longer period of time.

From various evaluation studies, we know that competencies can be acquired more easily by people with employment than by those without employment (Schmid 1996). Therefore, combating social exclusion has to start while people are employed. Protective training and competence development becomes increasingly important. This includes various forms of home training on the basis of multimedia technology. The realization of the concept of lifelong learning may be helpful in avoiding precarious employment and may even support people in starting a new career in a more promising work environment. For workers in precarious employment, so-called adaptive training can be seen as a possible measure to avoid unemployment. In the case of skills mismatch, employees have to acquire new skills through further training inside or outside the company. This strategy should also become a part of companies' human resource management.

For some risk groups, continuous learning becomes a heavy burden. Particularly, older people often have difficulties in acquiring the knowledge needed for them to participate in learning organizations; their position on the labour market may be gradually weakened and, in the end, they may become excluded from the labour market (Ernst and Lundvall 1997). In their case, it is possible to protect them from being fired and becoming unemployed through collective agreements or legal regulations. The problem here is that protective regulations for specific groups increase the risk of other groups becoming unemployed. 'Social protection schemes have—in part at least—had a negative impact on employment in that they mainly have tended to protect people already in work, making their situation more secure and consolidating certain advantages. They have in effect proved to be an obstacle to the recruitment of job seekers or of new entrance to the labour market' (European Commission 1993).

A five-stage model of social exclusion is presented and strategies of intervention are suggested (see Fig. 9.1). The process runs from full integration (stable employment), through forms of precarious, intermittent, or seasonal employment, to unemployment and long-term unemployment, and results in total exclusion from the labour market when people become unemployable and have to live on public assistance.

Stage 1: Stable and long-term employment

Intervention options: continuous further training

Stage 2: Precarious, fragile employment

Intervention options: protection agreements, training to overcome mismatch between needed skills and existing qualifications, home training using multimedia technology

Stage 3: Unemployment

Intervention options: wage subsidies, adjustment training

Stage 4: Long-term unemployment

Intervention options: job guarantees, promotion of employment outside the labour market, further training to acquire jobs in developing new industries, and wage subsidies for firms to create new jobs

Stage 5: Final exclusion from the labour market

Intervention options: training to keep workers employable, social aid

FIG. 9.1. *The process of social exclusion and options for political intervention*

9.8. General Strategies

Active labour market policy, including measures such as further training, wage subsidies, or the creation of employment outside the labour market, may help individuals to avoid social exclusion, but one may have some doubts whether this will solve the problem entirely. On the contrary, these measures are often seen as limited, particularly in a longer perspective. To approach the problem of social exclusion fundamentally, a new solidaristic approach or, as Lundvall and Borrás (1998) argue, a 'new new deal' is needed. This is not meant in the sense of guaranteeing material security, but of re-establishing bonds between excluded people and society.

The sharing of work can be seen as the key approach towards re-establishing solidarity. The general reduction of working time is discussed as one option to employ more people. Whether this strategy will have a significant impact on employment is still controversial; it is more often seen as an instrument to stabilize than to increase employment. Promoting part-time work is also discussed as a strategy for sharing work among a larger number of people. As part-time work is applied to low-skilled jobs in particular, it may help to reduce the problem caused by the rising need for skills and the increasing skills bias. The establishment of more flexible transitions from employment to other social spheres, such as education, leisure, family, community, and retirement, is also seen as a promising approach to divide existing jobs among more people. The idea of such an approach is that if people have a real choice between different activities without risking losing their jobs, the supply of labour will be reduced and more people can be employed.

Dividing the existing working time among more people is, of course, a defensive strategy to deal with the problem of social exclusion, as low demand for labour is taken as granted. The problem is that of restoring strong economic growth conducive to massive job creation. The need for applying an innovation-oriented growth policy is increasingly stressed in order to combat social exclusion. However, traditional innovation policy aiming at encouraging major technological breakthroughs seems to be less effective in creating a great number of new jobs. Instead, a policy is needed which creates the general conditions for continuous improvement, incremental innovations, and continuous learning in as many companies as possible. We can speak of the need for a conditions-enabling innovation policy (Schienstock 1999).

9.9. Conclusion

Global innovation competition puts a lot of pressure on companies to increase their learning capacity in order to be able continuously to produce incremental innovations. This transformation pressure has triggered techno-organizational change, moving firms towards learning organizations, and inter-organizational networking. The need for more flexibility, on the other hand, can be seen as the major factor behind increasingly unstable and inse-cure work careers for a growing number of people. This should not prevent politicians from supporting technological change and organizational restruc-turing; public intervention, however, should no longer rely on launching large research programmes in the first place. Instead a new, more catalytic, type of intervention is needed. The basic idea is to improve companies' capabilities to innovate by transforming them into learning organizations.

At the same time, innovation and labour market policies have to be linked more closely. This, however, implies a transformation of the traditional 'car-ing welfare state' into a 'co-operative social state'. Then the role of the state can be characterized more as an intermediary and enabler role than as a pro-ducer of benefits. The co-operative social state no longer concentrates on social aid as a compensation for resource deficits; rather, it supports self-organizing entities (Schmid 1996). This means that the main aim is to empower people to participate in the learning processes taking place within companies.

REFERENCES

AMIN, A. (1993). 'The globalization of economy: An erosion of regional networks?', in G. Grabher (ed.), *The Embedded Firm: On the Socio-Economics of Industrial Networks*. London: Routledge.

ATKINSON, J. (1995). 'New forms of work'. IES (Institute for Employment Studies). Brighton, Report no. 264.

BROWN, P. (1995). 'Cultural capital and social exclusion: Some observations on recent trends in education, employment and the labour market'. *Work, Employment & Society*, 9/1

CASTELLS, M. (1996). *The Rise of the Network Society*, The Information Age 1, Oxford: Blackwell.

DE FOUCAULD, J.-B. (1992). 'Exclusion, inegalités et justice sociale', *Esprit*, 182: 47–57.

ERNST, D., and LUNDVALL, B.-Å. (1997). 'Information technology in the learning economy—challenges for developing countries'. Danish Research Unit for Industrial Dynamics, Aalborg University, DRUID Working Paper 12.

Enquete Kommission Zukunft der Medien in Wirtschaft und Gesellschaft (1998) (ed.). *Deutschlands Weg in die Informationsgesellschaft*. Bonn: ZV Zeitungs-Verlag.

European Commission (1993). *White Paper: Growth, Competitiveness, Employment*. Luxemburg: European Commission.

FREEMAN, C., and SOETE, L., (1994). *Work for All or Mass Unemployment?* London: Pinter.

——and EFENDIOGLU, U. (1995). 'Diffusion and the employment effects of information and communication technology'. *International Labour Review*, 134/4–5: 600.

HEWITT, P. (1993). *About Time: The Revolution in Work and Family Life*. London: IPPR/Rivers Oram Press.

HUWS, U. (1998). *Flexibility and Security: Towards a New European Balance*. London: Citizens Income Trust.

KANTER, R. (1991). 'The future of bureaucracy and hierarchy in organisational theory: A report from the field', in P. Bourdieu and J. Coleman (eds.), *Social Theory for a Changing Society*. Boulder Colo: Westview.

LASH, S. (1994). 'Reflexivity and its doubles: Structure, aesthetics, community', in U. Beck, A. Giddens, and S. Lash (eds.), *Reflexive Modernisation. Politics, Tradition and Aesthetics in the Modern Social Order*. Cambridge: Polity Press.

LUNDVALL, B.-Å. (1996). 'The social dimension of the learning economy'. Department of Business Studies, Aalborg University, DRUID Working Paper, 1.

——and JOHNSON, B. (1994). 'The learning economy'. *Journal of Industrial Studies*, 2/1: 23–42.

——and NIELSEN, P. (1998). 'Competition, transformation and polarisation in the learning economy—illustrated by the Danish case'. *Revue d'Economie Industrielle*, 88: 67–80.

——and BORRÁS, S. (1998). *The Globalising Learning Economy: Implications for Innovation Policy*. Brussels: European Commission.

MILES, I. (1995) (ed.). 'Knowledge-intensive business services: Users, carriers and sources of innovation', in *European Innovation Monitoring System (EIMS)*, EIMS Publication 15.

NASSE, P. (1992). 'Exclus et exclusions. Connaitre les populations, comprendre les processus'. Paris: Commissariat Général du Plan.

OECD (1998). *Human Capital Investment. An International Comparison.* Paris: Centre for Education Research and Innovation.

PAUGAM, S. (1993). *La société française et ses pauvres.* Paris: Presses Universitaires de France.

REICH, R. B. (1991). *The Work of Nations: Preparing Ourselves for 21st Century Capitalism.* New York: Vintage.

ROBINS, K., and WEBSTER, F. (1997). 'From ICTs to information: Changing concepts of the information age'. Unpublished.

ROOM, G. (1995) (ed.). *Beyond the Threshold. The Measurement and Analysis of Social Exclusion.* Bristol: The Policy Press.

SCHIENSTOCK, G. (1997). 'Probleme der Koordinierung, Steuerung und Kontrolle einer globalen Ökonomie', in B. Blättel-Mink and O. Renn (eds.), *Zwischen Akteur und System. Die Organisation von Innovation.* Opladen: Westdeutscher Verlag.

——(1999). 'From traditional technology policy towards conditions-enabling innovation policy', in G. Schienstock and O. Kuusi (eds.), *Transformation Towards a Learning Economy. The Challenge for the Finnish Innovation System.* Helsinki: Sitra.

SCHMID, G. (1996). 'Reform der Arbeitsmarktpolitik. Vom fürsorgenden Wohlfrahrtsstaat zum kooperativen Sozialstaat'. *WSI (Wirtschafts- und Sozialwissenschaftlichen Institut) Mitteilungen*, 49. Jahrgang. Frankfurt am Main: Bund-Verlag.

SCOTT, A. (1996). 'From Silicon Valley to Hollywood: Growth and development of the multimedia industry in California', in H.-J. Braczyk, P. Cooke, and M. Heidenreich (eds.), *Regional Innovation Systems. The Role of Governances in a Globalized World.* London/Bristol: UCL Press.

SENGENBERGER, W., and PYKE, F. (1992). 'Industrial districts and local economic regeneration: Research and policy issues', in F. Pyke and W. Sengenberger (eds.), *Industrial Districts and Local Economic Regeneration.* Geneva: International Labour Organization.

SOETE, L. (1996). 'Social impacts of the information society—national and community level', in Finnish Institute of Occupational Health (ed.), *Proceedings of the International Symposium: Work in the Information Society*, 20–22 May, Helsinki.

TOURAINE, A. (1991). 'Face à l'exclusion'. *Esprit,* 169.

YÉPEZ DEL CASTILLO, I. (1994). 'A comparative approach to social exclusion: Lessons from France and Belgium'. *International Labour Review*, 133/5–6: 620.

10 (Europe)

Industrial Innovation and Sustainability—Conflicts and Coherence

FRIEDER MEYER-KRAHMER

10.1. Views on Technological Innovation and Environmental Sustainability

When the modern industrial economy emerged, the natural environment was considered an unlimited resource by industrial managers and most economists. Nowadays we know better: the industrial economy needs fundamental rethinking. A worldwide polluted environment, shrinking natural resources, and ever growing social problems call for radically new concepts for the future industrial society. Since 1987 'sustainable development' became a key notion for visions of a production and consumption system that is able to reduce the use of natural resources and to avoid pollution to the maximum possible extent, blaming the simple growth-oriented type of industrial technologies.

There are many definitions of sustainability. We use the term here in the sense of the UNWCED's report *Our Common Future* (1987): 'a development which meets the needs of the present without compromising the ability of future generations to meet their own needs'. The concept takes on a global perspective and aims to maintain economic development, to eliminate poverty and deprivation, to conserve the environment, and to enhance its resource base simultaneously. Furthermore, the opportunities for the less-developed countries should in the long term approach those of the developed countries.

While the implementation of 'sustainable development' as a concrete policy goal still has to be achieved, some ingredients are of common understanding:

(1) emissions and immissions have to be limited to the bearing capacity of the environment;
(2) in the future, primarily renewable resources should be used;
(3) the use of renewable resources must not be faster than the renewal rate;
(4) the total stock of non-renewable resources must not be depleted—technologies will need to use renewable resources or substitutes to replace non-renewable resources as they are used up.

In a different strand of discussion, industrialists and politicians in the leading industrial countries call for accelerated 'industrial innovations' as a powerful source of economic growth and wealth, and they usually mean by that technological innovations. Most existing government innovation policies are claiming to foster industrial (technological) competitiveness as a main target. There still seem to be hardly any policy approaches that aim explicitly at innovation processes conducive to sustainability, and at technical innovations which would achieve or maintain sustainability. At a first glance the goals of sustainable development and industrial innovations, respectively, seem to be conflicting. Even though for some ten or even twenty years there have been substantial efforts worldwide to raise resource productivity, the achievements since then seem to be far removed from the level of ecological sustainability (RMNO 1992; BUND/Misereor 1996). In many OECD countries industrial innovations aiming at competitiveness and growth are perceived as more important than those aiming at sustainability. But is this necessarily so? Under which conditions can the two concepts come to a significantly better agreement?

Research and technology (R&T) policies, and in their consequence industrial/technological innovations, cannot by themselves establish a socio-economic system which could guarantee sustainable development, but they might substantially contribute to this goal, first because of the need for innovations to solve problems of current unsustainable production methods and consumption patterns and, second, because of the need to develop and diffuse a wide range of environmental technologies.

There is a growing realization in the business community that high standards of environmental performance are not inconsistent with economic performance. At the same time, government and regulators began to appreciate that industry, albeit the source of pollution and waste, is also the agent through which cleaner production technologies could be applied and diffused. *Agenda 21*, one of the main outputs of the UNCED in 1992, crystallizes many of the strands of emerging thinking about the relationship between governments and industry with respect to environmental performance.

Agenda 21 proposes two programmes relating to business and industry—one on cleaner production, the other on responsible entrepreneurship. The programme to develop responsible entrepreneurship concentrates on the development of enterprises that are managed in line with the principles of sustainable development and calls for an intensification of R&D for cleaner technologies and an eco-cycle economy. The latter is the main point of the cleaner production programme, which aims to increase the efficiency with which natural resources are utilized by moving towards processes which generate less waste and increase the recycling and re-use of process wastes. Cleaner production technologies are viewed as being distinct from 'clean-up' processes which are applied end-of-pipe and often simply transfer pollution from one environmental medium to another.

Against this background, two views of the possibilities to solve the conflict between sustainable development and technological innovation can be found, a sceptical and an optimistic one. These views differ with respect to their assumptions on political lock-in factors (acceptance and implementation problems) and with respect to the extent of expected effects of resource productivity gains and a competition-driven structural change conducive to sustainability.

The *sceptical view*, for example, sounds as follows (OECD 1992: 206):

> As the 'green' discussion in OECD countries shows, there is only partial community of interest within countries, while the social and political mechanisms for articulating the conflicts are fragile and only slowly becoming institutionalized. Outside the OECD area these mechanisms are even more fragile, partly, perhaps, because the conflicts are greater, but, more importantly, because institutions are weaker.

Or Skea (1994: 424) criticizes: 'A cynical view would be that *Agenda 21* contains many laudable aspirations but has little to offer in the way of practical measures.'

The *optimistic view* assumes that challenges of sustainability, technological innovation, and competitiveness are compatible to a large extent—and therefore does not expect major political obstacles to implement a sustainability policy. For example Porter and van der Linde (1995: 133–4) argue:

> Using resources productively is what makes for competitiveness today. Companies can improve resource productivity by producing existing products more efficiently or by making products that are more valuable to customers—products customers are willing to pay more for. . . . Because technology is constantly changing, the new paradigm of global competitiveness requires the ability to innovate rapidly. This new paradigm has profound implications for the debate about environmental policy—about how to approach it, how to regulate, and how strict regulation should be. The new paradigm has brought environmental improvement and competitiveness together.

Countries which pre-emptively set high environmental standards, the optimists argue, can establish strong domestic markets for new technologies which may be used as a springboard for international trade when the standards are taken up elsewhere (concept of first-mover advantage). Business in Germany, Japan, and California has certainly benefited from this phenomenon. Because Germany adopted recycling standards earlier than most other countries, German companies have first-mover advantages in developing, for example, less packaging-intensive products, which are both lower in cost and sought after in the market-place. In the United States, Porter and van der Linde argue, Cummings Engine Company's development of low-emission diesel engines for such applications as trucks and buses—innovations that US environmental regulations spurred—are allowing it to gain position in international markets where similar needs are growing.

The optimistic view emphasizes the role of technology as having enough argumentative power to make concrete policies feasible. The sceptical one is

Frieder Meyer-Krahmer

focused on inabilities of the political system and lock-in effects of several sub-systems driven by 'Schumpeter dynamics' (Krupp 1992). Implicitly, Western policy favours the optimistic view. Though the importance of environmental goals is recognized, the Maastricht Treaty also indicates that policies to support environmental sustainability must be compatible with the goal of improving the competitiveness of European industry. The basis of these—highly simplified—views is a set of different concepts on innovation and sustainability. Table 10.1 gives a (selective) overview.

Underlying such concepts as well as innovation and environmental policies there are often implicit assumptions on different future development paths which must be discussed. These assumptions are dealing with:

(1) economic development: growth, trade, globalization, and competition;
(2) social and demographic assumptions: world population, family structures, and policies, availability of resources, patterns of societal organization;
(3) welfare and distribution: migration, international distribution of wealth and income, living opportunities, and consumption patterns;

TABLE 10.1. *Innovation and sustainability*

Approach	Main elements	Authors
Environmental economics	Application of neo-classical theory to environmental problems Concentration on allocation rules, internalization of external effects	Coase Baumol/Oates Siebert
Productivity approach	Resource efficiency	Porter Lovins v.Weizsäcker
Schumpeterian approach	Reorientation of trajectories Complex learning processes Institutional change Innovation strategies and qualitative growth	Freeman Krupp
Ecological economics	Co-evolution of human preferences, technology, organization, and ecological conditions Integration of ecological dimensions into economic theory (scale, time dynamics, carrying capacity) Distribution issues: equal living conditions of world's population, intergenerational equity	Daly Costanza Martinez Alier

Source: Kuntze, Meyer-Krahmer, and Walz 1998.

(4) the political system: adaptability, flexibility, lock-in effects;
(5) 'driving forces': capitalistic exploitation, irreversible processes, evolutionary processes, Schumpeter dynamics, public and private liberties.

Taking these dimensions of assumptions into consideration, three different development paths (scenarios) up to the year 2050 and beyond, with different conditions and consequences can be distinguished (Kuntze, Meyer-Krahmer, and Walz 1998: 7). These scenarios are highly simplified and should rather illustrate the range of alternatives than claim to be the results of a systematic and consistent analysis. They demonstrate the evidence that conclusions on the role of innovation policy, its design, and appropriate instruments are highly path-dependent.

(1) In the scenario of 'global crash' climate changes lead to the inundation of coastal zones and growing desertification, military conflicts for energy, water, food, etc., high migration movements, and the death of several billions of human beings because of hunger, epidemics, and wars. The role of innovation policy for sustainable development could only be characterized as insignificant in this scenario.
(2) The scenario of 'regionally limited crises' with growing north/south inequality. The role of innovation policy would consist of initiating technical *and* social solutions to adapt to climate change (e.g. relocation of cities, construction of large dams); furthermore, environmental technologies and solutions to increase resource productivity would be supported.
(3) The 'equality' scenario indicates the consequences of the main assumptions of the advocates of sustainability. The main role of innovation policy in this scenario would be to contribute to a very early change of technologies, organizations, behaviour, and frame conditions avoiding expected disasters and frictions. Social and institutional innovations would play a key role in this scenario, implying a substantial reduction in the material standard of living in industrialized countries.

10.2. Three Paths of Industrial Technological Innovation Towards Environmental Sustainability

At present, a fundamental and widespread dissociation of the consumption of resources from economic growth cannot foreseeably be achieved. Although a change of resource elasticities can definitely be observed over the last decade for some resources and pollutants, nevertheless, the specific efficiency successes are very often more than compensated for even by a moderate economic growth (Walz *et al.* 1992). In addition, it has to be kept in mind that even a reduced pressure on the environment might be much above the carrying capacity, especially when accumulating and persistent effects are taken into account.

Therefore new industrial models for an environmentally acceptable economy are needed which are not only desirable, but also (both for enterprises and consumers) economically attractive, so that they have a chance of being realized. We differentiate three models of this kind:

- more extensive use of environmentally acceptable technologies (end-of-pipe as well as integrated) as a traditional model
- the closing of materials cycles
- the integration of product policy and product use.

It has been shown that the more extensive use of environmentally acceptable technologies results in substantial environmental relief and has furthermore brought economic success to the Federal Republic of Germany, which for a number of years was the largest exporter of environmental technologies (now second). Table 10.2 provides several examples of the environmental benefits from cleaner processes and lower input/output ratios that could result from using information technology to develop real-time sensor devices. In another example, the authors (Jochem and Hohmeyer 1992) illustrate the argument with data for Germany which shows that German exports of

TABLE 10.2. *Selected examples of the potential environmental benefits from R&D investment in electronic sensor technology*

Technical measure	Environmental effects
A. Cleaner Processes	
Reduction of combustion air in rotary cement kilns	20% reduction of NO_x emissions
Improved control techniques for process heat and electricity generation	10%–20% reduction of SO_2 and NO_2 emissions
Improved control techniques for domestic hot water heaters	10% reduction of CO_2 emissions
B. Reduction of input/output ratios	
On-line control of chemical nickel baths in electro-plating by measuring the pH value and nickel content	2–3 fold increase in the lifetime of the bath
On-board control of following distance for vehicles on highways	2–3 fold increase in vehicle throughput (reduces need for new highway infrastructure)
Automatic dosing of separate detergent ingredients for washing machines	50% reduction of washing agents, 10% reduction of energy and water use
On-line measurement of plastic sheets	2%–10% reduction in consumption of raw materials

Source: ISI (Angerer 1992).

energy-saving products increased in the 1980s at twice the rate of all other industrial exports. These successes may be regarded as being due to congruent interests in activities of research efforts, environmental legislation, innovative enterprises, and existing acceptance of technology. The basic problem with this model is that, on its own, more extensive use of environmentally acceptable technologies does not produce enough of the necessary efficiency gains for an environmentally sustainable economy.

There are already several examples of the closing of materials cycles in production which represent economically interesting options (including utilization cascades). The present massive efforts towards establishing recycling economics also follow this model; its limits are set largely by the fact that the reconversion of products into raw materials and into secondary materials that are reintroduced into the production process still represents a relatively wide 'cycle', whereas for sustainability reasons the cycle should be as narrow as possible, meaning on as high a level as possible and with a possible minimum of additional transport demand. The shift from production responsibility to product responsibility, which is laid down in various waste management or 'eco-cycle' laws of some OECD countries, also entails a fundamental change in the model of 'integrated product policy'. In this context, environmentally acceptable management does not simply denote 'defensive' protection of the environment (for example, the observance of regulations) but also creates an opportunity for enterprises to adopt innovations and new business strategies. This strategic change can be made possible or supported by changes, for example, in the price system (internalization of external costs from the consumption of resources), public regulation, voluntary agreements, public procurement programmes, and changes in consumer behaviour. It is these entrepreneurial innovation strategies that will really determine the dynamics of the path towards an environmentally acceptable economy under conditions of partially regulated market economies.

10.3. **Sustainability and Learning: Innovation Strategies of Firms**

This shift in perspective will continue, as is to be expected in an evolutionary economic system. Environmentally sustainable economics means in this case not only 'defensive' environmental protection (for example, compliance with regulations), but makes possible innovation and new business strategies for enterprises. Impulses for this shift in strategy may be changes in the price system (internalization of external costs of resource utilization), state regulations, voluntary self-regulation, and changes in consumer behaviour. In my view, such entrepreneurial innovation strategies will determine the essential dynamics of the way towards environmentally sustainable economics under market economy conditions. To illustrate this view, innovation strategies to intensify product utilization and to prolong the life cycle will be treated in detail.

Generally speaking, the following strategies for designing an improvement of the utilization and life span of products can be distinguished (adapted from Stahel 1991):

• products designed to last longer
• increased use of maintenance and repair
• the upgrading of products in use through modernization
• the re-use of components from used products in manufacturing new products, as well as
• service strategies (sales of utilization instead of sales of products; divided, joint, or multiple use; selling the service 'function guarantee' instead of selling substitute products).

The changes in perspective contained in such strategies open up new market possibilities through introducing new consumer durables to the market, or through introducing new modes of usage for such goods (for example, by selling the function instead of the product itself). The benefits expected from usage will finally determine how the product is actually acquired (buying, rental, leasing, user co-ops, use on public offer), as well as the most suitable product design. Thus the strategy 'sales of results (practical use) instead of goods' means that the economic emphasis of the enterprises is shifted from manufacturing (production) to product management, that is from production companies to operating and leasing companies ('fleet management'). This is accompanied by a far-reaching manufacturer's liability, which requires the constructors to design products of great reliability, tolerance of misoperation, protection against unauthorized or improper use, which also inevitably means an extended life cycle for the goods. A holistic product policy also demands a substantial change in the requirements of continuous incorporation of technical change into the products.

A longer active life for products has considerable impacts on the economic structural change, the way of dealing with the existing stock of goods (stock management), as well as on R&D, for example:

(1) components and products that can be flexibly repaired and adapted to future requirements and technologies, open systems with a high degree of interchangeability, in order to continually integrate technical advances into existing systems (without having to exchange a complete system, thus slowing down progress), should be developed; 'life cycle engineering' is called for in product development, in order to close the loop of material flows;

(2) substitution of central manufacturing plants by decentral workshops staffed by specialist craftsmen (servicing, maintenance, technological upgrading);

(3) increasing significance of the insurance business through the growing importance of product liability;

(4) shift from a production-oriented industrial society to a utilization-oriented industrial service society.

Completely novel entrepreneurial strategies can be realized with this approach. They contain a variety of objectives such as cost-saving, quality improvement, new business fields, as well as combined product/service offers, and are at the same time compatible with the aim of an ecologically sustainable economy. There are already markets and companies that pursue these strategies. Examples are to be found in the aviation industry, manufacturers of photocopiers, drink vending machines and component manufacturers (Stahel 1994; Meyer-Krahmer 1998).

The speed with which such innovation strategies are adopted depends not least on the changes in the political framework conditions, the shifts in consumer preferences, and the 'mental structural change' in the enterprises. In any case these innovation strategies will bring about a radical sectoral structural change. Therefore, finally, the speed of dissemination of such innovation strategies is substantially influenced by the power of the winners and losers. Here lies the real line of conflict determining the speed with which these guiding principles assert themselves. This battle is not joined between left/right, ecological/non-ecological, employer/employee, but runs right through the economy, society, and politics.

10.4. Technology Policy and Environmental Sustainability

The use of science and technology policies to achieve environmental goals constitutes a new focus for technology policy (Soete and Arundel 1993). At a first glance, this requires a return to the emphasis in the 1950s and 1960s on public goals that were met through mission-oriented projects (Ergas 1987). However, there is a fundamental difference between older mission-oriented projects, for example, nuclear, defence, and aerospace programmes, and new projects to support environmentally sustainable development. The older projects developed radically new technologies through government intervention that was largely isolated from the rest of the economy, though it frequently affected the structure of related industries and could lead to new spin-off technologies that had widespread effects on other sectors. In contrast, modern mission-oriented environmental projects will need to combine many policies, including procurement, in order to have pervasive effects on the entire structure of production and consumption within an economy (Lahaye and Llerena 1996; Jaffe *et al.* 1995; Lévêque 1996).

The pervasive character of new mission-oriented projects to meet environmental goals calls for a systemic approach to policy. This approach results in substantial changes to the mission-oriented projects of the past. Table 10.3 summarizes the key characteristics and differences between the old and new models of mission-oriented projects. It is not difficult to denote the elements of such a policy. When discussing the constituent conditions for realization at the workshop, the empirical evidence made clear that these conditions are still not fulfilled. Many of these policy characteristics have been discussed since the beginning of the 1970s without significant effects on policy practice.

The achievement of the goal of environmentally sustainable development depends on the active participation of a wide range of institutions and firms in the search for new technologies. This requires a network approach to research and procurement to support the rapid diffusion and assimilation of information.

Policy intervention could guide the continuous search by industry for innovations towards environmentally beneficial directions and help to create a self-reinforcing process in which additional research for new technical solutions follows environmental pathways. There are four main policy tools for guiding investment and innovation:

TABLE 10.3. *Characteristics of old and new 'mission-oriented' projects*

Old: defence, nuclear, and aerospace	New: environmental technologies
The mission is defined in terms of the number of technical achievements with little regard to their economic feasibility	The mission is defined in terms of economically feasible technical solutions to particular environmental problems.
• The goals and the direction of technological development are defined in advance by a small group of experts.	• The direction of technical change is influenced by a wide range of actors including government, private firms, and consumer groups.
• Centralized control within a government administration.	• Decentralized control with a large number of agents involved.
• Diffusion of the results outside the core of participants is of minor importance or actively discouraged.	• Diffusion of the results is a central goal and is actively encouraged.
• Limited to a small group of firms that can participate owing to the emphasis on a small number of radical technologies.	• An emphasis on the incrementalist development of both radical and incremental innovations in order to permit a large number of firms to participate.
• Self-contained projects with little need for complementary policies and scant attention paid to coherence.	• Complementary policies vital for success and close attention paid to coherence with other goals.

Source: Soete and Arundel 1993: 51.

(1) direct regulation through emission and product quality standards and regulated limits for the permissible use of a product;
(2) economic instruments to attach the externality costs of pollution to the inputs and outputs of production;
(3) procurement policies to speed up the use or development of environmentally beneficial technologies within private firms;
(4) policies to influence the types of technologies that are socially and economically feasible. The latter include educational programmes, support for organizations that can influence consumer and producer behaviours, and Constructive Technology Assessment (CTA) to promote a dialogue among the users, producers, and social groups who will be affected by a new technology.

The goal of environmentally sustainable development requires a wide range of complementary policies to support investment in new environmentally benign technologies and the rapid diffusion of successful applications. The most comprehensive approach to formulate a coherent policy towards environmental sustainability can be found in the various 'green plans' (Johnson 1995). Green plans are long-term environmental strategies which replace traditional single-issue policies through a workable plan for environmental prosperity. A successful green plan is comprehensive: it aims at considering all aspects of the environment and is developed through consultation with all relevant actors in society.

The most prominent example, the Dutch National Environmental Policy Plan (NEPP and VROM 1993), is characterized by a management approach to environmental problems involving:

● adoption of quantified (measurable) targets and time frames
● integration of the environment into decision making by all sectors of society
● clear identification of responsibility for actions
● creativity in the design and use of policy instruments
● commitment to long-term reshaping of social and economic structures
● recognition of the Netherlands' dependence on international co-operation and action.

One of the elements of this action programme is to use technological innovation and technology policy, too. However: 'Technology can never be more than a tool, an instrument among others; and the type of technology that will be developed is very much dependent on the structural and cultural conditions that prevail in society. This is the starting point for a programme that aims to explore the unused potential of technology' (Vergragt and Jansen 1993: 136). This Dutch programme on Sustainable Technology Development (DTO, Duurzame Technologische Ontwikkeling) drafted an action plan for technology development under guidance of the long-term vision to achieve sustainability until the middle of the next century. This goal determines 'that in a sustainable world the per capita emissions of pollutants and consumption of resources will have to be reduced, generally, to something less than 10 per cent of the present levels practiced in the Western, industrialized world' (DTO 1994). Because such a dramatic goal cannot be achieved through further incremental progress in environmental technologies, the programme recognizes that developments are needed in the three dimensions: technology, structure, and culture. The first phase of the programme (1990–4) concentrated on developing an approach to innovations for sustainability. 'The result of the DTO-programme will not yet be "sustainable technologies", but "manuals" that teach the concerned parties how to innovate towards sustainability' (DTO 1994).

While new opportunities and indeed whole new paradigms could be opened up by technology, technological trajectories will be shaped by the decisions which determine future costs of production and patterns of economic activity. To the extent that environmental concerns occupy a central place in policy making, environmentally driven technologies (affecting innovation, diffusion, and technological paradigms) may shift industrial structures and competitive advantages, both nationally and internationally. At the same time, there is widespread evidence of market failure with existing price signals: much environmental investment would be profitable but is not undertaken, for reasons that seem to involve market structures, corporate cultures, and investment time horizons, given present price signals and rates of reward to environment-friendly measures by firms.

Technology policy can become an increasingly important instrument in attaining environmental objectives. More cross-sectoral, multidisciplinary approaches are called for. Consistent strategies for funding research on technologies to improve industrial and other sectors (for example, transport) performance and environmental quality need to be expanded, and co-operative research programmes among countries should be promoted. Funding R&D is, however, not sufficient. The appropriate mix of regulatory and market incentives that spur firms and consumers in environmentally desirable directions must be identified. This will require both shifts in political priorities and more research on how to target the incentives to obtain the desired results. However, a careful policy analysis has to include policy dilemmata (for example, lock-in-effects, symbolic policy) and the logic of political decision making to identify feasibility conditions and implementation obstacles more systematically than has been done in the past.

10.5. The Role of Regional, National, and International Policies

Environmental problems rarely respect national borders. The multinational character both of problems and solutions suggests a strong role for supra-national organizations. At the same time, the localized nature of many of the sources of pollution and differences in the institutions and solutions that have been developed to solve environmental problems, for example, to dispose of, or recycle, household and industrial waste, requires the extensive involvement of regional and national governments. For this reason, environmentally sustainable development can only be attained by active involvement of all levels of government.

In the European sphere an established criterion of the division of labour between regions, nations, and the European Union is the subsidiary principle. In the field of industrial innovation and sustainability, this is not a very helpful conceptual basis. From an evolutionary perspective it is more appropriate to distinguish between relevant actors, synergies, and learning processes. The regional level is most appropriate if face-to-face interaction of actors and learning processes are needed, the national (or European) level is most relevant when the legal, fiscal, or regulative frame conditions are involved, and the international is most appropriate if global solutions are needed.

The regional dimension of innovation depends greatly on the regional system of innovation (actors, competencies, networks, synergies). Especially interesting from the viewpoint of industrial innovation and sustainability are social experiments (see Majer and Seydl 1998). These experiments are often highly complex. The change from product-ownership consumption to use-oriented consumption is a good candidate for regions as an appropriate basis to implement social experiments, as well as to test options of changes and solutions. Social experiments often need a very close interaction between manufacturing, service, and trading companies, consumers and local or regional authorities. The aim is that private households change their patterns of behaviour significantly, that products are transformed into services and that research leads to new technical concepts. Regions can act as pioneers (in the Schumpeterian sense) because they are an ideal platform for such social innovation experiments. Further examples are eco-industrial parks. This concept has emerged from attempts to apply ecological principles to industrial activities and community design. An eco-industrial park is a community of manufacturing and service businesses seeking enhanced, environmental, and economic performance through collaboration in managing environmental and resource issues. By working together, a community of businesses seeks a collective benefit that is greater than the sum of the individual benefits each company would realize if it optimized its individual performance only. The involved local and regional actors are firms, regulatory authorities, regional developers, designers and builders, and other community authorities. The most well-known eco-industrial park is Kalundborg, Denmark. This example shows under which conditions a region can be a very successful platform for such types of complex experiments (Hiessl *et al.* 1998; Lowe *et al.* 1996).

The national (or European) level is the appropriate policy area if legal, fiscal, or regulatory frame conditions are involved. Typical examples of such kinds are environmental tax reforms. Making the exploitation of the environment more expensive while also reducing the costs of employment through a natural-yield reform of the tax and contribution systems promises to harmonize ecological, economic, and social interest, in line with the guiding principle of sustainable development. Liability is another candidate of national or European policy. Current environmental liability law is characterized by major shortcomings with regard to the prevention of damage to the environment, the recognition of those who cause the environmental damage, and compensation for damage to be paid to those who suffer from environmental damage. Thus it leaves significant gaps in liability compensation. Funds are an appropriate instrument in the event of collective responsibility for damages. Such a fund would be particularly well placed to internalize those costs to groups of polluters and to compensate those who suffer from pollution adequately. Besides such fiscal and legal frame conditions, the national and European levels are the appropriate space for other instruments, which are discussed by The Future Commission (1998).

In view of the global environmental threats and risks, far greater efforts must be made to achieve effective international consultation and co-operation in environmental policy. In particular, the use of new economic incentives and the introduction of institutional innovations in environmental policy provide opportunities for greater sustainability at the national, European, and global levels. According to the joint-implementation approach (Jepma 1995), countries will be able to comply with their own obligations to reduce emissions (for example, CO_2) both by action at home and in other countries. This will facilitate the reduction of emissions in places where action is most cost-efficient and ecologically effective.

The Kyoto Protocol that is part of the UN Climate Framework Convention explicitly mentions internationally tradeable emission certificates; this instrument must now be developed in more detail. Essentially, this instrument allows the regulation of a global volume of emissions, that is agreed in a binding manner, through issuance and trade in licensed and transferable emission rights (licences). This creates a market where none existed before— a market that introduces economically efficient solutions, gives incentives for innovative methods of protecting the environment, and guarantees real relief from the pressures on the evironment. Such a market can also be geared to produce a net transfer of resources from industrialized to developing countries through funding and technology in exchange for licences (UNCED 1994). There is much to be said in favour of such a market-based solution to steering emission volumes. This applies, in particular, to joint implementation in the initial phase and to tradeable certificates in the final phase of global environmental agreements (especially within the context of the climate convention) at both the European and global levels.

Institutions of international environmental policy exist mainly in the form of horizontal, national self-co-ordination, because of the lack of bodies capable of hierarchical direction. As regards international environmental policy, the decision making process traditionally takes the form of negotiations which are based on voluntary agreement to the development of problem-solving regulating mechanisms. The need for consultation and co-ordination has grown significantly with the rise in international environmental agreements and has led to many suggestions for institutional innovation and reform. In this respect, one can refer especially to the establishment of funds for the regulated transfer of technologies and finance from the north to the south as a direct steering instrument, and also changes in indirect procedural steering (such as capacity building and new forms of decision making). More far-reaching institutional reforms are under discussion, including the setting up of an international Council for Environmental Matters, similar to the UN Security Council, the creation of an ecological institution modelled on GATT, the environmental reform of the World Trade Organization (WTO), and the creation of an environmental court to decide on environmentally relevant disputes and to penalize those who damage the environment (Helm 1995). Leading industrial countries need to take a more active part in these discussions than hitherto. Their stance on these questions of international environmental policy is only credible and convincing if it is matched by domestic action, that is if there is a new drive for technical and social innovations in environmental protection at the national and regional level.

10.6. Conclusions: Contradictions, Inconsistencies, and Open Questions

In a selective and simplifying way the following contradictions and inconsistencies in the field of innovation and sustainability can be observed:

1. The term innovation was defined originally in a very broad sense, integrating technical, behavioural, organizational, and institutional change (Schumpeter). In the meantime the 'modern' terminology has become highly limited. Innovation is used mostly in terms of technical innovation, disregarding a broad range of economic, social, and political contexts (nevertheless, it is apparent that social innovation is as important as technical innovation (or even more so)). The situation is totally different in the field of sustainability. The various chapters of *Agenda 21*, the common basis for political discussions on sustainable development, contain a broad list of relevant problems rather than a precise definition. The search for indicators of sustainable development has produced a number of totally different approaches (Walz *et al.* 1995). The indicator list of the Commission for Sustainable Development (CSD), which perhaps comes closest to a consensus, contains much more than a hundred, partially extremely broad and complex, indicators covering economic, social, environmental, and institutional aspects on the one hand. On the other hand,

economists have taken another path, transforming sustainable development into an academic debate on the substitution between natural and man-made capital (weak or strong sustainability). Thus, the concept of sustainable development is still extremely broad and vague. This means on the level of terminology that both concepts are far from being compatible in terms of conceptional thinking, precision, and consistency.

2. Technology policy is focused mostly on R&D, hard-, or software. Sustainability requires an approach which is far beyond R&D and technology and includes economic and institutional change, new economic and social incentive structures, government regulation, etc. Technology and innovation policy in such a perspective needs an intersectoral (cross-sectional) approach. But in many countries technology policy is an element of a vertically fragmented policy system and stands in significant contradiction to such a systemic and integrative approach.

3. In many countries environmental policy is concerned primarily with short-term environmental problems and problems that translate into additional votes. The sustainability concept has, so far, not been translated into an operational environmental policy frame. Furthermore, the incentives for technology development affected by environmental policy are still not clearly defined. Therefore, environmental policies often ignore conditions and processes of innovations.

4. Radical ecologists demand a highly moral code of conduct (such as equal distribution of living opportunities in the world) and very often do not consider the consequences of social and world economic interdependencies. Wishful thinking dominates realistic visions. Ecological economics challenges traditional economics, but is still far from either establishing a new paradigm of economic thinking or being applicable for policy making (yet).

The main lessons to be drawn from these contradictions and inconsistencies are that an innovation policy for sustainability is still far from being adequately conceptualized. A systemic approach is needed which integrates change of behaviour, structural change, regulations, incentives, and technologies. Technology (and innovation) policy for sustainability has to overcome the inherent limitations of technology policy, developing a comprehensive approach to a broad range of different policies (technology, price system, attitudes and behaviour, incentives, regulations, etc.), different sub-systems and actors (public, semi-public bodies, firms, banks, research institutes, etc.) on different levels (regional, national, international). It is very necessary to promote a broad range of learning processes on different levels, by different actors and their attitudes and behaviour.

REFERENCES

ANGERER, G. (1992). 'The role of electronics in environmental technology and its impacts on the environment'. Paper presented to the international conference ECO WORLD '92. Washington, DC.

BUND/Misereor (1996) (eds.). *Zukunftsfähiges Deutschland. Ein Beitrag zu einer global nachhaltigen Entwicklung.* Studie des Wuppertal Instituts für Klima, Umwelt, Energie. Basel: Birkhäuser.

DTO (Programmabureau Interdepartementaal Onderzoekprogramma Duurzame Technologische Ontwikkeling) (1994). *Looking Back from the Future.* Dutch Governmental Programme for Sustainable Technology Development. Delft.

ERGAS, H. (1987). 'Does technology policy matter?', in B. Guile and H. Brooks (eds.), *Technology and Global Competition.* Washington, DC: National Academy Press.

THE FUTURE COMMISSION, FRIEDRICH EBERT FOUNDATION (1998). *Economic Performance, Social Cohesion, Environmental Sustainability. Three Goals—One Path.* Bonn: Dietz-Verlag.

HELM, C. (1995). *Sind Freihandel und Umweltschutz vereinbar? Ökologischer Reformbedarf des GATT/WTO-Regimes.* Berlin: Edition Sigma.

HIESSL, H., SCHÖN, M., KUNTZE, U., and DELAHAYE, F. (1998). *Vernetzungspotentiale von Unternehmen der TechnologieRegion Karlsruhe zur Schließung von Energie- und Stoffkreisläufen.* Karlsruhe: ISI.

JAFFE, A., PETERSON, S., PORTNEY, P., and STAVINS, R. (1995). 'Environmental regulation and the competitiveness of US manufacturing: What does the evidence tell us?' *Journal of Economic Literature*, 33: 132–63.

JEPMA, C. P. (1995) (ed.). *The Feasibility of Joint Implementation.* Dordrecht: Kluwer.

JOCHEM, E., and HOHMEYER, O. (1992). 'The economics of near-term reductions in greenhouse gases', in I. Mintzler (ed.), *Confronting Climate Change. Risks, Implications and Responses.* Cambridge: Cambridge University Press.

JOHNSON, H. D. (1995). *Green Plans. Greenprint for Sustainability.* Lincoln: University of Nebraska Press.

KRUPP, H. (1992). *Energy Politics and Schumpeter Dynamics.* Tokyo: Springer.

KUNTZE, U., MEYER-KRAHMER, F., and WALZ, R. (1998). 'Innovation and sustainable development—Lessons for innovation policies?', in F. Meyer-Krahmer (ed.), *Innovation and Sustainable Development.* Heidelberg: Physica-Verlag.

LAHAYE, N., and LLERENA, D. (1996). 'Technology and sustainability: An organisational and institutional change', in S. Faucheux, D. Pearce, and J. Proops (eds.), *Models of Sustainable Development.* Cheltenham: Edward Elgar.

LÉVÊQUE, F. (1996). *Environmental Policy in Europe: Industry, Competition and the Policy Process.* Cheltenham: Edward Elgar.

LOWE, E. A., MORAN, S. R., and HOLMES, D. B. (1996). *Fieldbook for the Development of Eco-Industrial Parks.* Oakland, Calif.: Indigo Development.

MAJER, H., and SEYDL, F. (1998) (eds.). *Pflastersteine. Ulmer Wege zur Nachhaltigkeit.* Sternenfels: Wissenschaft & Praxis.

MEYER-KRAHMER, F. (1998). 'Industrial innovation strategies—Towards an environmentally sustainable industrial economy', in F. Meyer-Krahmer (ed.), *Innovation and Sustainable Development.* Heidelberg: Physica-Verlag.

OECD (1992). *Technology and the Economy. The Key Relationships.* Paris: OECD, TEP. The Technology/Economy Programme.

PORTER, M. E., and VAN DER LINDE, C. (1995). 'Green and competitive—Ending the stalemate'. *Harvard Business Review*, 73: 120–37.

RMNO (Dutch Advisory Council for Research on Nature and Environment) (1992). *The Ecocapacity as a Challenge to Technological Development*. Rijswijk Publication RMNO 74a.

SKEA, J. (1994). 'Environmental issues and innovation', in M. Dodgson and R. Rothwell, (eds.), *The Handbook of Industrial Innovation*. Cheltenham: Edward Elgar.

SOETE, L., and ARUNDEL, A. (1993). *An Integrated Approach to European Innovation and Technology Diffusion Policy. A Maastricht Memorandum.* Luxemburg: Commission of the European Communities.

STAHEL, W. R. (1991). *Langlebigkeit und Materialrecycling—Strategien zur Vermeidung von Abfällen im Bereich der Produkte.* Essen.

——(1994). 'Produkt-Design und Ressourcen-Effizienz', in P. Zoche (ed.), *Herausforderungen für die Informationstechnik.* Schriftenreihe des Fraunhofer-Instituts für Systemtechnik und Innovationsforschung (ISI), Band 7. Heidelberg: Physica-Verlag.

UNCED (1994). *Financial Resources and Mechanisms for Sustainable Development: Overview of Current Issues and Developments.* UN-Dok. E/CN.17/ISWG.II/1994/2.

UNWCED (1987). *Our Common Future. The Brundtland Report.* Oxford: Oxford University Press.

VERGRAGT, P. J., and JANSEN, L. (1993). 'Sustainable technological development: The making of a Dutch long-term oriented technology programme'. *Project Appraisal*, 8/3. Den Haag: mimeo.

VROM (The Netherlands Ministry of Housing, Physical Planning and the Environment) (1993). *National Planning for Sustainable Development. The Netherlands Experience.* Report. Den Haag: mimeo.

WALZ, R., GRUBER, E., HIESSL, H., and REIß, T. (1992). *Neue Technologien und Ressourcenschonung.* Karlsruhe: ISI.

WALZ, R., OSTERTAG, K., and BLOCK, N. (1995). *Synopsis of Selected Indicator Systems for Sustainable Development.* Karlsruhe: ISI.

11

Organizational Innovation in European 531
Firms: A Critical Overview 532
of the Survey Evidence

BENJAMIN CORIAT

The purpose of this chapter is to provide an initial synthetical analysis of the lessons to be drawn from the study of the diffusion of organizational innovations in European firms.[1] This study is based on the exploitation of four major nationwide surveys that were respectively carried out in Germany, the UK, Denmark, and France.[2] Thus, the present chapter intends to complete and extend a series of studies aiming at making a thorough examination of the links existing between organizational innovation and firms' competitiveness, as part of a reflection already initiated on 'Made in Europe'.[3]

Before dealing with the content and analysis of the surveys, it seems useful to stress what the stakes of such an investigation are. Both empirical and theoretical reasons account for the recent interest in those themes.

Although several major works had long ago established the role of organizational dimensions in the understanding of firms' performances, it was not until the 1990s, and the spectacular emergence of Japanese firms on the international scene, that those themes were truly considered. Indeed, several studies then started to stress that the success of Japanese firms was first due to—among other factors—the fact that they originally represented a series of major organizational innovations, regarding work organization as such (just in time and all its protocols), product design (Clark and Fujimoto 1991), as well as inter-firm relations, particularly the relations between main contractors and suppliers (Asanuma 1989).[4] Such a particular context has made the

---

[1] A first version of this chapter was completed with the support of DG 'Enterprises' of the European Commission (see Coriat 1998). This chapter is a new enhanced version that has benefited from the support of DG 'Research' (under the DYANACOM TSER programme). The author is grateful to both institutions.
[2] Let us warn our reader that the results of the French surveys will not be directly presented in this chapter, since they are available, in their exhaustive version in Greenan (1996a) and (1996b).
[3] See the special issue 'Made in Europe' of the IPTS review (IPTS 1997a). Concerning the links between organizational innovation and European firms' competitiveness, cf. Andreassen et al. (1995: ch. 1), as well as the contributions by Coriat, Dosi, and Weinstein in IPTS (1997b) and IPTS (1997a).
[4] Cf. Aoki 1988, 1990 as well as our own essay (Coriat 1999) for a synthetical presentation of those innovations.

development of many empirical studies possible, both in Europe and the United States.

Quite naturally, the attention thus paid to firms' new practices has permitted a renewed theoretical—and often original—reading of the 'intangible' factors that account for firms' competence and performance. Some basic works, like Chandler's on firms' structures,[5] Penrose's vision of resource-based theory of the firm, or March's and Simon's (1958) have been revisited and have often led to major developments. In the end, the joint notions of *organizational learning* or *organizational competencies*, around which such evolutionist authors as Nelson and Winter (1982), Dosi and Marengo (1994), or Teece and Pisano (1994) focused their attention, have made possible the renewal of the classical visions of the scope of firms' competitiveness. This reflection is all the more sustained as it is nourished by representations asserting the transition towards a 'knowledge-based economy' (Foray and Lundvall 1996).

As far as we are concerned, we shall mostly insist on the fact that these various approaches all focus on the analysis of different modes of co-ordination as regards *information and competence* within firms, as well as in their relations with certain large institutions in charge of the production and diffusion of knowledge (schools and vocational training, research systems). Intra- and inter-organizational co-ordination patterns are thus thought to be unevenly efficient to ensure firms' satisfactory adjustment to their changing environment, or the development of their products or processes. Henceforth, *the relation between organization and performance* becomes the object of specific analyses and questionings. In such a context, the notions of 'best practices' or 'high performance work place' have appeared, and their development ought to be encouraged. Lastly, the OECD very recently (1999) dedicated a comparative study to this theme.

This empirical as well as theoretical debate, which first originated in the United States, has quickly reached Europe. In the context of a relative stagnation of Europe (compared to the United States or South Asia), the debate on organizational innovation has often been very heated. It has reached a kind of apex with the emergence of the theme of the 'European paradox'.[6]

Hence our desire to enter into the 'organizational black box' of European firms more thoroughly, using some of the major surveys that have been entirely dedicated to this theme these last years, in order to further the knowledge on some aspects of the discussion. More precisely, considering the vast array of the methods and measurement or evaluation tools that are commonly used (making it extremely difficult to compare results) and the largely

---

[5] For a synthesis of his own views on firm competencies see Chandler (1992).

[6] We have argued that in most cases Europe was lagging behind for organizational reasons more than technological ones (cf. Andreassen *et al.* 1995).

heterogeneous aspect of the different methods, goals, and consequently final results of those different studies, our ambition will remain limited. We have decided to focus our attention on the following three series of problems:

(1) the identification and nature of organizational innovations, as they stand out from the various surveys;
(2) an evaluation of the scope, levels, and modes of the diffusion of organizational innovations in the European firms;
(3) some preliminary findings as regards the appraising and measuring of the performances that can be directly linked to the dissemination of innovations.

In the final section we will offer some reflections on the results themselves, as well as on the means used to pursue the investigation on the various themes dealt with in the present study.

11.1. Identification and Content of Organizational Innovations

A close analysis of the various questionnaires, as well as of the use their authors have made of them, highlights the fact that the implicit concepts of organizational innovation largely differ from one survey to another. Our intention is to make things clearer on the following points.

11.1.1. 'Forms' Versus 'Organizational Traits': Two Alternative Approaches

A first contrast shows up in the questionnaires, whose aim is to trace organizational innovations by trying to identify the patterns of labour division and task co-ordination, that are generally clearly identified (for instance, the introduction of 'teamwork', 'just-in-time' methods, or the existence of 'quality circles'), considered as sufficiently recent, and representative of innovative practices, of approaches that essentially try to appraise some new 'organizational traits' of the firms, without really paying attention to the concrete means and patterns used to obtain them. Thus, the following two groups of approaches can be described.[7]

1. A first group of questionnaires is based on 'new', and supposedly well-identified 'forms' of organization. The most representative ones were used by the ISI (1996*a*) and (1996*b*).[8] Searching for '*new production concepts*', the ISI carried out several investigations. A first series of results (cf. ISI 1996*a*) is based on a list of eight items, most of which are directly focused on tracing the existence (or not), among the firms that were surveyed, of practices

---

[7] This distinction between the two approaches was first suggested by L'Huilery (1997).
[8] This chapter is based on information provided by different ISI newsletters published in 1996. This information are now gathered and published in a book (see Lay, Shapira, and Wengel 1999).

directly corresponding to clearly identified organizational forms: quality circles, Kanban systems, just-in-time with suppliers, team work, certification (see Table 11.3). The idea underlying this survey is that these new, recent patterns whose efficiency has been acknowledged (at least in certain environments and under certain conditions) constitute an accurate indicator of the firms' move towards a certain organizational state of the art and know-how that, at a given period (the 1990s) characterize a given industry.

2. Another group of questionnaires is based on what we call specific 'organizational traits' of the innovating firms. The most representative of the surveys based on such an approach is the Danish one (DISKO 1996*a* and 1996*b*), that appears as focused on the search for some 'organizational traits' *attached to the innovative firms*. Thus, contrary to the German survey approach, only one question in the Danish one (among the seven core questions making up the basic questioning relative to changes) deals with a codified and identifiable organizational form (namely: the presence of 'quality circles' groups). The majority of the other core questions (five in seven) mostly deal with the identification of the implementation of 'principles', corresponding to some traits of intra- or inter-organizational modes of coordination, such as the setting up of 'cross occupational working groups', 'systems for collection of proposals from employees', 'job rotation', 'delegation of responsibility', 'integration of functions', the last question dealing with 'wages based upon quality and results' (see Table 11.1). Such questions aim at pointing out some *organizational attributes* that are implicitly considered as so many positive indicators of an organization's abilities to react and evolve when faced with unstable environments. Hence, the insistence on some criteria relative to intra- and inter-firm modes of co-operation, within each organization. Indeed, the implicit concept underlying the questionnaire (cf. DISKO 1996*b*) is that an '*innovating firm*' is a '*flexible firm*'; the latter trait being defined as the dynamic capacity to adjust to changing environments, paying less attention to the organizational forms that make it possible. The degree of flexibility is thus gauged from 0 to 14, according to a double set of criteria that concern 'internal flexibility' indicators (i.e. intraorganizational changes), on the one hand, and 'external flexibility' (indicators of inter-organizational changes), on the other (for details on this issue see DISKO 1996*b*).

In practice, however, it is often a mixture of those two basic approaches that dominates, in which the different criteria are intertwined (see, for example, the UK or the French surveys).

11.1.2. On Methodology and Indicators

It is rather difficult to interpret the extent of the changes that have affected the division of labour with the available answers. The main difficulties can be presented as follows.

1. Firstly, it is impossible to identify the differences existing between various innovating patterns. For instance, if most questionnaires include questions relative to the introduction (or not) of 'teams', the answers do not permit to a full understanding of the nature of the changes that have taken place. Is it possible, for instance, to compare 'teams' that are set up after the Swedish model to those of the Japanese model?[9] In the same way, it is also impossible to have any idea about the nature and contents of the learning processes[10] that take place within and between work teams, since they largely vary according to how those teams are co-ordinated.

2. Similarly, we may question some of the indicators that are used in the different surveys. It is the case for example of the 'outsourcing' indicator used in the UK survey. In the absence of any information relative to the criteria applied by firms to such a process of outsourcing, it is indeed impossible to identify the concrete practices deployed by firms. If outsourcing consists of sub-contracting a certain kind of activities through classical and very old forms of 'bidding', then it certainly corresponds to an organizational change, but can we go as far as to say it is an organizational *innovation*?

Other works (particularly those of the French surveys, cf. Greenan 1996*a*, 1996*b*) explicitly deal with this subject and bring negative answers. Such is the case, for example, when, starting from the typology between four categories of firms established in Greenan (1996*a*), one of the categories brings together a group of firms that did undertake changes, but in order to introduce changes on line with the most traditional modes of the division of labour (i.e. of 'taylorist' and 'fordist' type). Such an approach thus poses the question of the legitimacy of considering any noticeable pattern change, whatever its nature, as an innovation.

The same kind of problem arises in the Danish survey with the indicators related to 'wages based upon quality and results, not piece work'. Let us note here that the indication 'not piece work' included in the questionnaire is highly interesting since it enriches the reflection already formulated about the difference to be established between organizational *change* and organizational *innovation*. The indication 'not piece work' is interesting in so far as it clearly indicates that the survey does not aim at identifying *any kind of change* (the introduction of wages based upon piece work would represent one), but *some particular types of changes* that are supposed to be sources of innovation. To put it differently, in the Danish survey, an implicit innovation concept exists which makes it possible to differentiate between two types of changes, clearly separating those that can be considered as innovations from those that cannot.

---

[9] On this point, please refer to Cole's founder works (1979).
[10] Cf. the discussion between Adler and Cole (1993) and Berggren (1994) on the comparison between NUMMI and UDDEVALLA, as well as a review of the debate in Coriat (1999).

These considerations confirm the necessity to have an *explicit* reflection and definition on the concept of organizational innovation which is used as a reference as well as a justification for the use of the indicators that are considered as relevant.

3. Lastly, some other questions ought to be mentioned, like, for instance, those related to the difficulty to estimate *the level of novelty* that can be associated with effective changes. This limit already exists when dealing with well-known and codified practices, but it is all the more important when dealing with practices that could be 'real' innovations (i.e. if they are different from the 'best practices' in the considered industry). Such radical new practices, once they have been designed and introduced, cannot be identified.[11]

11.1.3. A First Assessment: The Notion of Organizational Innovation and How it is Captured in Surveys

Is it possible to merge the various implicit or explicit notions of organizational innovation used in surveys into a sole notion? If so, can this sole notion enlighten the discussion and possibly be used as an anchor for the definition of pertinent and coherent indicators? To answer these questions we suggest proceeding by distinguishing between organizational *change* and organizational *innovation*.

Organizational innovation as a simple organizational change
The reason why organizational innovation is so difficult to identify is its *multidimensional character* which, from an empirical as well as a theoretical viewpoint, can only be approached and defined as a *joint* group of attributes.

If we limit ourselves to what we have learned from the questionnaires, it appears that 'innovative practices' are captured through

(1) some very clear-cut patterns of division of labour (i.e. the existence of 'teams', a question to be found in almost all surveys);
(2) through the ways tasks are co-ordinated between actors (for instance, the more or less 'co-operative' modes of distribution of information); or else, and more often
(3) through *a combination* of both types of indicators.

Matters get even more complex if we point out that the notion of mode of *co-ordination* itself, being very subtle, is not easy to define, since a given mode of co-ordination can be based on extremely diverse protocols and procedures. Following the seminal works by March and Simon (1958), and using the def-

---

[11] Only qualitative surveys might succeed in doing so. Some organizational innovations developed by US firms and relative to R&D management and product innovation could only be captured via qualitative, monographic surveys (cf. Iansiti and West 1997; and, more generally, Weinstein 1997*a*).

inition they give of what an organization is,[12] it seems possible to assert that co-ordination, as for its contents, encompasses the following three domains: the management and processing of *information*, of *knowledge* and of (conflicting) *interests*, they themselves being implemented through a different mix of authority, contracts, and incentives (Coriat and Weinstein 1997). In this light, the problem faced by the questionnaires is that the indicators selected by the surveys can, most of the time, provide only *one* of the constituent dimensions of organizational innovation, which, by itself, does not lead to understanding fully the very nature of the changes introduced, which impedes the formulation of any serious evaluation of the direction taken by the changes.[13]

To put things differently, if we consider that organizational innovation consists of a series of interrelated changes affecting the division of labour and the modes of co-ordination that prevail within a given organization (or between several organizations)—these very patterns possessing the triple dimension and content already mentioned (information, knowledge, and interests)—we then understand that each one of the implicit concepts of organizational innovation captures only one aspect of the changes introduced. This in turn explains the difficulty in interpreting the information delivered by the surveys. Thus, the lack of clarity resulting from the analysis of the different questionnaires is due to the fact that in the absence of a complete and coherent definition of organizational innovation (clearly stated *ex ante*), those questionnaires try to capture one or the other of the dimensions of organizational innovation, treating it as an indicator of the presence of organizational innovation itself. This implicit strategy is certainly efficient when considering its object: it clearly indicates the presence or the absence of organizational innovation, but it is not really informative about the content of the direction taken by the changes. Similarly, it does not tell us anything convincing either on the degree of *coherence* between the different dimensions of the change introduced (between level and type of division of labour and the related modes of co-ordination) or the real *depth* (or newness) of the change.

---

[12] According to March and Simon (1958) an organization is 'a system of co-ordinated action among individuals and groups whose preferences, information, interest and knowledge differ'. They add: 'Organization theories describe the delicate conversion of conflicts into cooperation ... the co-ordination of effort that facilitate the joint survival of an organization and its members.' In previous works (cf. Coriat and Weinstein 1995, 1997), we pointed out the benefits of an organizational approach based on the distinction between information, know-how, and interests, showing how the different theories relative to the firm finally depend on one or the other (or sometimes both) of these determinations. We think the same benefit can be had from these distinctions by applying it to the notion of organizational innovation.

[13] Our analysis makes it clear that the various approaches differ according to what they consider as innovations: either patterns of labour division (dominant in the German approach) or co-ordination specificities (i.e. the Danish approach), use mixed tools to capture the process of information, know-how, or interest co-ordination.

Organizational change and organizational innovation
From the above analysis, we certainly can infer that a key and constitutive element of any organizational innovation lies in a change of the division of labour and/or related modes of co-ordination. But does it necessarily mean that *any change* in these fields corresponds to an organizational innovation? Or, to put it even more bluntly, if an organizational change is a *necessary* condition to organizational innovation, is it a *sufficient* one?

The analysis of the different questionnaires fails to bring homogeneous answers. One part of the surveys implicitly brings affirmative answers to our questions, by implicitly saying that any organizational change corresponds to a form of organizational innovation. Such is the case with the UK survey, in which innovating practices include the mere existence of 're-engineering' (whatever the object) or outsourcing, even if, as it has been pointed out before, in both cases, nothing allows us to distinguish the meaning or the contents of the pattern of changes involved in such practices. The Danish survey, on the contrary, clearly shows *that only some changes* are regarded as factors of organizational innovations.

Is it possible to choose between these two options? If we follow the Danish intuition, an organizational change can be considered as innovating only in the presence of a list of pre-established best practices (or 'organizational traits' obtained thanks to their introduction within organizations). The UK survey, on the other hand, is more agnostic as to the existence of a supposed 'direction' for innovation, since any change is considered as an innovation indicator.

One of the difficulties of defining organizational innovations (and so to capture and measure them in surveys) lies precisely in the necessity of having to make a choice so as to decide which (and for what reasons) 'new'[14] organizational *practices* can be considered as innovative, thus excluding other practices that are not considered as representative of organizational innovations, in spite of the existence of changes introduced at one or another level of the firm.

11.2. Scope, Levels, and Process of the Diffusion of Innovation

In this section we analyse some of the results provided by various national surveys, country by country, before formulating some more general remarks.[15] As we shall illustrate, even if the population of firms taken into consideration by the different surveys is heterogeneous (cf. Box 11.1), a certain 'image' of the dissemination of innovative practices can be outlined.

---

[14] 'New' for the considered firm at a certain moment of its history, but not necessarily 'new' at all, if, for example the changes consist of well-known and old fashioned practices (i.e. introducing Taylorist or Fordist types of work organization in domains where they were not prevalent).

[15] The reader interested in the data can refer to the original surveys or to Coriat (1998).

Box 11.1. *The population of firms targeted by the different surveys*

Sector-related surveys: The German case. The German survey (ISI), whose scope is strictly restricted to the *machine tool sector*, is here the archetype. The survey offers the following advantages: (1) it is easier to interpret the collected data. Indeed, in this case, with a survey focused on the dissemination of a given number of patterns known for their innovative aspects, the analysis of the comparability of the dissemination of the various patterns and of the performances that are associated to them takes on a real meaning; (2) size effects are also significant. Some very accurate and pertinent remarks (if not conclusions) have been made regarding the dissemination of the various patterns and their effects, according to firms' sizes.

Multisector-related approaches corresponding to a given firm size: The British case. The British survey belongs to this category. It targets *all the medium- and large-sized firms*, classified in 4 categories (beyond 150–259, 300–499, 500–999, beyond 1,000), out of a sample taken from 15 sectors considered to be representative *of the whole manufacturing sector*. The initial ambition, partly fulfilled only because of the unequal rate of answers, was to interview 10 firms in each sector. In spite of the difficulties, this average was almost respected.

More generalist surveys: The Danish and French cases. The Danish survey is here a good illustration since its goal is to *cover the whole Danish private sector, in both manufacturing and services*. In this case, it has become possible to infer some lessons after comparing firms' behaviours in both sectors, and several unexpected aspects have shown up. It is worth noting that the French survey belongs to this category. Indeed, it deals with a wide range of manufacturing sectors, in order to establish a typology among four categories of firms.

11.2.1. In the UK, a Diffusion Less Extended than Expected, but 'Alive' and Bound to Develop

If we first consider the United Kingdom's case, the diffusion of the various practices among firms is *not as extended* as expected. A more precise idea can be obtained if we compare the results of the group of the most disseminated practices to those of the least disseminated ones (cf. Figure 11.1)

The most disseminated practices—'supply chain partnering', 'just-in-time', 'team-based working group', 'integrated computer-based technology' —have entirely or largely penetrated only about one third of all firms, while these same practices (even if they are the most widespread nationwide) are practically absent, most often in more than one third of firms. If we consider the least disseminated practices ('total quality management', 'outsourcing', 'concurrent engineering and manufacturing cells'), we notice that they are totally or practically absent in more than 60% of all firms. We should take into account the fact that the majority of the most widespread practices are

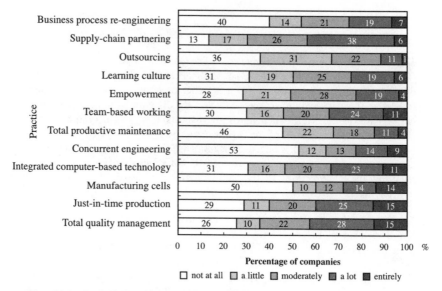

F IG . 11.1. *United Kingdom: Diffusion of different types of innovating practices*

Note: Please refer to the ESRC (1997) report for the data related to the three domains amalgamated in this figure.

Source: ESRC 1997

recent (the 1990s), whereas the least disseminated are generally older ones, for instance 'outsourcing' and 'manufacturing cells'. It is worth noting that *wherever these practices have been introduced, they are still alive* and have never been abandoned. It is even more encouraging to find out, through the questionnaires, that their massive extension is envisaged in the future. For all of the twelve practices, only less than 10% of all answers envisage their reduction, except for 'outsourcing', where the percentage proportion increases up to 22%. Finally, it seems, then, that the group of innovative firms (users), even if smaller than might have been expected, is deeply attached to its practices and undergoing changes, and even envisages their development and extension.

11.2.2. In Germany and Denmark, the Pace of Introduction is Fast, but Dissemination Remains Relatively Narrow

The German study, though conducted with different analysis and measurement tools, does not contradict these results. The following aspects are highlighted by this study.

Whereas the pace of diffusion is relatively fast, the scope of the dissemination remains moderate. Except for the changes that have been operated with a view to obtaining a 'certification' (the strong German trend towards changes aiming to improve or guarantee 'product quality' receives here a sort of confirmation), there is a wide gap between the presence of a new practice inside a firm and its extensive use, which means that new practices are often only locally developed, so as to obtain given and limited results. Hence the scope for their development and extension (cf. Table 11.1).

The Danish survey points out the same trend (cf. Table 11.2). Dissemination remains extremely contrasted: it is very uneven, depending on the practices concerned, and introduction paces themselves largely vary. In all cases, the number of firms showing little concern is important. Lastly, as in other national surveys, we can notice that when an innovative practice is present, the vast majority of answers indicate that the concerned populations remain below 50%. When such practices are effectively in use, however, they are developing fast.

To bring an intermediary conclusion to this point, it seems that beyond national specificity, some 'structural' traits of the dissemination of organizational innovation could be distinguished. This dissemination, though limited, is significant, both in the number of firms concerned as for the populations of workers concerned inside those firms. Lastly, the firms that have embarked on organizational innovation process intend to carry on and to develop and extend them.

TABLE 11.1. *Germany: Current and intended applications of individual elements of new production concepts* (n=1 305)

		Users in %	Intended application in %
New organizational principles	Teamwork	32	11
	Task integration	43	12
	Decentralization	25	5
	Development teams	41	8
Innovative quality management	No control of incoming goods	19	12
	Quality circle	40	19
	CIP	43	20
	Certificates (ISO 9000)	39	42
	Environmental audit	7	23
Redesign of the value added chain	Manufacturing segmentation	40	7,5
	Supplier concentration	25	7
	Kanban systems	18	11
	JIT supply	25	11
	JIT supply to customer	29	7

Source: ISI 1997.

TABLE 11.2. *Denmark: Diffusion of organizational innovations per types of practices* (percentage of work-force involved)

	No	Yes			
		Below 25%	25–50%	Above 50%	Don't know
Cross-occupational working groups	45.2	27.4	13.0	9.2	5.1
Quality circles/groups	54.9	19.1	9.0	9.9	7.2
Systems for the collection of proposals from employees (not quality circles/groups)	47.6	18.1	7.3	19.0	8.0
Planned job rotation	58.3	22.2	7.1	6.6	5.7
Delegation of responsibility	11.6	22.3	23.3	39.5	3.3
Integration of functions (e.g. sales, production/ service, finance)	34.7	29.4	14.4	13.2	8.3
Wages based upon quality or results (not piece work)	54.3	16.4	7.0	15.6	6.3

Source: DISKO 1996a.

11.2.3. Size and Sector-related Effects

The questionnaires have highlighted another dissemination trait, relative to identifying size and sector-related effects. As for size-related effects, the German study clearly states that whatever the nature of the considered innovation (three different ones were measured), the dissemination level of organizational innovation increases with the size of the firm. Likewise, if we consider the *firms' sector* or nature of activity (following a product/market type approach), dissemination levels vary, as well as the dissemination of each one of the patterns.

These results lead us to insist on the fact that if innovation choices (that is, of the different patterns introduced) are a key element in the firm's performance, they do not all have the same goals and cannot be developed in the same environments. The firms' characteristics (size, products/markets) thus imply the most relevant selection of innovation patterns, in accordance with the firms' capacities to absorb them.

Though it was conducted slightly differently, the Danish survey showed the same size and sector-related effects. As we know, in this study, innovation was measured according to a 'global flexibility index'. Using such a measurement tool, the following conclusions were reached:

(1) medium- and large-sized are more innovative (or 'flexible', as the authors of the questionnaires put it) than small ones;

(2) more surprisingly, the manufacturing sector seems more prone to innovate than the service sector.

Some additional illustrations of the existence of 'size' and 'sector' effects
could easily be provided. In so far as they seem clearly established (cf. L'Huilery 1997, which confirms these results on a wide sample of national surveys),
we shall limit ourselves to these indications.

11.2.4. To Sum Up: The Main Traits of 'a European Club of Innovative Firms'

Examined from the diffusion viewpoint, the different national surveys finally
convey the idea that innovative firms constitute a kind of 'club'. If we try to
tackle the main traits shared by the European innovative firms, the following
observations can be made.

(1) They represent a significant percentage (about 1/3)[16] of all the firms sur-
    veyed, but they do not make up a majority; and they are generally to be
    found among larger firms rather than in small and medium-sized ones;
(2) According to the Danish survey (the only one to question this point),
    they are mostly found in the manufacturing rather than in the service sec-
    tor, even if this result should be tempered by the fact that service indus-
    tries are more likely to be naturally flexible, which makes the need for
    organizational change less urgent and pressing.
(3) Innovating firms are not necessarily those that experienced the worst dif-
    ficulties, but are found among those that are most aware of the changes
    that have occurred in their environment and of the need for them to
    adjust to those changes.[17]
(4) A strong group of innovating firms applies organizational innovation in
    several areas and under different patterns: innovating firms thus seem to
    have mostly embarked on multidimensional and often 'cumulative'
    changes; thus the processes of organizational change seem to possess
    their own self-fuelled dynamism. The firms that have embarked on or-
    ganizational innovation processes are generally keen to persevere along
    this way, even if the first results, notably in terms of economic benefits,
    do not always measure up to previous expectations.

These outlines, even if they should be more precise, thus provide a first image
of what innovative firms are like.

---

[16] This percentage is largely indicative. Different results are obtained according to surveying
techniques and aggregation procedures. Still, this percentage seems to us not too far from reality since besides the differences in the methodology used by the questionnaires the same rough
percentage of innovative firm emerges (more on this in Coriat 1998).

[17] This point is made especially clear in the Danish survey: the most innovative firms are those
that are declaring feeling the highest level of 'competitive pressure' from their environment.

11.3. Performances

11.3.1. The Diversity and Relevance of the Chosen Indicators

The nature of the chosen indicators varies considerably according to the surveys, but such diversity represents a valuable source of knowledge. A first approach aims at establishing quantified performance measurements per type of organizational innovation. The German study clearly opted for this approach. It offers the following traits. The measurement is carried out by comparing, for each one of the chosen 'organizational forms', the performance obtained by the firms that use the given form with those that do not use it. The benefit of organizational innovation is thus distinctly quantified. Three performance criteria may be listed:

(1) the value added per head (between user and non-user firm);[18]
(2) the savings in terms of garbage and rejects;
(3) the effects on the reductions of the number of inventory days for outstanding bills.

It is worth noting that the cumulated effect of the three types of practices is also evaluated.

As it appears, most indicators refer to *the logic of cost reduction and thus of 'cost-competitiveness'*. Yet, as we will see later, the German survey uses also indicators that refer to non-cost factors of competitiveness.

Qualitative approaches combine cost and non-cost indicators of competitiveness. The UK survey opted for a unique and different approach. Indeed, the impact of different practices on different performance indicators is evaluated.

TABLE 11.3. *Germany: Value added per employee* (in German Marks) *and use of new production concepts* (comparison of average values, n = 1 305)

	Firms using	Firms not using
Quality circles	132	120
Certification	140	118
Kanban systems	143	120
JIT/Supplier	141	119
Manufacturing segmentation	130	121
Decentralization	140	120
Integration of responsibilities	132	120
Team work	133	122

Source: ISI 1996*a*.

[18] For reasons of space, only the results regarding this indicator are provided here (cf. Table 11.3). For more detailed results see ISI (1996*a*) and Coriat (1998).

The method consists of evaluating the different practices according to three series of goals:

- cost reduction,
- quality improvement, and
- *responsiveness* to the market.

This approach tries to assess cost and non-cost impacts before offering a more heterogeneous indicator such as *responsiveness*. Finally, a more 'comprehensive' evaluation is given by amalgamating the three series of answers obtained (cf. Figure 11.2). Yet, it should be mentioned that performances are evaluated after a very special criterion, i.e. '*the degree of conformity of performances compared to expected goals*' (in terms of cost, quality, or responsiveness).

11.3.2. Main Findings

'Cost' and 'quality' effects
Whatever the diversity of approaches and measurements, it is striking to notice that a common lesson can be drawn from the surveys: the effects of the introduction of organizational innovation are always significant, whether they be cost or quality effects, and the correlations between innovations and

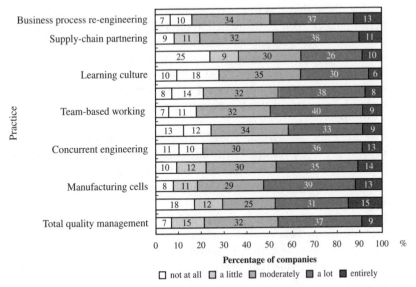

FIG. 11.2. *United Kingdom: Extent to which practices have met company objectives in respect of three amalgamated objectives (reducing costs, improving quality, increasing responsiveness)*

Source: ESRC 1997.

performances are always obvious. This element also accounts for the fact that in all surveys it clearly appears that innovating firms really intend, except for rare cases, to pursue the introduction of new practices when embarked in the first changes.

Four points of particular interest
The main lessons that can be drawn and be submitted to discussion are as follows.

1. One of the obvious results of the British survey is to establish that different practices seem respectively better adapted to specific goals: 'Thus for example Total Quality Management has been shown to perform relatively well at improving quality, whilst JIT is more successful for increasing responsiveness' (cf. ESRC 1997).

2. A 'grape-shaped' development: the UK and German surveys point to the existence of complementary effects between practices. Thus, in the UK survey supply chain partnering, work teams, integrated computer-based technology, and total quality management develop at fast and comparable paces, and are accompanied by good performances, so that innovations seem to call for one another, to reinforce one another in order to develop complementary effects between themselves.

3. The existence of a given pattern does not guarantee that its introduction took place in the required and efficient conditions. It is not surprising, then, that this practice should be associated with disappointing performances. As it is mentioned in the UK survey: 'For example, Team work based Working groups can take many different forms. An investment in this practice may have met with failure because the form implemented was not the "best". This may be further complicated because what is "best" may vary between situations. For example, one form of Team-Based Work may suit one company but not another' (cf. ESRC 1997: 31).

4. The 'systemic' dimension: some contrasting effects do not necessarily provide the same results. Each time surveys have tried to evaluate this aspect, they have stressed the fact that not only do different types of innovations or practices disseminate unevenly according to firms' sizes or sectors of activity, but the effects of identical practices in terms of performances distinctly vary according to the specificity of the firms that use them. This result was clearly pointed out by the German survey. In the same way, the UK survey shows that there may be a contradiction between different practices if their respective goals are taken into consideration.

11.3.3. **Some positive, obvious, but largely perfectible effects**

Finally, the following points emerge out of the collected data.

1. Firstly, however imperfect they may be regarded when taken individually, the diversity of the indicators that were used is, in itself, full of significance. It shows that different approaches may be pursued in such a task, from simple qualitative measurement tools (cf. the UK questionnaires relative to performances evaluated by managers), to accurate ones in terms of impact on the added value or the shortening of development periods (cf. German studies). Once more, the addition and complementarity are significant.
2. Basically, and even if each particular measurement tool is incomplete or disputable, it emerges that the introduction of organizational innovation really entails improved performances. The latter vary according to the category of firms, their size, or sector of activity, but the whole trend cannot be questioned.
3. These positive effects concern *cost competitiveness as well as numerous other factors related to non-cost competitiveness*. We will deal with this aspect later on because we think it is of special importance and should contribute to the forthcoming reflection on this theme.
4. Lastly, the systemic dimension of the effects of organizational innovation on performances should not be left aside. *Indeed, innovations appear all the more positive as they were introduced in complementarity one with the other,* and in accordance with the other organizational dimensions of the firms they penetrate.

11.4. **Concluding Remarks and Further Orientations**

If we set aside the questions posed by the definition of the very notion of organizational innovation, three series of final remarks can be made.

11.4.1. **Diffusion is not Extended as Expected, but it has Considerable Potentialities**

In spite of the heterogeneous aspect dealt by the questionnaires, it clearly appears that European firms are deeply concerned by the introduction of organizational innovating practices. On this particular aspect, we have outlined the emergence of a 'club' of European innovative firms, whose main characteristics have been analysed. We should like to insist on one essential conclusion: the considerable development potentialities still existing for organizational innovation. These potentialities clearly appear if we consider, whatever the survey, that about two-thirds of companies are only marginally or partially concerned with organizational innovations. It should also be noted that this percentage is much higher if we limit ourselves to small- or medium-sized firms. Thus, as far as small- and medium-sized firms are concerned, namely, the less innovating ones, it seems obvious that public policies should help them to take the plunge, so that they might join the 'club' of innovative firms. In the past, public policies managed to encourage technical innovation. Is it not time today to do so with organizational innovation?

11.4.2. Organizational Innovation is at the Crossroads Between Cost and Non-cost Competitiveness: New Arguments in Favour of 'Organizational Efficiency'

This part of the study is of paramount importance because it establishes the fact that organizational innovations are unique in so far as they impact on both cost and non-cost dimensions of firm's competitiveness.[19] From a theoretical viewpoint, this backs up the idea that organizational innovations should be analysed as *process innovations*.[20] These empirical results more generally back up the series of theoretical work based on the theory of organization, aiming at stressing the role of *'organizational—or "X"—efficiency'* (cf. Leibenstein 1982) *as a source of autonomous progress in performances* (cf. Coriat and Weinstein 1995; Gabrié and Jacquier 1994). A more systematic comparison between these theoretical works and empirical results could represent a possible development for the present study, helping to further the general knowledge on this crucial point. Taking all these elements into account, a final question emerges: if its benefits are so obvious, how can we explain the contrasted, if not limited, dissemination of organizational innovation? Why do firms often appear so reluctant and hesitant to introduce it?

11.4.3. Limits and Obstacles to the Development of Organizational Innovations

Several hypotheses can be formulated concerning the slowness or the difficulties with which organizational innovation is diffused. Some of them are directly provided by the questionnaires that have been analysed, whereas some others are deduced from them.

One of the key factors explaining the decision to introduce changes at the firm level seems to be the intensity with which the changes that have affected the environment are *perceived*. As the perception of this intensity varies, the necessity to innovate varies accordingly. Objectively, some sectors or companies

---

[19] These results confirm some prior studies on the same theme (cf. Taddei and Coriat 1993; as well as Andreassen *et al.* 1995). They also back up the development on the same problem to be found in *Made in Europe* (cf. IPTS 1997*a*), as well as Coriat end Dosis's contributions in IPTS (1997*b*).

[20] Even if (though it is a related question) several studies show (cf. those mentioned in ISI) an obvious and positive correlation between organizational innovations and product innovations.

are doubtlessly less exposed to competition than others, or else they develop their activities in such a way that external environmental changes are either insignificant for them or do not really concern them. Yet, *the 'subjective' dimension* should also be mentioned. Changes may be quite real without firms perceiving them, or perceiving the need to innovate in order to overcome their difficulties. Such seems to be the case with small- or medium-sized firms, whose managers, for lack of overtures, do not always think in terms of organizational innovation. An obvious obstacle to organizational innovation dissemination lies in the fact that know-how, in this field, is little codified and little disseminated. It often implies the necessity to resort to experts, which small and medium-sized firms are not used to. It should be noted that the most widespread practices correspond to relatively well-established codifications, for which a clear and visible 'supply' exists (provided by specialized consultants or organizations). Such is the case today, for instance, with certification and normalization to comply with ISO standards. To a certain extent, some Japanese practices (JIT), which are developing fast, are made available today, in the form of 'packages', by specialized organizations.

Another difficulty (partly linked to the absence of clear codification) lies in the fact that organizational innovation questions hierarchical and governance systems within companies. In this case, the whole social structure itself of the company is concerned, and any organizational change appears as a major risk for managers. Only if they are convinced of the necessity for their firms to undergo such changes will they take the plunge. As for 'middle management' (which the Danish survey studied more exhaustively), they see organizational changes as a complex mixture of *threats and opportunities*. Hence the risky aspect of organizational change for the company. Hence too, as noted in the Danish survey, the key role played by 'middle management' in the dissemination pace and the extent of the organizational changes that are introduced, and ultimately seen in the company's performances.

REFERENCES

ADLER, P. S., and COLE, R. E. (1993). 'Designed for learning: A tale of two auto plants'. *Sloan Management Review*, 34/3: 85–95.

ANDREASSEN, L., CORIAT, B., DEN HARTOG, F., and KAPLINSKY, R. (1995) (eds.). *Europe's Next Step—Organizational Innovation, Competition and Employment.* London: Frank Cass.

AOKI, M. (1988). *Information, Incentives and Bargaining Structure in the Japanese Economy.* Cambridge and New York: Cambridge University Press.

——(1990). 'Towards an economic theory of the Japanese firm'. *Journal of Economic Literature*, 28/1: 1–27.

ASANUMA, B. (1989). 'Manufacturer–supplier relations in Japan and the concept of relation specific skill'. *Journal of the Japanese and International Economies*, 3/1: 1–30.

BERGGREN, C. (1994). 'NUMMI vs. UDDEVALLA'. *Sloan Management Review*, 35/2: 37–50.

CLARK, K. B., and FUJIMOTO, T. (1991). *Product Development Performance*. Boston, Mass.: Harvard Business School.

CHANDLER, A. D. (1992). 'Organizational capabilities and the economic history of the industrial enterprise'. *Journal of Economic Perspective*, 6/3: 79–100.

COLE, R. E. (1979). *Work, Participation and Mobility: A Comparative Study of American and Japanese Study*. Berkeley: University of California Press.

CORIAT, B. (1995). 'Organisational innovation: The missing link in European competitiveness', in L. Andreassen, B. Coriat, F. Den Hartog, and R. Kaplinsky (eds.), *Europe's Next Step—Organizational Innovation, Competition and Employment*. London: Frank Cass.

——(1997). 'The new dimensions of competitiveness: Towards a European approach'. *IPTS Report*, 15, *Special Issue on 'Made in Europe'*.

——(1998). 'L'innovation Organisationnelle dans les Firmes Européennes—Nature, Diffusion, Performances—Premiers Jalon'. Rapport pour la DG 3, Document CREI, Université Paris 13.

——(1999). 'The Abominable System of Mr Ohno: Routines, Competences and Monitoring in the Japanese Production System'. Université Paris 13, CREI (Centre de Recherche en Economie Industrielle), Working Paper 99–04.

——and WEINSTEIN, O. (1995). *Les Nouvelles Théories de l'Entreprise*. Paris: Le Livre de Poche.

——(1997). 'Sur la théorie evolutionniste de la firme'. Contribution au Colloque: l'Evolutionnisme, Fondements, Perspectives, Paris.

DISKO (1996a). 'Organisational innovation in the Danish private business sector' by A. N. Gjerding. DRUID Working Paper, 96–16.

——(1996b). 'The flexible company. Innovation, work organisation and human resource management', by R. Lund and A. N. Gjerding. DRUID Working Paper, 96–17.

DOSI, G. (1997). 'The new socio-economics of organisation, competitiveness and employment'. *IPTS Report*, 15, *Special Issue, 'Made in Europe'*.

——and MARENGO, L. (1994). 'Some elements of an evolutionnary theory of organizational competences', in R. W. England, *Evolutionary Concepts in Contemporary Economics*. Ann Arbor: University of Michigan Press.

ESRC (1996). 'The performance of information technology and the role of human organisational factors', by C. Clegg, C. Axtel, B. Frabey, and R. Hull, Report to the Economic and Social Research Council (ESRC).

——(1997). 'The use and effectiveness of modern manufacturing practices in the United Kingdom', by P. E. Waterson, C. W. Clegg, R. Bolden, K. Pepper, P. B. Warr, and T. B. Wall, Report to the Economic and Social Research Council (ESRC) Centre for Organization and Innovation, Working Paper, June.

FORAY, D., and LUNDVALL, B.-Å. (1996). 'The knowledge based economy: From the economics of knowledge to the learning economy', in D. Foray and B.-Å. Lundvall (eds.), *Employment and Growth in the Knowledge Based Economy*. Paris: OECD.

GABRIÉ, H., and JACQUIER, J. L. (1994). *La Théorie Moderne de l'Entreprise, l'Approche Institutionnelle*. Paris: Economica.

GOLLAC, M. (1989). 'Les dimensions de l'organisation: Communication, autorité, pouvoir hiérarchique'. *Economie et Statistique*, 224: 27–34.

GREENAN, N. (1996*a*). 'Innovation technologique, changements organisationnels et évolution des compétences'. *Economie et Statistiques*, 298: 15–33.

——(1996*b*). 'Progrès technique et changements organisationnels: leur impact sur l'emploi et les qualifications'. *Economie et Statistiques*, 298: 35–44.

IANSITI, M., and WEST, J. (1997). 'Technology integration: Turning great research into great products'. *Harvard Business Review*, 75/3: 69–79.

IPTS (1997*a*). 'Made in Europe'. Institute for Prospective Technological Studies, JRC, European Commission. *IPTS Report, 15, Special Issue.*

——(1997*b*). 'Made in Europe: Employment through Innovation & Diversity'. Report of the Launching Seminar, Seville 6–7 October, Institute for Prospective Technological Studies, Working Paper Series, JRC, European Commission.

ISI (1996*a*). 'New production concepts help to save "Made in Germany" ', by G. Lay, C. Dreher, and S. Kinkel. Karlsruhe: Fraunhofer Institute for Systems and Innovation Research (ISI).

——(1996*b*). 'New production concepts: One discussion does make a summer', by S. Kinkel and J. Wengel. Karlsruhe: Fraunhofer Institute for Systems and Innovation Research (ISI).

——(1997). 'Process innovation as the key to innovative products—New production concepts for growth markets', by G. Lay. Karlsruhe: Fraunhofer Institute for Systems and Innovation Research (ISI).

LAY, G., SHAPIRA, P. , and WENGEL, J. (1999) (eds.). *Innovation and Production — The Adoption and Impacts of New Manufacturing Concepts in German Industry.* Series of the Fraunhofer Institute for Systems and Innovation Research (ISI). New York: Physica-Verlag Heudelberg.

LEIBENSTEIN, H. (1982). 'The prisoner's dilemma and the invisible hand: An analysis of intra-firm prodcutivity'. *The American Economic Review*, 72/2: 92–7.

L'HUILERY, S. (1997). 'Les enquêtes nationales sur l'innovation organisationnelle'. Université Paris 13, CREI (Centre de Recherche en Economie Industrielle), Working Paper 98–03.

MARCH, J. G., and SIMON, H. (1958). *Organisations.* New York: Wiley.

NELSON, R. R., and WINTER, S. (1982). *An Evolutionary Theory of Economic Change.* Cambridge, Mass.: The Belknap Press of Harvard University Press.

OECD (1999). 'Flexible working practices: Where are they found and what are their labour market implications'. Working Party on Employment, 29th Meeting held at the Château de la Muette, Paris.

TADDEI, D., and CORIAT, B. (1993). *Made in France: L'Industrie Française dans la Compétition Mondiale.* Paris: Libre de Poche.

TEECE, D., and PISANO, J. (1994). 'The dynamic capabilities of firms: An introduction'. *Industrial and Corporate Change*, 3: 537–56.

WEINSTEIN, O. (1997*a*). 'L'organisation de la R&D'. Université Paris 13, CREI (Centre de Recherche en Economie Industrielle), Working Paper 98–02.

——(1997*b*). 'New organisational concepts and practices at the firm level'. *IPTS Report*, 15.

PART V

Innovation Policy in the New Context

219- 38

631 632
638

12
Innovation Policy—A Systemic Approach

CHARLES EDQUIST

(Europe/

12.1. Definitions

Innovations are new creations of economic significance of either a material or an intangible kind. They may be brand new but are often new combinations of existing elements. A useful taxonomy is to divide innovations into new products and new processes. Product innovations may be goods or services. It is a matter of *what* is being produced. Process innovations may be technological or organizational. It concerns *how* goods and services are produced. Some product innovations (investment goods) are transformed into process innovations in their 'second incarnation', for example, an industrial robot.[1]

Innovation policy is public action that influences technical change and other kinds of innovations. It includes elements of R&D policy, technology policy, infrastructure policy, regional policy, and education policy. At the same time innovation policy is a part of what is often called industrial policy. Industrial policy is, however, a term that is burdened with a lot of dead wood in many countries because of vain efforts to provide public support to old and dying industries. The term innovation policy is naturally associated with change, flexibility, dynamism, and the future. Innovation policy should serve as midwife; not provide support towards the end of life.

12.2. Reasons for Public Policy Intervention

First, I want to point out that the market mechanism and capitalist firms best fulfil most economic functions in a modern society.[2] The market mechanism co-ordinates the behaviour and resources of private and public actors—often in a smooth and flexible manner. This concerns production of most goods, like bread and automobiles, and also a large proportion of service production, like cleaning and IT service provision. It is also true for many innovations, in particular incremental ones. Most of them occur in a spontaneous way through the actions of firms and in collaboration projects between firms.

---

[1] These distinctions are used in an analysis of the relations between innovations and employment in Edquist, Hommen, and McKelvey (2000).

[2] Capitalist firms include private firms, but also publicly owned firms which function in a similar way.

This is, however, less true for radical innovations, especially in the early stages of the development of new technology fields.

Sometimes there are reasons to complement—or correct—the market and capitalist firms through public intervention. This is true in the areas of law, education, environment, infrastructure, social security, income distribution, research, radical innovations, etc. In some of these fields there is no market mechanism operating at all and the functions are fulfilled through other mechanisms, for example, regulation. In other of these fields the market mechanism has for decades been complemented by public intervention in most industrial countries. What is at issue here is what should be performed by the state or public sector and what should not. This is an issue that is not only subject to ideological judgements, but could and should be discussed in an analytical way.

What, then, are the reasons for public policy intervention in a market economy? As regards, for example, technical change and other kinds of innovations, two conditions must be fulfilled for there to be reasons for public intervention in a market economy:

(1) the market mechanism and capitalist actors must fail to achieve the objectives formulated; a *problem* must exist (see below);
(2) the state (national, regional, local) and its public agencies must also have the *ability* to solve or mitigate the problem.

Let me discuss these two conditions in somewhat more depth.

1. There are no reasons for public intervention if the market and capitalist actors fulfil the objectives.[3] Innovation policy—or other kinds of public intervention—should be a complement to the market, not replace or duplicate it. In other words, there must be a *problem*—which is not automatically solved by market forces and capitalist actors—for public intervention to be 'considered'. Such problems can be identified through analysis (see section 12.4.2).

Note that I am here using the term 'problem' and not 'market failure'. This is because the approach here is different from traditional economics. The 'market failure approach' in economics is a part of a formal model: general equilibrium theory in an abstract economy. 'Market failure' in traditional economic theory implies a comparison between conditions in the real world (empirical facts) and an ideal or optimal system. As we shall see in section 12.4.1, however, innovation processes have evolutionary characteristics. The system never achieves equilibrium and the notion of optimality is irrelevant.

---

[3] I assume that the objectives—whatever they are—are already determined in a political process. It should be mentioned that they do not necessarily have to be of an economic kind. They can also be of a social, environmental, ethical, or military kind. They must be specific and unambiguously formulated in relation to the current situation in the country and/or in comparison to other countries. With regard to innovation policy the most common objectives are formulated in terms of economic growth, productivity growth, or employment (Edquist 1994: section 4).

Hence, comparisons between an existing system and an ideal or optimal system are not possible. Thereby the notion of 'market failure' loses its meaning and applicability.

It is normally considered advantageous to argue within the framework of a strict and formal model of some kind and use a theory-based criterion—for example, Pareto optimality—when formulating policy. However, for reasons mentioned, it is not meaningful to use the market failure approach in innovation policy design (Edquist 1994: sections 3.1 and 5). It is therefore necessary to take a step backwards as regards the degree of formality and rigour. Therefore, when I talk about a 'problem' I do so on an empirical basis and in a pragmatic way, not within the framework of a formal model. This is conscious and intentional. The reason is that this approach is more useful as a basis for policy design in the field of innovations and technical change. There is no alternative to a pragmatic basis for innovation policy design (Edquist 1993: 28).

2. If the public sector does not have the ability to solve or mitigate a problem, there should, of course, be no intervention, since the result would be a failure. Therefore, I spoke above about 'considering' intervention if a problem exists. Hence, this condition is an attempt to make sure that political failures are avoided to the largest extent possible. Adding this condition means that the existence of a 'problem', which is not automatically solved by market forces and capitalist actors, is a necessary but not sufficient condition for intervention.[4]

One difficulty in this context is, of course, that it is not possible to know for sure beforehand—*ex ante*—if public intervention can solve the problem or not.[5] The decision to intervene or not must thus be based upon whether it is likely or not that intervention mitigates the problem. Hence the decision must be taken in a situation of uncertainty. Then one can afterwards—*ex post*—determine through evaluations whether the problem was solved or mitigated. If this was not the case, we are talking about a political failure. In other words, political failures can never be completely avoided because of the uncertainty mentioned. We must accept some mistakes in public activity—as well as in private. They must, however, be exceptions and not the rule. In order to determine the success or failure of a given policy intervention through an evaluation, it is necessary that the objectives of the policy were clearly formulated *ex ante*.

There may be two reasons why public intervention cannot solve or mitigate a problem. One is that it is not at all possible to solve the problem from a

---

[4] As an alternative to calling for the fulfilment of these conditions for public intervention, one might argue that it should be discussed for each specific issue (from defence to bread production and radical innovation) whether markets or public actors can fulfil the objectives most efficiently—or if collaboration between them is called for.

[5] This is especially the case with innovation. Here, by definition, it is highly unlikely that there will be any clear-cut precedents for the problem to be solved.

political level. Then all types of intervention would, of course, be in vain.[6] The other reason is that the state might first need to develop its ability to solve the problem. A detailed analysis of the problems and their causes may, for example, be necessary means of acquiring this ability.[7] The creation of new organizations and institutions to carry out the intervention might also be necessary, that is, new policy instruments might need to be created. A patent office is an example of such an organization and a patent law is such an institution.[8] There are two main categories of policies to solve or miti- gate 'problems'.

1. The state may use *non-market mechanisms*. This is mainly a matter of using regulation instead of the mechanisms of supply and demand. One example is taxation of rich people and redistribution of income to poor people. Another is a subsidy to poor regions. The state might also provide edu- cational services free of charge or at a subsidized cost. Other kinds of regulation—particularly related to innovation activities—are the creation of technical standards, public subsidies to firm R&D, or tax incentives to R&D and to innovation activities.

2. Through various public actions the functioning of markets can be improved or the state may create markets. The improvement of the function- ing of markets is the objective of competition law and competition (anti- trust) policies. It is often a matter of increasing the degree of competition in a market. This might sometimes be achieved through deregulation, that is, getting rid of old or obsolete regulations.9 One example of market creation is in the area of inventions. The creation of intellectual property rights through the institution of a patent law gives a temporary monopoly to the patent owner. This makes the selling and buying of technical knowledge easier.[10]

---

[6] Hence, the problem is not solvable by the market mechanism and private actors or by pub- lic intervention.

[7] Hence, it might be necessary to carry out a detailed comparative empirical analysis, see sec- tion 12.4.2. in this chapter.

[8] Institutions as used here constitute the 'rules of the game', e.g. laws, rules, habits, routines, etc. Organizations are the actors or players, the actions of which are shaped by (and shape) the rules. See North (1990) and Edquist and Johnson (1997).

[9] However, markets are always institutionally embedded and there might be a contradiction between 'perfect competition' and innovation. If a market is 'perfect', in the neo-classical sense, the only information exchanged between producers and users relates to products already exist- ing in the market and it contains only quantitative information about price and volume. Anony- mous relationships between buyer and seller are assumed. Producers have no information about potential user needs and users have no knowledge about the characteristics of new products. 'If the real economy was constituted by pure markets, product innovations would be haphazard and exceptional' (Lundvall 1988: 350). Hence, markets supporting product innovation are normally not pure, but institutionally embedded. If policy makers are trying to create conditions that resemble perfect competition in their rule making, it may therefore constitute an obstacle to product innovation. Elsewhere, we have shown that this applies to the rules governing public technology procurement created by the European Commission: '. . . too great a stress on "per- fect competition" can undermine competitiveness' (Edquist, Hommen, and Tsipouri 2000: 307).

[10] Paradoxically, then, a monopoly is created by law, in order to create a market for knowledge, i.e. to make it possible to trade in knowledge. This has to do with the peculiar characteristics of

Public policy makers can also enhance the creation of markets by supporting legal security or the formation of trust. Another example is public technology procurement—to be discussed below.

In both cases, public policy is very much a matter of formulating the 'rules of the game'. These rules might have nothing to do with markets, or they might be intended to create markets or make the functioning of markets more efficient. In other words, policy is very much a matter of creating, changing, or getting rid of institutions in the form of rules, laws, etc.

The example of market creation through the institution of patent law mentioned above indicates that a 'problem' that motivates public intervention might concern the future; a problem might be something that has not yet emerged. In other words policy might well be proactive—and should often be! A *problem-solving* policy of this kind might alternatively be called an *opportunity-creating* policy.[11] One of the problems to be solved might be that uncertainty prevents new technologies from emerging. One example of such a problem is the case where public funding of basic R&D might be necessary because capitalist actors do not have the incentive to fund it. Another example could be that training people and stimulating research in public organizations in a certain field—for example, multimedia—could create new opportunities that would not be realized without policy. I will come back to these opportunity-creating kinds of innovation policies when discussing lock-in situations in section 12.4.1.

Another example pointing in this direction is the public creation of standards, which decreases the uncertainty for firms. For example, the creation of the Nordic Mobile Telephony Standard (NMT 450) created by the Nordic PTTs in the 1970s and 1980s was absolutely crucial for the development of mobile telephony in the Nordic countries. This made it possible for the private firms to develop mobile systems. Ericsson and Nokia would not have assumed global leadership in this field without the NMT 450 (which later developed into the NMT 900 and the digital GSM standard).[12]

A further example of policy leading to market creation is public technology procurement, namely, the public buying of technologies and systems, which did not exist at the time. Public technology procurement was used in combination with NMT 450 in Finland and Sweden to provoke Nokia and Ericsson to enter the new field—which they were reluctant to do in the beginning (Fridlund 2000 and Palmberg 2000). In this way public innovation policy might take the role of a 'midwife' in the emergence of new technology fields and whole production sectors. It could even be argued that

knowledge as a product or commodity. It is hard to know the price of knowledge as a buyer, since you do not know what it is before the transaction. And if you know what it is you do not want to pay for it. In addition, knowledge is not worn out when used—unlike other products.

[11] There might even be reasons to treat the solving of existing problems and the creation of future opportunities as two different situations calling for public intervention.

[12] The NMT story is told in Fridlund (2000) and Palmberg (2000).

most innovation policies should take this proactive approach—an issue that will be further discussed in section 12.4.

12.3. Selectivity in Innovation Policy

When state intervention is intended to improve the functioning of markets, it is often a matter of increasing the degree of competition rather than increasing the rate of innovation. This kind of policy can be argued to be 'general' in the sense that it tries to achieve the same thing everywhere. When applied, however, this kind of competition policy has to be specific to certain sectors—or even products—of the economy in certain countries or regions. The degree of competition has to be estimated, and if means to increase it are needed, they must be appropriately designed and implemented. When markets are created by public action the policy is also specific to various functional areas, whether they concern inventions or the right to pollute. The creation of standards or public technology procurement is always technology specific.

In most other kinds of public policy, the state does not use the market mechanism. Instead, it complements the market or influences the consequences of its operation. This applies to the lion's share of all public policy. Most public policy of this kind is selective, rather than general. It is selective in the sense that its consequences are not uniformly distributed among different activities. This actually follows from the first of the two conditions that constitute reasons for public intervention (see section 12.2): if a certain 'problem' is to be solved, this has to be targeted in a selective manner. This is, for example, true for devaluations. A devaluation of a country's currency (in a fixed exchange rate regime) means favouring export production and production exposed to competition from imports. Devaluations mean a preservation of the existing structure of production. They contribute to higher profits in established sectors while decreasing the relative incentives to invest in new areas.

Public policy for basic research is also selective. Politicians and policy makers must, for example, allocate public research funds among fields of research. Someone must decide which fields of research shall be given priority. Should the funds be used for nuclear physics or biotechnology? Regional policies are selective in a similar manner. Someone has to decide which regions to favour, why, and how. Hence, it is not relevant to discuss whether innovation policy measures and instruments are selective or not in an absolute sense. It is only relevant to talk about degrees of selectivity. Public funding of basic research and direct support to specific companies can be seen as extremes in this respect.[13] Other innovation policy instruments are

---

[13] Public funding of basic research is provided in all countries, but direct support to specific companies only in some. This is probably because direct support to individual firms has negative side effects, for which reason it should be avoided, to the largest extent possible.

located in between them. To divide industry into two parts and favour one of them—for example, through devaluations—is, of course, less selective than providing direct support to specific firms. It is natural that public policy—for example, innovation policy—is selective. Policy is a matter of governing, directly or through influencing the structure of incentives of other actors (and thereby their behaviour). To influence and govern is the *raison d'être* of politics and policy. The degree to which public policy meets its objectives is much more important than its degree of selectivity.

12.4. Policy Implications of the System of Innovation (SI) Approach

'Systems of innovation' (SI) is a new approach for the study of innovations as an endogenous part of the economy. The SI approach has emerged only during the last decade or so. An SI can be defined as encompassing all the important factors that influence the development, diffusion, and use of innovations as well as the relations between these factors. These factors can be studied in a national, regional, or sectoral context; that is, national, regional, and sectoral systems of innovation coexist and complement each other. The SI approach can also be said to synthesize much of what we know today about innovation processes, their determinants and consequences.[14]

The SI approach places innovations at the very centre of focus; they are not treated as exogenous phenomena. Less obvious is that this is also true for other learning processes of various kinds. This is because learning in the form of formal education and searching through R&D is behind much of innovation. This is why there is currently so much talk about 'the learning economy'. The SI approach has diffused surprisingly fast in the academic world as well as in the realms of public innovation policy making and firm innovation strategy formulation.[15] 'Systems of innovation' is simply at the centre of modern thinking about innovation and its relation to economic growth, competitiveness, and employment.

[14] The first two books exclusively devoted to analyses of 'national systems of innovation' were Lundvall (1992) and Nelson (1993). However, Chris Freeman (1987) first used the expression in published form. Regional systems of innovation have been addressed, for example, in Braczyk *et al.* (1998). Sectoral systems of innovation have been analysed in Carlsson (1995), Breschi and Malerba (1997), and Nelson and Mowery (1999). All these books—and others—are reviewed in the introduction to Edquist and McKelvey (2000) which is a collection of 43 central articles on systems of innovation of various kinds.
[15] For example, EU policy makers have adopted some elements of the systems of innovation approach, which is evident in the broader view of innovation policy that was adopted in the 1995 Green Paper on Innovation. Prime Ministers Paavo Lipponen (Finland) and Antonio Guiterres (Portugal) also used the concept of 'innovation system' when they were outlining the immediate future agenda of the EU in terms of 'a Europe of innovation and knowledge' (letter to the Members of the European Council of 16 October, 1999). The OECD also uses the approach intensively (e.g. OECD 1998). The SI approach is also used as a framework for designing innovation policy at the national level in some EU member countries, e.g. Finland and Ireland.

12.4.1. **Characteristics of the SI Approach and General Policy Implications**

In the SI approach, a long-term perspective is natural and important. This is because innovation processes take time, sometimes decades. They also have evolutionary characteristics, that is, the processes are often path-dependent over time and—still—open ended; it is not clear—even to the actors involved—what the end result will be, that is, which path will be taken. History matters! The SI approach has adopted this major contribution from evolutionary theory.

Since innovations occur everywhere, to a larger or smaller extent, in a system of innovation and because of the evolutionary character of innovation processes, an innovation system never achieves equilibrium. We do not even know whether the potentially 'best' or 'optimal' trajectory is being exploited at all, since we do not know which one it would be. This means that the notion of optimality is inappropriate in a system of innovation context. We cannot specify an optimal or ideal system of innovation. Even if it exists, we are unaware of it. As mentioned in the discussion of reasons for public policy intervention in section 12.2 above, 'the market failure approach' implies a comparison between conditions in the real world and an ideal or optimal system. Since such comparisons are not possible in our field, we have instead used the notion of 'problem'. We can identify two main kinds of policy implications of the systems of innovation approach.

1. The SI approach contains *general* policy implications (just like standard economic theory), that can be extracted from the characteristics of the approach. They are 'general' in the sense that they are of a 'signpost' character. In the rest of this section some further characteristics of the SI approach will be discussed.[16]

2. The Systems of Innovation approach provides a framework of analysis for identifying *specific* policy issues. It is helpful in identifying 'problems' that should be the object of policy and for specifying how innovation policies to solve or mitigate these problems could be designed. Since this cannot be based on comparisons between existing systems of innovation and an optimal one, it will have to be based upon comparisons between different existing ones—geographically and/or historically. These issues will be addressed in section 12.4.2.

Organization
Most innovations occur in firms. The SI approach stresses, however, that firms do not innovate in isolation but in interaction with other *organizational actors* (other firms, universities, standard-setting agencies, etc.) and that this interaction is shaped by (and shapes) the framework of existing *institutional*

---

[16] The discussion of the general characteristics of the SI approach is based upon the more detailed discussion thereof in Edquist 1997: 15–29.

rules (laws, norms, technical standards, etc.). Hence, interaction and interdependence is one of the most important characteristics of the SI approach, where innovations are considered to be determined not only by the elements of the system but also by the relations among them. Innovations emerge, therefore, in systems where organizational actors and institutional rules are important elements. The importance of institutions and organizations is stressed—albeit to varying degrees and with different degrees of clarity—in all versions of the SI approach (Edquist 1997; Edquist and Johnson 1997).

The *organizations* with which innovating firms interact—to gain, develop, and exchange various kinds of knowledge, information, and other resources—may be other firms (suppliers, customers, and competitors). Of particular importance are inter-firm relations involving sustained interaction between users and producers of innovations. Here the argument is that inter-firm linkages are far more than arm's length market relationships; they involve more than exchange of quantitative information about prices and volumes. They often constitute ongoing co-operative relationships that also involve the exchange of other kinds of knowledge and information that shape learning and technology creation. Firms also interact with non-firm organizations such as universities, standard-setting agencies, research institutes, private foundations, financing organizations, schools, government agencies, policy organizations, etc.

A general policy implication of the fact that much learning and innovation is interactive is that this interaction should be targeted much more directly than is normally the case in innovation policy today.[17] Innovation policy should not only focus on the elements of the systems, but also—and perhaps primarily—on the relations among these elements. This includes the relations among various kinds of organizations, but also those between organizations and institutions. For example, the long-term innovative performance of firms in science-based industries is strongly dependent upon the interactions of these firms with universities and research institutes. Hence these interactions should be facilitated by means of policy—if they are not spontaneously functioning smoothly enough. The laws and rules governing the relations between universities and firms also shape these interactions—and it is therefore important that these are appropriate for enhancing collaboration.

Organizations are consciously created formal structures with an explicit purpose. They are the players or actors in systems of innovation. Some organizations are created by public policy makers and can therefore serve as policy instruments; others are not. In periods of structural change, a country might have to redesign many of its organizations; this has been the case recently in Eastern Europe. The design of new organizations was very important also in

---

[17] For example, public technology procurement policies could be used more systematically to shape patterns of user–producer interaction. Or the knowledge infrastructure (including the system of intellectual property rights) could be used to develop R&D co-operation more fully, and so on (Edquist *et al.* 1998).

the innovation policies and more general development strategies of Japan, South Korea, and other Asian economies.

Some general policy implications of this view of organizations are the following. It is important to study how firms and non-firm organizations interact with each other and how they perform in relation to innovations. A number of relevant questions can be posed in relation to this area of research and analysis. Is the support that public organizations give to innovation appropriate? Should new public organizations be created? Are the technological support organizations doing the right things and doing them reasonably well? How can the formation of new firms be enhanced? How can the relations between organizations be influenced in order to facilitate innovations? In relation to these questions, it should be emphasized that some of the key tasks of public policy are to create new organizations, to change some, and to wipe out others.

Institution

Laws, social rules, cultural norms, routines, habits, and technical standards constitute the institutional context within which organizations interact. Institutions are not organizations. Rather, institutions are the rules of the game; they shape the behaviour of firms and other organizations by constituting constraints and/or incentives for innovation (North 1990). Some institutions are designed or created by public agencies, for example, patent laws or (some) technical standards. These institutions may serve as important innovation policy instruments. Others evolve spontaneously over extended periods of time, as do various kinds of social rules, habits or routines (Edquist and Johnson 1997). Policy makers cannot directly influence these. A general policy implication of this view of institutions is that a country or a region might need to redesign the institutional rules in the field of innovation and learning (namely, those that policy makers can influence). Of particular importance might be those institutional rules that influence interaction among firms and between firms and other organizations in the field of learning and innovation. Much innovation policy takes this form.

In any system of innovation it is important, from a policy point of view, to study whether the existing institutions are appropriate for promoting innovation. How should institutions be changed or 'engineered' to induce innovation? How can organizations be influenced by changing the institutional structure (framework conditions) around them? Are the incentives for innovation appropriate and strong enough? This dynamic perspective on institutional change is crucial in the SI approach. Not only organizational change but also the evolution and design of new institutions was very important in the development strategies of the successful Asian economies mentioned above, as well as in the ongoing transformation of Eastern Europe. These general policy implications of the SI approach are no surprises. To change organizational actors and institutional rules is what innovation policy makers already do in their efforts to develop the ability of the public sector to pursue innovation policy. Such changes are important engines in the development of whole systems of innovation. These instruments are the most important ones at the disposal of policy makers in the field of innovation and learning. Such creation or redesign of organizations and institutions might be more important policy instruments than subsidies and other financial instruments (which are, of course accompanied by rules, that is, institutions).

Lock-in situations
Earlier in this section we saw that the SI approach considers innovation processes to be evolutionary and path-dependent. From this follows the danger of (negative) 'lock-in' to existing patterns of innovation, for example, trajectories leading to low growth, decreasing employment, etc. This may apply to patterns of learning and production specialization of firms, industries, regions, and countries. We also know that large-scale and radical technological shifts—that is, shifts to new trajectories—have rarely taken place without public intervention.[18] In addition, a minor intervention at an early stage in the product cycle may have a tremendous impact, as we saw in the case of the NMT 450 mobile telecommunications standard. At the same time, a major effort at a mature stage might have only a small impact; the large support to the shipyard industry in Sweden in the 1970s only marginally prolonged the life of that industry.

These are obviously arguments for early policy intervention and for supporting the emergence of new technological systems, which would facilitate transitions from dead-end trajectories for regions, countries, and firms. Negative lock-in situations imply a role for policy in adapting to shifts in technologies and demand. Policy issues in this context might be the following. How can policy makers contribute to the development of alternative patterns of learning and innovations and the nurture of emerging sectoral systems of innovation? A key issue here is the choice between supporting existing systems (with their historically accumulated knowledge bases) and supporting the development of radically new technologies and sectoral systems.

Demand-side instruments
Another consequence of the interdependent and non-linear view that characterizes the SI approach, as discussed earlier, is that it is natural to bring in *demand* as an important determinant of innovation (Edquist and Hommen 1999). This widens the traditional, supply-side oriented, view on innovation policy to include also instruments working from the demand side. They include various laws, regulations, and standards—that is, institutions—influencing suppliers from the angle of the product that is developed and

---

[18] Lipsey and Carlaw (1998) have shown this for the case of the United States.

produced. They also include public technology procurement as an innovation policy instrument. Such procurement means that a public agency, as a sophisticated customer, places an order for a product or system that does not (yet) exist. It can trigger innovation, create a market, lead to the satisfaction of previously unsatisfied needs, and solve previously 'unsolvable' socio-economic problems.

The SI approach can be characterized as 'holistic' in the sense that it has the ambition to encompass a wide array—or all—of the determinants of innovation. Many—or perhaps even most—innovations emerge outside the formal R&D system in a narrow sense, for example, through the learning processes immanent in ordinary economic activities (learning-by-doing, learning-by-using, learning-by-interacting). In addition, innovations are not only developed but also produced, diffused, and used. They also change during these processes. All the factors and processes mentioned here are included in a system of innovation—but not in an R&D system. The general policy implication is that it is necessary to go beyond R&D as a determinant of innovation when designing innovation policies.

The determinants of innovation—as seen by the SI approach—include not only economic factors, but also institutional and organizational factors (both discussed earlier), as well as political and social ones. One general policy implication of this is that it is obviously important to take all these different determinants into account when designing policies. Another is that it is important to integrate and co-ordinate policy areas like R&D policies, education policies, regional policies, and even macroeconomic policies when formulating innovation policies. This also has to do with the fact that innovation is only one integrated part of more general processes of learning in society, which also include formal education, training, and R&D.

Summing up
The general policy implications of the SI approach discussed in this section provide signposts that can inform detailed comparisons of systems of innovation (to be discussed in section 12.4.2). They can serve as rules of thumb, suggesting where to look for problems and possible solutions in innovation policy making. In this capacity they can aid innovation policy makers to 'learn by doing'—that is, to improve their performance as problem solvers by comparing it with past performance. In other words, policy can be used to improve the functioning of systems of innovation without there being any notion of optimality, given certain socio-economic objectives such as economic growth and employment creation. Such objectives can be achieved, for example, by creating incentives for changes in the production structure promoting sectors characterized by rapid growth and a high degree of employment creation.

The policy implications discussed in this section have been of a general character. They do not tell a policy maker exactly how to intervene in order to improve the functioning of the system of innovation. It would be much more interesting if we could provide some of the answers to the many questions formulated in this section! Which organizations and institutions should be changed, and in what way, if the objective is to get an efficient and adaptive system of innovation? How could policy ensure that negative lock-in situations are avoided? What should the balance be between supporting existing innovation activities and promoting the emergence of new sectoral systems of innovation? Which new sectoral systems should be supported? Which demand-side policy instruments should be used, and in what way? The SI approach as such cannot provide answers to these specific questions. Neither can any other approach nor theory. However, in section 12.4.2 we shall discuss how the SI approach can be helpful in finding answers to such specific questions.

12.4.2. The SI Approach as a Framework for Identifying Specific Policy Problems and for Designing Policies to Mitigate These

As seen above, certain general policy implications can be extracted from the characteristics of the SI approach. However, this is certainly not sufficient as a basis for designing specific innovation policies. In this section, I will indicate how the SI approach may serve as a framework for identifying problems that should be the object of policy and for designing specific innovation policies. In this work, the general policy implications may be helpful by serving as signposts and rules of thumb.

To decide on the appropriate division of labour between private and public actors in the field of innovation is a very complicated task. In section 12.2 we concluded that a necessary (but not sufficient) condition for public intervention in processes of innovation is that a 'problem'—which is not automatically solved by market forces and private actors—must exist. This means that neutral or general policies are normally irrelevant (see section 12.3). Substantial analytical and methodological capabilities are needed to identify problems— whether policies are being made at the regional, national, or EU level. Such capabilities are also needed to design policies that can mitigate the problems.

Problem identification by means of comparisons
There is no way to identify these problems specifically enough, for purposes of policy making, on the basis of theory alone. This is true for all existing theoretical perspectives and not only for the SI approach. No theory or approach can tell a politician or policy maker exactly how to use 100 million ECU to enhance innovation processes. Let us take standard economic theory as an example. The market failure analysis argues that a completely competitive, decentralized market economy would provide suboptimal investment in knowledge creation and innovation. Firms underinvest in R&D because of uncertainty and appropriation problems. This leads, for example, to a case for

public subsidies for knowledge creation, or for the creation of intellectual property rights. This nicely links up with the 'linear model' approaches and economists and policy makers often consider this to be a justification—or theoretical foundation—for governments to subsidize R&D.

However, the policy implications that emerge from the market failure theory are actually not very helpful for policy makers from a practical and specific point of view. They are too blunt to provide much guidance. They do not indicate how large the subsidies should be or within which specific area one should intervene. And they say almost nothing about how to intervene, namely, which policy instruments that should be used. The conclusion is that standard economic theory is not of much help when it comes to formulating and implementing specific R&D and innovation policies. It provides only general policy implications; for example, that basic research should sometimes be subsidized. As we have seen, the same is true for the SI approach.

The general policy implications of the SI approach are different from those of standard economic theory. This has to do with the fact that the characteristics of the two frameworks are very different. The SI approach shifts the focus away from actions at the level of individual, isolated units within the economy (firms, consumers) towards that of the collective underpinnings of innovation. It addresses the overall system that creates and distributes knowledge, rather than its individual components.

Systems of innovation can be quite *different* from each other, for example, with regard to specialization of production, resources spent on R&D, etc. For example, industrial production in the United States and Japan is much more specialized in the production of R&D intensive ('hi-tech') products than is industrial production in the EU (Fagerberg in this volume, Edquist and Texier 1996). Further, within the EU, R&D intensities vary greatly between countries. In addition, organizations and institutions constituting elements of the systems may be different. For example, research institutes and company-based research departments may be important organizations in one country (for example, Japan) while research universities may perform a similar function in another (for example, the United States). Institutions such as laws, norms, and values also differ considerably between systems.

An important characteristic of the SI approach is that these differences are stressed, rather than abstracted from, as is the case in neo-classical economics. This makes it not only natural but also vital to *compare* different systems. Without such comparisons it is impossible to argue that one system is specialized in one or the other way, or that a system performs well, or badly. Comparisons are the most important means for understanding what is good or bad, or what is a high or a low value for a variable in a system of innovation. However, as argued in section 12.4.1, we cannot specify an optimal or ideal system of innovation, since innovation processes have evolutionary characteristics. Therefore, comparisons between an existing system and an ideal or optimal system are not possible. A 'problem' cannot be identified in this way.

The only possible system comparisons are between existing systems. Historically pre-existing systems can be compared with current ones, or different currently existing ones can be compared with each other.[19] The comparisons must be genuinely empirical and very detailed. They would then be similar to what is often called 'benchmarking' at the firm level. Such comparisons are crucial for policy purposes, for example, for the identification of 'problems' that should be subject to policy intervention.

There are several reasons why such comparisons are better pursued with the help of the systems of innovation approach than within the framework of traditional economics. These include the fact the SI approach places innovation at the very centre of focus and that differences between systems of innovation are stressed—rather than abstracted from—in the SI approach. Another reason is that the SI approach allows for the inclusion not only of economic factors influencing innovation, but also institutional, organizational, social, and political factors. Hence, the SI approach can fruitfully serve as a framework for developing specific policy issues. These can, for example, indicate to policy makers when, where, and how to use financial resources for innovation purposes. This might also indicate how to devise institutions and organizations, how to organize education and learning, etc.

I shall now provide an example of how a comparative analysis can identify a problem that should be subject to innovation policy. Through empirical comparisons we know that industrial employment in the Swedish economy decreased by 27% between 1975 and 1996. Among 17 countries (the 15 EU member states, USA, and Japan), only two countries had a larger decrease (Pianta and Vivarelli 1999). Sweden's employment in services increased by 21% during the same period. It was the lowest figure among the 17 countries (Pianta and Vivarelli 1999).

The Swedish economy has been very successful in the diffusion of process technologies during the latest decades. Sweden has not been as successful with regard to product innovations, as shown by the following comparisons. The proportion of Swedish industrial production that took place in the growth industries was in 1990 approximately 60% of the average for all OECD countries.[20] Hence, Swedish industry was not specialized in production of growth products. Employment in the growth sectors has grown much slower in Sweden than in other OECD countries. In fact it has decreased. In the growth industries there were 210,000 jobs in Sweden 1975 and 190,000

---

[19] This includes comparisons against averages for more than one, or all, systems for certain variables. A final kind of comparison would be between a value for a certain variable in an existing system and some norm, or goal. However, this would, of course, not be a comparison with another existing system, nor with an optimum.

[20] Growth industries are defined as those industrial sectors that grew most rapidly in the OECD world as a whole during 1975–1990. They are, to a large extent, the same as the so-called hi-tech industries, i.e. those sectors where the R&D intensity is high (Edquist and Texier 1996). Some of the data presented here are not up to date, but the example still serves the purpose of identifying a 'problem'. The data are, however, updated in an ongoing project.

jobs in 1991. In the other OECD countries there was an average increase of 50% in employment in the growth industries during the same period. These jobs were characterized by high productivity and relatively high wages (Edquist and Texier 1996).

If employment in Swedish industry had grown as rapidly as in the other OECD countries (on average) in the growth sectors during 1975–91, then there would have been 315,000 jobs in these sectors in Sweden in 1991. That is 125,000 more than the actual number. This should be related to the fact that there were only about 870,000 employees in manufacturing in Sweden in 1991 (Edquist and Texier 1996). This means that Swedish industry has not exploited the possibility of creating 125,000 'real' high productivity, high wage jobs in the growth industries. The structural change in the direction of more knowledge-based activities has been considerably slower in Sweden than in the surrounding world. Thereby, the production structure of Swedish industry has become more obsolete. It can be argued that this is a major explanation for the fact that Sweden had an unemployment rate of about 10%, meaning about 500,000 unemployed, in the late 1990s.[21]

This empirical and comparative analysis has identified a 'problem' in the Swedish national innovation system that should have been subject to public intervention, since it seems not to have been solved spontaneously by market forces and private actors during a long period of time.[22] It should only be so, however, if the public agencies also have the ability to solve or mitigate the problem. The policy recommendation emerging from this discussion is that explicitly comparative empirical analyses should be carried out as a basis for policy making in countries (and regions). They can serve the purpose of identifying 'problems' that should be the object of policy.

Causal explanation and policy design
However, an identification of a 'problem' by means of benchmarking is certainly not sufficient as a basis for designing innovation policies; it is only a first step. First of all, the existence of a 'problem' is only a necessary condition for pursuing an innovation policy. The public sector must also have the ability to solve or mitigate the problem. A detailed analysis of the problems and their causes might be necessary and new organizations and institutions might be necessary for creating this ability. To know *that* there is reason to consider public intervention is not enough. A symptomatic description of a problem only indicates *where* and *when* intervention is called for. It says nothing about *how* it should be pursued. In order to be able to design appropriate innovation policy instruments it is necessary to also know the causes behind the problem identified, at least the most important ones. A causal

---

[21] It is often said that every new manufacturing job creates 3–4 service jobs, i.e. 125,000 manufacturing jobs might mean 500,000 jobs in total.

[22] A similar analysis identifying a 'problem' in Europe as a whole with regard to the structure of production has been carried out by Jan Fagerberg, in this volume.

analysis might also reveal that public intervention might be unlikely to solve the problem identified, due to lack of ability.

The combination of a symptom describing (problem identifying) analysis and a causal explanation may be called a 'diagnostic' analysis (Edquist 1993, 1994). Such an analysis can provide a basis for an efficient therapy or treatment, namely, a policy. Without a diagnosis it is impossible to know which prescriptions to make, and without timely prescriptions there is a risk that we shall become pathologists—that we shall try to find the diagnosis after the patient has passed away. However, satisfactory causal explanations in the social sciences are rare phenomena. Therefore, an inability to explain in detail might not be a reason to abstain completely from intervention in the process of innovation. Because problems identified may sometimes be very severe— for the economy, for the environment, or for the social conditions—trial-and-error intervention may be necessary. However, it is still necessary to have some clue about the most important causes behind a problem.

Within a systems of innovation framework an identification of the causes behind the problems is the same as identifying deficiencies in the functioning of the system. It is a matter of identifying functions that are missing or inappropriate and which lead to the 'problem' in terms of comparative performance. Let us label these deficient functions 'system failures'. When we know the causes behind a certain 'problem' (for example, low performance), we have identified a 'system failure'. The OECD has addressed what they call 'systemic failures' and defined them as 'mismatches between the components of an innovation system' (OECD 1998: 102). Let me try to be somewhat more specific with regard to what a 'system failure' might be. On the basis of the discussion of the characteristics of the SI approach, at least three main categories of systems failures can be mentioned:[23]

- organizations in the system of innovation might be inappropriate or missing
- institutions may be inappropriate or missing
- interactions or links between these elements in the SI might be inappropriate or missing.[24]

We pointed to an area of low performance of the Swedish economy which is likely to be closely associated with the functioning of the national system of innovation, namely, too little product innovation and insufficiently rapid change in the structure of production in the direction of a higher proportion of R&D intensive goods in manufacturing production. However, a detailed causal analysis of the problem identified is necessary to find out which kind

---

[23] Two of these three categories (organizations and interaction) were mentioned by Andersen, Metcalfe, and Tether (2000), in their short discussion of system failures.

[24] The interactions might, for example, lead to lock-in situations. This could be a consequence if conservative users with a weak technical competence put their suppliers at a competitive disadvantage, as a result of the interaction between the two.

of system failure is behind this problem.[25] Not until they know the character of the system failure do policy makers know whether to influence or change organizations, institutions, interactions between them; or something else.[26] Hence, an identification of a problem should be supplemented with an analysis of its causes as a part of the analytical basis for the design of an innovation policy. Benchmarking is not enough.

'Problems' and 'system failures' are different from 'market failures' in that they are identified through comparisons between existing systems. The result is that the identification of 'market failures' and 'system failures' can be expected to point in different directions, or at different issues—at least partly. It is also likely that there are more systems failures than market failures in most innovation systems (of course depending on their performance). Hence, the resulting innovation policies will be different.

12.5. Conclusion

In summary, concrete empirical and comparative analyses are absolutely necessary for the design of specific policies in the fields of R&D and innovation. The SI approach is an analytical framework suited for such analyses. It is appropriate for this purpose because it places innovation at the very centre of focus and because it is able to capture differences between systems. In this way specific problems that should be objects of innovation policy can be identified.

In order to design specific policies, it is also important to identify the causes—or system failures—behind the problems. These problems and their causes do not come out of the SI approach as such, but from the empirical and comparative analyses that can be carried out with the help of it. There is no substitute for concrete analyses of concrete conditions in an effort to design innovation policy. However, the general policy implications of the SI approach may be helpful as signposts in carrying out the empirical comparisons between systems of innovation.

REFERENCES

ANDERSEN, B., METCALFE, J. S., and TETHER, B. S. (2000). 'Distributed innovation systems and instituted economic processes', in J. S. Metcalfe and I. Miles (eds.), *Innovation Systems in the Service Economy*. Dordrecht: Kluwer Academic Publishers.

[25] Such a causal analysis was attempted in Edquist (1993).

[26] It should be mentioned that a certain system failure might be solved in several different ways, since, for example, different organizations may perform the same function. For example, research institutes and company-based research departments may, in one national system, perform the same function as research universities in another.

BRACZYK, H.-J., COOKE, P. , and HEIDENREICH, M. (1998). *Regional Innovation Systems: The Role of Governances in a Globalized World.* London: UCL Press.

BRESCHI, S., and MALERBA, F. (1997). 'Sectoral innovation systems: Technological regimes, Schumpeterian dynamics, and spatial boundaries', in C. Edquist (ed.), *Systems of Innovation: Technologies, Institutions and Organizations.* London: Pinter/ Cassell Academic.

CARLSSON, B. (1995) (ed.). *Technological Systems and Economic Performance: The Case of Factory Automation.* Dordrecht: Kluwer.

EDQUIST, C. (1993). 'Innovationspolitik för förnyelse av svensk industri'. Tema T Report 33, Linköping: Department of Technology and Social Change, Linköping University.

——(1994). 'Technology policy: The interaction between governments and markets', in G. Aichholzer and G. Schienstock (eds.), *Technology Policy: Towards an Integration of Social and Ecological Concerns.* Berlin: Walter de Gruyter.

——(1997a) (ed.). *Systems of Innovation: Technologies, Institutions and Organizations.* London: Pinter/Cassell Academic.

——(1997b). 'Systems of innovation approaches—their emergence and characteristics', in C. Edquist (ed.), *Systems of Innovation: Technologies, Institutions and Organizations.* London: Pinter/Cassell Academic.

——and HOMMEN, L., (1999). 'Systems of innovation: Theory and policy from the demand side'. *Technology in Society*, 21: 63–79.

—— ——and TSIPOURI, L. (2000) (eds.). *Public Technology Procurement: Theory, Evidence and Policy.* Boston: Kluwer Academic Publishers.

——and JOHNSON, B. (1997). 'Institutions and organisations in systems of innovation', in C. Edquist (ed.), *Systems of Innovation: Technologies, Institutions and Organizations.* London: Pinter/Cassell Academic.

——HOMMEN, L., JOHNSON, B., LEMOLA, T., MALERBA, F., and SMITH, K. (1998). *The ISE Policy Statement: The Innovation Policy Implications of the 'Innovation Systems and European Integration' (ISE) Research Project*, Linköping. Also available at the ISE home page at the following address: http://www.tema.liu.se/sirp/ise and on a CD-ROM, which can be ordered from the following e-mail address: Charles.Edquist@tema.liu.se.

——HOMMEN, L., and MCKELVEY, M. (2000). *Innovations and Employment in a Systems of Innovation Perspective: The Role of Process and Product Innovations.* Cheltenham: Edward Elgar.

——and MCKELVEY, M. (2000) (eds.). *Systems of Innovation: Growth, Competitiveness and Employment* (2 vols.). Cheltenham: Edward Elgar.

—— and TEXIER, F. (1996). 'The growth pattern of Swedish industry 1975–1991, in O. Kuusi (ed.), *Innovation Systems and Competitiveness.* Hesinki: Taloustieto Oy Publishers.

FREEMAN, C. (1987). *Technology Policy and Economic Performance: Lessons from Japan.* London: Pinter.

FRIDLUND, M. (2000). 'Switching relations and trajectories: The development procurement of the AXE Swedish switching technology', in C. Edquist, L. Hommen, and L. Tsipouri (eds.), *Public Technology Procurement: Theory, Evidence and Policy.* Boston: Kluwer Academic Publishers.

LIPSEY, R. G., and CARLAW, K. (1998). 'A structuralist assessment of technology policies—Taking Schumpeter seriously in policy'. Working Paper 25, Ontario: Industry Canada. (Also published in Edquist and McKelvey 2000.)

LUNDVALL, B.-Å. (1988). 'Innovation as an interactive process: From user–producer interaction to the national system of innovation', in G. Dosi, C. Freeman, R. Nelson, G. Silverberg, and L. Soete (eds.), *Technical Change and Economic Theory*. London: Pinter.

—— (1992) (ed.). *National Systems of Innovation: Towards a Theory of Innovation and Interactive Learning*. London: Pinter.

NELSON, R. R. (1993) (ed.). *National Innovation Systems: A Comparative Study*. Oxford: Oxford University Press.

—— and MOWERY, D. (1999) (eds.). *Sources of Industrial Leadership: Studies of Seven Industries*. Cambridge: Cambridge University Press.

NORTH, D. C. (1990). *Institutions, Institutional Change and Economic Performance*. Cambridge: Cambridge University Press.

OECD (1998). *The OECD Jobs Strategy: Technology, Productivity and Job Creation. Best Policy Practices*. Paris: OECD.

PALMBERG, C. (2000). 'Industrial transformation through public technology procurement? The case of Nokia and the Finnish telecommunications industry', in C. Edquist, L. Hommen, and L. Tsipouri (eds.), *Public Technology Procurement: Theory, Evidence and Policy*. Boston: Kluwer Academic Publishers.

PIANTA, M., and VIVARELLI, M. (1999). 'Employment dynamics and structural change in Europe', in J. Fagerberg, P. Guerrieri, and B. Verspagen, *The Economic Challenge for Europe: Adapting to Innovation-based Growth*. Cheltenham: Edward Elgar.

239-52

13

The Need for New Perspectives in European Commission Innovation Policy

MARGARET SHARP

13.1. Introduction

The purpose of this chapter is to consider the policy implications of the perspectives on socio-economic development in Europe opened up by the work on the globalized learning economy. It raises questions first, about what sort of policies are needed; secondly, about the current focus of innovation policies in Europe; and, finally, about the changes in policy needed to face up to the challenges of the next two decades. It draws upon the research summarized in Bengt-Åke Lundvall's and Susannah Borrás's volume *The Globalising Learning Economy* (Lundvall and Borrás 1998) but also on research on industrial policy currently under way in the TSER project, 'Science, Technology and Broad Industrial Policy' (SOE1-CT97-1053), and on my own work on the European Union's research and technological development (RTD) policies summarized in the book published in 1998 with John Peterson (Peterson and Sharp 1998).

13.2. The New Policy Agenda

Let us start by summarizing the main strands of argument emerging from the Lundvall and Borrás (1998) volume. The key features of the globalizing learning economy are as follows.

1. *Intensification of competition.* A number of factors, among which are the liberalization of trade and financial markets, the end of the Cold War, and, not least, developments in technologies themselves, especially in information and communication technologies, have combined to create an era of intense competition between companies located in all parts of the world. Whether large or small, home-based or multinational, most companies today find themselves involved in global networks of one sort or another. Supply chains, forward and back, rapidly involve overseas companies with whom any company may well find themselves competing for market share 'on their own patch'. At the same time, rapidly changing technologies make almost all companies vulnerable to competition if they fail to keep pace with new developments. There may be small pockets of, for example, domestic service-based

sectors of the economy still shielded from this competition but, in general, protection is limited and policies based on protection of little lasting value.

2. *Ability to adapt and innovate a key attribute.* The only way to survive in a world of such intense competitive pressures is flexibility, which implies an ability to adapt and change rapidly and easily. This requires, *within* the company, high levels of technological capability (to be able to understand and 'translate' for use within the firm developments at the leading edge of new technologies), mechanisms for keeping up to date and learning about new product and process developments, and methods of rapidly disseminating and acting upon this information. *Externally* it means that the company must be 'plugged into' key information and learning networks (since learning is essentially an interactive process). *Internally* it demands high levels of delegation, short chains of responsibility and reciprocal loyalty and trust among key decision takers.

3. *The uneven distribution of costs and benefits.* Although it is fairly obvious that the gainers from such a system will be the well educated (especially in science and technology) who can learn fast and adapt quickly, the distribution of costs and benefits within society is less predictable and more random. Yet the very pace of change makes is essential for society to safeguard those who for one reason or another are excluded from the benefits. Large numbers excluded from benefit not only makes for a highly inequitable society but also for social unrest and disillusion, which in turn can threaten the democratic way of life.

If these are the key features of the globalizing learning society, then there are five main policy messages. First, *education and training are essential.* To participate effectively in this globalizing, learning world, any economy has to possess a modicum of those who are well versed in up-to-date science and technology and a large number who are capable of learning rapidly from others. A strong basic education system with a reasonable number of good quality students going on to undergraduate and post-graduate studies in science and engineering is a prerequisite. So too is good research base, for it is through training at post-graduate and post-doctorate levels in research that key skills in state-of-the-art techniques are acquired. With technology moving so fast, lifelong learning includes the recognition that training and retraining have to continue throughout working careers.

Secondly, because much knowledge is tacit and passed on within and between organizations by word of mouth and learning-by-doing, *networking both within and outside organizations becomes an important part of the learning process* (see, in this volume, the chapters by Mytelka, and Archibugi and Iammarino). Academics have known this for a long time, hence the importance of the 'common room', where they can meet and talk, and the academic conference, where new ideas are discussed among peers. In the same way business executives from small firms learn best from those who have handled the same problems and with whom they feel they can empathize. Increasingly large firms are also learning that they are not self-sufficient but need to access new ideas and new skills by linking into specialist networks. Co-operative structures and co-operative institutions which genuinely foster such networking have an important part to play—whether chambers of commerce or research organizations. Equally institutions which merely have intermediary status but which do little to bring institutions together—as happens, for example, with some science parks—are often of little value.

Thirdly, *protection does not help.* The isolationist is self-defeating. Protection for the short term is rapidly overtaken by the pace of change. What is initially seen as a breathing space too often becomes an excuse for doing nothing, which exacerbates the longer run problem of catch-up. Rather than protection, policy needs instead to stimulate change and adaptation. Hence a tough competition policy, accompanied by deregulation and privatization, has its part to play (and has indeed added considerably to the intensification of competition during the 1990s). Likewise measures to ensure a lively small and medium-sized enterprise (SME) sector from which, in time, larger firms may grow are also important. In this regard, measures to encourage the provision of seed corn capital and to facilitate the raising of venture capital and equity capital at later stages of development are helpful, but so too are the networking and mutual support mechanisms mentioned above.

Fourthly, *the macroeconomic environment must be perceived as among the pressures for transformation.* In this respect the period of preparation for EMU in the 1990s, with its pressures for meeting the relatively stringent convergence criteria may be seen as adding to the intensity of competition. In the same vein, the tough stability pact that now accompanies the single currency may also be seen as a stimulant to competition and, via competition, for innovation. The reverse side of this coin, however, goes in the opposite direction. The over-stringent restraint of demand hits sales and business confidence and results in low levels of investment in plant and equipment (as indeed has been the case in the EU in the 1990s). Since new plant and equipment embodies much incremental innovation, the state of the macroeconomy has knock-on effects on innovation. The successful launch of the euro in 1999 and the run-up to its full assimilation in 2002 may in this regard push in two directions. Success may raise business confidence, especially in economies such as Italy which have suffered from considerable instability, stimulate investment, and with it innovation. Vice versa, too stringent a monetary policy from the ECB could lead to recession, dis-investment, and continued failures in innovation. As yet it is too early to say which force will be the stronger. But it is vital to recognize the interrelationship that exists between micro- and macroeconomic policy.

Finally, *cohesion and structural policies remain important.* The faster the pace of innovation, the greater the risks of social exclusion *as a result of technological development* (see, in this volume, Schienstock's chapter). In particular, those social groups and regions which are already lagging are likely to attract few resources to upgrade infrastructure and skills in such vital areas as ICT. This argues for continuing emphasis on the cohesion issue and continuing pressure for policies which not only redistribute resources and provide the hardware for infrastructure improvement, but also pay attention to the necessary software improvements. In other words, roads, bridges, even telecom infrastructures are not enough: investment in human capital is just as, if not more, important.

These ideas set the framework for the sort of policy required to meet the demands of the modern, open, globalizing, learning economy. Before going on to consider how they might apply to the European Union and its member states, it is worth looking briefly at the main features of the Commission's current efforts to promote innovation in the European Union.

13.3. Current Commission Policies Promoting Innovation

Current policy efforts in the EU need to be considered within two contexts: first, the multi-annual Framework Programme, and specifically the Fifth Framework programme which is just beginning its first phase of implementation; secondly, the Green Paper and subsequent Action Plan on Innovation.

13.3.1. The Multi-annual Framework Programmes

The multi-annual Framework Programmes were first introduced in the early 1980s by Commissioner Narjes as a means of regularizing the community's growing science and technology responsibilities. The concept was legitimized in the Single European Act of 1987 and subsequently extended in the Maastricht Treaty, which was ratified in 1993.

Table 13.1 compares the main lines of expenditure through the successive Framework Programmes. These incorporated the community's research activities in the energy and nuclear power areas inherited from the 1960s and 1970s, putting them together with the new programmes initiated by Davignon in the early 1980s. Spending under the older programmes had been divided between 'direct' research activities in the community's own Joint Research Centre(s) (JRC) and 'indirect' programmes which operated by contracting research from existing research laboratories belonging to member states. The new Davignon programmes of the early 1980s were dominated by ICT, especially ESPRIT and RACE (note the rising ICT expenditures and falling share of energy during these years), but it is notable that in the 1990s industrial technologies (mainly the BRITE–EURAM programmes), the life sciences, and the environment have all increased their share of expenditures at the expense of ICT. The other main growth area has been the Training and Mobility for Research (TMR—earlier known as Human Capital and Mobility)

TABLE 13.1. *RTD priorities and the Framework Programmes*

Framework Programme	I	II	III	IV	V
Years	1984–7	1987–91	1991–94	1994–8	1998–2002
Total million ECUs	3,750	5,396	6,600	13,100	14,960
EU RTD spending as % EU budget	2.5	3.1	3.5	3.9	4.6[a]
EU RTD spending as % Member state govt RTD spending	1.1	2.3	3.3	5.9	–
Priorities (%)					
ICT[b]	25	42	38	28	24
Industrial technologies[c]	11	16	15	16	17
Environment	7	6	9	9	10
Life sciences	5	7	10	13	16
Energy	50	22	16	18	18
Others[d]	2	7	12	14	15
Total	100	100	100	100	100

Notes:
[a] Based on 1999 budget
[b] Information and communication technologies
[c] Includes industrial processes and new materials
[d] Includes human capital and mobility, development, diffusion, and exploitation and social economic research

Sources: European Commission 1994, 1997*a*; Peterson and Sharp 1998, Table 7.4.

programmes funding exchange programmes for post-graduate students and research personnel.

The new programmes of the 1980s were all 'indirect', in that the money was spent on research contracts not in the JRC, but they also shared a number of other characteristics which marked the new programmes out from the earlier research initiatives of the Commission.

(1) *they were competitive*—while the Commission identified broad areas of research, project bids within each area could be submitted by any laboratory within the EU and were assessed by peer review according to scientific and technological excellence;

(2) *they were collaborative*—funded projects had to involve at least two firms and/or research institutes from different EU countries;

(3) *they were shared cost*—firms had to contribute 50% of research costs: universities and research institutes were expected to meet fixed costs and charge only for the actual costs involved in doing the research;

(4) *they had a considerable element of bottom-up choice*—while the Commission identified broad priorities, the detailed projects submitted reflected the views of researchers as to where work was best directed.

The Commission also consulted widely with the relevant research community in setting its broad priorities;

(5) *the research involved was supposedly pre-competitive*—aimed at generic research problems rather than research specific to particular products or processes.

As Table 13.1 shows clearly the scale of the EU's activities expanded considerably over these years (although the figures include both an expanded coverage of activities and an increasing number of countries involved). In the early 1990s a series of studies was undertaken detailing the 'impact' of these programmes within individual member states. Although there were criticisms, in general the programmes were welcomed by both academic and industrial participants, both identifying in particular the value of the collaborative experience. Once established, however, each programme developed its own constituency which lobbied hard for its continuation. In addition, the requirement under the Maastricht Treaty that the main lines of action under the Framework Programme be agreed by unanimous vote in the Council, and then be subject to co-decision with the European Parliament, increased the resistance to change. It was easier to add an extra line to the programme rather than drop existing commitments. By the late 1990s the Davignon evaluation of the fourth Framework Programme argued that 'It is time for a change because times have changed' (European Commission 1997*b*) and came out with a number of clear criticisms of the way the programmes were then operating.

The Davignon criticisms fed into a wider debate that emerged in the run-up to the formulation of Framework V. The main lines of criticism can be summarized as follows.

1. *The programme had become too diverse and lacked focus.* Framework IV, for example, had eighteen separate lines of action. This fragmented action and scattered resources too widely.

2. *It was still too dominated by big programmes.* In spite of the shift away from ESPRIT and the telecommunications programmes, too much money still went to a small number of large firms and not enough to SMEs.

3. *Too much emphasis was still on the production of new technologies and not enough on diffusion of new technologies.* Again, the lack of involvement of SMEs was notable, but also the emphasis in many programmes on developing new technologies rather than improving competencies in the use of up-to-date techniques.

4. *Pre-competitive research meant RTD without any obvious use.* Pre-competitive was, it was argued, by definition 'use-less' (that is, without any immediate application). Too much money, it was alleged, was wasted on this 'use-less' research. It would be much better to devote it to helping firms, especially SMEs, launch products and processes which had commercial potential.

5. *Cohesion has been used to justify 'mediocrity'.* This was the view put bluntly by Sir William Stuart in his evidence to the House of Lords Select

Committee (1997: para. 2.32) but echoed also in the German position paper on Framework V. Their worry was that the quality of research being undertaken within the Framework Programme was being compromised in order to accommodate research groups from the less-favoured countries and regions. This meant that the original principle of selection by research excellence no longer held sway. Both the British and the Germans argued that cohesion should play no part in the Framework Programme decisions. The Spanish, by contrast, argued that not enough attention was paid to cohesion.

6. *Procedures were too inflexible.* A combination of unanimous decision in the Council and enforced co-decision between Council and Parliament led to a situation in which decisions were so complicated they could never be revised. Yet over the course of the four to five years that any Framework Programme operated, times changed and priorities needed to be revised. There was no mechanism for doing this.

7. *Administration was poor and payment slow.* The most pervasive criticism of the Framework Programmes was of their administration. Many complaints were received of unduly bureaucratic procedures, capped by a poor record of payment which left many small companies (and research groups) in deep financial trouble.

Framework V set out to answer many of these criticisms. There was a determined effort to simplify the structure—initially to be only six lines of action in contrast to the eighteen of Framework IV. But these soon expanded under the influence of various pressure groups and although the Commission managed to retain only seven main action lines, by the time various key actions and generic programmes within each line had been defined, the structure was almost as complicated as any earlier programme. More effort was made to fund demonstration and pilot programmes, to show the 'relevance' of the research, and, once again emphasis was put on attracting more applications from SMEs, with the CRAFT and similar programmes which simplify application procedures. In addition, the Commission made considerable efforts to accelerate decisions and ensure that contracts and payments were on time.

13.3.2. The Green Paper and Action Plan on Innovation

At the same time as the debate about Framework V was taking place, the Commission issued their Green Paper on innovation (European Commission 1995). The Green Paper itself derives from the criticisms of the community's innovative capacity incorporated in the Delors White Paper on Growth, Competitiveness, and Employment (European Commission 1993). This was made explicit in the following extract from the White Paper:

In the Commission's opinion Europe's research and industrial base suffers from a series of weaknesses. The first of these is financial. The Community invests proportionately less than its competitors in RTD . . . A second weakness is the lack of coordination at various levels of RTD activities, programmes and strategies in Europe . . . The greatest weakness, however, is the comparatively limited capacity to convert scientific break-throughs and technological achievements into industrial and commercial successes. (European Commission 1993, ch. 4)

Much of the Green Paper (European Commission 1995) was devoted to an extended diagnosis of this analysis. The EU's problem was 'innovation in a straitjacket'; it had too small and too fragmented an R&D effort and, in particular, its record on industrial R&D was poor with industry failing to anticipate new trends and technologies. Its education and training systems were too academic, and lacked practical and experimental content. There was too little mobility of researchers and cross-fertilization of ideas; too much regulation and red tape. Intellectual property rights were more difficult and expensive to enforce than in the US, and both tax and financial systems viti-ated against enterprise.

The Green Paper (and the Framework V discussions) initiated a wide debate about innovation and what the community should do. This cul-minated in the publication in 1997 of the commission's *First Action Plan for Innovation* (European Commission 1997c). This identified three main fields for action.

1. *Fostering a climate for innovation*—which highlighted opportunities in education and training, especially management training, the aim being to stimulate people to think more creatively and innovatively.

2. *Establishing a framework conducive to innovation*—with emphasis on easing the procedures of innovation, including obtaining patents and finance and limiting regulation. Finance for SMEs was seen as particularly impor-tant, especially the provision of seed corn capital for high-tech start ups.

3. *Gearing research to innovation*—where the key issues were technology transfer and awareness. The Commission proposed to encourage technology watch (foresight) activities, campus companies (university-based SMEs), more demonstration projects, and general encouragement to all companies, large and small, to strengthen research activities.

Implementation of the action plan was the responsibility of both the Com-mission and EU member states. For the Commission, it was mainly a matter of using instruments and procedures already set up, largely within the Framework Programmes, and cajoling and persuading member states to fol-low suit. For member states, there was no compulsion to follow the Commis-sion's lead. It was a question, really, of how far the domestic agenda reflected the same priorities. For some (for example, Ireland, Finland, Denmark) the two coincided. For others (the UK, for example) there was fortuitous overlap (for example, in the pursuit of foresight studies) but otherwise little beyond exhortation and sympathy with the general sentiments discussed.

The publication of the Green Paper and the action plan nevertheless raised the core issue of how the EU should pursue the innovation agenda. The diagnosis was right. The key problem did not lie on the supply side with the failure to *produce* new technologies (although as recent studies including Laursen 1999; Dalum, Laursen, and Villumsen 1998; and Fagerberg in this volume, have indicated, Europe's lagging capabilities in electronics may have affected performance) but on the demand side with the failure to make *use* of new technologies. What, however, could the Commission do? Measures to encourage industry to invest more in R&D lay mainly with member states, some of whom already gave R&D privileged tax status. The Commission had influence in areas such as IPR and regulation but, as the biotechnology debate illustrated, easing regulations was easier said than done when the views of all sides among fifteen nations had to be reconciled in both council and parliament. On technology transfer and finance, the Commission could and did take action. But is it really appropriate for Brussels, rather than the relevant national or regional authority, to run a seed corn capital fund for use by SMEs? Should Brussels-funded technology transfer centres be running publicity campaigns among local firms extolling the virtues of community-funded innovations and urging participation in European collaborations? Is collaboration with SMEs in other EU countries really the best way for locally based firms to learn how to use and exploit the potential of new technologies?

13.4. The Need for New Perspectives

Where, then, should innovation policy be going? Can we bring together the policy lessons from the TSER studies with current trends in policy to suggest new ways forward?

First, it might be worth noting that, in spite of the criticism, there are a number of areas where the EU does seem to have got things right. The emphasis on *collaboration and networking*, initially introduced to enhance the European nature of the programmes, has proved to be exactly right. For many nationally based firms and research institutes the European programmes took them down the learning curve of new collaborative methodologies before they became common practice. The value of this experience is reflected in the almost unanimous verdict of users in the impact studies and other evaluations (see Peterson and Sharp 1998: ch. 9 for a summary of these studies) which give the highest valuation on the benefits gained from collaboration and especially the access it afforded for learning new skills and technologies. The question now is whether such collaborations should be limited to linkages within the EU and associated states, or whether more encouragement should be given to linkages with US or East Asian firms? The emphasis placed in many programmes on *bringing together firms and academic institutions* working in particular fields of research to work on specific projects again proved to be the right way of trying to bridge the academic industry gap rather than the (essentially linear) model of science parks and technology transfer centres. The question here is whether such collaborations should become a required element in programmes—perhaps too many projects, particularly those involving partners from cohesion countries, involved only research institutes?

If the key innovation issue in Europe is the take up and use of new technologies by firms of all shapes and sizes, then the Commission is also right to *concentrate on the diffusion issue*, and SMEs in particular. Among these, technology-based small firms are in fact a relatively small minority and their problem is not failure to use new technologies (except by their potential customers) but primarily the financial difficulties of start up and the valuation put by banks and financial markets on intellectual assets. These are a wholly different set of issues which need to be treated separately. Finally, in spite of the unhappiness of the British and Germans, the Commission has been quite right to insist upon *participation by cohesion partners* in mainstream Framework Programme projects. Such participation is an important 'avenue for learning' by partners in cohesion countries and one mechanism for helping to counter all too apparent forces of social and economic exclusion at a time of fast technological change and intense competition. As Lundvall and Borrás (1998) emphasize, trickle down has not worked. This said, there is a strong case for a switch in emphasis within the structural funds from concentration on physical infrastructure— new roads, bridges, and town centres—to the software necessary to provide an infrastructure for innovation.

It is also important to keep a sense of perspective. The total sum being spent under Framework V amounts to only euros 3 billion per annum, spread across fifteen member states and some dozen new applicants from Eastern and Central Europe. It amounts to less than 3% of total R&D expenditures across all member states, approximately 5% of all public sector support for R&D in the EU15. In other words, it is really a very small sum of money which, although it has greater leverage than might appear, especially in the cohesion countries, is nevertheless by itself relatively insignificant. The other side of this coin, however, is that where EU money is joined by national and/or regional resources, it can create a critical mass of resources which can change things. A good example here is the German Bio-Regio programme, where federal and Länder money has been mobilized alongside EU resources to stimulate a whole new area of activity, bringing in also local private sector funding to help with start-up finance for new firms. Another example is Ireland, where the government has made deliberate use of both EU Framework and EU structural funds as a central plank in its own innovation programme. The lesson here is that EU funds may not be large in themselves, but they can be a useful catalyst for wider action, and in particular where national and regional governments are pushing in the same direction and actions are mutually reinforcing the policy impact can be substantial.

Nevertheless, while the criticism can be overdone, there remain many things that are wrong with EU programmes when judged from the 'learning globalizing' point of view. Too much money is still focused on the production of new technologies in *'grands projets'* by Europe's big firms and erstwhile national champions. The task force initiative, mooted in the Green Paper on innovation and subsequently subsumed within various 'key actions' in Framework V, showed all these traits. Projects such as 'the car of the future' clearly run into the danger of funding Europe's large motor car companies to undertake research which they should be doing anyway.

There remain also far too many shibboleths associated with the Commission's programmes. Why this continued concentration on pre-competitive research? Why not fund more basic research? Is there any reason why this should be the preserve of national governments? And why not more support for competitive, pre-production R&D where there is an acknowledged financing gap? Again, would there not be sense in more co-operation with the United States, especially if reciprocal deals could be brokered? Does collaboration have to be inter-country collaboration? Might the Framework Programme not learn something from the structural funds about the value of regional R&D networks in helping SMEs to upgrade competencies?

The previous paragraph begins to map out the sorts of new policy perspectives that are emerging. Putting together the lessons from the 'learning globalizing' framework and the debate on innovation, the main elements for a new European level innovation policy might be as follows.

1. *More support for basic research.* Given the degree to which the boundaries between basic and applied research are already becoming blurred, it seems absurd for the EU to maintain the pretence that it should not fund basic research. Indeed, projects such as those under the biotechnology programme which have concentrated on sequencing various genomes have in essence been basic research programmes. The key issue is not just that this funding helps to push forward the frontiers of knowledge, but that it also trains high-grade minds in state-of-the-art techniques when such knowledge is crucial to being able to use new technologies developed elsewhere. The benefits from high levels of federal funding for basic research in the US have been apparent for some time. At a time when national government support has been waning, EU funding could provide a useful catalyst to reverse the trend. One possibility would be for the EU, working together with national governments, to help endow a 'super-league' of research universities. Another might be to create in the sciences a series of senior research fellowships akin to the Monnet Fellowships, which have been so successful in promoting European studies within universities in the EU. As with the Monnet Fellowships, these would be for a limited, five-year period, after which national governments

would assume responsibility for funding the positions through the normal university channels. As such, they would be a useful way of making sure that more resources went over the longer term from national budgets into basic research.

2. *Enhanced support for TMR.* The TMR has already made its mark as an important element within the Framework Programmes. It is particularly important for training young researchers, especially from the cohesion countries, in modern research methodologies. But the programme also creates linkages and friendships which survive for a lifetime and are the stuff of successful academic endeavour. There is much to be gained and very little to lose from such support.

3. *Continued emphasis on collaborative, shared-cost projects*—but widening the focus to encourage collaboration (with appropriate sharing of financial costs) with countries outside the EU. Such collaborations are already extended through associate status to countries such as Israel and it would be a comparatively short step to shift towards worldwide collaboration. This might be particularly appropriate in some of the more scientifically oriented projects.

4. *Shift the focus of SME support to the regional level.* It is not appropriate for Brussels to be co-ordinating either seed corn capital initiatives for high-technology start ups or regional technology transfer centres for local SMEs. Both initiatives are better co-ordinated at the local level. In this regard both the Framework and the SPRINT (Innovation) Programmes could learn from the structural funds where the Regional Innovation Strategies have led to successful local initiatives which bring together national and regional governments to help promote an innovation programme. These help to create local networks of firms (large and small), research institutes, universities, and technical colleges to promote learning about and using new technologies specific to the needs of local industry. With new technology-based small firms the network may well include local bankers and businessmen, capable of helping with the finance of start ups. The difference in this case is that the initiative would not be limited to the less-favoured regions. EU funding would be available to help catalyse activities in any region, the qualifying criteria being that it must be an initiative to help SMEs and must involve equal funding from national and local sources.

5. *Continued emphasis on cohesion.* As was made clear earlier, the structural and cohesion programmes are important ways of limiting the social exclusion costs imposed by the intense competition of the globalizing learning economy. However, much more emphasis needs to be given, within these programmes, to the innovation initiatives and less to the provision of physical infrastructure.

6. *Improve macro–micro co-ordination.* The successful launch of the single currency puts the onus of adjustment on the supply side of the economy. Although wrapped up in euphemisms about structural reform and/or labour

and capital market flexibility, the issue remains the same as with the 'adjustment and adaptability' requirement of the 'learning globalizing' economy. An economy that is flexible and adaptable will be better able to meet the intense competition of the new global economic market-place; and better able to adjust, itself, to the new world of the euro. What most commentators forget (because most are brought up in the neo-classical tradition of economics which treats technology as exogenous) is that the two are interdependent. Successful structural reform—creating an economy that is flexible and adaptable—requires a macroeconomic climate that is conducive to investment and risk taking. An economic stance that is too stringent in holding down demand can have the opposite effect of freezing investment and, with it, the take up (and use) of new technologies. Vice versa, economic management that is too loose can lead to inflation, which equally destroys business confidence and vitiates against risk taking. There is a balance to be struck between the two. But the message for policy makers, especially in an era when inflation has retreated from being a major problem, is that the onus cannot all be put on the supply side: those responsible for demand-side management must be aware of, and sensitive to, the interdependencies between the demand and supply sides of the economy.

13.5. Conclusion

Innovation remains a key issue for policy makers. Europe's main problem lies not in the production of new technologies but in their take up and use. As they stand, current EU policies, run by the Commission, hardly touch these problems. In their times, they had their point. In particular, they were seminal in stimulating collaboration between all kinds of different firms and institutions within Europe. But collaboration alone is not enough. Nor can the EU and member states go on ignoring each other's policy efforts. There are many things the EU is trying to do—for example, to stimulate innovation in SMEs—which would be more effectively organized at national or regional level. The priorities that emerge from the 'learning globalizing' economy—education, training, networking, promoting new enterprise, cohesion, and macroeconomic balance—cut across EU and member-state responsibilities. In this the EU has a unique role to perform in setting the agenda and mobilizing action among and between the different tiers of government. It has few funds at its disposal, but it can use them to catalyse action by member state and regional governments which, if mobilized to work in the same direction, can be very effective—as has happened in Ireland. The EU is also uniquely well placed to ensure that the interdependence of the demand and supply sides of the economy are well understood. In all these ways, there is a new agenda which is both feasible and forward looking and where the Commission can begin to carve out a new role for policy.

REFERENCES

DALUM, B., LAURSEN, K., and VILLUMSEN, G. (1998). 'Structural change in OECD export specialisation patterns: De-specialisation and stickiness'. *International Review of Applied Economics*, 12: 447–67.

EUROPEAN COMMISSION (1993). 'Growth, competitiveness and employment: The challenges and the ways forward into the 21st Century'. The Delors White Paper. Brussels: European Commission.

—— (1994). 'The European report on science and technology indicators 1994'. Brussels: European Commission.

—— (1995). 'Green paper on innovation'. Brussels: European Commission.

—— (1997*a*). 'The European report on science and technology indicators 1997'. Brussels: European Commission.

—— (1997*b*). 'Five year assessment of the European Community RTD framework programme'. Report of an independent panel chaired by Vicomte Davignon. Brussels: European Commission.

—— (1997*c*). 'First action plan on innovation: Innovation, growth and employment'. Brussels: European Commission.

HOUSE OF LORDS SELECT COMMITTEE ON SCIENCE AND TECHNOLOGY (1997). 'EU Framework programme for European research and technological development, 2nd Report'. London: HMSO.

LAURSEN, K. (1999). 'The impact of technological opportunity on the dynamics of trade performance'. *Structural Change and Economic Dynamics*, 10: 341–57.

LUNDVALL, B.-Å., and BORRÁS, S. (1998). *The Globalising Learning Economy: Implications for Innovation Policy*. Brussels: European Commission.

PETERSON, J., and SHARP, M. (1998). *Technology Policy in the European Union*. Houndmills: Macmillan.

14
Innovation Policy in the Knowledge-based Economy— Can Theory Guide Policy Making?

JENS NYHOLM, LARS NORMANN, CLAUS FRELLE-PETERSEN, MARK RIIS, AND PETER TORSTENSEN

14.1. Introduction[1]

One of the most fundamental features characterizing the transition from the industrial era to more knowledge-based economies is the growing importance of innovation. It is a change both in scale and scope. Scale, because the rate of innovation is accelerating in almost all sectors (Lundvall 1998); and scope, because innovation strategies now have to integrate a wider set of activities such as marketing, services, brands, and organizational change. The knowledge-based economy presents a qualitatively new agenda for society. Understanding the fundamental challenges that the knowledge-based economy impose on firms, policy makers, and analysts cannot be done by extrapolating past developments. We are faced with a broader range of innovation issues and new factors of competition.

There is no doubt that current changes challenge the traditional policy strategies in EU countries. As a result, the policy agenda has shifted from large-scale, policy programmes applying uniform principles across sectors to more flexible schemes, reflecting differences in the innovative capability of firms. At the same time, the institutional set up for policy making is changing. The knowledge-based economy calls for more coherent innovation policy strategies, often including several ministries and institutions in the implementation. Further, a dialogue with business on critical framework conditions has become a major tool in designing innovation policy. Policy makers are, however, still at a stage of 'muddling through'. So far, they have primarily responded to the signals they get from market-leading firms and less to theory. Policy makers, therefore, need a better sense of the underlying rationales and directions for the initiatives they implement. Economic research can help governments in formulating the visions that strategies and initiatives should follow. Until recently, mainstream economic theory, including neo-classical theory and new growth theory, dominated the formulation

---

[1] Any opinions expressed in the chapter are those of the authors and not necessarily those of the Ministry of Industry and Trade.

of both economic and structural policy in most advanced economies. Lately, the traditional theoretical approach has been challenged by evolutionary economics, and in particular by the 'national innovation system' approach.

The purpose of this chapter is to discuss the features of the evolving knowledge-based economy as perceived from a policy maker's perspective and to confront these features with those two different economic research traditions. Special attention will be given to two issues or questions. First, do the theories give a realistic picture of knowledge development, innovation, and business dynamics? And secondly, how much guidance do the theories provide for the direction of policy making? As policy makers, we believe that these questions are relevant to raise within the context of the EU programmes for socio-economic research. There has always been a strong focus on how technological research can help business. We welcome this opportunity to consider how socio-economic research can contribute to policy making and indirectly to economic performance.

The discussion will show that mainstream economic theory is more concerned with issues of allocation and market clearing than with the complexity of innovation processes and business dynamics. As a consequence, the resulting 'market failure' approach to business and innovation policy has led to policies that seem to be misguided in light of the features that characterize the knowledge-based economy. Evolutionary theory is more successful in capturing the characteristics of the innovation process and of the factors leading to failures and successes in the current complex competitive environment. However, the policy recommendations remain somewhat too abstract and general to provide policy makers with a clear sense of direction. The solution, as we see it, lies in the expansion into new areas of research and in new co-operative patterns of interaction between social scientists and policy makers. At the very end, the Danish LOK initiative is presented as an example of such a new type of interaction.

14.2. Competitiveness in the Knowledge-based Economy

14.2.1. New Factors of Competition

In the 1950s 90% of the market leading firms were able to remain so throughout the decade. In the 1960s the proportion was 85%. However, between 1985 and 1995 only 20% of the market leaders in the beginning of the decade were still market leaders by the end of the decade (Holten Larsen and Schultz 1998: 6). These numbers illustrate an increasingly volatile business environment and the need for flexible business strategies. International surveys and analyses indicate that new factors of competition are emerging in this more turbulent environment. Firms implementing new

strategies based on innovation, flexible organizations, and social responsibility seem to perform better than firms with more traditional strategies
(OECD 1998: 17). As illustrated in Figure 14.1, new competition parameters have been added to traditional factors such as cost and technological
competence.

At the bottom of the pyramid we find the traditional competition parameters related to price competition. In the 1960s and the 1970s parameters
such as cost effectiveness and quality control gave firms a competitive
advantage. In the current economy these parameters remain basic conditions for remaining in the market, but they are far from sufficient to create
a strong competitiveness. Firms that rely mainly on price competition will
as a matter of fact compete with firms from low-cost countries.

At the middle of the pyramid, we find the parameters that created the
winners in the 1980s. Today, however, parameters such as technological
competence, international profile, and time to market are other preconditions for maintaining market shares, but they are not sufficient to become
a market leader. At the top of the pyramid, we find the parameters that
create winners in the market-place today. Firms in this category rely not
only on cost effectiveness and technological competence to be competitive; they have developed strategies for continuous innovation. Furthermore, the market leaders of today emphasize the communication of
values and emotional aspects of the company and its products to its
internal and external stakeholders. Such strategies may also involve taking
social and environmental responsibilities in the local community and
global society.

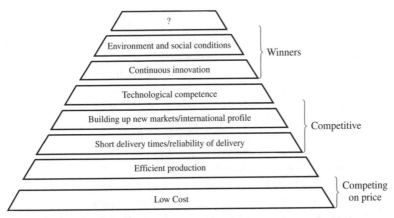

FIG 14.1. *The 'competition pyramid': Development since the 1960s*
Source: Ministry of Business and Industry 1998.

14.2.2. **Innovation Across Functions and Sectors**

The new factors of competition imply that innovation must be viewed with a far broader lens than hitherto. Innovation in the knowledge-based economy has to be seen as a value-creating process in the broadest sense. It is a process that takes place across a range of functions. An example is the role of marketing in overall innovation. Marketing provides a strategic tool for the firm. It can add further value to its products, position the firm on the market, and further affect the preferences of consumers through image-building activities. Marketing tends to interact with other activities of a firm. For firms operating on consumer markets, marketing activities and branding, in particular, tend to get integrated into product development and become innovative activities in line with product and process development.

Product-related services in business-to-business markets is another example of the increasing importance of cross-functional innovation. Rather than relying solely on price, functionality, and the quality of the product, producers attempt to differentiate their products and create closer relations with customers through service packages attached to the physical product. For instance, the pharmaceutical industry provides doctors with vocational training, courses, seminars, test facilities, and results, etc. The industry becomes in effect a knowledge provider and attempts to build close knowledge networks characterized by feedback mechanisms from its customers. Another example can be drawn from the IT sector. The comeback of IBM was to a great extent based on activities such as advisory and training services linked to their physical products. Today IBM sells its products as much through the additional value and knowledge inherent in the services as through the physical product as such.

Figure 14.2 illustrates how a range of activities and functions in firms becomes integrated in the innovation process in the knowledge-based economy. As innovation activities increasingly integrate different functions in the process, innovations increasingly take place across sectors. Intuitively, we still tend to view innovation as something that takes place primarily in high-tech industries, where formal R&D are performed. A result is that the importance of market-oriented innovation activities in low-tech manufacturing and in service sectors are underestimated.

Today a broad range of industries in the manufacturing sector has become far more technology and knowledge intensive, even though the industries cannot be considered high-tech on the basis of their final products or R&D intensities. Also in the service sector a range of new, innovative, and fast growing branches are emerging. Business and communications services as well as finance and insurance services are highly knowledge intensive sectors. And firms from the business services sectors have—together with firms in the machinery sector—been identified as the most important knowledge providers to the overall Danish business sector (Dreier 1998: 4).

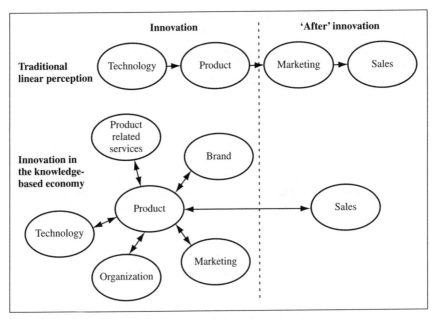

FIG. 14.2. *Innovation in the knowledge-based economy*

14.2.3. **Shift in Firm Strategy—From Division of Labour to Sharing of Knowledge**

The tendency for innovation to go on across sectors and functions has gone hand in hand with a change in firm strategy. Empirical studies and signals from market leading actors indicate how firms have introduced dramatic changes in firm strategy to 'reinvent' the firm on more globalized and know-ledge-intensive markets. The strategic responses take two interrelated forms. First, firms introduce greater internal organizational flexibility; and secondly, firms develop closer external networks with partners.

Increased competition has pushed firms to change their internal organiza-tion in order to increase the capacity to adapt to changes in the environment and become more innovative. Good habits simply turn bad when the external environment changes. A Danish survey showed that more than 84% of the firms introducing more flexible work organizations have experienced increased competition (Gjerding 1997: 5). Another dimension of this devel-opment is the strengthened tendency for firms to outsource activities that do not hold the potential to differentiate the firm from its competitors (Maskell *et al*. 1998: 11). This implies a focus on core competencies that form the 'his-torical backbone' of the firms' competitive position.

The tendency to develop closer relations with customers, suppliers, know-ledge institutions, and universities also represents a striking feature of changed business strategies in the knowledge-based economy. There are several reasons for the empirical finding that firms co-operate when they innovate (Madsen 1998: 9). An important reason is that innovation tends to become more complex (Lundvall 1998: 7). Often innovation involves a range of technologies and knowledge from different sectors. The firm is forced to seek knowledge and complementary competencies through partners and to co-ordinate the different activities that go into the final product. Also, economic considerations may push the firm into closer co-operation, even with competitors. Innovation involves greater economic risk, which the firm may seek to share with partners.

In an overall perspective, the division of labour and specialization is increasing in the knowledge-based economy. But at the same time the process of division and specialization in the economy transforms and adds new dimensions to existing relations. Firms build closer networks and promote co-operation internally in the organization and externally with other firms or knowledge institutions. These activities are centred on *sharing* knowledge and the co-ordination of activities aimed at improving specific competencies and learning abilities, as illustrated in Figure 14.3.

The networking firms of the knowledge-based economy should be perceived as creators, organizers, and exploiters of knowledge in constant change and with unique characteristics, as opposed to the standard economic picture of the company as a user of tangible resources—human and physical capital—in the production of goods and services (Drake 1998: 3). The fundamental challenge for the business sector is to master the process of learning and unlearning[2]—in the sense of using knowledge, experiences, and competencies drawn internally and in networks.

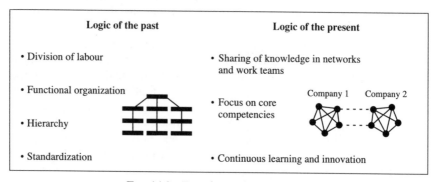

FIG. 14.3. *From hierarchy to network*

---

[2] Old habits and customs often have to change in order to be really open to new learning.

14.2.4. **Towards a New Business and Innovation Policy**

The transition to a more knowledge—and learning—based economy is reflected in business and innovation policy reforms throughout the EU and OECD. At the present stage, however, the most important source to policy changes is not theory but rather practical experience and empirical observations. Market-leading firms are often the observatories for policy makers together with fairly well-documented changes in innovative firm behaviour as the ones cited above. As a result, reforms are often less co-ordinated and based on trial and error learning processes. At the international level, the speed of policy adjustment varies significantly between countries. The new conditions outlined in the previous section mean that the success of business policy reforms depends on the ability to deal with the following issues:

(1) a flexible and differentiated approach to innovation dealing with the needs in different sectors, including the service sector, and tailor-made to the needs of the large number of slowly adapting firms;
(2) support of a broader range of innovation activities from technological, organizational, service to marketing innovation activities; the biases towards technological innovation need correction;
(3) focus on inter-firm co-operation as a means of increased learning and pooling of competencies;
(4) support of the implementation of improved principles for organizational learning and for the development of competencies;
(5) reforms in the intermediary knowledge transfer institutions such as technological service institutions and training institutions;
(6) promotion of co-operative research networks and knowledge transfers between universities and the business sector (see, in this volume, the chapter by Conceição and Heitor); especially in the most knowledge intensive sectors, time is becoming a powerful competitive factor; and there is still room for improving the transfer mechanisms for knowledge between universities and business firms; research indicates that the time from developing new research-based knowledge to its commercial application has not decreased significantly in certain strategic sectors;
(7) promote other important framework conditions; such as venture capital and other capital sources to start ups.

The new reality also has a great impact on what kind of measures and policy approaches can lead to business success. Table 14.1 sums up some of the main features underlying business policy in the past and in the future.

In general, the new business and innovation policy paradigm can be characterized as being more process oriented than the former paradigm. Unstable markets, shorter product life cycles, and the growing importance of mutual

TABLE 14.1. *Old and new features of business and innovation policy*

Business policy in the industrial society	Business policy in the future
Large scale programmes employing uniform principles across sectors and firms	Intermediary institutions that are able to serve firms according to their specific needs
Subsidies to individual firms	No direct subsidies to firms, but to institutions co-operating with firms
No incentives to institutional co-operation	Supporting institutions co-operating across sectors (research, education, labour market)
Supporting process and product innovation	Supporting organizational innovation, service innovation, and marketing innovation as well
Low degree of co-ordination between ministries	High degree of co-ordination between ministries
Dialogue with business organizations and labour market organization representing sectors	Dialogue with cutting-edge enterprises belonging to business clusters in order to identify critical framework conditions

learning makes it impossible for policy makers to design policy without a close interplay with cutting-edge companies. The design of new initiatives needs to be flexible and market oriented in order to be adjustable to the specific needs of businesses.

14.3. Theoretical Rationales for Business and Innovation Policy

In this section, we confront the picture of the emerging economy drawn in section 14.2 with the assumptions and rationales of modern economic theory. From a policy maker perspective, theories should ideally meet two criteria in order to be useful for policy purposes. First, theory should provide a model of the economy that deals with the relevant issues, makes intuitive sense, and generally corresponds to empirically observed phenomena. Secondly, theory should deduce rationales that give direction for deciding what policy efforts are needed. One specific challenge for theories dealing with business and innovation policy in the knowledge-based economy is to be of help in identifying barriers in knowledge development, diffusion, and use in business and society. We can identify six critical issues/questions and concepts:

- what is knowledge?
- how does knowledge and innovation develop?
- where does the development of knowledge and innovation take place?

- what are the costs or difficulties in diffusing, adopting, and using knowledge and innovation in different contexts?
- how is co-operation between firms perceived?
- are company differences significant? Is there a scope for firm strategy?

14.3.1. Mainstream Economic Theory and Business and Innovation Policy

The basic economic argument in mainstream economic thinking and in particular in new growth theory is that knowledge is a peculiar good that implies increasing returns to society because of spillover effects. Private incentives to invest in activities that lead to innovation and learning explain the level of knowledge accumulation that subsequently explains differences in growth among regions and nations. The theory predicts that countries specializing in technologically progressive industries experience more rapid growth than others. The policy strategy offered by mainstream economic thinking is that public action should compensate for market failures due to insufficient private incentives to invest in R&D. Therefore, policy makers should intervene to induce firm's investment in R&D to the benefit of the whole economy. For policy makers it would be particularly attractive to allocate resources to R&D intensive sectors such as biotechnology.

Table 14.2 to some extent simplifies the positions of mainstream economics on knowledge, innovation, and alternatives to 'pure' markets. And recent

TABLE 14.2. *How mainstream economics deals with six key issues for innovation policy*

Key issues in the knowledge-based economy	Mainstream economics
1. What is knowledge?	Equivalent to codified knowledge or information, as well as intermediate forms
2. How does knowledge and innovation develop?	Through R&D activities
3. Where does the development of knowledge and innovation go on?	Primarily the R&D function of advanced/ 'high technology' manufacturing
4. Are there any costs or difficulties in diffusing, adopting, and using knowledge and innovations in other contexts?	The question is not specificly addressed, but it is assumed costless (Pavitt 1991: 18).
5. How is co-operation between firms perceived?	Since 'pure' markets are assumed, this is not really an issue
6. Are company differences significant? Scope for firm strategy?	Agents are assumed homogenous. Therefore, there is no real scope for strategies except to 'optimize'. However, knowledge protection is a key issue

theories within the tradition address, for example, issues such as market structure, firm behaviour, and learning. Mainstream economic theory does not really dwell on the first three issues, namely the what, how, and where of knowledge and innovations. Furthermore, mainstream economic theory in general 'assumes away' the last three issues on the costs of diffusion, firm interaction, and firm differences. This is not because mainstream economists do not acknowledge the complexity surrounding these issues. It is rather because the objective of mainstream economics is different. Addressing the characteristics of knowledge and business dynamics has not been a central concern to mainstream economics. Mainstream economics has been more concerned with issues of allocation and market clearing for the whole economy than with qualitative aspects of business dynamics and differences between sectors, firms, and technologies. As a consequence, the main policy lessons to be drawn from mainstream economics have been within the areas of monetary and fiscal policy. Mainstream economics has been strong in providing policy makers from ministries of finance and economics with models covering the whole economy that focus on a few monetary or fiscal variables such as interest rates, inflation rates, trade balance, and balance on public budgets. For these policies it has not been a significant drawback that the models neglect most of the underlying qualitative aspects of the economy.

For business and innovation policy makers, however, this is obviously different. Innovation policy makers need a theoretical body dealing with the complex processes of knowledge development and business dynamics. But since, until the early 1980s, there was no fully articulated alternative to mainstream economic thinking on knowledge and innovation, policy makers have still looked for rationales for business and innovation policy within the paradigm of mainstream economics. Therefore, the market failure framework has been and still is very influential in OECD countries, not least because civil servants in core economic ministries have been 'brought up' within the mainstream tradition. The misperceptions inherent in the market failure framework have in some areas led to policies that are misguided in the light of the empirical circumstances in the knowledge-based economy. We can give three examples that elaborate on traditional economic thinking on specific topics and its implications for policy practice in some instances.

1. *Innovation is non-linear.* The mainstream theoretical approach to technological change is based on a linear model of innovation, whereby investment in formal R&D is regarded as input into applied technology, which subsequently gets commercialized (Mowery and Rosenberg 1989: 13). Often this approach tends to view innovation and learning processes as something taking place exclusively in high-tech sectors, where formal R&D is performed. In particular, most new growth theory models operate with a specific R&D producing sector within the economy, which supplies other sectors with productivity-raising new technological knowledge (Romer

1990). A crucial endogenous factor then becomes the amount of resources devoted to that sector.

This linear approach possesses a number of drawbacks. First of all, it may be difficult or meaningless for the policy maker to identify a specific knowledge-producing sector in the knowledge-based economy. Instead of thinking of a specific narrowly defined knowledge or R&D producing sector in the economy, it is nowadays more suitable for the policy maker to think of learning and knowledge production as something taking place across the whole economy. Secondly, a theory of innovation cannot mechanically be translated into a theory of output and growth. The linear approach to technological change takes for granted that R&D and innovation contribute directly to economic growth. How innovation is effectively adopted, diffused, and used in the economy also depends on the effectiveness of the supporting institutional system as well as the interaction among the institutional actors.

The massive public funding of R&D in Europe through the EU Framework Programmes illustrates the point that we attempt to make. It can be argued that from the outset the Framework Programmes were based on a linear logic. The EU allocated substantial subsidies to research centres and large enterprises with the aim of developing new generic technologies and standards. The expected technology push effect should lift Europe onto a level comparable to Japan and the US in terms of technological application and innovation. In later generations of the Framework Programmes a more market-oriented focus has been adopted to facilitate the diffusion of knowledge among smaller companies.

2. *Innovation and learning is interactive.* In the neo-classical theoretical scheme the communication among firms takes the form of simple anonymous economic transactions. In reality, however, innovation in most cases requires qualitative communication in terms of other categories of information than price and quantity. Since much knowledge is tacit and therefore difficult to transfer, face-to-face communication is often needed when external knowledge has to be integrated with internal capabilities of firms. Since mainstream theory in general assumes that firms operate anonymously on 'pure' markets, it is abstracted from this kind of interactive learning processes. In this context one may argue that the mainstream conception of markets has influenced the design of the prevailing procurement policy within the EU countries. As a consequence the prevailing policy may contradict an innovation policy that emphasizes interactive learning and collaboration. Box 14.1 discusses the issue in more detail.

3. *Firms differ and have different needs in the innovation process.* The factors determining a firm's competitiveness have changed over time. Today it is not necessarily the cost of traditional inputs that determine whether a firm is competitive or not, but its organizational competence, its ability to understand and adopt new knowledge, to read market signals, and to adjust to customer needs. This implies that firms not only differ across sectors but also

Box 14.1. *Procurement policy may limit innovative collaboration and learning*

Public procurement is a central policy area in relation to the implementation of the single European market. The rules applied to public procurement aim at opening national markets to competition from other member states by giving suppliers equal opportunities to bid. The rules also guarantee that the public sector applies market-based principles in relation to procurement.

Public sector demand as expressed through public procurement can in many cases spur innovation in private enterprises. The 'critical' demand for solutions by a public institution that is expressed through procurement is actually a case of interactive learning and knowledge diffusion. This learning and knowledge diffusion may stimulate new thinking in private firms when trying to meet the requirements set up by a public institution and may be a central factor behind firm innovations.

However, in securing fair competition among participants in public procurement, the formal rules may have a negative impact on knowledge creation and diffusion. The rules will in many cases limit the dialogue between the procurer and the private firm. It is, however, a dialogue which is almost a precondition for innovative solutions since it involves knowledge diffusion, combination of competencies, and learning.

The consequence of rigid procurement rules may be that procurement processes give rise to solutions that are price competitive, but do not spur innovation and the dynamic development for firms and society as a whole.

within sectors. The main reason is that learning and competencies tend to be localized and path dependent. But despite these differences, public investments in labour-market training systems has aimed at strengthening *general* qualifications in the labour force. The rationale has been to upgrade labour market mobility and invest in qualifications that are less firm specific, and therefore would suffer from under-investments in the absence of public support. However, the key source of competitive strength in the knowledge-based economy lies in specific core competencies and in the methods for employing human resources. It can be argued that more specialized courses would strengthen mobility even more, since courses adapted to the needs of individual firms generally would be better at linking learning and training to job functions, which significantly improves employee's skills and attractiveness on the labour market (Stern 1996: 24). The rigid distinction between general and specific qualifications seems to have lost its relevance in the highly differentiated knowledge-based economy, *where 'neutral' policies are likely to be so abstract, that they have little effect* (Smith 1997: 23), as discussed in Box 14.2.

One might argue that the policy failures resulting from the market failure paradigm is out of the hands of academic researchers. It is a theoretical

Box 14.2. *General versus specific qualifications in the labour market training system*

For many years, Denmark has been investing in a widespread publicly funded system for vocational and adult training. The policy rationale for financing adult training is that companies tend to under-invest in human resources because of possible spillovers and that adult training is important to labour-market flexibility. Employees may change jobs and the benefits of investment in training, in terms of higher productivity and higher skills, may not be fully obtained by the company itself. The prerequisite for public funding of adult training is that the qualifications obtained are useful for the labour market in general. Public funded adult training therefore focuses on general qualifications such as technology, mathematics, reading, and writing.

It can be argued that qualifications such as co-operation-skills, communication, and awareness of quality are also useful qualifications for employees in general; especially in recent years where new, more flexible types of organizational forms have been diffused. These new types of organizations are characterized by co-operation, delegation of responsibility, and cross-functional communication. However, these skills are most effectively learned within the framework, where they are used. For example, it may be less meaningful to attend courses on co-operation without the colleagues with whom the daily co-operation takes place.

Skills such as co-operation, communication, and quality awareness, however, are perceived as specific qualifications that are only useful to the company itself and therefore not publicly funded. The distinction between general and specific qualifications has been made according to the way the qualifications are obtained rather than how they can be used.

framework providing broad guidance and in concrete circumstances it is not a substitute to sound judgements and careful thinking by policy makers themselves! One cannot expect researchers to participate in the policy process. Policy making is another activity involving compromises and knowledge about how firms react. And the concept of market failures has still guided the thinking about business policy and provided overall direction to the question of when government intervention may be justified. However, the fundamental agenda of distribution and market clearing in mainstream economic theory remains insufficient for business and innovation policy makers in the knowledge-based economy.

For innovation policy purposes it was a significant step forward when evolutionary theory, as articulated in Nelson and Winter (1982: 14), began to challenge mainstream economic thinking in the 1980s. Evolutionary theory represents important progress by providing a better description of key issues for business policy such as the circumstances surrounding innovation processes and the business needs that follows. Therefore, evolutionary theory, as we shall see in the following section, is better equipped to deal with the complexity of the real world issues that concern company strategists and business policy makers.

14.3.2. Evolutionary Rationales for Business and Innovation Policy

The starting-point of evolutionary theory is that knowledge and innovation are the key forces determining the competitiveness of firms and countries, and that knowledge and innovation are developed through *search* and *learning* across firm functions, sectors, and institutions. The search and learning goes on through *interaction* within firms, between firms, and between firms and other institutions. The assumption of 'pure markets' without any contact between supply and demand is replaced by a perspective that perceives interaction between firms—particularly between suppliers and users—as almost a precondition for innovation. The feedback from users or access to complementary expertise from competing firms or other *institutions* is the central driving force of knowledge development and innovation according to evolutionary theory. The important concept of *institutions*[3] is usually defined within the framework of *national innovation systems*. National innovation systems consist of the national institutions that are important for developing and diffusing knowledge in society. The key idea behind the innovation system concept is that the innovative capacity of an economy depends on more than the sum of firms and other institutions. It depends on their *interaction* in knowledge development, distribution, and use.

A critical assumption underlying evolutionary thinking is that knowledge is perceived as being partly *tacit*. In addition to codified knowledge or information, knowledge also embodies a tacit element that is built into routines and competencies that firms develop over time. This assumption has a tremendous impact on other allied or derived assumptions that constitute evolutionary thinking and ways of perceiving reality. Among those, two will be mentioned. First, learning tends to develop cumulatively and follow specific *path-dependent trajectories*. The accumulated competencies and routines are not consciously chosen among alternatives but evolve through incremental steps of trial and error. The learning path may open some and close other options for future developments. Since learning is cumulative, the capacity for learning depends on the complexity of what has already been learned. Secondly, competencies to develop, absorb, and use knowledge are *differentiated*

---

[3] Institutions can be formally organized or codified entities with an explicit purpose such as the national education and training system, the research system, the financial system, etc. But institutions can also be less formal and involve issues such as norms for co-operation in society, relations between employers and employees, principles for firms' internal organization, etc. It appears that institutions in this broad understanding of the concept ranges from 'rules of the game' to physically manifested organizations in the national innovation system.

TABLE 14.3. *How evolutionary theory deals with six key issues for business and innovation policy*

Key issues in the knowledge-based economy	Evolutionary theory
1. What is knowledge?	Comprises both codified and tacit knowledge
2. How does knowledge and innovation develop?	Through search, learning, and interaction across company functions and sectors
3. Where does the development of knowledge and innovation go on?	Across firms and institutions in the economy, including 'low-tech' and services
4. Are there any costs or difficulties in diffusion, adoption, and use of knowledge and innovations in other contexts?	It is demanding a lot of knowledge just to absorb, adopt, and use both codified and tacit knowledge developed elsewhere (Cohen and Levinthal: 1989). It requires competencies to use codified knowledge effectively. And it requires interactive learning and experience sharing to adopt and use tacit knowlege. The effective diffusion/absorption and use therefore depends on training, interaction, and organizational issues.
5. How is co-operation between firms perceived?	Often a precondition for innovation, since learning is interactive. Further, few firms possess all the necessary knowledge inputs it takes to innovate on their own. Finally, since tacit knowledge is 'tied' to firms, those are less at risk to lose their key competencies to competitors than assumed in neo-classical thinking.
6. Are company differences significant? Scope for firm strategy?	Yes. The differences are severe and exist at the level of the individual company, sector, and country. Differences exist when it comes to learning, developing, adopting, and using knowledge and innovations. The implication for firm strategy is a focus on internal coherence across functions and departments to stimulate interactive learning. Further, a focus on the interaction with other firms and institutions. And, finally, on avoiding lock in into 'wrong' learning routes..

between firms and locations. The diversity and variability in learning trajectories followed by firms means that the competencies and routines accumulated by each firm tend to be highly differentiated. As a result, firms tend
to develop highly differentiated patterns of specialization depending on
firm-specific, sector-specific, and location-specific aspects (Cantwell 1991). In
relation to the main reference points from the innovation policy makers' perspective, Table 14.3 sums up the evolutionary positions.

It is clear that the key assumptions and way of modelling the economy
in evolutionary theory is significantly different from the mainstream economic model. And by integrating the central concepts and issues of the
knowledge-based economy into a coherent framework, evolutionary theory
has contributed significantly to a better understanding of the circumstances surrounding the innovation processes. Evolutionary theory deals
intensively with issues like: what is knowledge?; how does it develop? Furthermore, it gives intuitively reasonable answers to some of the questions
where mainstream economic thinking has gone wrong, namely, the issues
of diffusion, firm co-operation, and firm differences. As a consequence, the
implications and general attitude towards business and innovation policy
are also significantly different from what can be deduced from mainstream
economic theory.

1. On the one hand, the approach towards the ability of policy makers to
    intervene correctly and in the right scale is more humble (Malerba 1997:
    10). The speed, complexity, and diversity of the competitive environment
    of firms make it difficult for policy makers to design interventions appro-
    priately. Centrally planned and dirigistic policies will fail when trying to
    influence business structures, capabilities, and routines that are strongly
    path dependent, specialized, and context-specific. Instead, *policy learning*
    and the development of information systems to policy co-ordination are
    key priorities (Smith 1997: 23).
2. On the other hand, the breadth of areas where failures might appear is
    greater and in this sense the need for public intervention is greater. Pol-
    icy should also work to correct 'institutional failures', 'co-ordination fail-
    ures', 'lock-in failures', 'transition failures', and 'learning failures'. Since,
    for example, institutions are very broadly defined in evolutionary think-
    ing, the policy actions aimed to correct them are also broad.[4] Moreover,
    interactive learning and the search for new technological options in all
    parts of the economy should be encouraged. Finally, government inter-
    vention should be sensitive to diversity between firms and sectors.

---

[4] Policy actions to correct 'institutional failures' could, for example, be initiatives aimed at
improving organizational flexibility within firms, improving incentives for co-operation between
firms, improving interaction between firms and public research institutions, improving the functioning of formal institutions themselves such as financial institutions, technological infrastructure, etc.

The difficulties for evolutionary theory arise when theory is to be operationalized into political action. From a policy maker's perspective the theory remains somewhat too abstract when it comes to identify the circumstances where intervention may be justified. Although opening the 'black box' of firms, knowledge, and innovations, one could argue that the black box to some extent remains in evolutionary theory, when it comes to political action. How does one, for example, avoid getting into positions of technological 'lock-in'? How can we avoid institutional failures? Which institutions are relevant to look at? How do we in practice encourage interactive learning? What is learning? And how do we learn? Consider the example of 'institutional failure'. Policy should be directed towards improving the functioning of institutions. But since there is no clear boundary between institutions that are important for innovation, and those that are not, evolutionary theory opens up for all kinds of policy initiatives.[5]

14.4. Looking Ahead

The complexity, pace, and knowledge intensiveness of business life has increased rapidly. And as things have changed the traditional rationales for business and innovation policy have become more and more out of touch with reality. In this context the rise of evolutionary economics has served as a significant advance. But also in the evolutionary articulation of business and innovation processes one might argue that theory followed practice rather than vice versa. It is therefore less surprising that evolutionary theory is in a better correspondence with the real world circumstances and challenges currently facing firms. From a policy maker's perspective, there has thus been a tendency for theory to react to reality. For innovation theory to catch up and move ahead of practice, theory needs to address new questions and expand into new areas. Four areas for future research seem to be particularly important in the knowledge based and learning economy:

- research on providing better *indicators* for the knowledge economy
- research on how people and organizations *learn*
- research on improving techniques on how to *measure the effects of policies*
- research on *new co-operation patterns between academic researchers and policy makers* and diffusion of best practice.

In addition to addressing these areas, innovation theory could deal more with the boundaries for relevant and less-relevant policy intervention. Academic research should not become politicized and policy making is not a

---

[5] And since institutions in evolutionary thinking range from formally organized or physical entities with an explicit purpose to 'rules of the game' such as norms for co-operation in society, institutional failures would tend to be ubiquitous in the economy, just as market failures are ubiquitous in relation to innovative activities.

scientific activity, but the boundaries for justified government intervention in business life can still become clearer. And for this undertaking we need new forms of interaction between academic researchers and policy makers. Further, we need to break down some of the walls between research and policy making, just as the walls between R&D and strategy functions have already been broken down within firms in the knowledge economy.

The project 'Management, Organization, and Competencies', which was launched by the Danish Government in 1997, can illustrate how research and policy can go hand in hand in practice. The five policy initiatives that eventually emerged involved close co-operation between four different ministries and defined a new agenda for business policy. The collaboration between research and policy making is described in Box 14.3.

Box 14.3. *Management, organization, and competencies—the new agenda of innovation policy*

In 1997 the Danish government earmarked 237 million Danish crowns in a four–year period to start five new initiatives under the project-heading Management, Organization, and Competencies (the LOK project). The initiatives aim at supporting change in management and work organization to the requirements of a more knowledge-based and global economy. The project involves close co-operation with researchers.

At the beginning of 1996 scholars at the University of Aalborg started a three-year research project on the Danish innovation system in a comparative perspective titled *The Danish Innovation System: Comparative analyses of challenges, positions of strength, and bottlenecks*—in short, the DISKO project. The starting-point for the research project was the research on 'National Innovation Systems' as initiated by Lundvall, Freeman, and Nelson. The first part of the project analysed change in management and work organization in Danish firms.

The co-operation between the researchers and the Danish Ministry of Business and Industry involved the establishment of steering groups, reference groups, and the organization of continuous feedback between the parties. The ministry also financed two Ph.D. students from Aalborg University and the DISKO project. The two Ph.D. students worked at the ministry for nine months, and in this period they participated in the design and implementation of the LOK project. The project contributed to the development of political initiatives in at least in three different ways.

First and foremost, the DISKO project contributed with analyses of the correlation between new forms of work organizations and the performance of firms and the kind of activities that firms had started in relation to new forms of organizations. The analyses played a central role in providing the analytical foundation for developing political initiatives aiming at supporting firms' transition to new and more flexible organizational designs. The analyses gave a rationality for implementing political initiatives in an area that so far had been almost untouched by business and innovation policy. Moreover, the analyses contributed with new knowledge about the barriers and problems that firms are facing when changing organizational structures. This contributed to the process of pinpointing the main areas for political priorities within the LOK project.

Finally, the DISKO project contributed to defining the concept of flexible organizations. Before the analyses of the DISKO project, there was only a sketchy understanding on how to define and understand flexibility and changes in organizational design. In the DISKO project, a number of specific organizational features characterizing flexible firms were identified as crucial for performance. In the following policy formulation process, this contributed to defining criteria and principles in the specific policy initiatives.

REFERENCES

CANTWELL, J. (1991). 'The theory of technological competence and its application to international production', in D. G. McFetridge (ed.), *Foreign Investment, Technology and Economic Growth*. Calgary: University of Calgary Press.

COHEN, W. M., and LEVINTHAL, D. A. (1999). 'Innovation and learning: The two faces of R&D', *Economic Journal*, 99: 569–96.

DRAKE, K. (1998). 'Firms, knowledge and competitiveness', *OECD Observer*, no. 211: 24–7.

DREIER, I. (1998). 'Den videnbaserede økonomi—En analyse af vidensintensitet og vidensstrømme i det danske innovationssystem'. Copenhagen: Business Development Council.

GJERDING, A. N. (1997) (ed.). 'Den fleksible virksomhed: Omstillingspres og fornyelse i dansk erhvervsliv'. Copenhagen: Business Development Council.

HOLTEN LARSEN, M., and SCHULTZ, M. (1998). 'Den udtryksfulde virksomhed'. Copenhagen: Klampenborg Bergsøe.

LUNDVALL, B.-Å. (1998). 'The learning economy—Challenges to economic theory and policy', in B. Johnson and K. Nielsen (eds.), *Institutions and Economic Change*. Cheltenham: Edward Elgar.

—— and BORRÁS, S. (1998). *The Globalising Learning Economy: Implications for Innovation Policy.* Brussels: European Commission.

MADSEN, P. T. (1998). 'Den samarbejdende virksomhed'. Copenhagen: Business Development Council.

MALERBA, F. (1997). 'Public policy in industrial dynamics: An evolutionary perspective'. ISE Working paper. Milan: CESPRI–Bocconi University.

MASKELL, P., ESKELINEN, H., HANNIBALSSON, I., MALMBERG, A., and VATNE, E. (1998). *Competitiveness, Localised Learning and Regional Development: Specialisation and Prosperity in Small Open Economies.* London: Routledge.

MINISTRY of BUSINESS and INDUSTRY (1998). *Erhvervsredegørelsen 1998.* Copenhagen: Ministry of Business and Industry.

MOWERY, D., and ROSENBERG, N. (1989). *Technology and the Pursuit of Economic Growth.* Cambridge: Cambridge University Press.

NELSON, R. R. (1959). 'The simple economics of basic scientific research'. *Journal of Political Economy*, 67: 297–306.

NELSON, R. R. and WINTER, S. G. (1982). *An Evolutionary Theory of Economic Change.* Cambridge, Mass.: Harvard University Press.

OECD (1998). *Technology, Productivity, and Job Creation: Best Policy Practices.* Paris: OECD.

PAVITT, K. (1991), 'What makes basic research economically useful?' *Research Policy,* 20: 109–19.

ROMER, P. M. (1990). 'Endogenous technological change'. *Journal of Political Economy,* 98: 71–102.

ROTHWELL, R. (1983). 'Difficulties of national innovation policies', in D. Lamberton, S. Macdonald, and T. Mandeville (eds.), *The Trouble with Technology,* London: Pinter Publishers.

SCHMOOKLER, J. (1962). 'Economic sources of inventive activity'. *The Journal of Economic History,* 22: 1–20.

SHARP, M., and PAVITT, K. (1993). 'Technology policy in the 1990s: Old trends and new realities'. *Journal of Common Market Studies,* 31/2: 129–51.

SMITH, K. (1997). 'System approaches to innovation: some policy issues'. Report of the ISE Sub-project 'Systems Theories of Innovation: Policy Implications'. Brussels: European Commission.

STERN, D. (1996). 'Human resources in the knowledge-based economy: roles of firms, schools and governments', in OECD, *Employment and Growth in the Knowledge-based Economy.* Paris: OECD.

TASSEY, G. (1991). 'The functions of technology infrastructure in a competitive economy'. *Research Policy,* 20/4: 345–61.

TEECE, D. (1991). 'Reconceptualising the corporation and competition', in G. R. Faulhaber and G. Tamburini (eds.), *European Economic Integration,* Dordrecht: Kluwer.

ZYSMAN, J. (1994). 'How institutions create historically rooted trajectories of growth'. *Industrial and Corporate Change,* 3: 243–85.

273 - 91

(OECD)

f62
538
531
532

15
Innovation Policy in the Globalizing Learning Economy

BENGT-ÅKE LUNDVALL

15.1. The Learning Economy

As pointed out in the introductory chapter, a fundamental trend in the last decade has been the speeding up of the rate of change. This reflects a combination of changes in technology and international trade with political deregulation initiatives. At the level of the firm, it is registered as an intensification of competition in sectors already involved in international trade, while firms in formerly protected sectors become more exposed to competition.

Change and learning are two sides of the same coin. The speed up of change confronts agents and organizations with new problems and to tackle the new problems requires new skills (OECD 2000). The process is characterized by cumulative circular causation. The selection by employers of more learning-oriented employees and the market selection of change-oriented firms accelerate further innovation and change. There is nothing to indicate that the process will be slowed down in the near future. Rather, the deregulation of markets for services and the entrance of new competitors from Eastern Europe will give new momentum to the process.

In this new context the major policy objective of innovation policy must be to contribute to the learning capability of firms, knowledge institutions, and people. Here we shall point to human resource development, new forms of firm organization, network formation, and to a new role for knowledge-intensive business services and universities as key elements in promoting learning. In the introductory chapter it was argued that an even broader set of policies needs to be integrated in a strategy to cope with the challenges of the learning economy. In this chapter the focus is on policies aiming directly at enhancing the capability to adapt and innovate.

As illustrated by the permanent and apparently irreparable weakness of Europe in information technology products and services, it is difficult to catch up once you have been left behind (the fact that competencies as well as product and trade specialization patterns are cumulative and sticky gives a first mover advantage—see Archibugi and Michie 1998). Therefore there should be a focus also on the formation of the next techno-economic paradigm. It will be argued that building new technological systems aiming at attacking problems inherent in the globalizing learning economy such as social and ecological sustainability may be a key to open up the next techno-economic paradigm in the same way as the US engagement in the Cold War played a central role in creating the basis for the present one around information technology.

15.2. A New Theoretical Rationale for Innovation Policy

As the focus through the last decade has moved from science policy with broad social objectives towards innovation policy more narrowly focused on the impact on economic performance, the connection between innovation policy and economic theory has become stronger and more direct. Increasingly policy makers are under the influence of economic theory and the distance from new theoretical results in economics to new policy ideas has been shrinking. Therefore it is useful to confront the policy implications of different theoretical approaches to innovation and learning.

The standard arguments for government policy developed within neo-classical economics have been developed on the basis of a specific definition of knowledge as technical information that is codified and therefore a public good (see Cohendet and Joly in this volume). Further, it is assumed that knowledge is a good characterized by scale economies in its production and use, and that its use gives rise to positive externalities. On the basis of this definition of knowledge, it is clear that some of the fundamental policy issues have to do with intellectual property rights. The fact that information is easy to copy and distribute makes it less attractive for private agents to invest in producing it and the new technology is often more useful for society as a whole than it is for the private investor (the social rate of return is higher than the private).

These standard arguments for government intervention in terms of guaranteeing intellectual property rights are certainly valid in their neo-classical theoretical context and actually they take on a new importance in the new economy where the transaction of pieces of knowledge and information becomes core economic activities. Still the analysis gives a lop-sided understanding of the learning economy because it neglects that tacit knowledge remains fundamental for the core competencies of individuals, organizations, networks, and regions. Therefore the agenda for innovation policy it ends up with will be correspondingly biased and incomplete.

15.2.1. Tacit Knowledge—Individual, Organizational, and Networked

The classical examples of tacit knowledge quoted in the literature are typically individual practical skills (like biking and swimming) that cannot be made explicit and that cannot be transmitted through, for instance, telecommunication networks. But it is important to note that there are other kinds of tacit knowledge that are more at the core of the economic dynamics. Managers use experience-based tacit knowledge when taking complex decisions, and scientists use personal and tacit knowledge in their research. In both cases it is a question of interpreting complex sets of information and seeing patterns that less-experienced managers and scientists would not be able to see.

While both the practical and the analytically oriented tacit knowledge is impossible to codify and to transfer through telecommunication media, it can be learned through experience. It will typically be learned in an interaction with other people, through a master–apprentice or collegial relationship. This also implies that tacit knowledge can be shared through a process of interaction and co-operation. Simple forms may be accessed through imitation of behaviour, but mostly the learning is strongly facilitated if the master or colleague co-operates and communicates with the apprentice. People and organizations that solve problems together will typically, at the end of a specific project as a result, share some of their partners' original knowledge, and some of the new tacit knowledge produced by the interaction. Interactive learning is a key to shared tacit knowledge and this implies, of course, that the social context is important for this kind of learning—an observation to which we shall return below.

Tacit knowledge is not to be found only at the level of the individual. An organization, with its specific routines, norms of behaviour, codes of information, etc., may be regarded as a unit that carries within it knowledge, a substantial part of which is tacit. Management may have an incentive to codify the knowledge that constitutes the organization—for instance, in order to make it less vulnerable to the risk that key persons leave the organization. But normally they will realize that it can only be done sucessfully when the firm operates in a simple and static environment. They might also experience that very ambitious efforts in this direction bring the organization to a standstill while the rest of the world keeps moving on and also moves on in new directions where the codified knowledge proves to be a burden rather than an asset.

Industrial networks and inter-firm co-operation may also be seen as repositories of tacit knowledge layered into common procedures and codes, not reflected in formal contracts or any other documents. Some of these procedures might be possible to codify while others, actually, would lose their meaningfulness if they were written down (playing golf, drinking cocktails, flirting with professionals from the other organization, sharing political, religious, and literary tastes may be fundamental elements in bringing people from different organizations together in projects of interactive learning but they do not look impressive on paper and they undermine their own function if they become part of an explicit and purely instrumental strategy). This is a problem similar to the formation of trust in a market economy. Arrow has made the point that trust cannot be bought and if you could buy it would have no value whatsoever. There would always be someone around to pay more for friendships and trust relationships if they were for sale (Arrow 1971). The informal and tacit character of 'know-who' (Lundvall and Johnson 1994) kind of knowledge is crucial for the strength of networks.

Information technology and the new economy has a contradictory impact on the codification of knowledge. On the one hand, it makes it less costly to codify knowledge and in some areas also much more attractive to do so. The Internet economy where the market for information explodes gives new incentives to codification. On the other hand, the use of information and communication technology has as its major impact that it speeds up change and it increases complexity in the knowledge base. This is why tacit knowledge becomes even more important than before. This is especially true for tacit knowledge that is helpful in locating, selecting, and using information. Therefore tacit knowledge and interactive learning becomes not less, but more, important in 'the new economy'.

The fact that knowledge that is crucially important for economic success is tacit has important implications for the principles from which innovation policy should be designed. It means that the process of interactive learning will not take place in pure markets where individually optimizing agents meet. It becomes obvious that the capability to learn is not the same across individuals and organizations. The learning process is socially embedded and organizational forms and institutional set ups are crucial to the outcome of the interactions. This is why innovation policy needs to have a social dimension where the *quality of interaction* between people and organizations are important and where *enhancing the competence of firms* becomes a legitimate objective.

15.2.2. Spillovers and Knowledge-sharing in the Learning Economy

In neo-classical analysis it is a major policy issue to make sure that intellectual property rights are respected. Spillovers are regarded as a policy problem. The concepts of externalities and spillovers take as their starting-point the idea that all knowledge originally is produced by one individual unit and that a main concern for the producer is to avoid others getting access to it. This peculiar perspective does not correspond to the realities of the learning economy since, in this context, networking, co-operation, and learning by interacting are necessary elements in most successful strategies. Agents do try to keep some strategic information for themselves in specific situations, and from time to time some of them even enter law suits when their property rights have been illegally impinged upon. But they also enter into a complex set of relationships where the aim of the network is to create, to share, and to pool knowledge.

Sometimes the objective is even to stimulate the diffusion of knowledge to as many users as possible—for example IBM's strategy of allowing the cloning of PC-technology in order to diffuse the standard worldwide. In most of these relationships the main focus of the agents is not on hindering others from access to knowledge but rather to create a relationship that makes interactive learning possible. This implies that in this context instrumental behaviour will become mixed with 'communicative rationality', where the common goal is for the involved partners to understand better what the problems are and what solutions can be developed (Lundvall 1992).

This implies that the broader social context—the presence and form in society of 'social capital'—will affect the learning process. In a society that is extremely individualistic or where the loyalties are narrowly related to the family, it might be especially difficult to engage in interactive learning. The present state of the Russian economy illustrates that production and intellectual capital has little value if not based on 'social capital'. The neglect among Western experts of the need to build social capital in civil society and in terms of institutionally supported trust relationships has contributed to the present situation.

15.2.3. **Some General Implications for Innovation Policy**

The standard neo-classical analysis points to the need to establish strong intellectual property rights in order to stimulate private investments in technical information, and possibly to the need for governments to subsidize R&D-efforts in relation to basic research. When we shift the focus to include tacit knowledge, interactive learning, and knowledge sharing the task of policy makers becomes more complex. In the new context of the learning economy the international competitiveness of firms, regions, and nations will reflect to what degree they are good at building and using competences.

What matters most is, of course, competencies that are directly or indirectly in demand in the market and that cannot easily be copied or reconstructed by competitors. Competencies can be constructed through different mechanisms and to specify these mechanisms is a way of defining some of the major tasks for innovation policy. As we shall see below, it gives priority to policies aiming at enhancing human resource development, creating new forms of organization, building innovative networks, reorienting innovation policy towards service sectors, and integrating universities in the innovation process.

The first set of mechanisms has to do with the *development of human resources*. The firm can increase its competence through hiring skilled employees or it can develop the skills of its workers in-house. Most firms combine these two methods of human resource development but the emphasis will differ and is a crucial aspect of the strategy of the firm. The labour market and education system surrounding the firm will affect the strategic choices made in this respect. But also in a given labour market context there is some leeway for variation in firm strategies.

The *organization of the firm* is a major factor conditioning the competence building taking place inside the firm. The specific mode of learning may emphasize individual learning or collective learning as well as explicit or tacit knowledge. It may be focused on formal training versus learning by doing, etc. Today the design of 'learning organizations' may be the single most important factor determining the fate of the firm and even of national economies (Andreasen *et al.* 1995; Coriat 1997; Weinstein 1997). Again the location and the context in which the firm operates will affect its organizational set up. Pharmaceutical firms will be more dependent on building competencies through R&D, while firms in the sector producing furniture will depend more on learning by doing and design capabilities. The geographical location of the firm in a wider context of education and labour market institutions will further restrict its choice of strategy in this respect.

Building *innovative networks* with other firms that are suppliers, users, and competitors has become increasingly important for competence building. This reflects the combination of a highly developed division of labour and the fact that products and technologies become more complex in terms of their knowledge base. There is no single firm that controls all the elements necessary to develop a new product, process, or service. Competence building increasingly has become a collective effort, reflecting the co-operation and networking between formally separate firms.

One of the most dramatic changes that has taken place in the last decade relates to the role of *knowledge-intensive service sectors* in the learning economy (see Tomlinson in this volume). A rapidly increasing proportion of the labour force is employed full time with creating, disseminating, and using new competencies. These activities are important in terms of their growing direct contribution to the value creation, but their indirect impact on firms belonging to other sectors may be even more important. The sector tends to become the most important node in competence building networks and to design innovation policy accordingly becomes a key isssue.

Obviously *universities* are important repositories of knowledge. So far the firms interacting directly and regularly with universities have belonged to a rather small segment of 'science-based' firms in chemistry, electronics, and instruments, or they have been big firms in sectors such as automobiles and mechanical engineering. New developments indicate a new role of universities and it is a crucial issue how the knowledge base of universities can be made more accessible to private firms without undermining the relative autonomy of universities (see Conçeicão and Heitor in this volume).

15.3. Increasing the Capacity to Innovate—Moving More Rapidly Along the Technological Trajectory

By starting from an analysis of different sources of competence building at the firm level we have located five areas where there is a special need to intervene in order to enhance the learning capability of the economy. Below we shall briefly discuss policies aiming at human resource development, creating new forms of organization, building innovative networks, reorienting innovation policy towards service sectors, and integrating universities in the innovation process.

15.3.1. Human Resource Development

There is growing consensus that there is a need for radical change in policies aiming at human resource development and for giving them a stronger priority. The distance between the rhetorics and what is actually taking place in the area is substantial, however. The movement in the education system towards promoting the capability to learn and the formation of new combinations of theoretical knowledge and social skills is slow. Financial pressures on governments trying to qualify for the EMU result in a resource scarcity that makes experimentation and radical reform difficult. The response to the generally accepted need for lifelong learning and new pedagogical forms better suited to slow learners is weak and unevenly distributed among European countries. There is still a big gap between the public and private investments made in the upgrading of the skills of the active working population and the needs for upgrading. It is a worrying paradox that it is so much easier to reach agreement at the European level on subsidizing agriculture than it is to agree on a forward-looking community-wide human resource development strategy.

Formal training of youth needs to give strong emphasis on the forming of the capability to learn. This implies that certain fields of knowledge related to communication skills, such as mastering languages and computer use, should be given priority in all parts of the education system. It also implies that pedagogical methods using problem-oriented and project-organized learning become important. Finally, the growing importance of social capital points to the need to make sure that the education system is organized in such a way that it promotes ethical and collaborative behaviour among students.

Lifelong learning is an area where there is a need for a combination of private and public initiatives. Below we shall emphasize the importance of learning organizations in the private sector. But empirical data show that firms left to themselves will invest primarily in competence building of employees with a good formal training. This 'Matthews syndrome', where more is given to those who already have a lot, points to a need for public responsibility to make sure that unskilled workers get a proper upgrading of their skills. Trade unions need to develop 'solidaric competence policies' and to make stronger efforts to integrate clauses emphasizing skill upgrading in collective agreements and employment contracts.

In the field of human resource development, the EU could play an important role in establishing a kind of discipline that corresponds to the one established around financial and monetary issues. Benchmarking efforts aiming at developing more adequate practices might be helpful in promoting policy learning in the field.

15.3.2. New Forms of Organization

While it is generally accepted that the public sector has a role to play in enhancing human resources, at least in organizing the training of young people, it has been assumed that firms by themselves will easily find the best way to organize themselves. Contrary to this assumption, we recommend a much more active role for government in this area.

Currently, an organizational revolution is taking place and there is an enormous unexploited potential among European firms in this respect. The full positive impact of information technology on productivity can only be harvested if the organizational forms develop. New forms of organization that increase connectivity and interaction between departments are key elements in accelerating innovation. Forms of organization will always reflect national specificities and the broader social and institutional context, including industrial relations, education systems, and industrial structures. Still, new broadly defined better practice organizational trajectories can now be discerned and policy makers should stimulate and help management and workers to move ahead along these. It will involve a movement towards more horizontal communication, more intense communication inside and outside the firm, and the delegation of responsibility to workers. In the chapter by Nyholm *et al.* in this volume, there is discussed an ambitious Danish policy initiative creating better framework conditions for organizational change (the LOK-project). The EU should stimulate research and establish a forum for the exchange of policy experiences in this field.

Efforts in this field may start by establishing a stronger knowledge base through research on the economic performance of firms that have chosen different organizational forms. Integrating new research results in the training of managers and forms of dissemination that aim at active managers is another important element. Other areas where the public sector may stimulate efforts are action research within organizations, benchmarking efforts, and other forms where the success stories are communicated widely to the population of firms. These may be combined with giving small and medium-sized firms access to the services of consultancy firms specialized in distributing good practices.

15.3.3. **Building Innovative Networks**

One of the most dramatic changes in the learning economy is the growing importance of networking and inter-firm co-operation in connection with innovation. It reflects the speeding up of change, but also the growing complexity of the innovation process, where each single innovation has to build upon several disparate technologies and where each technology has to combine several separate scientific disciplines. Public policy has different roles in this context. Competition policy needs further changes in order to respond to the full implications of the new regime. The formation of networks of firms and of firms and knowledge institutions should be stimulated at different levels. At the regional level the formation of knowledge-intensive networks is a key to promote regional development (Cooke 1997). The formation and renewal of industrial districts where network relationships over-layer local labour markets characterized by special competencies in the labour force may be stimulated. At the European level, the formation of networks and consortia may help to create a more interdependent and coherent innovation system and promote the competitiveness of European industry. But in this area there are two caveats.

First, the design of effective public policies is especially difficult in this area. What is needed is to bring the right parties together in minor co-operative activities so that they can start to build trust (Lazaric and Lorenz 1997). Public policy may try to support the formation of organizational routines that reduce the risks involved and support initiatives from below to form new network relationships. The formation of 'social capital' is crucial for the development of networking and here the role of government policy is both complex and diffuse. Consequent legal efforts to reduce corruption both in the private and the public sphere may be important prerequisites for establishing effective learning in society. Also in this field there is a need for further research, including analyses of the basic roles of, and reasons for, network formation.

Secondly, it should be noted that, given the high rate of change, networks that are geographically closed may, in the long run, hamper rather than stimulate innovation. This corresponds to the perspective on social capital proposed by Woolcock (1998), where it is taken into account that socially dense interactions may become conservative if they are not open to the environment. Both at the regional and the national level *outward* networking may be crucial in order to remain at the front of the innovation race. The experiences from ESPRIT and the weak state of the European electronics industry point to the need for extra-European networking. Industrial districts may need stronger interaction with external parties in order to avoid lock in into stagnating product areas. This implies a role for public policy in promoting the internationalization of firms and the positioning of big European firms in global networks (Storper 1997).

15.3.4. A New Role for the Service Sector

TSER-research indicates that the service sector is the one where the rate of change is currently most dramatic and that this will remain so also for the near future. A better analytical understanding of the service sector is of key importance for policy making. The preliminary results indicate that parts of the service sector—business services, communication services, and other knowledge-intensive services—increasingly tend to become key sectors in relation to the overall industrial dynamics. They become central nodes in the innovation system gathering and codifying knowledge, connecting users and producers of knowledge, and distributing knowledge, worldwide, between different localities. Antonelli (1996), Tomlinson (1997), and Tsounis (1997) demonstrate how certain business and communication services become key sectors in relation to the overall industrial dynamics. With the growing importance of the Internet and of e-commerce this will become even more the case in the future.

The traditional focus of industrial policy on the competitiveness of manufacturing firms is becoming correspondingly less relevant. Services become increasingly important in their own right as providers of wealth and jobs, and as strategic elements in innovation systems. Rethinking regulatory systems, including quality control systems, so that they promote rather than block innovation in these sectors is one policy task. Another one is to promote access to knowledge-intensive business services for SMEs and marginal regions.

15.3.5. Integrating Research Institutions in the Innovation System

Gibbons *et al.* (1994) have proposed that we have entered a new mode of knowledge-creation (mode II), where there is a much stronger connection between science and technology and where innovation typically will be the outcome of an interaction among a multitude of actors distributed between many different institutions and locations. These developments point to the need to integrate the knowledge base of universities more closely with the innovation process.

There is a great diversity in attempts in Europe to get universities more effectively engaged in innovation. The TSER-thematic network on High Technology SMEs illustrates different regional and national models in this respect, and shows how university research increasingly gives rise to technology based spin-offs. In the case of Chalmer University in Sweden the building of new technology-oriented transdisciplinary centres seems to have been a major element of a successful strategy (Holmén and Jacobsson 1997). It is obvious that local conditions are important but certain common principles seem to correspond to good practices in this field. Matrix forms of organizations (combining discipline-organized departments with temporary interdisciplinary centres) buffer organizations connecting universities with SMEs and incentives to support circulation of scholars between basic, applied, and development research tasks are obvious policy initiatives in the new context.

In this field it is, as already stated by Conçeicão and Heitor in this volume, necessary to raise a warning against solutions that completely break down the protection of academic autonomy. The major function of universities is to train students and scholars in skills that are crucial for the development, absorption, and use of technology and this calls for a certain degree of autonomy. Also, autonomous basic research is becoming increasingly important as competition and new governance forms tend to promote applied and short-term development work in the private sector. For excellent overviews of the complexity of the contribution of academic research to economic development, see Pavitt (1995) and Martin and Salter (1996). It is also too simplistic to see this as a problem to be solved unilaterally from the supply side by universities themselves. It can be shown that firms that have no personnel with an academic degree only seldomly interact with universities. Stimulating small and medium-sized firms to appoint their first academics may be one of the most efficient ways to increase the interaction between industry and university.

15.4. Innovation Policy in a Wider Perspective

So far the focus has been on a set of policies that will increase the capability to innovate and adapt in a rapidly changing environment. As indicated in the introductory chapter, the costs of rapid change and the negative effects of the learning economy may be substantial (Carter 1994, 1996). There are a number of factors that make it more and more difficult to leave these changes to 'repair' policies. Large-scale income transfer is becoming more and more difficult in the context of globalized monetary regimes and Internet transactions. Environmental damage is difficult to repair. This is one reason for proposing a wider perspective on innovation policy. The other reason has to do with the fact that the market-led speed up of innovation may be effective in the short run but in the longer view the crucial issues have to do with creating a new techno-economic paradigm and here non-market intervention in the form of a need-oriented technology policy may be a key element (see also Edquist in this volume). There are many indications that the present acceleration along a well-established technological trajectory (where Europe trails behind) based on information technology discriminates against long-term efforts to create the basis for the next one. The kind of innovation policy referred to below responds to the first problem and it may also help to solve the second one.

This distinction between two different types of innovation policies relates to *the exploration–exploitation dilemma* (Lundvall and Borrás 1998). In the learning economy the selection regimes will be tough and together with short termist governance regimes they will make firms pursue narrow strategies (Chesnais and Serfati 1997). Rather than looking for radically new innovations and for deep change they will move rapidly ahead in a kind of *strip-mining* fashion. This reflects the fact that to follow narrow trajectories is the most efficient when it comes to moving rapidly ahead in terms of incremental innovation and diffusion and efficient use of innovations.

15.4.1. Designing an Innovation Policy Aiming at Social and Environmental Sustainability

The policies presented above emphasize the importance of human resource development and the integration of the different parts of the innovation system in networking and interaction. They will prove more helpful when it comes to catch up along the information technology trajectory than traditional science and technology programmes that focus exclusively on the support of basic science and the protection of intellectual property rights. But they should be supplemented by a need-oriented innovation policy that explicitly aims at tackling issues raised by the speed up of innovation and transformation. It would be possible to list numerous such needs but here we shall focus on two issues.

- social and regional polarization
- environmental threats from rapid transformation.

Social and regional polarization is not a new phenomenon in the history of capitalism. In the present era polarization between people and regions has become rooted in differences in skill, competence, access to, and participation in, interactive learning to an extreme degree (Fagerberg and Verspagen 1996; Fagerberg, Verspagen, and Caniëls 1997). Education systems and learning organizations should therefore be designed so that they strengthen the learning capability of the weak learners (the new new deal—see Lundvall 1996). New ways of using the potential of advanced user-friendly information technologies such as multi-media is one element in a policy tackling these issues. Regulating the equal and effective access to information technology and communication systems in marginal regions is another.

The environmental threats call for immense transdisciplinary and multitechnological efforts and they need to be realistically anchored in an understanding of the role of social movements and interest groups (Jamison and Østby 1997; see also Meyer-Krahmer in this volume). Just measuring and analysing what is going on in terms of pollution and biological degradation at the global level is a major challenge. Developing pure technologies in manufacturing and transports is another. Social innovations that change the incentive structures in agriculture and forestry so that more environmental friendly techniques become in demand are also needed. Social innovations affecting the mode of everyday life is also an element in a strategy aiming at sustainable growth.

15.4.2. The Parallel with the Post-war US Military Procurement of Information Technology and Software

In this context it is interesting to consider the historical role of government in connection with the formation of the current techno-economic paradigm around information and software technologies. The major player in this field was, of course, the US military. The impact from military demands were dramatic especially in the early history of the formation of the new technological system. While the impact of direct procurement was important in this phase, the most important influence came through the construction of knowledge institutions, academic training, and subsidized access to computers. The fact that universities were used as the base for developing new knowledge in the field was critically important for the wide and rapid diffusion of the new technologies in the economy as a whole. According to Mowery and Langlois (1997), the direct procurement of software became less and less effective in terms of spillovers as it became increasingly oriented towards very specialized military needs. The authors also argue that attempting to design separate organizations outside universities and pursuing applied research aiming at specific private needs actually undermines the wide distribution of knowledge.

The US software example illustrates a case where massive intervention had long-term effects on the overall dynamics of economic growth through fostering a new techno-economic paradigm. It is important that the idea was not to designate the technological winners of the future—nobody in charge of building the first elements of the software knowledge infrastructure, or the embryo of the Internet, had any idea that this specific technology would revolutionize the world economy and give the US a lead in the field. But the massive concentration of knowledge power, which could not have happened through a market-led incremental approach, to solve a set of collective needs related to the Cold War had the indirect effect to open up radically new technological avenues.

This is not to argue that any kind of massive government intervention would result in new dynamic trajectories. The example of nuclear technology demonstrates that this is not at all the case. When considering the possible impact of a strong effort to develop social and technical innovations in the environmental field, both the technologies involved and the relation to market demand should be taken into account. Environmental problems call for combining biological processes and control technologies. It is also interesting to note that the new technologies developed will actually be closer to the needs expressed in private markets than were military technologies. As new regulations are introduced, for instance through making the polluter pay, new markets for 'green products' are created. Also, the preferences of private and collective consumers are affected by 'environmental learning' as the non-sustainability and the private and collective risks of following present strategies are realized. As Europe moves ahead in directions that others have to follow later on, new and growing markets are created. National and European procurement policies may be crucial for the success of such a strategy. Among the policy instruments analysed in the TSER-projects, they seem to be especially effective when it comes to creating products with new green qualities. TSER-projects show, for instance, that new forms of procurement policies where public agencies organize private users in procurement aiming at energy savings have been highly effective in affecting the direction of technical change (Edquist 1996; Edquist and Hommen 1997; Westling 1996).

15.4.3. Building New Technological Systems

In this context it is useful to think in terms of 'technological systems' as a special version of innovation systems. A technological system is a combination of interrelated sectors and firms, a set of institutions and regulations characterizing the rules of behaviour and the knowledge infrastructure connected to it. Most innovation policies referred to above are well suited when it comes to supporting existing technological systems, but much less so when it comes to stimulate the creation of new ones (Carlsson 1995).

In the case of environmental innovation the following three elements may be crucial for success:

(1) establishing flexible but demanding standards in an interaction between users and producers—this implies creating markets for green products and procurement policies activating private as well as public users; creating a green competition regime where national governments get incentives to establish more demanding standards than the average;

(2) establishing institutes in charge of systematically measuring and evaluating the crucial parameters related to the environment; stimulating experimental new initiatives in building training and research centres in crucial fields—such initiatives may represent different new combinations of scientific disciplines;

(3) strengthening the links between environmental policy, innovation policy, and general economic policy.

Such a model, where the core elements are market creation, building new knowledge infrastructure, and policy co-ordination, might be used also in other areas where the globalizing learning economy tends to undermine its own logic.

15.5. A European Agenda for Innovative Policy

Taking into account all the different aspects of innovation policy discussed in this chapter, we recommend that innovation policy at the European level should at least include the following elements. Europe should:

(1) use its strength in world trade negotiations to avoid trade and competition regulations that are obstacles to need-oriented innovation policies, including procurement strategies aiming at enhancing environmental standards;

(2) stimulate international openness in knowledge production and distribution, and position European firms in global production networks and in global competition;

(3) build learning economies in Europe—that is to stimulate local experiments, assess outcomes, and stimulate European policy learning in the fields of human resource development, organizational change, network formation, and coupling of industry to knowledge-intensive services and universities;

(4) initiate need-oriented innovation policies, create new markets, and build new technological systems focused on creating social and environmental sustainability.

Many of these elements are already on the European agenda as specified in the Green Paper on innovation and in the outline of the Fifth Framework Programme. Actually, it might be argued that while the Green Paper takes on the first task of promoting innovation along the trajectory, the Framework Programme corresponds to the wider perspective on innovation policy, including its need orientation. On the background of the TSER-projects covered by this policy action we find that the Green Paper tends to underestimate the soft aspects of innovation, such as the role of human resources, competent users, demand factors, network building, and organizational change. A major criticism of the actions proposed in the Framework Programme is that they are too partial in their focus on science and technology, remaining in a linear understanding of innovation and not achoring the formation of technological systems in their socio-economic context.

One factor that has delayed the development of appropriate policies has been the old plan versus market controversy. As indicated above, an analysis with focus on innovation demonstrates that 'pure markets' are problematic when it comes to stimulating innovation. It also shows that modes of interaction between firms which represent a mixture of competition and cooperation are more efficient than 'pure competition'. The invisible hand is not so invisible and what is at stake is not government interference in a next-to-perfect market economy. This is not an argument for massive and detailed government intervention but rather for a pragmatic and realistic assessment of what governments could and should do.

A favourite specific theme in the 1980s was the argument that governments cannot 'pick winners' and that this implies a move away from selective policies and a stronger focus on framework conditions—that is, conditions that are in principle common to all firms in a national economy. This argument has a sound base but it may go too far. On the one hand, there is always a risk that governments become captives of specific industrial interests and detailed interventions and specific subsidies may create a culture of 'clientelism' among firms (cf. the government support to old industries in steel, shipbuilding, and not least the Common Agricultural Policy). On the other hand, the concept of 'general framework conditions' is misleading in the sense that any set of framework conditions will affect different types of firms differently. This should be especially obvious when the focus is on learning and knowledge. Learning regimes and the characteristics of the knowledge base differ strongly between sectors (cf. the taxonomy in Pavitt 1984). While some sectors benefit directly from public investments in science, others are much more dependent on the skill level of workers, etc.

An interesting compromise between, on the one hand, moving towards framework conditions and, on the other, taking into account that the most important framework conditions differ among firms has been developed in some of the small OECD countries. In the Netherlands there has been a growing focus on industrial clusters which encompass vertically organized subsystems of firms, while the Danish analysts and policy makers have broken down the whole economy to nine 'resource areas'. For each of these areas a forum including policy makers, analysts, trade unionists, and industrialists has been established. In these fora informal debates go on regarding what changes in the existing framework conditions are the most strongly needed and there is a close connection from these debates to new law proposals.

One major problem with such a model has to do with the exploration/exploitation dilemma. In general, industrial policies are normally more efficient when it comes to confirm the exploitation of existing opportunities than in opening up new avenues. This is something that can be seen when national systems of innovation and the role of governments in this context are compared (Edquist and Lundvall 1993). And normally policy is most successful when it comes to reinforce patterns of connectivity and linkages that are already there. Bringing policy makers into a close dialogue with groups of industrialists who belong to a common stronghold in the economy will normally reinforce these tendencies. What may be needed is that such institutional set ups are complemented with new bodies with a responsibility for economy-wide policy issues related to competence building and innovation both at the national level (Lundvall 1999) and at the European level (Lundvall 2000).

The Lisboa Summit (March 2000) may be seen as a move in the direction of a stronger co-ordination at the European level. The summit focused thematically on 'a Europe based on Knowledge, Innovation and Social Cohesion' and it gave the European Council and prime ministers a more important role than ministers for specific policy fields in the process of developing the common platform. In order to cope with the challenges of the globalizing learning economy similar institutional innovations are needed at the national and regional level. And in order to cope with the new challenges of the globalizing learning economy it is absolutely necessary to break down the very segmented feudalist structure of the Commission where directorates now tend to serve as local and often competing kingdoms. The present debate about institutional reform of the Commission now focusing mainly upon the power balances between different groups of countries might actually be unlocked by bringing in the need for a new vision and a new kind of co-ordination. For instance it might result in programmes that are heavy in terms of administration of funds being located in specific agencies, separated from departments responsible for the political co-ordination of competence building and innovation.

REFERENCES

ANDREASEN, L., CORIAT, B., DEN HARTOG, F., and KAPLINSKY, R. (1995) (eds.). *Europe's Next Step—Organisational Innovation, Competition and Employment*. London: Frank Cass.

ANTONELLI, C. (1996). 'Localised technological change, new information technology and the knowledge-based economy: The European evidence'. Mimeograph in the context of *TSER-project on Innovation in Services*. Sassari: Department of Economics, University of Sassari.

ARCHIBUGI, D., and MICHIE, J. (1998) (eds.). *Trade, Growth, and Technical Change*. Cambridge: Cambridge University Press.

ARROW, K. J. (1971). 'Political and economic evaluation of social effects of externalities', in M. Intrilligator (ed.), *Frontiers of Quantitative Economics*. Amsterdam: North Holland.

CARLSSON, B. (1995) (ed.). *Technological Systems and Economic Performance: The Case of Factory Automation*. Dordrecht: Kluwer Academic Publishers.

CARTER, A. P. (1994). 'Change as economic activity'. Working Paper 333. Boston: Department of Economics, Brandeis University.

——(1996). 'Production workers, meta-investment and the pace of change', in E. Helmstädter and M. Perlman (eds.), *Behavioral Norms, Technological Progress and Economic Dynamics*. Ann Arbor: University of Michigan Press.

CHESNAIS, F., and SERFATI, C. (1997). 'Long horizon investment under a globalised finance dominated accumulation regime: An interpretation of the levelling off and decline of R&D in the 1990s'. Paper presented at the DRUID Summer Conference on Competition and Industrial Dynamics, 1–3 June, Skagen.

COOKE, P. (1997). 'Regions in a global market: The experiences of Wales and Baden Württemberg'. *Review of International Political Economy*, 4/2: 349–81.

CORIAT, B. (1997). 'Made in Europe—Context and Objectives'. Paper presented at the Launching seminar of 'Made in Europe', 6–7 October, Sevilla.

EDQUIST, C. (1996). 'Government technology procurement as an instrument of technology policy', in M. Teubal, D. Foray, M. Justmein, and E. Zuscovitch (eds.), *Technological Infrastructure Policy*. Amsterdam: Kluwer Academic Publishers.

——and HOMMEN, L. (1997). 'Government technology procurement and economic theory'. Report for sub-project 3.2.2. 'Government technology procurement as a policy instrument' in the TSER-project on Innovation Systems and European Integration, Department of Technology and Social Change, Linköping: Linköping University.

——and LUNDVALL, B.-Å. (1993). 'Comparing the Danish and Swedish systems of innovation', in R. R. Nelson (ed.), *National Systems of Innovations: A Comparative Analysis*. Oxford: Oxford University Press.

FAGERBERG, J., and VERSPAGEN, B. (1996). 'Heading for divergence? Regional growth in Europe reconsidered'. *Journal of Common Market Studies*, 34: 431–48.

——VERSPAGEN, B., and CANIËLS, M. (1997). 'Technology, growth and unemployment across European regions'. *Regional Studies*, 31/5: 457–66.

GIBBONS, M., LIMOGES, C., NOWOTNY, H., SCHWARTZMAN, S., SCOTT, P., and TROIW, M. (1994). *The New Production of Knowledge*. London: Sage.

HOLMÉN, M., and JACOBSON, S. (1997). 'Characterising the competence-base of a region—The case of Western Sweden'. TSER/TEIS Working Paper 10, MERIT.

JAMISON, A., and ØSTBY, P. (1997). *Public Participation and Sustainable Development, Comparing European Experiences*. Aalborg: Aalborg University Press.

LAZARIC, N., and LORENZ, E. (1997). 'Trust and organisational learning during inter-firm co-operation', in N. Lazaric and E. Lorenz (eds.), *The Economics of Trust and Learning*, Cheltenham: Edward Elgar.

LUNDVALL, B.-Å. (1992) (ed.). *National Systems of Innovation: Towards a Theory of Innovation and Interactive Learning*. London: Pinter Publishers.

——(1996). 'The social dimension of the learning economy'. Department of Business Studies, DRUID Working Paper 96-1. Aalborg: Aalborg University.

——(1999). *Det Danske Innovationssystem (The Danish Innovation System)*. Copenhagen: Erhvervsfremmestyrelsen.

——(2000). 'The challenge of the learning economy and the need for a new type of policy co-ordination at the European level', in International Hearing for the Portuguese Presidency of the European Union. The Prime Minister's Office: Lisbon.

——and BORRÁS, S. (1998). *The Globalising Learning Economy: Implications for Innovation Policy*. Brussels: European Commission.

——and JOHNSON, B. (1994). 'The learning economy'. *Journal of Industry Studies*, 2/1: 23–42.

MARTIN, B., and SALTER, A. (1996). 'The relationship between publicly funded basic research and economic performance'. *A SPRU Review* (July). Report prepared for HM Treasury. Falmer: SPRU.

MOWERY, D., and LANGLOIS, R. N. (1997). 'Spinning off and spinning on (?): The federal government role in the development of the US computer software industry'. *Research Policy*, 25: 947.

OECD (2000). *Knowledge Management in the Learning Society*. Paris: OECD, Centre of Education Research and Innovation.

PAVITT, K. (1984). 'Sectoral patterns of technical change: Towards a taxonomy and a theory'. *Research Policy*, 13: 343–73.

—— (1995). 'Academic research, technical change and government policy', in J. Krige and D. Pestre (eds.), *Science in the 20th Century*. Harwood: Academic Publishers.

STORPER, M. (1997). *The Regional World: Territorial Development in a Global Economy*. New York: Guilford Press.

TOMLINSON, M. (1997). 'The contribution of services to manufacturing industry: Beyond the deindustrialisation debate'. CRIC Discussion Paper 5, September.

TSOUNIS, N. (1997). 'Knowledge intensive business services and productivity growth: The Greek evidence', contribution to SI4S-TSER-project.

WEINSTEIN, O. (1997). 'New organisational concepts and practices at the firm level'. Paper presented at the Launching seminar of 'Made in Europe', 6–7 October, Sevilla.

WESTLING, H. (1996). *Co-operative Procurement. Market Acceptance for Innovative Energy-Efficient Technologies*. Stockholm: NUTEK.

WOOLCOCK, M. (1998). 'Social capital and economic development: Toward a theoretical synthesis and policy framework'. *Theory and Society*, 27/2: 151–207.

INDEX

Note: page references in **bold** indicate chapters.

Index